THE UNIVERSITY OF WINCHESTER

Martial Rose Library
Tel: 01962 827306

Twentieth Century Poetry

TWENTIETH CENTURY POETRY

Selves and Situations

PETER ROBINSON

OXFORD
UNIVERSITY PRESS

This book has been printed digitally and produced in a standard specification
in order to ensure its continuing availability

OXFORD
UNIVERSITY PRESS

Great Clarendon Street, Oxford OX2 6DP

Oxford University Press is a department of the University of Oxford.
It furthers the University's objective of excellence in research, scholarship,
and education by publishing worldwide in

Oxford New York

Auckland Cape Town Dar es Salaam Hong Kong Karachi
Kuala Lumpur Madrid Melbourne Mexico City Nairobi
New Delhi Shanghai Taipei Toronto
With offices in
Argentina Austria Brazil Chile Czech Republic France Greece
Guatemala Hungary Italy Japan South Korea Poland Portugal
Singapore Switzerland Thailand Turkey Ukraine Vietnam

Oxford is a registered trade mark of Oxford University Press
in the UK and in certain other countries

Published in the United States
by Oxford University Press Inc., New York

© Peter Robinson 2003

The moral rights of the author have been asserted

Database right Oxford University Press (maker)

Reprinted 2009

ISBN 978-0-19-927325-6

Preface

Twentieth Century Poetry: Selves and Situations is a series of interconnected studies. Though shape and cohesion are aimed for in the book, no attempt has been made at military discipline, vanguard or rearguard, in the way these explorations of individual works, oeuvres, and human histories proceed. Early drafts of three chapters were in existence before the completion of *In the Circumstances: About Poems and Poets* (1992). All but two were written before *Poetry, Poets, Readers: Making Things Happen* (2002) found its form. While this book was not produced exactly to develop or reconsider published work, there have inevitably been changes in the writer's outlook during the time that they were composed and revised. As regards guiding ideas on relations between poems, people, and places, the introductory chapter, for example, expresses qualms about what 'circumstance' and 'context' may haplessly imply. With regard to ways of approaching individual cases, I hope the reader will find in the following chapters more grateful understanding and less anxious moralizing than in some earlier work.

The selves and situations of twentieth-century poems could not conceivably achieve anything without the collaborative involvement of readers, each one of us an evolving self in changing situations. Alongside its various concerns, this sequence of chapters looks at ways in which poets can create, and create out of, relationships of a more or less trusting kind with their poems' implied and, by those means, actual readers. It also includes cases that reveal the relative absence of, or wish to do without, such relationships. In the first chapter this range of possible relations, or their absence, is introduced through an exploration of complexities in ways by which selves and situations interact and become imaginatively identified with each other in poems. Each subsequent chapter shares an interest in how poems can be both attached to and detached from the culture, society, and conditions in which they were written. It also sketches the ubiquity and elusiveness of the self in the situation of the text. Poems are, furthermore, seen to be focal points for relationships between readerly and writerly selves and their situations in and over time.

Of the poets treated in this book only Louis MacNeice was dead when I began to write and publish. I am old enough to have been able to pen a student elegy for Ezra Pound, and to have talked with his companion Olga Rudge. All the poets in the second half of the book are alive or were when I wrote on their work. Two or three of them I like to think of as friends. In such a situation a canonical justification for critical attention is neither to be had nor particularly to be desired. Among the many things that can be said for the works of these poets is that they have sustained the attention given to them. If readers are already familiar with their names or writings then I am happy, and I hope that my discussions add to appreciation. If the names are unfamiliar then I hope that after reading about them an interest will have been kindled. These poets do not belong to a single school or clique. They might well not have admired each other's work. Born in the fifty or so years between 1885 and 1938, they seem to me to make an illuminating sequence.

The emphasis in these studies of twentieth-century poetry's selves and situations serves to underline the conviction that its capacities arise in necessary, yet often complexly attenuated, relationships—with both experience and the experience of reading. Such poetry's distinctive qualities and powers are found within immensely variable, shifting relations. In following out some of these issues through readings of poems that I variously admire, I hope to have provided pleasure and insight. As I see it, these poems are engaged with our most pressing concerns as encountered by other selves in situations that are experienced as very close at hand.

P. R.

18 February 2004

Acknowledgements

Aside from the first, these chapters have appeared in earlier versions, and I gratefully acknowledge the help and permission of their first publishers and editors: 'Not a Villanelle: Pound's Psychological Hour', *Shiron* [Sendai], 31 (1992); 'Basil Bunting's Emigrant Ballads', in R. Caddel (ed.), *Sharp Study and Long Toil: Basil Bunting Special Issue, Durham University Journal* supplement (1995); 'MacNeice, Munich, and Self-Sufficiency', *Shiron* [Sendai], 40 (2002); 'Dependence in the Poetry of W. S. Graham', *Review of English Literature* [Kyoto] 60 (1990), and, revised, in H. Jones and R. Pite (eds.), *W. S. Graham: Speaking Towards You* (Liverpool: Liverpool University Press, 2004); 'Elizabeth Bishop's Art', *Perversions* [London], 1/3 (1994), and, revised, in S. Sakurai (ed.), *The View From Kyoto: Essays on Twentieth-Century Poetry* (Kyoto: Rinsen, 1998); '"The bliss of what?": Bishop's Crusoe', in L. Kelly (ed.), *Poetry and the Sense of Panic: Critical Essays on Elizabeth Bishop and John Ashbery* (Amsterdam/Atlanta, Ga: Rodopi, 2000); 'Allen Curnow Travels', *English* 49/193 (2000); 'Charles Tomlinson in the Golfo dei Poeti', *Review of English Literature* [Kyoto], 58 (1989) with passages added from 'Received Accents', *London Review of Books*, 8/3, 20 Feb. 1986; '"Absolute circumstance": Mairi MacInnes', *Cambridge Review*, 31/2 (2002), here including passages from a review of *Clearances* published in *The Reader* 11 (Sept. 2002), and *The Sewanee Review*, 61/2 (spring 2003); 'Tom Raworth and the Pop Art Explosion' *The Gig*, 13–14 (2003) (*Removed for Further Study: The Poetry of Tom Raworth*); 'Roy Fisher's Last Things', in J. Kerrigan and P. Robinson (eds.), *The Thing about Roy Fisher: Critical Studies* (Liverpool: Liverpool University Press, 2000).

Colleagues, acquaintances, friends, and family have provided long-term support, generous encouragement, and specific help. They know who they are, and I thank them all very warmly.

Contents

CHAPTER 1

Selves and Situations

I

In his 'Réflexions sur la poésie', dated 'Paris, janvier 1944', the poet and member of the resistance Robert Desnos wrote that 'La grande poésie peut être nécessairement actuelle, de circonstances . . . elle peut donc être fugitive' (Great poetry may necessarily be of the present day, the circumstances . . . it may therefore be fugitive.)[1] The philosopher Thomas Nagel, delivering the 1990 Locke lectures almost a half-century later, suggested that 'We must turn our attention to the circumstances in which people act and by which they are formed, and we must change the question from "How should we live, whatever the circumstances?" to "Under what circumstances is it possible to live as we should?"'[2] Desnos's fate between the writing of those reflections on poetry and his death from typhus and malnutrition in a concentration camp the following June is enough to start thoughts about adequate circumstances. This fate both sharpens the urgency of Nagel's alternative questions and casts shadows of doubt upon their adequacy to the situations of life in which human selves will be shaped and in which they will be obliged to act.

A few painful war years before Desnos's remark on the fugitive nature of great poetry T. S. Eliot, lecturing in England, wrote that the music of a word 'arises from its relation to the words immediately preceeding and following it, and indefinitely to the rest of its context' and from the relation 'of its immediate meaning in that context to all the other meanings which it has had in other contexts'.[3] What these three passages have in common is a dependence on the uses, meanings, and associations of 'contexts' and 'circumstances', words that share the idea of a subject around which everything else circulates. Both 'context' and 'circumstance' are, like 'surroundings', words no one would want to be without.

---

[1] Robert Desnos, *Destinée arbitraire*, ed. M-C. Dumas (Paris: Gallimard, 1975), 237.

[2] Thomas Nagel, *Equality and Partiality* (Oxford: Oxford University Press, 1991), 52.

[3] T. S. Eliot, 'The Music of Poetry', in *On Poetry and Poets* (London: Faber & Faber, 1957), 33.

Yet they may suggest the existence—even when being used to qualify such an idea—of a subject, whether it be 'word', 'people', a 'text', or 'we', about which, to quote a phrase of Eliot's, 'the worlds revolve'.[4] This understandable way of talking, and the words that sustain it, can also serve to reinforce misleading assumptions. These words, if taken at face value, suggest that the subjects of our attention can only be thought and felt about when experienced from somewhere beyond them—as if they could only be experienced, as it were, ecstatically. Yet, as the title of a previous book had it, we are always and inescapably 'in the circumstances'. The words, and others like 'surroundings' or 'environs', may encourage us to mistake the representation of an experiencing subject, a represented self. We may be encouraged to suppose the existence of such an ecstatic self rendered or implied by the occasion of a poem. We may also find ourselves misreading that poem as it both arises in a situation of history and survives it through the changing situations of historical time.

Ludwig Wittgenstein's *Tractatus Logico-Philosophicus* was first published accompanied by an English translation by C. K. Ogden and an introduction by Bertrand Russell in 1922—the year that one of Russell's other acquaintances, the poet Eliot, published *The Waste Land*. This poem, a collage of selves suffering from and, some of them, seeking a way out of imprisoning situations, helped sponsor the poet's impersonality theory of individual talent and its relation to a tradition, as well as his notion of an objective correlative.[5] Both of these ideas are attempts to manage the relations of a learnedly troubled self to a complex cultural and historical situation. In the only book he published during his lifetime Wittgenstein addresses the problem of a 'self' around which 'worlds' may or may not 'revolve' by seeming to collapse the two terms. Thus, he asserts that: 'The world and life are one', 'The thinking, presenting subject; there is no such thing', 'Where in the world is a metaphysical subject to be noted?', and 'Here we see that solipsism strictly carried out coincides with pure realism. The I in solipsism shrinks to an extensionless point and there remains the reality co-ordinated with it.' Wittgenstein's early conclusion to this line of thought preserves 'the metaphysical subject' and the 'philosophical I' as 'not the man, not the human body or the human soul of which psychology treats' but 'the limit' of the world.

---

[4] T. S. Eliot, 'Preludes', in *Collected Poems 1909–1962* (London: Faber & Faber, 1963), 25. For the poet's philosophical studies and influences see M. A. R. Habib, *The Early T. S. Eliot and Western Philosophy* (Cambridge: Cambridge University Press, 1999).

[5] See T. S. Eliot, *The Sacred Wood: Essays on Poetry and Criticism* (London: Methuen, 1920), 48–50, 100.

I wouldn't be able, or want, to follow him to his early conclusion with its indebtedness to Kant's criticism of the Cartesian subject, and to a rereading of Schopenhauer—from which he himself later withdrew assent.[6] What I can do is to draw on some implications about the place of the non-metaphysical subject in the world. Are they, the subject and the world, one and the same? 'I am my world', Wittgenstein asserts towards the end of his book, and, in one of its most memorable paragraphs:

> If I wrote a book 'The world as I found it', I should also have therein to report on my body and say which members obey my will and which do not, etc. This then would be a method of isolating the subject or rather of showing that in an important sense there is no subject: that is to say, of it alone in this book mention could not be made.

Later he adds that 'The world is independent of my will.'[7] Everything that we are aware of has to be either perceived or understood by a unique human being. Yet this unique self as a non-metaphysical subject must, at the same time, be a contingent fact among the innumerable other facts in the world. To be aware of the world—and for it thus to be 'your world'— cannot, of course, mean that you have anything resembling absolute power of will over it. This is among the conditions that produce the common experience of feeling that, for example, earthquakes and politicians are doing things that I do not, and did not, want to happen to my world. It brings us back to Nagel's questions about how we should live and the circumstances in which we can live. That Wittgenstein worked at his book on active service during the First World War also casts its shadow over the limits within which Nagel's questions may well have to be asked.

In this introductory chapter I look at how poets have addressed themselves to this crucial relationship between the 'I' that writes the book about 'The world as I found it'[8] and the 'I' that seems both to be in the world and yet, somehow, not in it. My inclination is to understand the realm of individual consciousness as entirely coordinated with, and

---

[6] Ludwig Wittgenstein, *Tractatus Logico-Philosophicus*, trans. C. K. Ogden (London: Routledge & Kegan Paul, 1922), 151, 153. For a commentary on these remarks see P. M. S. Hacker, *Insight and Illusion: Themes in the Philosophy of Wittgenstein* rev. edn. (Oxford: Oxford University Press, 1989), ch. 4 and, for an account of the philosopher's evolving thought, ch. 8. For a study of how Wittgenstein's example has influenced vanguard poetry see Marjorie Perloff, *Wittgenstein's Ladder: Poetic Language and the Strangeness of the Ordinary* (Chicago, Ill.: University of Chicago Press, 1996).

[7] Wittgenstein, *Tractatus*, 151, 181.

[8] Ibid. 151.

inseparable from, the contingent fact of an individual body, with its vicis-situdes, in the world. Yet when reading the past century's poetry it is necessary to bear in mind that others have understood these relations within various conflicting strands of philosophical and literary thought. Nevertheless, cubist doctrines of vision, imagist pronouncements on complexes in instants of time, and their later evolutions, have this in common. They are situated conceptually at the point where a perceiving subject, a self, seeks to make meaning-filled form from what is experienced in a field of vision, a human situation.[9]

Reducing the sweep somewhat, I will be putting the words 'self' and 'situation' through their paces so as to point in directions which will, I hope, qualify misleading implications in words like 'context' and 'circumstance'. It is 'ecstatic' of us to assume that the words of a poem, and the poem itself, are somehow selected from, and so detached from, their language. We might be tempted to imagine that poets choose words and set them in their poems as shoppers select products in a department store. Yet the verbal context can't circulate beyond the text, like a shop window of alternative lexical possibilities. The words of a poem remain in the learnt language and require the embedded present consciousness of that language to be understood at all. Nor can poets, both as and as not inscribed subjects of poems, be separable from the circumstances within which they both live and represent themselves as living. I am suggesting that however impersonal or transpersonal or non-personal an outlook any of us attempts to adopt, it must, nevertheless, be a view (that's to say, a self) from somewhere (in a situation).[10]

But are there selves in poems?[11] Roy Fisher's 'The Memorial Fountain' begins by representing a situation: 'The fountain plays | through summer dusk in gaunt shadows'. Here there is already the written trace of a self,

[9] See e.g. Ezra Pound, *The Literary Essays of Ezra Pound*, ed. T. S. Eliot (London: Faber & Faber, 1954), 3–4, and Pierre Reverdy, 'L'Image', *Nord-Sud* (March 1918), cited in M-L. Astre and F. Colmez (eds.), *Poésie Française* (Paris: Bordas, 1982), 379.

[10] For an account of the self as necessarily conscious of being a body among other such bodies see Quassim Cassam, *Self and World* (Oxford: Oxford University Press, 1997). But see also Thomas Nagel, *The View from Nowhere* (Oxford: Oxford University Press, 1986) and, for a recent defence of the 'no point of view' account see A. W. Moore, *Points of View* (Oxford: Oxford University Press, 1997).

[11] The philosophical literature on the self is vast. For an introduction to some of its themes see Jonathan Glover, *I: The Philosophy and Psychology of Personal Identity* (Harmondsworth: Penguin, 1988). For an account that draws on the evidence of twentieth-century literature see Charles Taylor, *Sources of the Self: The Making of the Modern Identity* (Cambridge: Cambridge University Press, 1989), ch. 24.

underlined in the interpretive choice of the verb 'plays' and the adjective 'gaunt'. At the end of the long first sentence comes the brief exclamation 'Harsh | skyline!'. This phrase too underlines the presence of a represented self embedded in the poem. Then it turns to the other people in the scene, represented as 'darkening | intelligences of what's visible; | private, given over, all of them—'. Every one of these selves is then granted a situation of its own: 'Many scenes.' Nonetheless, they also all belong to the same atmosphere: 'Still sombre.' Yet now a conundrum is introduced. Are the scenes 'sombre' because the inscribed self of the describing poet still sees them that way? Or are all the darkening intelligences seeing them as 'sombre'? Or is 'sombre' simply a truthful report? Fisher's poem concludes by putting the presence of the poet into the poem. The effect of this might be, willy-nilly, to imply the existence of a further removed 'self' that has stepped back to watch itself watching, even as it simultaneously steps forward into its scene:

> And the scene?
> a thirty-five-year-old man,
> poet,
> > by temper, realist,
> watching a fountain
> and the figures round it
> in garish twilight,
> > > working
> to distinguish an event
> from an opinion;
> > > this man,
> intent and comfortable—
> Romantic notion.[12]

Yet the tendency to assume that there must be a further removed 'self' doing the describing may be precisely the false step I'm writing to identify. For the embedded self of the poet writing is as present in word choices, all of them, but particularly of verbs and adjectives, as at the start of the poem. Fisher commented on this poem in an interview once:

It's a mock meditation on external space poem, a mock Gray's 'Elegy' or a 'Westminster Bridge', the *paysage moralisé*, the simple meditative man in landscape. I do a very crude thing. I put a man in a landscape and if you walk seriously three steps into the job of describing the landscape, and then work out a technique

---

[12] Roy Fisher, *Poems 1955–1987* (Oxford: Oxford University Press, 1988), 60–1.

appropriate for describing the man as he finally attempts the landscape, then problems and ironies arise thick and fast.[13]

Though Fisher calls this 'a very crude thing', it's the sort of poetic occasion with attendant problems and ironies—ones of self and situation—that has attracted a great many twentieth-century poets. All of the writers whose work is explored in the following chapters have written poems that directly address such encounters. Elizabeth Bishop's 'The Bight', subtitled significantly '*On my birthday*', is a poem similarly engaged with a self self-consciously rendering a situation. Bishop too glances back to the work of a poet from the nineteenth century. Of 'the water in the bight' she writes that 'if one were Baudelaire | one could probably hear it turning to marimba music'.[14] Yet while these problems and ironies were certainly foreshadowed in Romantic and symbolist poetry of the earlier century, and might even be traced back to Gray's 'Elegy' and before, Fisher's word 'mock' in 'mock meditation' signals a distinct difference of degree, if not actually of kind. Both Bishop and Fisher in the second half of the twentieth-century were also revisiting in their poems the modes of earlier modernists, poets who would locate an isolated self in an alienated and alienating, frequently urban, situation.[15]

II

Some might say my ideal of a poem is, to make a hash of Wordsworth's phrase, a real person speaking to real people. Yet I don't think that Dr Zhivago's poems were actually written by the fictional character in Pasternak's novel. Nor do I believe that Andrea del Sarto composed his dramatic monologue conventionally attributed to Robert Browning. I don't believe that Fernando Pessoa's heteronymic poet Álvaro de Campos really studied engineering in Glasgow.[16] No, I'm one of those

[13] Roy Fisher, *Interviews Through Time and Selected Prose*, ed. T. Frazer (Kentisbeare:: Shearsman, 2000), 72–3.

[14] Elizabeth Bishop, *The Complete Poems 1927–1979* (New York: Farrar, Straus and Giroux, 1983), 60.

[15] The indebtednesses of Roy Fisher to William Carlos Williams and of Elizabeth Bishop to Marianne Moore are evident and widely discussed. Williams's debts to cubist poetry have also been explored. See e.g. J. Kerrigan and P. Robinson (eds.), *The Thing about Roy Fisher* (Liverpool: Liverpool University Press, 2000); David Kalstone, *Becoming a Poet: Elizabeth Bishop with Marianne Moore and Robert Lowell*, ed. R. Hemenway (London: Chatto & Windus, 1989), 1–76; and Bram Dijkstra, *Cubism, Stieglitz, and the Early Poetry of William Carlos Williams* (Princeton, NJ: Princeton University Press, 1969).

[16] For the 'biography' of Álvaro de Campos and his creation by Pessoa see 'The Advent

people who understand that Vladimir Nabokov constructed both the novel *Pale Fire* and the poem 'Pale Fire'.[17] I see how he attributes the poem to its imaginary poet John Shade, said to be not quite as cold—and therefore good—as Robert Frost (and not quite as convincingly a self either). Of course, I don't believe that the speaker of a poem has to be a living, or once living, person. Nor do I think that the representations of the poet in a lyrical poem appearing to be uttered by the poet (Browning's sonnet 'To Edward Fitzgerald', for instance) are anything other than representations.

Yet for communication to take place representations have to be understood as representations of something. Indeed, the significance of dramatized speakers in non-lyric poems does so frequently require our understanding of the authorial representation implied in the dramatic mask. The poem is not a play, and the speaker lacks a convincing referent. So we supply a more plausible one, and are meant to do so. 'Andrea del Sarto' is an expression of a Victorian poet's problems with love and art, not, in any sustained sense, a Renaissance artist's. The poem is not written in period Italian. Álvaro de Campos is an authorial device for Pessoa's own deployment of futurist-style verse. The timbre of a represented person will, if it is successful, be produced by such poems with dramatized speakers. Such poems, if we are to be convinced, have to be issued with dual aspects. They are uttered by a speaker (usually taken to be a human being) and issued by the only apparently removed poet—one usually manifested by the signature style of, for example, Browning's blank verse. In the case of apparently autobiographical lyrics the double aspect is no less in evidence, and very similar assumptions will be in play. The biographical facts of the assumed person can be taken, quite harmlessly, as bearing upon the represented figure evoked in the reading. Such facts won't mislead; they may illuminate; and many will be assumed—even necessary to grasping the poem.

This is most patent in poems where the known author is named. César Vallejo's 'Piedra negra sobre una piedra blanca' (Black Stone on a White Stone) is a nuanced instance of such poems, for the statement about the named poet cannot be true in the moment of the poem's utterance:

of the Heteronyms', in E. Lisboa and L. C. Taylor (eds.), *A Centenary Pessoa* (Manchester: Carcanet, 1995), 214–18.

[17] Nabokov admitted that 'The American poem discussed in the book by His Majesty, Charles of Zembla, was the hardest stuff I ever had to compose' (*Strong Opinions* (New York: Vintage, 1990), 55).

> César Vallejo ha muerto, le pegaban
> todos sin que él les haga nada;
> le daban duro con un palo y duro
>
> También con una soga; son testigos
> los días jueves y los huesos húmeros,
> la soledad, la lluvia, los caminos . . .[18]

[César Vallejo has died, they beat him, | all of them, though he's done them no harm; | they hit him hard with a stick and hard | with a rope as well; witnesses | are the Thursdays and the humeri bones, | the loneliness, the rain, the roads . . .]

It is part of the learned skills of poetry readers that they understand the poet is talking about himself while still alive. We know this from the future tense of the verb in the first line of the sonnet's octave ('Me moriré en Paris . . . (I will die in Paris . . .)). In imagining himself as no longer alive, the poet also calls upon the situation in which he has died to be his 'witnesses'—and this is a situation which includes the poet's self as a vulnerable body ('son testigos | los días jueves y los huesos húmeros, | la soledad, la lluvia, los caminos . . .'). Similarly, in 'Paris, Octubre 1936' Vallejo uses the phrase 'di mi gran situación . . . de todo esto yo soy el único que parte' (of my great situation . . . of all this I'm the only one who leaves). And just as in the sonnet he turned to the language of crime and justification ('testigos'), so in this poem too he looks to objects in the immediate surroundings of his 'great situation' to act as his alibi ('coartada'):

> Y me alejo de todo, porque todo
> se queda para hacer la coartada:
> mi zapato, su ojal, también su lodo
> y hasta el doblez del codo
> de mi propia camisa abotonada.[19]

[And I go far away from all of it, because all of it | stays to form the alibi: | my shoe, its lace-hole, its mud as well | and even the elbow joint | of my own buttoned-up shirt.]

Situations are where selves will be obliged to make their constrained, life-shaping and perhaps death-producing, decisions—and these situations will, in turn, be, or have been, shaped by the presence or absence of other selves. Parting in Vallejo's poem probably means dying, but it might

---

[18] César Vallejo, *Selected Poems*, ed. S. Hart (London: Duckworth, 2000), 42.
[19] Vallejo, *Selected Poems*, 59.

include leaving on travels or going to Spain, where the Civil War had recently begun. The poet on the point of leaving becomes the situation he leaves behind. Vallejo's lines have general point too, because we are all always the only one to leave a situation, for that is one thing a situation is felt to be—a self *and* the world in which it is alive. Such an externalizing of a self as a situation instances a familiar process of concretion in writing poetry. So, in a book review, a young poet is compared to Elizabeth Bishop when 'she evinces a knack for the restrained accumulation of physical description to adumbrate mental geographies'.[20]

The 'gran situación' of Vallejo's two poems is not rare in twentieth-century poetry. The Italian poet Vittorio Sereni names himself at the close of his 'Paura seconda' (Second Fear): 'Con dolcezza (Vittorio, | Vittorio) mi disarma, arma | contro me stesso me.' (With tenderness (Vittorio, | Vittorio) it disarms me, is arming | me myself against me.) He also has a poem entitled 'Situazione' in which he identifies himself with his immediate surroundings: 'Sono io tutto questo, il luogo | comune e il suo rovescio | sotto la volta che più e più imbruna.' (I am all of this, the common | place and its reverse | beneath the vault as the last light withdraws.)[21] Bishop herself works a variation on such moments of self-identification. 'In the Waiting Room' begins with a careful location of the situation 'In Worcester, Massachusetts' where she 'went with Aunt Consuelo | to keep her dentist's appointment'. She has to wait a long time, and towards the end of the poem its speaker announces:

> But I felt: you are an I,
> you are an *Elizabeth*,
> you are one of *them* ...
> *Why* should you be one, too?[22]

The first-person singular pronoun and the given proper name are the means of representation. They are plainly not fixed to their referents. All English speakers refer to themselves as 'I' and there are an enormous number of people called 'Elizabeth'. Nevertheless, to be a person at all 'I' have to identify 'myself' by and with my name. That there may be many others who must make, in their specificities, exactly this identification only serves to underline the uniqueness of habitual associations between pronoun, proper name, and referent. The words may look the same, and

[20] Carrie Etter, 'The Life of a Desk', *Times Literary Supplement*, 5235, 1 Aug. 2003, 24. The poet reviewed is Julia Copus.
[21] Vittorio Sereni, *Poesie*, ed. D. Isella (Milan: Mondadori, 1995), 252, 138.
[22] Bishop, *Complete Poems*, 160.

they may sound the same, but 'they' are not the same people. It will not improve our ability to appreciate written art if in the literary situation, and the literary situation only, we imagine that such relevant identifications and distinctions cannot be made.

It is of note that Vallejo's poem in which he named himself as dead was written not long before his death in Paris. Sereni's poem in which his given name is repeated appears in the last section of his last book. 'In the Waiting Room' too is a late poem. The mature poet has become the relevant biography of the work in the process of living the life out of which the poetry comes. André Breton's 'Tournesol' (an early poem dated 26 August 1923) ends with 'le grillon' that 'M'a jeté un coup d'oeil d'intelligence | André Breton a-t-il dit passe' (the cricket . . . threw me a knowing look | André Breton it said go by). The poem also constitutes part of its author's sustained attempt to become just such a relevant biography.[23] The poetry will have then come out of the relevant life of such a conceived human being, a human being known about, learned about, and then assumed in further reading. This is as true for an apparently impersonal poet like T. S. Eliot. It is evidently true for a poet who patently acts a role in his poems, a poet like the writer of 'I, the poet William Yeats'[24]—or the Ezra Pound who quotes 'another man's note' as conclusion to his 'Villanelle: The Psychological Hour': 'Dear Pound, I am leaving England.'[25] It is no less true for a seemingly self-effacing writer like Marianne Moore, as for a reserved but often casually present poet like Bishop. Indeed, Moore's poem 'Silence' offers a memory of her father, while her note to it reveals that the two quotations attributed to the supposed parent are lifted from the poet's reading of Miss A. M. Homans and Edmund Burke. The candour of the note hardly settles—given the poet's often-noted commitment to truth telling—a problem of poetic ethics. It more probably exacerbates one.[26]

As poets continue to write and publish, if they do, one of the given elements in their creative situation is a consciousness of the self that has been in part created by the previous writing of poems. Thus, the history

[23] André Breton, *Oeuvres Complètes*, i, ed. M. Bonnet et al. (Paris: Gallimard, 1988), 187–8, and see 1213 n. for this poem's peculiar significance in Breton's life.
[24] W. B. Yeats, 'To be Carved on a Stone at Thoor Ballylee', *The Collected Poems*, 2nd edn., ed. R. J. Finneran (Basingstoke: Macmillan, 1991), 190.
[25] Ezra Pound, *Personae: The Shorter Poems*, rev. edn. ed. L. Baechler and A. Walton Litz (New York: New Directions, 1990), 156.
[26] Marianne Moore, *The Complete Poems*, ed. C. Driver (Harmondsworth: Penguin, 1982), 91, 276 n. James Fenton discusses the poem and these issues in *The Strength of Poetry* (Oxford: Oxford University Press, 2001), 106 ff.

of the poet as a poet comes to be an element in the situation within which the composition of poems takes place. Browning may have thought that if *'Shakespeare unlocked his heart'* in his sonnets then 'the less Shakespeare he!'. The husband of the poet who wrote *Sonnets from the Portuguese* penned the poem 'House'. Elizabeth Barrett Browning's sequence is one where, if in transparently 'translated' guise, 'I sonnet-sing you about myself' and my love for my husband.[27] That same husband allowed himself to be the less Browning—though I'm not inclined to make such a judgement myself—when stung by 'words I read | —Some six or seven at most' about his dead wife, who, for the words to have point, had to be a poet too. 'To Edward Fitzgerald' is the sonnet of a famous old widower, using the first person to refer to himself, defending his wife's literary and human reputation against a posthumously published sneer from the now dead friend of Tennyson. Its author could joke about his identity too, as in this—also uncollected in his lifetime—'Inscription for a Sketch': 'Here I'm gazing, wide awake, | Robert Browning, no mistake!'[28]

III

Poems are quite usually occasioned in a unique matching of selves and situations. William Empson's 'Aubade' was written—according to a much later comment of the poet's—in Tokyo during, probably, 1933, but not published until 1937. An aubade is a song at dawn, a lament that the lovers of the poem are forced to part by the rising sun—and in the Land of the Rising Sun this traditional theme is given an extra political twist. Empson had some things to say about the flag. In a letter of about March 1932 he writes from Tokyo that 'The Japanese flag (a poached egg, or clot of blood on a bandage, which gives the insanely simple and self-centred effect of an amoeba when drugged) is very much in evidence'.[29] In his poem the rising sun of the flag is also going to part the lovers. 'Aubade' contains a variety of pronouns. The opening line of the poem ('Hours before dawn we were woken by the quake') gives us, as well as the situation of an earthquake in the early hours of the morning, the as-yet-unspecified plural selves of a 'we'. One of those must be the lyric speaker

---

[27] Robert Browning, 'House', in *The Poems*, ii, ed. J. Pettigrew and T. J. Collins (Harmondsworth: Penguin, 1981), 438–9.

[28] Browning, *Poems*, ii, 972.

[29] William Empson, Letter from *c.* Mar. 1932, cited in John Haffenden, 'Sexual Types of Ambiguity: William Empson in Japan', *Areté: The Arts Tri-Quarterly*, 6 (autumn 2001), 104.

(who, in this instance, is identified with the poet); and in the next line he steps forward with 'My house was on a cliff'. After repeating this pronoun in line 6, the poet introduces the first-person singular in line 7: 'I hoped that various buildings were brought low.' The last line, a repeating one, of this second verse includes the unspecific second person—which functions to generalize the experience being reflected upon: 'The heart of standing is you cannot fly.' The third verse then narrows the 'we' down to two characters:

> It seemed quite safe till she got up and dressed.
> The guarded tourist makes the guide the test.
> Then I said The Garden? Laughing she said No.
> Taxi for her and for me healthy rest.
> It seemed the best thing to be up and go.[30]

The poem's speaker is not worried until the woman he's in bed with gets up. That he is the 'tourist' and she the 'guide' implies a good deal about their relative relations to the local situation. The third line above tells us that the speaker's house has a garden, and that the woman doesn't think it's necessary to go into the garden to escape the dangers of the earthquake. She has to get a taxi, and can leave him to take a rest after what the title implies have been his sexual exertions.

Empson's next stanza begins by commenting on this dialogue of the parting lovers. They note the difficulties of communicating ('The language problem but you have to try') and the suggestion that not only must there be some communication, but there has to be some deception too ('Some solid ground for lying could she show?'). As has been frequently pointed out, the word 'lying' puns in the manner of Shakespeare's 'When my love swears that she is made of truth, | I do believe her, though I know she lies'[31]—on being recumbent and telling untruths. Yet the second of these senses seems the more significant in Empson's line, because it raises the question of why something needs to be concealed by lies. You could think that this is just the usual position of the lovers at dawn in an aubade—the relationship is traditionally an illicit one, hence the need to part, and all these things are true of Empson's poem too. However, the next verse pushes on the story and fills in more of the situation:

---

[30] William Empson, 'Aubade', in *The Complete Poems*, ed. J. Haffenden (London: Allen Lane, 2000), 69–70, for this and subsequent citations.

[31] William Shakespeare, *Shakespeare's Sonnets*, ed. K. Duncan-Jones (London: Nelson, 1997), 391.

None of these deaths were her point at all.
The thing was that being woken he would bawl
And finding her not in earshot he would know.
I tried saying Half and Hour to pay that call.
It seemed the best thing to be up and go.

Here the third-person-singular masculine pronoun introduces another character—one whose identity has caused problems of ambiguity not discussed in Empson's classic volume of 1930. The problem is created by the word 'bawl', which, like 'cry', can mean both to shed noisy tears and to shout in a pained or angry fashion. Sidney Bolt was surely not the only reader of this stanza to think that the 'he' must be the husband of the woman. After all, that too is a convention of the situation in an aubade. Indeed, you could feel that it was illegitimate for Empson to feel angry about the assumption, as if a critic were casting aspersions on the poet's character by making such a suggestion. Yet this is exactly how he seems to have responded to the reading. Empson was reported to be 'indignant at the suggestion that the woman was another man's wife, affirming that she was a nursemaid employed by the German Ambassador'.

Bolt adds the further suggestion that perhaps the 'he' was 'a small boy in the charge of the nursemaid who was the poet's companion'.[32] Yet even this detail doesn't wholly solve the problem of 'story' here, for if the first 'he' is the small boy who would 'bawl'—cry out for his nurse—then, she not being in earshot, 'he' would know. Who would know? And know what? If 'he' were a small boy, then he would be able to know that she was not at her post, and this might be bad enough if reported to the parents. Yet 'he' could presumably not know, and not be likely to jump to the conclusion, that she had been absent because she was having sex with the young British poet and critic living about a fifteen-minute walk from the German embassy. So there is the possible, but slightly strained, reading that the first 'he' is the little boy, and the second 'he' the ambassador, his father. Equally, there is the possibility that the situation is so delicate because the mere fact of her not being there to quiet him would be enough to lose her the job. This would have been a financial and social disaster for her in the early 1930s. Whatever understanding we opt for, the literary-critical situation has moved on. We are dealing with a poem in which the 'I' is a representation of the empirical Empson during his three years in Japan from August 1931 to July 1934, and the 'she' is a representation of a real self too.

---

[32] Sidney Bolt, cited in Empson, *Poems*, 320.

One more slight ambiguity of story comes up in the next to last line in the poem's penultimate stanza:

> Tell me more quickly what I lost by this,
> Or tell me with less drama what they miss
> Who call no die a god for a good throw,
> Who say after two aliens had one kiss
> It seemed the best thing to be up and go.

The odd phrase is the 'two aliens'. If you teach this poem in Japan, all the students think that the two lovers must neither be Japanese, because in that country a Japanese woman could not be an 'alien'. Empson in his 1940 notes for *The Gathering Storm* was at pains to indicate that the Japanese poet 'C. Hatakeyama' whose work he translated in the same collection 'has nothing to do with the Aubade poem'.[33] Yet if his bedfellow were really an 'alien' in 1930s Tokyo, then she couldn't—presumably—be Japanese anyway. However, the 'Haru' identified as his girlfriend was, it appears, Japanese. So what the poem means by the phrase 'two aliens' is that each of the lovers is an 'alien' to the other.

Empson never saw the potential narrative ambiguity in his 'two aliens' phrase. Another of his recorded comments about the poem makes it clear that he didn't think of himself as engaging in the relationship as an exotic pastime. As John Haffenden puts it:

The relationship meant more to Empson—and to Haru—than just an easy or exploitative sexual encounter . . . Thirty years later, in an interview, he glossed the poem to reveal honourable and well-intentioned hopes. 'When I was in Japan, from 1931 to 1934, it was usual for the old hand in the English colony to warn the young man: don't you go and marry a Japanese because we're going to be at war with Japan within ten years; you'll have awful trouble if you marry a Japanese, and this is what the poem is about.'[34]

So that is what the 'two aliens' phrase signified for Empson. The people in bed making love are fond enough of each other to be considering or even discussing a life together. However, they are from nations that within a decade will be making war—and that's why the Rising Sun will part them.

---

[33] Empson, 'Note to "The Fool", etc.', in *Poems*, 322. See also my 'Very Shrinking Behaviour: The Poetic Collaboration of William Empson and Chiyoko Hatakeyama', *Times Literary Supplement*, 5233, 18 July 2003, 13–15.

[34] John Haffenden, 'Sexual Types of Ambiguity', 109, citing 'William Empson in Conversation with Christopher Ricks' (1963), in *Poems*, 119.

Empson didn't hear the ambiguity in his 'two aliens' phrase because as well as writing about a situation that seems to have occurred during 1933–4 in the poem he is also writing from the situation of an Englishman sometime slightly later. He is not, it would seem, thinking of the poem being read by Japanese students at the end of the twentieth-century—and identifying themselves racially with one of the protagonists of the poem, someone who, even then, in Tokyo, was definitively not an 'alien'. Here too we can see examples of 'The language problem but you have to try'. The words of the poem need to be understood not against the background of the historical context or with the social and cultural circumstances surrounding them. They have to be understood as representing and being spoken by selves who are present in the situations, and who represent themselves as from the perspectives that were available to such people at such a time and in such a place.

Empson dropped a stanza from 'Aubade' after its magazine publication. It is one that casts an oblique light on the ambiguities of story under discussion:

> This is unjust to her without a prose book.
> A lyric from a fact is bound to cook.
> It was more grinding; it was much more slow.
> But still the point's not how much time it took.
> It seemed the best thing to be up and go.[35]

Empson may have cut this stanza because its third and fourth lines signal a desire to be less 'unjust to her' with a line that appears, in the absence of that 'prose book', even more unjust. Their break up was 'more grinding'. The need to get a rhyme word for the refrain will have helped produce 'more slow', a mildly ungrammatical variant of 'slower'. What's more, line four admits that the second half of the previous line is irrelevant to the point of the poem. Yet, despite these flaws, I regret the loss of this acknowledgement that lyric poems can invite commentaries that do justice to one or other of the protagonists, as I do of the additional fact that short poems are bound to cook the book of facts from which they are composed. Empson's cutting the verse improves his poem, but its first two lines succinctly count the costs that may be incurred when composing the selves and situations of a life into those of a poem. It is tempting, and many have been tempted, to abolish these problems and ironies by

---

[35] Empson, *Poems*, 319.

recourse to a theory of poetry as wholly fiction. I prefer to keep poetry itself situated firmly in the difficulties.[36]

The fugitive nature of both the situations and the selves in poetry can also be sensed from Empson's poem. The self in relation to its situations can seem both the situation and not it, as in the expression 'my situation'. It is also a part of 'Aubade' that the selves—as in 'Paris, Octubre 1936' by Vallejo and 'Situazione' by Sereni—are in a position to leave. Indeed, the two refrain-like lines in Empson's poem indicate the two basic options, the options of staying or going: 'The heart of standing is you cannot fly' and 'It seemed the best thing to be up and go.' The repeated lines are adapted from the villanelle structure—a form that Empson employed on a number of occasions. His experiments with stanzas that require multiple rhymes on the same sounds and repeated refrains attempt to apply complex axiomatic formulae to a situation or a range of related ones. They also provide readers with the portable equipment to apply these axioms in other cases. As we have seen, the two overlapping situations of 'Aubade' are the romantic embroilment with 'Haru', and the larger embroilments of what we call 'foreign affairs' or 'international relations'. Extremely precarious they were too in a three-year period that saw the beginning of the Manchurian Incident on 18 September 1931 and the coming to power of Adolf Hitler in January 1933.

The device of the alternative refrains requires for its successful deployment that the implications each time either is used should be at least different, and at best cumulatively complex. The complexity is then doubled by the significance generated if the two contrary refrains are taken together. This multiplication of senses is emphasized by their appearing as a couplet at the end of the poem. In 'Aubade' the refrains begin by seeming to be comments on the specific situation of the earthquake. Then, as the reason for her having to leave is brought out, the situation enlarges to one involving the politics and cultural assumptions of the times. Behind the initial uses is an explanation for why they had to part on that occasion. Later the phrases offer much wider political and cultural explanations for why they must separate. These, in turn, evolve from what might be excuses into positions of dignified principle. Yet behind this evolution of explanation and justification lies the ineradicable

---

[36] For further discussion of issues involving facts and lyric poems see my 'Robert Lowell and "Moral Luck"', in *In the Circumstances: About Poems and Poets* (Oxford: Oxford University Press, 1992), 83–104, and 'Matters of Fact and Value', in *Poetry, Poets, Readers: Making Things Happen* (Oxford: Oxford University Press, 2002), 83–108.

shadow of self-criticism on the part of the poet for a relationship that ended unhappily. Thus, 'The heart of standing is you cannot fly' begins as a potential rebuke to the poet for abandoning the girl. It ends as his justification for standing by his country in the gathering war situation. 'It seemed the best thing to be up and go' begins as self-concerned prudence and ends as historically justified wisdom.

Empson humorously renders their communication problems during the earthquake. The difficulties of interpretation, the ambiguities of the two repeating lines, are also a part of the 'language problem', a problem which never goes away and which Empson would spend his life as a writer on poetry and literature exploring. Towards the poem's close he draws together perceptions about the European conflicts, both present and to come, and his awareness of related developments in China and Japan:

> Tell me again about Europe and her pains,
> Who's tortured by the drought, who by the rains.
> Glut me with floods where only the swine can row
> Who cuts his throat and let him count his gains.
> It seemed the best thing to be up and go.
>
> A bedshift flight to a Far Eastern sky.
> Only the same war on a stronger toe.
> The heart of standing is you cannot fly.[37]

'Only the same war on a stronger toe', he writes, and this points to the real wars that were happening when he first published the poem (the Sino–Japanese War and the Spanish Civil War). Nevertheless, the phrase 'bedshift flight' also hints at a 'sex war'—not that between the sexes, but the one fought in the twentieth century to increase public knowledge of, and honesty about, the varieties and complexities of human desire.[38] Empson's 'Aubade' is engaged with problems of Japanese society in an intimate fashion—in that he explicitly comments on the problems of interracial sexual relationships in conflictual political situations. Empson is able to expand considerations relating to his personal experience to the

[37] See also Christopher Ricks, 'William Empson: The Images and the Story', in *The Force of Poetry* (Oxford: Oxford University Press, 1984), 213–14 and, for helpful explications, Philip and Averil Gardner, *The God Approached: A Commentary on the Poems of William Empson* (London: Chatto & Windus, 1978), 163–8.

[38] Empson lost his fellowship at Cambridge for a sexual misdemeanour in 1927 and his teaching contract was not renewed in Japan thanks to another such episode in 1934 (see *Poems*, 252–6, 288).

stands that others are being asked to make in different parts of the globe. His poem's large perspectives and combinations of the intimate with the public make for some problems of clarity and unity in the poem. However, disunities and lacunae in 'Aubade' are crucial marks of its attachment to those very situations and selves that went into constituting it.

IV

Just as selves and situations are fugitive, so can the words be used to refer to a great variety of human predicaments. The flexibility of the term 'situation' is allowed its range in the chapters that follow. It will be found signifying a cultural moment of poetic inspiration, the atmosphere of a political crisis, the mood of a decade, the state of a nation, a condition of exile, an artistic vogue, and a lifetime. The degree of importance that supportive situations have in the writing and reading of poetry is brought into sharper light by moments of historical and personal crisis—as Empson's 'Aubade' also attests. In the next chapter the study of Ezra Pound's 'Villanelle: The Psychological Hour' reveals a poem directly and complexly concerned with the collapse of such a supportive milieu. This collapse is the result of forces external to the poem: the loss of friends and the alterations in cultural atmosphere caused by the outbreak of war in 1914. Yet these are forces which must be contained in the poem too. Thus, a poem's relevant context will be understood, in large measure, from the implications of words in the text. Similarly, the chapter on Louis MacNeice's *Autumn Journal* and the Munich crisis examines the relationship between a long poem's formal resources and the situation of its composition, both public, in the political climate of the late 1930s, and personal, in the poet's emotional life. The arguments for attachment stated or implied there are then challenged and qualified by the piece on W. S. Graham, he being a poet who cultivated his independence and struggled with various forms of weak and strong dependence in both his writings and his life.

The studies of work by Basil Bunting, Elizabeth Bishop, and Allen Curnow are each concerned with the poetic shaping of the often painful or difficult insights which may come of expatriation or travel. Both of these are conditions of life in which the relation of the self to its situations is likely to be attenuated. The piece on Bunting examines poems about enforced expatriation because of grinding poverty. That on Bishop finds her Brazil period to have been largely beneficial and, to an extent, reparative of her manifold losses and bereavements. Nevertheless, the second of two chapters on her work takes the measure of just how much and how little her work could do with such burdens, ones which are often added to by the creative efforts required to relieve them. The chapter on Curnow draws attention to the many and various benefits his work has received from travel abroad. The study of some earlier poems and a translation by Charles Tomlinson analyses various stylistic indicators of the poet's unfortunate detachment from the scenes he renders. The work gathered here was written to develop an appreciation of the losses and gains in such movements across the great distances and minute details of a treated scene. The chapter on Mairi MacInnes's work underlines the conflictual relationship of fidelity to and detachment from place in the poetry of writers whose lives and works have been shaped by great imaginative and actual displacements.

The work on Tom Raworth's early poetry and its links to the moment of pop art explores the relationship between a self in its domestic and affective situations and the ways in which such materials will be shaped by the available styles and manners of an art movement. Such a movement is a set of situations that takes place within the confines of cultural and historical developments. Since all the poets and their works studied here have complex relationships to modernism, this chapter also examines the renewal of interest in early and classic modernist procedures during the 1950s and 1960s. It then considers the possibility that this renewal of interest, far from being a return to the main current of twentieth-century creativity, was a further chapter in the crisis of how poetic art is itself situated in relation to the selves of writers and readers.

The study of Roy Fisher's work concludes the book by exploring related concerns with last things and the treatment of the dead in poems. The death of others is one of the key situations when we feel ourselves, by contrast, to be located, and in places that impinge more sharply through the presence of death in the absence of the dead ones. Fisher's many writings on the treatment of the dead share such an intensified sense of situated meaning. This is the case not least because Fisher's work has been largely exercised by questions of perspective, groundedness, and location. Though, unlike some of the other poets read here, Fisher is not much of a traveller, his attention to the rendering of locations has been profoundly inflected by styles associated with movement, displacement, alienation, and conflict. His work provides an occasion for a resolving consideration of the book's issues.

On 18 September 1823 Goethe told Eckermann that 'Alle meine Gedichte sind Gelegenheitsgedichte, sie sind durch die Wirklichkeit angeregt und haben darin Grund und Boden. Von Gedichten, aus der Luft gegriffen, halte ich nichts.' (All my poems are occasional poems, they have been prompted by reality and thus have ground and foundation. I don't hold with poems plucked out of the air.)[39] It is likely that Eugenio Montale's second volume of poems, *Le occasioni* (1939), was titled thus with Goethe's remark in mind. These examples should discourage us from ever thinking that an 'occasional poem' is—by definition—a trivial one, limited by the constraints of its situation. A similar service was performed for the expression 'vers de circonstance' by Robert Desnos when in January 1944 he wrote that 'La grande poésie peut être nécessairement actuelle, de circonstances . . . elle peut donc être fugitive.' Thus, the only way for a poem to take to the air is for it to be well grounded. In times of violent public confusion, as equally in times of individual uncertainty and distress, we need this kind of poetry.

Finally, there remains Thomas Nagel's proposal. He suggested that we change the question asked from 'How should we live, whatever the circumstances?' to 'Under what circumstances is it possible to live as we should?' Returning to these questions now, we can see that, given our being able to move from one set of circumstances to another, to live and work in different cultures, it cannot be practically possible (aside from the undesirable establishment of a globally homogenous ethical totality) to abandon his first question. After all, it is one test of a self (one we mostly don't want to be tested by in the final end) that there are actions we would feel we would have to do, and others we would feel we could never do, *under any circumstances*, in whatever situation.

Equally, his second question ('Under what circumstances is it possible to live as we should?') cannot help but toy with a fiction of omnipotent will and fantastic choice. It is impossible to imagine ourselves as independent of all circumstance—aside from being dead, and even then, as Vallejo's sonnet suggests, the represented situation may remain as our witness. What's more, we can only imagine morally better or more promising situations as evolving, or emerging, or even being metamorphosed from existing situations. They cannot be conjured, as God was once thought to have created the world, from nothing. So how could

[39] Johann Peter Eckermann, *Gespräche mit Goethe in den Letzten Jahren seines Lebens*, in Johann Wolfgang von Goethe, *Gedenkausgabe der Werke, Briefe und Gespräche*, xxiv, ed. E. Beutler. (Zürich: Artemis, 1948), 48.

we ever be deconditioned enough exactly and realistically to ask in what precise circumstances we could sense ourselves able to act more morally and with less conflict-ridden selves? My point is not that political philosophers and everyone else should abandon the project of world amelioration. On the contrary, I'm suggesting that this needs to be done with as full an understanding and acceptance of the historical and cultural situatedness of selves as is possible.

Though thoroughly well intentioned, neither of Nagel's questions appears quite the right one to be asking; if, that is, both are taken as exclusive questions. Given the world we find ourselves in, we should not want wholly to abandon the first, while we can never extricate ourselves from situations sufficiently to be able to ask the second. These questions of Nagel's are not the subject of the following chapters. However, writing these studies has helped lead to this thought. If we are going to ask ourselves more realistically nuanced questions about how and where we may live as we should, it will be necessary to achieve and work with more complex, multi-perspectival understandings of what it is to be in the world. Since there is no way to experience this world but by means of our own minds and senses, it will inevitably seem to each of us, as Wittgenstein saw it, 'my world'. Yet this world, he also understood, is only minimally subject to 'my' will at all. It is both not my world, and, as the philosophy of language makes plain, other people's world too.[40] It is also a world that can be perceived by human beings as not only theirs. One of the ways (among others) to gain a textured understanding of our selves in their situations, so as to ask questions about the world and how to live in it, is to read poetry. Most urgently for us, we would find it beneficial to read with understanding the poetry written in our present day and in our recent past.

---

[40] See Ludwig Wittgenstein, *Philosophical Investigations*, 3nd edn., trans. G. E. M. Anscombe (Oxford: Blackwell, 2001), sects. 243–315, 75e-88e. For an explication see Hacker, *Insight and Illusion*, ch. 9. See also Bernard Williams, 'Wittgenstein and Idealism', in *Moral Luck: Philosophical Papers 1973–1980* (Cambridge: Cambridge University Press, 1981), 144–63.

CHAPTER 2

Not a Villanelle: Pound's Psychological Hour

I

Ezra Pound experienced disturbing collapses of creative situation at least four times before his final silence. The first of these may have been his sojourn at Wabash College, Indiana.[1] The poem 'In Durance' with its repeated phrase 'I am homesick after mine own kind'[2] dates from this period. The most dramatic of such crises was that initiated by Pound's remaining in Italy during the Second World War and precipitated by Benito Mussolini's fall from power in July 1943.[3] His two years of isolation in what remained of Italy under Axis control culminated in Pound's imprisonment at Pisa, out of which came *The Pisan Cantos*. The poet's transfer to Washington for trial and his incarceration at the mental institution of St Elizabeth's were then the most prolonged state of relative seclusion in a life so shaped by writing and corresponding that isolation and self-doubt might seem odd words to characterize Pound's life or work. 'Villanelle: The Psychological Hour' is another poem prompted by a collapse of creative situation, that produced by the first year of war in 1914–15, and shaped by isolate and uncertain reflections upon the poet's relations to the lives and works of artists who were then his colleagues.

Burton Raffel has described Pound's 'Villanelle' as 'pleasant, careful,

---

[1] See Charles Norman, *Ezra Pound* (London: MacDonald, 1969), 22–4; Noel Stock, *The Life of Ezra Pound* (Harmondsworth: Penguin, 1974), 46–55; Humphrey Carpenter, *A Serious Character: The Life of Ezra Pound* (London: Faber & Faber, 1988), 71–83.

[2] Page references in the text are to Ezra Pound, *Personae: The Shorter Poems* rev. edn., ed. L. Baechler and A. Walton Litz (New York: New Directions, 1990). For 'In Durance' see pp. 19–21.

[3] See the opening of 'Gold and Work 1944', in *Selected Prose 1909–1965*, ed. W. Cookson (London: Faber & Faber, 1978), 306; *The Cantos of Ezra Pound*, 4th coll. edn. (London: Faber & Faber, 1987), 478; Stock, *Life*, 511–14; Carpenter, *Serious Character*, 626–9; Mary de Rachewiltz, *Discretions* (London: Faber & Faber, 1971), 184–7.

but essentially dithering verse'.[4] By offering a reading I want to counteract a widespread underestimating of the work. Peter Brooker notes that 'Pound's poem is obviously only loosely a villanelle',[5] but 'loosely a villanelle' would not be one, and the poem is not 'made up of five three-lined stanzas and a quatrain—all using only two rhymes—and with the lines repeated according to a regular pattern'.[6] K. K. Ruthven calls it 'a villanelle in name only'.[7] Why is 'Villanelle: The Psychological Hour' called a villanelle when it does not have the structures and expectations of such a form? Conflicting exegesis of the poem's relations to Pound's milieu and his sense of himself with regard to his contemporaries links the poem to T. S. Eliot and Vivien Haigh-Wood, Henri and Sophie Gaudier-Brzeska, James Joyce, and W. B. Yeats. Exploring these possibilities will lead to some observations about an ambiguity in the presentation of its subject.

'Villanelle: The Psychological Hour' appears in the 'Poems of Lustra 1915–1916' section of *Personae*.[8] It was probably composed during the summer or early autumn of 1915, and first published in the December 1915 issue of *Poetry* (Chicago). This text has some different readings from the 'Poems of Lustra' version, which I touch on later. Burton Raffel's description of the poem ('pleasant, careful, but essentially dithering verse') takes a diagnosis for a symptom, as if echoing the opening stanza's 'middle-ageing care' with 'careful'. Yet, far from 'dithering', Pound's phrasing has a definitive, sure-footed, and unobtrusive accuracy. The first five lines pitch the confession of a troubled consciousness:

> I had over-prepared the event,
>   that much was ominous.
> With middle-ageing care
>   I had laid out just the right books,
> I had almost turned down the pages.

Hyphenated compounds often mark a distinctive verbal inventiveness. Here 'over-prepared' offers a nonce verb, and 'middle-ageing' a newly

---

[4] Burton Raffel, *Ezra Pound: Prime Minister of Poetry* (Hampden, Conn.: Archon, 1984), 46.
[5] Peter Brooker, *A Student's Guide to the Selected Poems of Ezra Pound* (London: Faber & Faber, 1979), 108–9. To another critic the poem is 'not a villanelle at all' (William Harmon, *Time in Ezra Pound's Work* (Chapel Hill, NC: University of North Carolina Press, 1977), 78).
[6] James Joyce, *A Portrait of the Artist as a Young Man*, ed. C. G. Anderson (New York: Viking, 1968), 538.
[7] K. K. Ruthven, *A Guide to Ezra Pound's Personae* (1926) (Berkeley and Los Angeles, Calif.: University of California Press, 1969), 242.
[8] *Personae*, 155–6.

calibrated epithet, creating a phase between the end of youth and the start of middle age. Perhaps it is a 'care' that indicates the approach of middle age, or one which brings on that time of life. The word 'care' here oscillates between loving attention and wearying worry; it is nudged in the direction of the second sense by an internal rhyme with 'over-prepared'. Creative engagement may decline into fussy perfectionism: Pound's phrasing performs the former by evoking thoughts of the latter. In 'that much was ominous' the expected phrase 'was obvious' is hauntingly deflected; in 'just the right books' can be heard: only and precisely those books which will create the best impression. This is verse about dithering, not 'dithering verse'. It does not suffer from Yvor Winters's 'fallacy of imitative form: the attempt to express a state of uncertainty by uncertainty of expression'[9]—at least not in the precision of its phrasing.

The speaker had dithered over opening his books at the most suitable pages, but decided against it; or, then again, perhaps not:

> *Beauty is so rare a thing.*
> *So few drink of my fountain.*

With these lines, which function as a pseudo-refrain, the 'middle-ageing care' is associated with a style of verse writing. This is largely achieved by the repeated 'so' and by the period diction: '*Beauty*', '*rare*', '*few*', '*fountain*'. Yet Pound's poem does not suffer from the inclusion of these lines as if they were lapses by a clumsy performer with an incorrigible taste for dated idiom. The lines don't rhyme. They deploy a fundamentally trochaic cadence, spurred on by the intonation pattern of 'pages', followed by a basically iambic one, but with an equivocal first foot. If the second 'so' (in 'So few') is to be an intensifier, and thus have an anaphora-like relation to 'so rare', then this 'So' at the beginning of the line must be stressed. However, the move over the line-end from 'pages' to '*Beauty*' has set up an expectation of inertial continuity: since '*thing*' is stressed, the next line will begin with an unstressed syllable. This makes 'So' into a logical connecting particle, and produces the buried syntax: it is because '*Beauty is so rare a thing*' that '*few drink of my fountain*'. This implication is drawn out by the second appearance of the lines, when no full stop separates them into two sentences.[10] An intonational ambiguity allows for both a complaint and an explanation.

[9] Yvor Winters, *In Defence of Reason* (Athens, Ohio: Ohio University Press, 1947), 87.
[10] This is true of the revised edition I am using. It is not true for the text in *Selected Poems*, ed. T. S. Eliot (London: Faber & Faber, 1948), 149, where the refrain is exactly the same on its two appearances. Nor is it true of the text in E. Pound and M. Spann (eds.), *Confucius to Cummings:An*

A speaking voice, as distinct perhaps from one reading, takes up the tune of 'So':

> So much barren regret,
> So many hours wasted!
> And now I watch, from the window,
>   the rain, the wandering busses.[11]

The self-understanding appears to change from 'regret' to annoyance, and then back to a wistful passivity. With the first of these lines we are in the psychological territory of Prince Rasselas in the Happy Valley: 'He, for a few hours, regretted his regret.'[12] The speaker has lost valuable time, has exhausted his youth in the pursuit of a worn-out manner. This is the moment when the word 'passéism' was in vogue.[13] 'And now I watch' has the implication that even at this moment he could be working, but is using up his time in pointless worry about where his expected guests could be. The detachment of the objects of 'watch' from their verb by the comma'd-off 'from the window' serves to isolate the speaker. The phrase 'wandering busses' locates him between the lyrical impressionism of 'wandering' and the modern urbanity of London 'busses' which— beyond their appearance to a troubled sensibility—do not wander: they follow routes and timetables. As with 'ominous' for 'obvious', there is a 'dance of the intellect among words'[14] in the disjunction between 'wandering' and 'busses', a disjunction present too in the title's shift from 'Villanelle' to 'Psychological Hour' and indicating that the poem is about just such points of change. These unobtrusive instances of logopoeic intelligence locate the poem in a frame of mind more capaciously self-aware than that of its apparent speaker.

Anthology of Poetry (New York: New Directions, 1964), 309, where the first of the two lines in its second manifestation is punctuated with a comma.

[11] Though Baechler and Walton Litz note that 'It has been our general policy to preserve Pound's punctuation and spelling, however idiosyncratic, unless there is clear evidence of errors by the compositor' (Pound, *Personae*, 275), perhaps 'buses' would be better, as in *Selected Poems*, 149, since 'busses' might be the plural of 'buss', a kiss.

[12] Samuel Johnson, *The History of Rasselas, Prince of Abissinia*, ed. D. J. Enright (Harmondsworth: Penguin, 1976), 48.

[13] See *Pound/Joyce: The Letters of Ezra Pound to James Joyce*, ed. F. Read (New York: New Directions, 1970), 113.

[14] Ezra Pound, *The Literary Essays of Ezra Pound*, ed. T. S. Eliot (London: Faber & Faber, 1954), 25.

II

The next passage in the poem is obscure, and this is because it alludes
meaningfully to matters it does not spell out:

> 'Their little cosmos is shaken'—
> the air is alive with that fact.
> In their parts of the city
> they are played on by diverse forces.
> How do I know?
> Oh, I know well enough.
> For them there is something afoot.
> As for me;
> I had over-prepared the event . . .

For many years it has been conventional to link this poem to Pound's
friendship with Henri and Sophie Gaudier-Brzeska.[15] In his memoir of
the young sculptor who had been killed in a charge at Neuville St Vaast on
5 June 1915 Pound describes his anxiety that the younger man would find
him, now thirty years of age, a tired and insufficiently radical figure. He
mentions a visit that Gaudier paid to Pound and how he read him early
poems because he thought they would be 'just the right . . . pages':

I was interested and I was determined that he should be. I knew that many things
would bore or disgust him, particularly my rather middle-aged point of view, my
intellectual tiredness and exhaustion, my general scepticism and quietness, and I
therefore opened fire with 'Altaforte,' and 'Piere Vidal,' and such poems as I had
written when about his own age. And I think it was the 'Altaforte' that convinced
him that I would do to be sculpted.

Pound's phrase 'opened fire' is sadly deaf to its implicating the violence of
the avant-garde with that of the Western Front, the vitality of youth with
a killing energy. This deafness confuses the purpose of Pound's prose.
The aggressive note is also an indication of isolation and a concomitant
need to belong, for Pound has picked up the tune from his milieu. It is a
common characteristic of the pre-war art movements, most pronounced
in the Italian futurism[16] from which the London vorticists had attempted

---

[15] See e.g. Peter Robinson, 'Ezra Pound and Italian Art', in R. S. Humphries (ed.), *Pound's
Artists* ed. (London: Tate Gallery, 1985), 123–4.

[16] Walter Benjamin noted that 'Marinetti . . . expects war to supply the artistic gratification of
a sense perception that has been changed by technology. This is evidently the consummation of
"L'art pour l'art." Mankind, which in Homer's time was an object of contemplation for the
Olympian gods, now is one for itself. Its self-alienation has reached such a degree that it can

to distinguish themselves. The poet then returns to the subject of his 'middle-ageing care':

He even tried to persuade me that I was not becoming middle-aged, but any man whose youth has been worth anything, any man who has lived his life at all in the sun, knows that he has seen the best of it when he finds thirty approaching; knows that he is entering a quieter realm, a place with a different psychology.[17]

The visit of the two friends, the differences in age, the fear of not being sufficiently aggressive, and the middle-ageing theme, together with the importance of the sculptor's death in Pound's life, have seemed sufficient grounds for assuming that the poem recalls a lost member of the vorticist group. It seems to be recounting an occasion when these allies failed to meet, which later came to have 'ominous' reverberations.

Omar Pound and Robert Spoo challenge this association of Gaudier with the poem in their account of Pound's friendship with Margaret Cravens. They suggest that the couple is Thomas Stearns Eliot and Vivien Haigh-Wood:

John Peale Bishop, in a letter of November 1922 to Edmund Wilson (Beinecke), mentions learning from Ezra Pound himself that 'Villanelle' records an occasion on which Eliot and his fiancée failed to turn up for tea, deciding instead to go to the registrar's office to be married. Gaudier-Brzeska and his companion are not the subjects of the poem, as frequently suggested.[18]

The Eliots were married on 26 June 1915 in a register office in Hampstead, and Pound's advice probably had an influence on Eliot's decision to marry an Englishwoman and attempt to establish himself in the literary world of London.[19] No source is known for 'Their little cosmos is shaken'[20] and it may well be that the composed phrase is in inverted commas to produce some Laforguian irony,[21] in the manner of Eliot's

---

experience its own destruction as an aesthetic pleasure of the first order' (in 'The Work of Art in the Age of Mechanical Reproduction', in *Illuminations* (New York: Schocken, 1969), 244).

  [17] Ezra Pound, *Gaudier-Brzeska: A Memoir* (New York: New Directions, 1970), 45–6.
  [18] *Ezra Pound and Margaret Cravens: A Tragic Friendship 1910–1912*, ed. O. Pound and R. Spoo (Durham, NC: Duke University Press, 1988), 143.
  [19] Valerie Eliot notes that 'Shrewdly realizing that his future as a writer lay in England, Pound encouraged him to settle there, and to marry an Englishwoman, Vivien Haigh-Wood, which he did after leaving Oxford in June' (in T. S. Eliot, *The Waste Land: A Facsimile and Transcript of the Original Drafts Including the Annotations of Ezra Pound*, ed. V. Eliot (London: Faber & Faber, 1971), p. ix).
  [20] K. K. Ruthven notes 'Quotation unidentified' in *A Guide to Ezra Pound's Personae*, 243.
  [21] 'Laforguian' may be premature. Pound's translation of 'Pierrots' was first published in 1918. However, he would have known the Laforguian mode of early Eliot when he wrote

early poems. Its words indicate that the small world created by the couple has been disturbed, and that this disturbance has reached the speaker in the form, perhaps, of their non-appearance: 'the air is alive with that fact'. The contrasting epithet and noun also serve to mock faintly 'Their little cosmos'. What has shaken the couple is hinted in the phrase 'their parts of the city'—where 'parts' implies that the pressures of the different social strata in London conflict in them: 'they are played on by diverse forces'. There may be suggested here some difficulty for the couple in sustaining their 'little cosmos', perhaps in the form of parental opposition.[22] Then come the four lines that Pound added after the poem's magazine publication, beginning: 'How do I know? | Oh, I know well enough.' The problems that Pound himself had gone through in gaining consent to marry the Englishwoman Dorothy Shakespear have been detailed in the volume of their letters.[23]

III

'For them there is something afoot. | As for me': in revision Pound turned the speaking voice back upon its own little cosmos and thence to the villanelle-like refrain: '*Beauty is so rare a thing | So few drink of my fountain.*' Though there are many instances of repeating forms in the poem, the returning italicized lines are what most suggest its being called a villanelle. Some have been hesitant about the fact that it is not a villanelle. Pound knew that it was not one, and commented on what he had intended by that part of the title: 'I wanted the effect of a recurrence of theme and meant "Villanelle" to mean generally the feel of the villanelle form in a modern subject.'[24] Does 'a modern subject' mean 'an up-to-date topic' or 'a contemporary sensibility'? Probably both. The title's 'Psychological' suggests a sensibility, but 'Hour' could signal a topic.

This very phrase appears in Henry James's 1903 tale 'The Papers'. Maud Blandy watches Howard Bight play upon the vanity of Mr Mar-

---

'Villanelle: The Psychological Hour'. A French source for the poem is likely to be Charles Vildrac's 'Visite', which Pound praises in 'A Retrospect', in *Literary Essays*, 13, and cites in a lineated prose translation (including the line 'He promised to come again') in 'The Approach to Paris: Vildrac', in *Selected Prose 1909–1965*, 336–8.

[22] See Ezra Pound's letter to T. S. Eliot's father, postmarked 28 June 1915, two days after the Eliots' marriage, in *The Letters of T. S. Eliot*, ed. V. Eliot (London: Faber & Faber, 1988), 99–104.

[23] See e.g. Henry Hope Shakespear's letter to Ezra Pound dated 12 October 1912 and the poet's reply, in *Ezra Pound and Dorothy Shakespear: Their Letters*, ed. O. Pound and A. Walton Litz (London: Faber & Faber, 1984), 72, 87–8. The Pounds were married on 18 April 1914.

[24] Cited in Raffel, *Ezra Pound*, 46.

shall, the author of *Corisanda*, to make him imagine his future fame by means of the journalistic manipulation of his rumoured death—from which, like Sherlock Holmes, he is miraculously to 'return'. James's story maps quite closely over Pound's poem: a young couple being befriended by a foolish older writer anxious about his social standing. Here Marshall asks the gormless question, and Bight replies:

> 'To step in?' His visitor hung upon his lips.
> 'To do the thing better, so to speak—to do it right; to—having raised the whirlwind—really *ride* the storm. To seize the psychological hour.'[25]

James has Bight exploit a cant phrase, 'To seize the psychological hour', meaning, in the words of an older idiom: 'to strike while the iron is hot'. Given the difference of dates between James's story and Pound's poem it may well be that the latter's title phrase is signalling itself as an 'hour' now decidedly past. Pound briefly mentions 'The Papers' in his 1918 essay on the writer. He calls the tale 'a fantasia, diverting', and explains:

> By fantasias I mean sketches in which the people are 'real' or convince one of their verity, but where the story is utterly unconvincing, is not intended to convince, is merely a sort of exaggeration of the fitting situation or the situation which ought to result in order to display some type at its apogee.[26]

'Villanelle: The Psychological Hour' looks, in this light, to be an attempt to condense real occasions and people from Pound's London life into a 'fitting situation' which, unlike a 'fantasia', dispenses with all but a trace of 'story' and would be thus the more convincing.

Similarly, Pound's phrase describing his poem's 'recurrence theme' can indicate both a musical phrase's return and the return of a subject. There are various formal recurrences: the italicized lines beginning '*Beauty* . . .', the anaphora 'I had . . .', and 'So much', 'so many'; and repeated phrasing: 'How do I know? | Oh, I know well enough' or 'Two friends . . . Friends? . . . less friends'. There is the use of diurnal recurrence as a structural marker: '*Between the night and morning?*', 'The first night? | The second evening?', '"To-morrow at tea-time"' , and 'Now the third day is here—'. There are also recurrences of regret about the speaker's

---

[25] Henry James, *Maud-Evelyn, The Special Type, The Papers, and Other Stories* (London: Macmillan, 1923), 160. James's tale contains other possible prompts for Pound's poem, such as: 'If she kept to herself, from the morrow on, for three days, her adoption of that course was helped, as she thankfully felt, by the great other circumstance and the great public commotion under cover of which it so little mattered what became of private persons' (p. 177).

[26] *Literary Essays*, 321–2.

'works', of unease about personal contacts, of self-concern about ageing, and of anxiety about a suitable milieu for making art.

Pound's best work is composed in a thematically significant rhythm, and he is able here to combine a rhythmic and stylistic experiment with a personal and cultural situation so that the word 'theme' may aptly cover both the poem's music and its matter. Here Pound's ear for tones of speech and cultural conditions, as well as for cadence and incantation, is at its best. In his preface to the *Poetical Works of Lionel Johnson* he notes that 'The villanelle, even, can at its best achieve the closest intensity, I mean when, as with Dowson, the refrains are an emotional fact, which the intellect, in the various gyrations of the poem, tries in vain and in vain to escape.'[27] In Pound's poem the emotional fact might be the effect of the figure's isolation, the intellect attempting to explain the couple's non-appearance as an escape from that emotion, in vain because the poem's conclusion reinforces the figure's predicament with its unexpected 'other man's note'. The poet has discovered a 'subject' that he can create out of the rhythmic suggestiveness in a villanelle's reiterations, without being bound to sustain its usually unified tone and enclosing form. This formal disruption can itself indicate a large-scale shift similar to that of 'wandering' and 'busses'.

A source for the oscillation of a stiff italicized loftiness and a more fluidly mundane roman text may be *A Portrait of the Artist as a Young Man.* The magazine instalment where Stephen Dedalus is represented as composing 'The Villanelle of the Temptress'[28] is printed like the novel with verse in italic and prose in roman. It was published in *The Egoist* on 1 July 1915, less than a month after Gaudier's death, and five days after the Eliots' wedding:[29]

> *Your eyes have set man's heart ablaze*
> *And you have had your will of him.*
> *Are you not weary of ardent ways?*

And then? The rhythm died away, ceased, began again to move and beat. And then? Smoke, incense ascending from the altar of the world.

[27] *Poetical Works of Lionel Johnson* (London: Elkin Matthews, 1915), p. xvii, and *Literary Essays*, 369.
[28] This is the name Stanislaus Joyce gave the poem, which is included among Joyce's own 'Youthful Poems' in James Joyce, *Poems and Shorter Writings*, ed. R. Ellmann, A. Walton Litz, and J. Whittier-Ferguson (London: Faber & Faber, 1991), 72.
[29] *The Egoist, An Individualist Review*, 2/7, Thurs. 1 July 1915 (New York: Kraus Reprint, 1967), 107–9.

Joyce's poem is a villanelle in the style of the fin de siècle. It is first broken up between passages describing the young artist's composing mind, and then the whole poem is cited. *The Egoist* instalment ends at this point, a pause indicated in the novel text by an asterisk. The prose then shifts into an invocation of the Dublin scene:

> *Are you not weary of ardent ways?*
> *Tell no more of enchanted days.*

*

What birds were they? He stood on the steps of the library to look at them, leaning wearily on his ashplant. They flew round and round the jutting shoulder of a house in Molesworth Street. The air of the late March evening made clear their flight, their dark quivering bodies flying clearly against the sky as against a limp-hung cloth of smoky tenuous blue.[30]

Joyce's novel also contrasts a literary weariness with crisp evocations of the urban environment, itself touched with a stylistic beauty. Joyce's brief questions, 'And then?' or 'What birds were they?', may have suggested Pound's 'How do I know?', 'Friends?', 'The first night? | The second evening?' And it is such contrasts as are found in his own 'Villanelle' that Pound praised in Joyce's prose: 'On almost every page of Joyce you will find just such swift alternation of subjective beauty and external shabbiness, squalor, and sordidness. It is the bass and treble of his method.'[31]

In Pound's poem the return of the refrain moves the theme back to the speaker's anxieties about his creative isolation, his literary reputation, and his ageing:

> Two friends: a breath of the forest . . .
> Friends? Are people less friends
>   because one has just, at last, found them?
> Twice they promised to come.
>
>   *'Between the night and morning?'*
>
> *Beauty would drink of my mind.*
> Youth would awhile forget
>   my youth is gone from me.

In an earlier poem called 'The Plunge' Pound associates 'the new' with 'New friends, new faces' and opposes them to 'walls, streets, stones, | All

---

[30] James Joyce, *A Portrait of the Artist as a Young Man* (Harmondsworth: Penguin, 1960), 217, 223–4.

[31] *Literary Essays*, 412.

mire, mist, all fog' with 'Grass, and low fields, and hills' (p. 66). Similarly, 'In a Station of the Metro' presents a contrast of urban and natural in the move over the line end from 'crowd' to 'Petals' (p. 111). So too in 'Villanelle' Pound connects the reviving idea of new literary friends with a natural vitality: 'Two friends: a breath of the forest . . .'. The touching note in 'just, at last, found them', rather than 'met them', suggests that the speaker imagined this couple were particularly valued as the sorts of colleagues and companions he had long needed. As early as 1907 'In Durance' had announced:

> I am homesick after mine own kind,
> Oh I know that there are folk about me, friendly faces,
> But I am homesick after mine own kind. (pp. 19–20)

The assistance that Pound gave to Eliot in helping to establish him both in London and in a transatlantic literary world is well documented, and gives the impression that Pound saw his younger compatriot in precisely this light. On 30 September 1914, in a letter to Harriet Monroe, Pound wrote:

He is the only American I know of who has made what I can call adequate preparation for writing. He has actually trained himself *and* modernized himself *on his own* . . . It is such a comfort to meet a man and not have to tell him to wash his face, wipe his feet, and remember the date (1914) on the calendar.[32]

This recognition of Eliot as one who had become a 'modern' writer in isolation contrasts starkly with the lengthy and published self-education displayed in 'just the right . . . pages' of Pound's early volumes.

IV

First readers of the next line, *'Between the night and morning?'*, may be forgiven for imagining that the couple had promised to come in the early hours. That is so eccentric a call for London in 1915 it must be ruled out, as must the supposition that 'The Psychological Hour' is in fact in the small hours. The allusive obscurity of the line prompted James Longenbach to comment: 'When Pound first published it in December 1915, the secret society of readers capable of identifying the allusion to Yeats's "The People" would have been very small: Yeats's poem was not

---

[32] Ezra Pound, *The Selected Letters of Ezra Pound 1907–1941*, ed. D. D. Paige (New York: New Directions, 1950), 40.

published for another two months. These were not poems written for the people at large.'[33] Alluding to a poem by one of the most famous poets alive in 1915, even if it had not yet been published, is less 'elitist' if we assume, as Pound had reason to do, that though the line was unknown that December it would become familiar soon enough:

> 'What have I earned for all that work,' I said,
> 'For all that I have done at my own charge?
> The daily spite of this unmannerly town,
> Where who has served the most is most defamed,
> The reputation of his lifetime lost
> Between the night and morning...'[34]

Yeats is writing about the failure of the Abbey Theatre audiences to appreciate what he had been trying to achieve for them and Ireland, as well as his own sense of time lost for the composition of poetry. Later in the poem his 'phoenix' (probably Maud Gonne) rebukes him for losing faith with the people when in adversity. James Longenbach argues that Pound's obscure allusion makes his poem one designed (citing Pound himself) for 'an actual, if almost imperceptible aristocracy'. While not wishing to debate Longenbach's conclusions about Pound's clannish sense of his own and his friends' superiority, I would say that he over-emphasizes the implications of the allusion, noting that

Like Yeats's 'The People,' Pound's 'Villanelle' is about the artist's right to choose his own company. But unlike Yeats, Pound is not conscious of a second voice rebuking his dismissal of the people. He is more desperately concerned with differentiating his art from the 'common' world of Amy Lowell and Vachel Lindsay.

Perhaps so, but it is also possible to be rebuked by silence. The 'Villanelle' has the rebuke of the friends' non-appearance, and it has the reinforcing challenge of the other man's note arriving on the third day. Longenbach suggests that the allusion to Yeats's 'The People' brushes aside the anxiety created by the two people not coming to tea. 'Without knowledge of Yeats's "The People"', he writes, 'the point of Pound's poem is all but imperceptible, for "The People" tells us that the poet should not worry about his fickle friends and the reputation that could be lost "between the night and morning."'

[33] This and two further quotations are from James Longenbach, *Stone Cottage: Pound, Yeats, and Modernism* (New York: Oxford University Press, 1988), 152–3.

[34] *The Variorum Edition of the Poems of W. B. Yeats*, ed. P. Allt and R. K. Alspach (New York: Macmillan, 1971), 351.

This is unlikely. 'Villanelle: The Psychological Hour' gives no indication that the friends are 'fickle'. It explains that they are 'played on by diverse forces' and that for them 'something is afoot'. Nor is there indication in Yeats's poem that the 'unmannerly town' is composed of Yeats's friends; quite the contrary. The allusion to Yeats's poem raises the question, for the speaker of the 'Villanelle', of whether the reason why the two people stayed away is because the man who had 'over-prepared the event' is no longer a significant figure in the London literary scene, and therefore not worth visiting. Far from brushing aside the behaviour of the friends, it focuses the speaker's anxiety on the matter of his reputation.

Pound's quotation of the line, or slight misquotation if you are pedantic about the question mark inside the quotes, involves the original context in 'The People', but only lightly. Pound had not written for the theatre; he had not then been seriously embroiled in nationalist politics; he had not been involved in a frustrated love for the person who rebukes the speaker's elitism in Yeats's poem. Where Yeats is confronting his wasted time in relation to public issues, Pound is presenting an isolated writer concerned about his colleagues and allies.

The three lines following the citation seem then to explain that he had hoped the younger people, both still in their twenties, would learn from him, would '*drink of my mind*'. This is to take '*Beauty*' as paralleled by 'Youth': both referring to the friends. It is also possible for '*Beauty*' to be the abstraction, and so refer to art, as in Laurence Binyon's remark,[35] or Beardsley's.[36] The self-caressing pathos of the final two lines from part I of the poem should be enough to recall that the 'Villanelle', however significant its autobiographical base, is also the portrait of a state of mind—and not one necessarily fully endorsed by the writer, who has here made the speaker sound close to the ones in Eliot's early poems.[37]

---

[35] 'Slowness is beauty', in Ezra Pound, *Guide to Kulchur* (New York: New Directions, 1970), 129.

[36] 'Beauty is difficult', in *The Cantos*, 511. See also Geoffrey Hill's discussion of Pound's use of this word in *The Enemy's Country: Words, Contexture, and other Circumstances of Language* (Oxford: Oxford University Press, 1991), 96, 101–2.

[37] For a discussion of relations between 'Villanelle: The Psychological Hour' and 'The Love Song of J. Alfred Prufrock' see M. L. Rosenthal, *Sailing into the Unknown: Yeats, Pound, and Eliot* (New York: Oxford University Press, 1978), 69–75.

V

Vivien Eliot was keen on dancing, and a number of outings to halls in
London are recorded. Perhaps part II of the poem is derived from one of
them:

> ('Speak up! You have danced so stiffly?
> Someone admired your works,
> And said so frankly.
>
> 'Did you talk like a fool,
> The first night?
> The second evening?'
>
> '*But* they promised again:
> "To-morrow at tea-time".')

The poem turns sharply from the 'dying fall', the mere murmur of 'my
youth is gone from me' to the vigorous colloquial: 'Speak up!' Once again
the tune of 'so' emerges: 'so stiffly' and 'so frankly', where the second 'so'
is not, of course, an intensifier. The grammar of self-doubt has been
skilfully turned here. A statement has a tagged-on question mark to alter
the intonation pattern. The added 'And said so frankly' introduces, as if to
banish, the possibility that it may have been a piece of polite flattery. The
italicized '*But*' allows the suspicion to remain that he had talked 'like
a fool', and that they had been good enough to overlook the fact by
promising again though perhaps thinking better of it later. The parenthesis which encloses these lines serves to indicate that the whole section
is to be understood as interior self-questioning and remembered dialogue, dialogue which actually took place before section I of the poem.

The conclusion is an example of how to make an unexpected and
apparently unconnected occurrence serve as the strike of the hammer
that mints the coin:

> Now the third day is here—
> no word from either;
> No word from her nor him,
> Only another man's note:
> 'Dear Pound, I am leaving England.'

It is a great touch that the poet should have his own name referred to in
the poem's final line. This distinguishes Pound's 'Villanelle' from the
strategies of T. S. Eliot's early poems and James Joyce's *A Portrait of the*

Artist as a Young Man, in which sustained voices and characters are interposed between the writer and readers. Nevertheless, naming 'himself' in the poem's conclusion Pound 'says "I am" this, that, or the other, and with the words scarcely uttered one ceases to be that thing'.[38] Thus, he emphasizes the inevitable doubling in lyric poems where the 'I' of the speaker, however autobiographically motivated, is nonetheless a representation.

One reason for the decisiveness of Pound's close is that it has been rhythmically prepared for. There is, throughout, a skilful building up of unstressed or part-stressed terminal syllables, a tune somewhere between a spondee and a trochee.[39] A decisive and significant-sounding end which seems to introduce an irrelevant circumstantial fact is yet pregnant with meaning for the entire occasion. It leaves us with little way of knowing who the other man might be, and, as with the 'Two friends', it may help but it is strictly unnecessary to an understanding of the poem. The speaker, now identified as Pound, a persona of himself, senses in the coincidence of the non-appearances and the note a collapse of his creative milieu. The date of the poem's first appearance (and the fact that it now appears in the 'Poems of Lustra 1915–1916' section of *Personae*) should not fail to recall the Great War, and the likelihood that this note is from someone who is reporting for duty overseas. Even if the direct association of the 'Two friends' with Gaudier and his sister is dropped, the sculptor's death in the summer of 1915 took its toll on Pound. Taken together with disturbances in the Eliots' life, and with thoughts of Yeats and Joyce, it came to signify the permanent dispersal of what might have been, for Pound, a supportive and vitally creative situation.

The war had come and ruined everything. That phrase, 'The Psychological Hour', may have been a variation on a current cliché, meaning 'the most suitable moment', but its function as a means of 'placing' the self-concern of the poem would not have anything to 'place' without a hinterland of urgent and critical disturbance. 'Villanelle: The Psychological Hour' can be read as a technical exercise or the presentation of a sensibility, a 'portrait' in which the first-person speaker is viewed with third-person detachment. The appearance of Pound's name in the final line

---

[38] *Gaudier-Brzeska: A Memoir*, 85.

[39] The end-words are: 'pages', 'fountain', 'wasted', 'window', 'busses', 'shaken', 'city', 'forces', 'forest', 'found them', 'morning', 'from me', 'stiffly', 'frankly', 'evening', 'tea-time', 'either', and then 'England'. They work by being interspersed with lines and phrases ending in stressed terminal syllables.

locates this object of study in the context of what may also be understood as a crucial moment in the poet's own life.

For Pound the writer that cliché, 'The Psychological Hour', serves as a pointer for other elements in his poem that locate its speaker as a person suffering from a loss of confidence deriving from disturbances in his world of writers and artists. This loss of confidence as it is displayed in introspective anxieties about reputation and ageing instances a neurotic response to the cultural disruptions of 1915. Pound's poem is a diagnosis of a problem that he may have felt himself to be suffering from; namely, a too aestheticized, psychologized, and depoliticized concept of good art. In this sense, the 'Villanelle: The Psychological Hour' is a forerunner of *Hugh Selwyn Mauberley*, the first poem of Pound's to contain the word 'usury', and a definitive criticism both of an English aestheticism and of E. P.'s involvement with it.

Much may be said of Pound's activities as a poet with a political programme.[40] All that needs noting here is that the American poet's later work, with his promotion of a personal idea of Mussolini,[41] involved a rejection of psychology and an introspection which Pound associates with weakness. The 'psychology' of the speaker in Pound's poem is seen in a perspective shaped by the poet's devices of style. This distancing externalizes the problems that the 'Villanelle' touches. It attaches them to the persona of the poet, in this instance called 'Dear Pound'. This framing is part of Pound's way of developing as a stylist, his 'casting off, as it were, complete masks of the self in each poem'.[42] The problems of style are thus not carried forward as clarifications to problems of a self which, despite Pound's remark about ceasing 'to be that thing', must be conceived as existing over time for moral reflection to be possible: '"Master thyself, then others shall thee beare"',[43] as he wrote in the autumn of 1945.

---

[40] I have said something about it in both 'Ezra Pound and Italian Art', in *Pound's Artists*, 159–72, and 'Ezra Pound: Translation and Betrayal', in *In the Circumstances: About Poems and Poets* (Oxford: Oxford University Press, 1992), 173–97.

[41] The most succinct summary of this phase in the poet's life may be Luigi Barzini's: 'Ezra Pound's ideas about Mussolini and his government, before and during the war, are perhaps the most illustrious example of this kind of utter but honest confusion' (*The Italians* (Harmondsworth: Penguin, 1968), 28).

[42] *Gaudier-Brzeska: A Memoir*, 85.

[43] *The Cantos*, 521. The line may be an adaptation of Chaucer's from 'Truth, Balade de Bon Conseyl': 'Reule wel thyself, that other folk canst rede' in *The Works of Geoffrey Chaucer*, 2nd edn., ed. F. N. Robinson (London: Oxford University Press, 1966), 536. Chaucer's line may mean: 'Rule yourself well so that you can advise others'; Pound's seems to mean: 'Learn how to manage yourself and then other people will either put up with you or will sustain you'. Both lines

The 'youth' and 'beauty' of Pound's poem could hardly constitute a proper, full, or correct analysis of the 'relation of the state | To the individual' (p. 199). Yet they do contribute to an emblem of what may be defeated by 'diverse forces', something for whose loss a personal, emotive, even neurotic, response might well be the suitable one. It is the technical accuracy and thus sincerity of response in the poem's style which constitutes its permanent contribution to political culture, for, as Pound had noted, '"Only emotion endures"',[44] and this trace of a state of mind remains as a perpetual counter to such 'diverse forces' as seek, in one way or another, to cut us off in our prime.

assume a knowable self that exists over time. Carroll F. Terrell says the line is a 'Paraphrase of the rhythm' of the Chaucer, though he cites a variant reading and a variant title to those given in Robinson's edition (see *A Companion to the Cantos of Ezra Pound*, 2 vols. (Berkeley and Los Angeles, Calif.: University of California Press, 1980/1984), ii. 454).

[44] *Literary Essays*, 14.

CHAPTER 3

Basil Bunting's Emigrant Ballads

I

Basil Bunting wearied of 'Gin the Goodwife Stint' and 'The Complaint of
the Morpethshire Farmer'. Victoria Forde reports a letter to Louis
Zukofsky in which the poet compares his feelings about the latter to
Yeats's for 'The Lake Isle of Innisfree',[1] while Peter Makin implies that it
is for their overt political content that Bunting 'eventually distanced himself from these poems'.[2] A late ode in which the matter of sheep farming
returns is frankly quietist:

> Lambs and gimmers and wethers and ewes
> what do you want with political views?
> Keep the glass in your windows clear
> where nothing whatever's bitter but beer.[3]

Bunting's ballads have been linked to 'They say Etna', partly perhaps
because the longer poem contains the following lines:

> Item, the Duke of Slumberwear can get more
> by letting the shooting although there is nothing to shoot
> but a dozen diseased grouse and a few thin leveret
> than by cleaning the ditches to make the ground healthy for sheep.[4]

Makin observes of this poem that it 'is a political statement that works by
art. And art gives it not only force, but accuracy.'[5] Bunting's editor,
though, describes this as 'Pound-pastiche'.[6] It is; even to the fake precision of 'a dozen diseased grouse', where insistent assonance and allitera-

[1] Victoria Forde, *The Poetry of Basil Bunting* (Newcastle upon Tyne: Bloodaxe, 1991), 88.
[2] Peter Makin, *Bunting: The Shaping of his Verse* (Oxford: Oxford University Press, 1992), 61.
[3] *Basil Bunting, Uncollected Poems*, ed. R. Caddel (Oxford: Oxford University Press, 1991), 23.
[4] Ibid. 4.
[5] Makin, *Bunting*, 57.
[6] Ibid. n.p. Bunting's models for the poem may have been sections such as Canto XII and the
'Hell Cantos' XIV and XV (see Ezra Pound, *The Cantos of Ezra Pound*, 4th coll. edn. (London:
Faber & Faber, 1987), 53–7, 61–7.

tion are gained at the price of a plausible accuracy. Nevertheless, the lines indicate an early political programme of Bunting's: 'I began with a wish to limit my aims (abolish the protection of "game" in England and extend the range of black-faced sheep), and they were still far too abstract and ambitious to do anything but harm if I persisted.'[7] Poems outlast political programmes, but, as in the pre-eminent case of *The Divine Comedy*, it is frequently a political involvement that energizes the poetic forms whose memorable shape persists.

Does the following quatrain from 'The Complaint of the Morpethshire Farmer' make the same political statement as the four lines quoted above?

> Sheep and cattle are poor men's food,
> grouse is sport for the rich;
> heather grows where the sweet grass might grow
> for the cost of cleaning the ditch.[8]

Or does this one from 'Gin the Goodwife Stint'?

> The ploughland has gone to bent
> and the pasture to heather;
> gin the goodwife stint,
> she'll keep the house together.[9]

Bunting was fond of insisting on the pre-eminence of sound in poetry. The second quatrain quoted above is three trimeters and a dimeter (the second line); it half rhymes on the first and third, fully on the second and fourth lines; it alternates stressed and unstressed terminal syllables. Comparison with the four unrhymed free-verse lines from 'They say Etna' reveals an audibly more focused sound in the later poem. 'Poetry is just making noises, you know, it's mouthfuls of air. The meaning is hardly ever of any importance.'[10] Still, the cast of Bunting's statement is designed to tease a journalist: notice the 'just', the 'you know', and the 'hardly ever'. What makes the difference on those rare occasions when the meaning is of some importance? Despite Bunting's preference for 'making noises', I will be taking it for granted here that the sound of a

---

[7] Letter to Dorothy Pound, 11 Dec. 1954, cited in Peter Quartermain, *Basil Bunting: Poet of the North* (Durham: Basil Bunting Poetry Archive, 1990), 14.

[8] Basil Bunting, *Collected Poems*, 2nd edn. (London: Fulcrum, 1970), 105.

[9] Ibid. 100.

[10] Sally Beauman, 'Man of Plain Words', *Daily Telegraph Magazine*, 244, 13 June 1969, 32, cited in Quartermain, *Basil Bunting*, 15.

poem is its meaning, and that the meaning is its sound. Thus, the lines
from 'They say Etna' and the first verse of 'Gin the Goodwife Stint' mean
quite different political things, despite the apparent similarity of their
concerns. My subject is what the sound of Bunting's ballads means, how
and what their meanings sound.[11]

Victoria Forde describes the two ballads as 'in the Northumberland
dialect',[12] but this is misleading. Bunting's poems show no sustained
attempt to render in written form the accents, the regional vocabulary,
and non-standard syntax of a dialect. They have little in common with
Tennyson's 'Northern Farmer' poems, or with the work of William
Barnes. That they seem dialect poems is an impression which perhaps
derives from the way Pound gave translations of some of the words into
a more familiar English when he anthologized the two ballads.[13] Pound
later commented that 'No one since Burns has used the old simple meters
with such force.'[14] This too is an inexact observation which mischarac-
terizes Bunting's forms, draws attention to some elements of Burnsian
diction, and conceals the relevance of Wordsworth, a poet whom
Bunting acknowledged as one of his early influences.[15] Makin observed
that 'The "Goodwife" has of course a compression quite unlike the
structure of the "Morpethshire Farmer", yet also Burnsian.'[16] The word
'compression' points to a distinct difference in metre and rhythm, but
there is similarity of matter and diction. Burns uses the word 'Guidwife'

[11] Peter Makin's appendices 5(a) and (b) are essential documents in this discussion, and in
particular the two, for me, uncontentious observations that 'the sound gives us something as
complex, as internally differentiated, and therefore as structurable (by the maker) as that semantic map, with all its finenesses', and that this semantic map and the sound structure 'may have an
ironic relationship and so forth' (Makin, *Bunting*, 338). To say that the sound is the meaning and
the meaning the sound is to call attention to the absolute identity of these arbitrarily separable
elements. The 'meaning' of a poem includes the supposed relationships between its sounds and
meanings, just as these supposed relationships can only be properly experienced by hearing the
poem as a totality of sounds.

[12] Forde, *Basil Bunting*, 89.

[13] See Ezra Pound (ed.), *Active Anthology* (London: Faber & Faber, 1933), 106–8, and Ezra
Pound and Marcella Spann (eds.), *Confucius to Cummings: An Anthology of Poetry* (New York: New
Directions, 1964), 313–16.

[14] *Ezra Pound and Japan: Letters and Essays*, ed. S. Kodama (Redding Ridge, Conn.: Black Swan,
1987), 168.

[15] In a lecture on 'Wordsworth and the XIX Century' Bunting asserts that 'Burns, Ramsay,
Blake, however good their work, however singable, used well-worn rhythms and sound effects
that were part of the common stock. Their songs were new examples of the old mode.
Wordsworth made his music new' (*Basil Bunting on Poetry* ed. P. Makin (Baltimore, Md.: Johns
Hopkins University Press, 1999), 103). Writing to Louis Zukofsky on 6 Aug. 1953 he stated that
'Wordsworth, when I was a small kid, showed me what it [poetry] was' (cited in Quartermain,
Basil Bunting, 9).

[16] Makin, *Bunting*, 60 n.

on numerous occasions.[17] Here is a stanza from his 'The Shepherd's Wife':

> What will I get to my supper,
>> Gin I come hame, gin I come hame?
> What will I get to my supper
>> Gin I come hame again een, jo?[18]

Burns's poem is written in a recurrent metrical pattern with repeating lines so that music written for one verse will fit the others. The poem is a song. Even if Bunting had sung ballads such as this in mind as he composed, what he achieved in these two poems is a varied spoken rhythm. They thus take their place in a tradition of literary adaptations of folk songs, the most well known of which appear in Wordsworth and Coleridge's *Lyrical Ballads*.

II

Pound's reference to 'the old simple metres' is not quite accurate enough:

> Gin the goodwife stint
> and the bairns hunger
> the Duke can get his rent
> one year longer.

Pound describes Bunting's 'deeper concern with basic human problems in relation to the state of the times' as displaying a 'glum sobriety'.[19] In the second stanza of 'Gin the Goodwife Stint' the glum note derives from a lengthening by one syllable of the penultimate line and the shortening of the two-stress final line to four syllables. Bunting is likely to have learned such an effect not from Burns's ballads, but from *Hugh Selwyn Mauberley* where, in the final verse of 'Yeux Glauques', a woman's gaze is

> Bewildered that a world
> Shows no surprise
> At her last maquero's
> Adulteries.[20]

---

[17] e.g. 'The Guidwife of Wauchope-House, to Robert Burns, the Airshire Bard. Feb. 1787' and 'The Answer', in *The Poems and Songs of Robert Burns*, 3 vols., ed. J. Kinsley (Oxford: Oxford University Press, 1968), i. 324–7; or 'The Guidwife count the lawin', in Burns, *Poems*, ii. 606–7.

[18] Ibid. ii. 632.

[19] *Confucius to Cummings*, 316.

[20] Ezra Pound, *Personae: The Shorter Poems*, rev. edn. ed. L. Baechler and A. Walton Litz (New York: New Directions, 1990), 189.

Yet while quatrains from the first sections of Bunting's 'Villon', written five years earlier, are directly imitative of *Mauberley*'s stanzas,[21] his ballads have digested the influence and turned it to their own ends. The use of stressed monosyllables flush against each other, for example, is distinctly Bunting's own in 'bairns hunger' and 'one year longer'. Nevertheless, though his rhythm in the final two lines is different, the metrical arrangement of three then two stresses, and the syllabic pattern of six then four, appears in both poems' stanzas. In each case the shortening line produces a 'dying fall', Bunting's tight-lipped monosyllables effecting a rhythm of their own and, simultaneously, a dictional context quite unlike the faded glamour of Pound's Pre-Raphaelite epitaph.

Makin describes 'Gin the Goodwife Stint' as 'a cunning wave pattern, developing power out of calmness: effective as a political statement because of its form'.[22] This 'wave pattern' refers to the recurrence of the third line from stanza one, which also forms the title, as the first line of stanza two. There is a similar repetition, this time of the third line to the second quatrain, 'the Duke can get his rent', as the opening line of the final verse. The repeating form also means that the third-line end-words of each stanza beat out, as if inexorably, the relation between the protection of game and rural depopulation: 'bent', 'stint', 'stint', 'rent', 'rent', 'emigrant'. None of these is a full rhyme as encountered in the separate quatrains, yet the full rhyme of 'bent' and 'rent', linking two aspects of the Duke's power, binds the three verses. Meanwhile, the end words with unstressed syllables indicate a contrary motion. First, there is an apparently uncomplaining endurance: though the pasture is gone 'to heather', if the housewife is thrifty 'she'll keep the house together'. This full rhyme gives place to the faint disparity heard in the children who 'hunger' and the Duke getting his rent 'one year longer'. The strain of their effort to survive shows in the off-sounding rhyme. Finally, loyalty to the home place is taxed beyond endurance, and the closing rhyme, instead of keeping the verse together one stanza longer, points outward and away in a decisive discrepancy of sound:

> The Duke can get his rent
> and we can get our ticket
> twa pund emigrant
> on a C.P.R. packet.

[21] The following stanza from 'Villon' (1925): 'know nothing, are nothing, save a fume | driving across a mind | preoccupied with this: our doom | is, to be sifted by the wind' (*Collected Poems*, 15) seems a direct adapting of Pound's 'Drifted . . . drifted precipitate, | Asking time to be rid of . . . | Of his bewilderment' (*Personae*, 197).   [22] Makin, *Bunting*, 60.

The appearance of a first-person-plural pronoun in the second line means that the speaker is probably the goodwife's husband. This orients the viewpoint from which the woman's scrimping, the children's hunger, and the family's saving is to be seen: a father forced into a situation where he is unable to provide. Pound explained the last line in 1933: 'C.P.R. = Canadian Pacific Railway. It was recently, and may still be, possible for an emigrant pledged to agricultural labour to cross to Canada on C.P.R. boats for two pounds.'[23] Thus, the anthologizer elucidates the clash of two registers in Bunting's close. His 'twa pund' is the only occasion in the poem when spelling is used to indicate a regional accent; 'C.P.R.', on the other hand, is the acronym of a then remote transcontinental transport company. Though Bunting's ballads are not written in a sustained dialect, they do deploy regional diction and pronunciation as part of their sound-meaning.

In 'Gin the Goodwife Stint' the second line of each verse begins with the conjunction 'and'. In the first there is a simple addition of examples: 'the ploughland has gone to bent | and the pasture to heather'. In the second, when the repeated third line comes into play, a contrast is effected between the goodwife's hoping to 'keep the house together' and what this involves: 'Gin the goodwife stint | and the bairns hunger'. So, in this case, the conjunction yokes together two obligations with an implicit violence: the Duke's indifference to the fates of his tenants, all the more sharply felt for not being stated. In the third quatrain the turn into the second line also effects a contrast. This time it is with the oppressed compliance in 'the Duke can get his rent | one year longer', for, despite the appearances, the goodwife's family is saving up to resist their oppression in the only way it can: 'The Duke can get his rent | and we can get our ticket'. This development shaped upon the conjunction 'and' is articulated in the differing implications to be drawn from giving the monosyllable first less then more stress. Makin described the poem as 'developing power out of calmness' and called it 'effective as a political statement because of its form'. Yet is this brief lyrical ballad with its almost toneless, mute resistance a political statement at all?

Bunting may have found a hint for his final line's acronym in the close of T.S. Eliot's 'A Cooking Egg':

> Where are the eagles and the trumpets?

---

[23] *Active Anthology*, 108. In *Confucius to Cummings* this becomes 'In 1920 it was still possible' (p. 314). 'Gin the Goodwife Stint' is dated 1930 in Bunting's *Collected Poems*, 100.

> Buried beneath some snow-deep Alps.
> Over buttered scones and crumpets
> Weeping, weeping multitudes
> Droop in a hundred A.B.C.'s.[24]

'A.B.C.'s' are tea shops, and Eliot's rhyme of 'trumpets' and 'crumpets' signals a general irony about post-war London. The European empires are gone and all that remain are weeping widows and survivors. Yet there is also nostalgia for the lost grandeur in the contrasting rhyme words. Eliot, like Pound, gave Bunting hints for renovating diction and rhythm. However, by adapting these hints to the ballad stanza and to a matter apt for such a form, Bunting produced a specificity of rhythmic and structural implication that reveals the quatrains of Pound and Eliot to be largely cosmopolitan literary-critical exercises. Capital cities are places where wide ironic perspectives and political statements may find a hearing. Bunting's poems are located far from such vicinities of power. When Pound came to make his most sustained attempt at political statements he was obliged to go to Rome.

III

'The Complaint of the Morpethshire Farmer'—ten quatrains to the earlier poem's three—is a sustained sequence of variations on the ballad stanza. Bunting's rhythmic invention and variety can be sensed by comparison with this half stanza from James Hogg's 'The Highlander's Farewell':

> The glen that was my father's own,
>   Maun be by his forsaken;
> The house that was my father's house
>   Is levell'd with the braken.[25]

These four lines alternate iambic tetrameters and trimeters, with (as in 'Gin the Goodwife Stint') stressed then unstressed terminal syllables, and rhyme only on the trimeters. Bunting's opening quatrains offer reminiscences of this pattern, though in contrast to his other ballad here the quatrain's closing rhymes are never on weak syllables, and the metrical variations make each verse a gallery of technical accomplishment:

---

[24] T. S. Eliot, *Collected Poems 1909–1962* (London: Faber & Faber, 1963), 47.
[25] James Hogg, *Songs by the Ettrick Shepherd 1831*, in J. Wordsworth (ed.), *Revolution and Romanticism, 1789–1834* (Oxford: Woodstock, 1989), 134.

> On the up-platform at Morpeth station
> in the market-day throng
> I overheard a Morpethshire farmer
> muttering this song:
>
> Must ye bide, my good stone house,
> to keep a townsman dry?
> To hear the flurry of the grouse
> but not the lowing of the kye?
>
> To see the bracken choke the clod
> the coulter will na turn?
> The bit level neebody
> will drain soak up the burn?

While Bunting's first stanza alternates tetrameters and trimeters, never-theless his stress pattern does not settle into a steady iambic like Hogg's. The opening three words prepare readers for variable, spoken patterns: 'On the up-platform' is unstressed only on the elided definite article, 'up-' and 'form' having distinguishably different medial stresses, while 'On' and 'plat' take the beat. In the second verse, the fourth line substitutes a tetra-meter, and the third quatrain has an irregular trimeter as its third line.[26]

As its title might suggest,[27] the poem appears (even to its use of ques-tion and exclamation marks) a more expressive, dramatized voicing than the tight-lipped 'Gin the Goodwife Stint'. Yet the first stanza's 'I over-heard a Morpethshire Farmer | muttering this song' equivocally distin-guishes the reception and timbre of what follows from the traditional sung ballad which it nevertheless recalls. The first stanza has no dialect pronunciations or border diction. The narrating first person singular characterizes this as a variant of the encounter poem in which an inscribed poet-figure, using an educated and literary English, relates the tale of a local person in an adjusted speech that indicates the presence of a dialect without the poem's being in it.

The diction Bunting then adopts resembles Hogg's in that it appears in largely standard grammar and spelling but is interspersed with local land-

---

[26] The metrical variations of the ten stanzas are as follows: 4343/4344/4333/4343/3343/4344/3343/3433/4343/4343.

[27] This generic title has a long lineage including poems by Chaucer and Villon, a lineage mod-ishly revived by Jules Laforgue in *Les Complaintes* (1885) and so having its echo in poems by Pound and Eliot. It is also used to entitle a literary ballad in Wordsworth's 'The Complaint of a Forsaken Indian Woman', a poem which, like 'The Last of the Flock' may have helped Bunting when young to an awareness of what poetry is. Both poems first appeared in the *Lyrical Ballads* (1798) (see *The Poetical Works of William Wordsworth*, 5 vols., ed. E. de Selincourt and H. Darbishire (Oxford: Oxford University Press, 1940–9), ii. 40–6).

scape terms. Where Hogg has 'glen', 'braken', and the dialect word 'Maun', Bunting's poem includes 'ye', 'bide', 'kye', 'na', and 'neebody'. Still, this is a smattering of selected diction, not a fully-fledged dialect. Bunting's poem is again distinguished by its stressed monosyllables:

> And thou! Thou's idled all the spring,
> I doubt thou's spoiled, my Meg!
> But a sheepdog's faith is aye something.
> We'll hire together in Winnipeg.

A stanza from Wordsworth's 'The Tables Turned' has a strikingly similar opening line:

> And hark! how blithe the throstle sings!
> He, too, is no mean preacher:
> Come forth into the light of things,
> Let Nature be your Teacher.[28]

Hogg's lines contain a single variation on its regular iambic, a spondee at the opening of its second line: 'Maun be'. Wordsworth does this with his second foot, 'how blithe', the second line's opening 'He, too,' and the third's 'Come forth'. Yet in each case the underlying iambic pattern is enlivened by variation without being destabilized. Bunting's monosyllables are more radical presences. In 'thou! Thou's idled' only the second syllable of the verb can be weak, and comparison with the same pronoun on the next line shows that each time the word appears it takes a minutely different degree of stress; its subtle modulation dramatizes the working relation between the farmer and his sheepdog. But the most winning moment in Bunting's stanza is the 'aye something'. The inserted 'aye' defines the line's shape by preparing the necessary emphasis on 'something', meaning 'a great compensation', rather than 'an unspecific thing'. Simultaneously this emphasis on the word 'something' draws attention to the rhyme 'spring', where a stressed monosyllable rhymes with a necessarily unstressed second syllable. The discrepant stressing of the rhyme sound insinuates the limited comfort in the loyalty of the dog, for this farmer is leaving his family behind—perhaps until he is settled enough to send for them. Let this single phoneme 'aye', and all it does in 'The Complaint of the Morpethshire Farmer', stand as an emblem for how the sound of a poem and its meaning cannot be understood in separation.

Of this ballad Pound observed: 'Bunting is aware not only of the

---

[28] First published in the *Lyrical Ballads* (1798) (see *Poetical Works of William Wordsworth*, iv. 57).

tragedy and the infamy back of the tragedy but of the mode in which it works.'[29] The American poet's conviction that 'the love of money is the root of all evil' probably explains his distinction between, here, first the infamy then the tragedy:

> Sheep and cattle are poor men's food,
> grouse is sport for the rich;
> heather grows where the sweet grass might grow
> for the cost of cleaning the ditch.

> A liner lying in the Clyde
> will take me to Quebec.
> My sons'll see the land I am leaving
> as barren as her deck.

Yet Pound's comment also suggests a qualification. 'Bunting is aware...', he notes, and this poem along with its companion are not political statements in the manner of the lines from 'They say Etna' with which I began. They are works of art made from incidents narrated with a political awareness. Their resistance sounds in the stressed syllables rising against an inertial iambic pattern, as above in 'sweet grass might grow', or 'land I am leaving'. The sound operates upon what Pound's loose emotive terms brand as 'infamy' and 'tragedy', making permanent example of an injustice, and rendering the experience of dispossession in a form which resembles, but is not the same as, the country people's own attempts to retain their dignity in humiliating circumstances.[30] Yet in both cases these ballads are laments, poems about a defeat, and, like the straitened country people whose fates are spoken through them, their resistance is a making of what they can from loss. Their engagement involves a withdrawal. Nevertheless, it is an engagement, and the two ballads have the impetus of a political concern giving urgency to their shaping of voices. Bunting wearied of these poems, perhaps for their 'bitter' political views. Yet, along with his great masterpiece *Briggflatts*, which also centres upon the matter of the North, it is not least for his revivals and renovations of the literary ballad that Basil Bunting will be remembered.

---

[29] *Ezra Pound and Japan*, 168. A similar conjoining of what is taken to be tragedy with infamy produces the opening of *The Pisan Cantos*: 'The enormous tragedy of the dream in the peasant's bent | shoulders' which quickly dovetails into 'Thus Ben and la Clara *a Milano*' (in *The Cantos of Ezra Pound*, 425).

[30] For a discussion of such operations upon an encounter involving cultural differences in language and a political awareness see the account of Wordsworth's 'The Sailor's Mother' in my *In the Circumstances: About Poems and Poets* (Oxford: Oxford University Press, 1992), 1–23. For Bunting's views on the same poem see *Basil Bunting on Poetry*, 100–2.

CHAPTER 4

MacNeice, Munich, and Self-Sufficiency

I

In *Modern Poetry: A Personal Essay* Louis MacNeice makes 'a plea for impure poetry', which is 'conditioned by the poet's life and the world around him'. A poet is also to be a community's 'conscience, its critical faculty, its generous instinct'.[1] The Munich crisis of September 1938 was a situation in which both conscience and criticism were engaged. The political analyses of the immediate moment and the retrospect of the following three months helped shape the character of MacNeice's *Autumn Journal* as an object and a reading experience. The poet's desire for an impure poetry conditioned by 'the world around him' is qualified by his sense that the way circumstance is articulated in a poem must be mediated by 'the question of Form'.[2] A poet's technique then becomes a negotiation with situation in which both dependence and independence are exercised. These issues are informed by MacNeice's debate with Aristotle in *Autumn Journal* about the desire to be 'spiritually self-supporting' or to recognize that 'other people are always | Organic to the self'. It is a debate whose terms are relevant both for questions in the poet's private life and for the policy of appeasement adopted in the face of Hitler's territorial ambitions.

An aim of this chapter is to consider how when MacNeice writes that 'the sensible man must keep his aesthetic | And his moral standards apart'[3] the lines calculatedly travesty the poet's manifest beliefs about ethics and art. Further, it explores how these beliefs are demonstrated in the formal ordering of the poem—ones which, nevertheless, MacNeice

---

[1] Louis MacNeice, *Modern Poetry: A Personal Essay* (Oxford: Oxford University Press, 1938), preface (n.p.), 5.

[2] Ibid. 2.

[3] Louis MacNeice, *Collected Poems*, ed. E. R. Dodds (London: Faber & Faber, 1979), 135 (twice), 147.

has 'refused to abstract from their context'.[4] At the close of *Modern Poetry* MacNeice, writing in early 1938, imagined that

> When the crisis comes, poetry may for a time be degraded or even silenced, but it will reappear, as one of the chief embodiments of human dignity, when people once more have time for play and criticism.[5]

Yet, in the event, poetry was neither silenced nor degraded. Nor did it need to wait until people had 'time for play and criticism'—itself a phrase which faintly and haplessly degrades the place poetry can and does have in life, whether there is a crisis going on or not. So I look at the *Autumn Journal* and Munich as a relationship between the individual poet and a dramatic public situation to underline how, by means of its formal and thematic procedures, a poem can play a role in its times. Yet such an exploration must also delineate, at the very least by implication, ways in which poems cannot undo the damage done by various politicians' errors of judgement in late September 1938.

On 27 May 1992 the British Prime Minister John Major signed a document formally nullifying the Munich Agreement. Neville Chamberlain had put his signature to the original document at 2 a.m. on 30 September 1938. First rumours of a Czech putsch had begun on 21 May of the same year, when the Czech army, in response to well-founded rumours of German aggression, had partially mobilized. Resulting diplomatic pressure had obliged Hitler, much to his annoyance, to postpone his plans. In August, the month *Autumn Journal* begins, Lord Runciman visited the Sudetenlands to pressurize the Czech government into appeasing German interests there. On 15 September Neville Chamberlain flew to Berchtesgaden. He met Hitler again on 22–3 September at Godesberg, where Hitler presented what amounted to an ultimatum, the Godesberg Memorandum. On the 25th the British Cabinet decided it could not accept the terms of this memorandum, nor urge them on the Czech government. On the 26th preparations for war began, and Chamberlain sent via Sir Horace Wilson a personal letter to Hitler. At 10.30 p.m. on 27 September Hitler directed a reply to Chamberlain asking him to judge if he could 'bring the Government in Prague to reason at the very last hour'.[6]

---

[4] Louis MacNeice, *Collected Poems*, 101. For a succinct summary of the historical and biographical context for MacNeice's *Autumn Journal* see Jon Stallworthy, *Louis MacNeice* (Oxford: Oxford University Press, 1995), 227–38.

[5] MacNeice, *Modern Poetry*, 205.

[6] Cited in Alan Bullock, *Hitler: A Study in Tyranny* (Harmondsworth: Penguin, 1962), 466.

On 28 September, 'Black Wednesday', the day war seemed inevitable, the British fleet was mobilized. Further diplomatic efforts involving British appeals to Mussolini[7] and ambassadorial visits to Hitler from France, Britain, and Italy produced the suggestion of a conference. Thus, on 29–30 September came about the historic Munich Pact, which effectively acceded to Hitler's Godesberg Memorandum, with its 1 October deadline for the secession of the Sudetenlands. It also produced Chamberlain's scrap of paper, a private agreement between himself and Hitler, which promised 'Peace for our time'. Alan Bullock sardonically observes that after the agreement was reached 'the two dictators left to the British and French the odious task of communicating to the Czechs the terms for the partition of their country'.[8] On 1 October German troops marched into the Sudetenlands. The Czechs went down, 'and without fighting' (p. 117),[9] in MacNeice's words.

'No case of this kind can be judged apart from its circumstances', Winston Churchill wrote, and 'The facts may be unknown at the time, and estimates of them must be largely guesswork'.[10] Indeed, Chamberlain had himself explained that 'we must adjust our foreign policy to our circumstances',[11] meaning that our straitened finances justified appeasement. It came to light at the Nuremburg trials, however, that while Chamberlain assumed that Hitler's final territorial demand in Europe was that involving the Sudeten Germans, the 'objective in Hitler's mind was, from the first, the destruction of the Czechoslovak State'.[12] Similarly, the German readiness for war may have been overestimated: 'Some of his generals were so convinced that it would not be possible to carry out a successful invasion . . . that they were apparently ready to overthrow Hitler'.[13] According to Churchill's highly partisan account this plot was postponed when Chamberlain flew to Berchtesgaden on 14 September,

---

[7] For an Italian poet's responses to Munich see Vittorio Sereni's 'In una casa vuota', in *Poesie*, ed. D. Isella (Milan: Mondadori, 1995), 190, and *Selected Poems of Vittorio Sereni*, trans. M. Perryman and P. Robinson (London: Anvil, 1990), 122.

[8] Bullock, *Hitler*, 469.

[9] Page references in parenthesis are to MacNeice, *Collected Poems*.

[10] Winston Churchill, *The Second World War*, 6 vols. (1948, rev. 1949) (Harmondsworth: Penguin, 1985), i. 287.

[11] Keith Feiling, *The Life of Neville Chamberlain* (London: Macmillan, 1946), 324; see also 366–8.

[12] Bullock, *Hitler*, 444.

[13] T. O. Lloyd, *Empire to Welfare State: English History 1906–1985*, 3rd edn. (Oxford: Oxford University Press, 1986), 208; and see Churchill, *Second World War*, 280–1; Bullock, *Hitler*, 452; and, for a full account of Munich from the *Wehrmacht*'s viewpoint, John W. Wheeler-Bennett, *The Nemesis of Power: The German Army in Politics 1918–1945* (London: Macmillan, 1954), 393–435.

and abandoned when the Munich Pact seemed to prove that Hitler's bluff had succeeded. That there was a plot appears beyond doubt. John Wheeler-Bennett, however, in his detailed version, notes that this theory for the plotters' failure to act, which was 'circulated by interested parties, does not hold water for a moment'.[14]

Wheeler-Bennett does, nevertheless, note that 'it was manifestly evident that conditions for such an enterprise were vastly less favourable after the signing of the Munich Agreement'.[15] Immediate events quickly proved Chamberlain wrong about peace for our time. When on 2 November Ribbentrop and Ciano dictated the new Czech–Hungarian frontier, the other two signatories of the Munich Pact were not invited. On 15 March 1939, two weeks after MacNeice had composed the head note to *Autumn Journal*, Hitler annexed the remaining parts of Czechoslovakia. Two days later, in a speech in Birmingham, the British Prime Minister abandoned appeasement. The Czech leader in London, Thomas Masaryk, had pointed to the gamble taken by Chamberlain at Munich by agreeing to allow Hitler to absorb the Sudetenlands. 'If you have sacrificed my nation to preserve the peace of the world,' he stated, 'I will be the first to applaud you; but if not, gentlemen, God help your souls.' Haile Selassie more wryly observed: 'I hear you have the support of the British government. You have my profound sympathy.'[16]

In *Fellow Travellers of the Right* Richard Griffiths suggests that 'The immediate aftermath of the Munich agreement was, for most people, either disgust or relief.'[17] On the back of a postcard showing a photograph entitled 'The Pilgrim of Peace | Bravo! Mr. Chamberlain' Ludwig Wittgenstein wrote with evident disgust: 'In case you want an Emetic, there it is.'[18] Christopher Isherwood admitted to a secret relief: 'What do I care for the Czechs? What does it matter if we are traitors? A war has

---

[14] *The Nemesis of Power*, 421.

[15] Ibid. 424.

[16] See Lloyd, *Empire to Welfare State*, 204–8; Feiling, *Life of Neville Chamberlain*, 324: John W. Wheeler-Bennett, *Munich, Prologue to Tragedy* (London: Macmillan, 1966), 171; Franklin R. Gannon, *The British Press and Germany, 1936–1939* (Oxford: Oxford University Press, 1971).

[17] Richard Griffiths, *Fellow Travellers of the Right, British Enthusiasts for Nazi Germany 1933–1939* (Oxford: Oxford University Press, 1983), 304.

[18] Ray Monk, *Ludwig Wittgenstein: The Duty of Genius* (London: Jonathan Cape, 1990), illus. 44–5. See also Fania Pascal, 'A Personal Memoir', in R. Rhees (ed.), *Recollections of Wittgenstein* (Oxford: Oxford University Press, 1984), 39–40: 'It was the days before Munich; Mr Chamberlain was making a stand, acting as though the country was preparing for war. We looked on in silence at the diggers' efforts. I turned to Wittgenstein to protest, to cry out that it's all a sham, that we are lost, but he silenced me by raising his hand forbiddingly. He said: I am as much ashamed of what it happening as you are. But we must not talk of it.'

been postponed—and a war postponed is a war which may never happen.'[19] William Empson, who explained later that 'the point is to join up the crisis-feeling to what can be felt all the time in normal life', had written 'Courage Means Running' in 1936. Many years later he felt obliged to alter his final verse's 'wise patience' to 'flat patience' in the light of the shame that had descended upon the entire policy of appeasement after Munich:

> As the flat patience of England is a gaze
> Over the drop, and 'high' policy means clinging;
> There is not much else that we dare to praise.

Christopher Ricks, echoing Empson's own alignment of the poem with inter-war foreign policy, describes 'Courage Means Running' as 'about what can be said for Munich'.[20] Patrick Kavanagh, in the interests of a felt and vital parochialism, counterposes a local and international border dispute in 'Epic', first published in 1951:

> I heard the Duffy's shouting 'Damn your soul'
> And old McCabe stripped to the waist, seen
> Step the plot defying blue cast-steel—
> 'Here is the march along these iron stones'
> That was the year of the Munich bother. Which
> Was more important?[21]

While Kavanagh uses the contrast to state a case for his sort of poetry, the thrust of my argument is that there must be similarities of principle involved in both disputes, similarities that MacNeice explores in *Autumn Journal*. One problem with Ricks's phrase 'what can be said for Munich' is that Empson himself did not write his poem with Munich in mind, and, not being inclined to appease Germany at any point, assumed, like MacNeice, that war would come and should be fought. At the time everyone will have felt what could be said for Munich: we have been spared the endurance of another war. Yet many, including Empson, will have also understood the cost of what could be said for that piece of paper.

---

[19] Christopher Isherwood, *Christopher and His Kind 1929–1939* (London: Eyre Methuen, 1977), 241, cited in Peter McDonald, *Louis MacNeice: The Poet in his Contexts* (Oxford: Oxford University Press, 1991), 90.
[20] William Empson, *The Complete Poems*, ed. J. Haffenden (London: Allen Lane, 2000), 336, 77, 125.
[21] Patrick Kavanagh, *Selected Poems*, ed. A. Quinn (Harmondsworth: Penguin, 1996), 101–2. The poem is cited in a brief discussion of MacNeice and contemporary Irish poetry in the introduction to P. Fallon and D. Mahon (eds.), *The Penguin Book of Contemporary Irish Poetry* (Harmondsworth: Penguin, 1990), pp. xvii–xviii.

MacNeice appears to have experienced both disgust and relief. He writes in *The Strings are False* of first fear. 'The terror that seized London during the Munich crisis was that dumb, chattering terror of beasts in a forest fire'. Then came a sense of relief. 'Chamberlain signed on the line and we all relapsed'. Then, he records something less sharp than Wittgenstein's contempt: 'Newsreels featured the life of Chamberlain—the Man of Peace after 2,000 years.[22] Yet there is a further complex of feelings in *Autumn Journal*, for out of this slide through fear and relief to an empty disbelief comes a sense of shame and inadequacy.

II

The threat of war is insinuated into the opening passage of *Autumn Journal*. Where 'summer is ending in Hampshire' there are 'retired generals and admirals'—

> And the spinster sitting in a deck-chair picking up stitches
>> Not raising her eyes to the noise of the 'planes that pass
> Northward from Lee-on-Solent.   (pp. 101–2)

The retired military men will have seen service in the First World War, and the planes are from a naval air station. At this point the political situation seems a noise off-stage. By section V of the poem MacNeice is exploring the attempt to deal with the 'chattering terror', an attempt to which the poem's mock garrulousness acknowledges a complicity that two of the poem's most recent critics have called 'an immensely winning demonstration of how not to "stop talking", though all the time behind the talk lurks fear':[23]

> The latest? You mean whether Cobb has bust the record
>> Or do you mean the Australians have lost their last ten
> Wickets or do you mean that the autumn fashions—
>> *No, we don't mean anything like that again.*
> No, what we mean is Hodza, Henlein, Hitler,
>> The Maginot Line,
> The heavy panic that cramps the lungs and presses
>> The collar down the spine.   (pp. 108–9)

[22] Louis MacNeice, *The Strings are False: An Unfinished Autobiography* (London: Faber & Faber, 1965), 174–5.
[23] Michael O'Neill and Gareth Reeves, *Auden, MacNeice, Spender: The Thirties Poetry* (Basingstoke: Macmillan, 1992), 183.

Milan Hodza was a Slovak statesman and Prime Minister of Czechoslovakia from 1935 to just before the Munich Pact. Konrad Henlein was the Sudeten leader, who had visited London on 12 May 1938 to press the claim that his people had been oppressed by the Czech government.[24] The issue of Czechoslovakia is taken up again in section VII, which opens by listing 'Conferences, adjournments, ultimatums, | Flights in the air, castles in the air, | The autopsy of treaties . . .' (p. 113). 'Flights in the air', with its hint of escape in the offing, almost certainly refers to Chamberlain's meetings with Hitler in mid-September. There was possible folly even in Chamberlain's taking to the air. Bullock notes that Hitler's 'vanity was gratified by the prospect of the Prime Minister of Great Britain, a man twenty years older than himself, making his first flight at the age of sixty-nine in order to come and plead with him'.[25] The 'autopsy of treaties' probably refers to the argument justifying Hitler's foreign policy as a necessary correction to the Treaty of Versailles.[26]

The passage usually cited in discussions of Munich and MacNeice's poem is that describing 'cutting down the trees on Primrose Hill'.[27] Later in the section, though, there is this sequence of lines:

> But one—meaning I—is bored, am bored, the issue
>   Involving principle but bound in fact
> To squander principle in panic and self-deception—
>   Accessories after the act,
> So that all we foresee is rivers in spate sprouting
>   With drowning hands
> And men like dead frogs floating till the rivers
>   Lose themselves in the sands.   (p. 114)

There is a vertiginous enjambment in this passage, where the phrase 'Involving principle but bound in fact' shifts sense, taking from 'in fact' its substance as a statement and turning it into a colloquial filler, as if the line end read: bound, in fact, to squander. This shift may be related to Chamberlain's 'we must adjust our foreign policy to our circumstances'

---

[24] For details of the proposals see Churchill, *Second World War*, 256.

[25] Bullock, *Hitler*, 454.

[26] See Griffiths, *Fellow Travellers of the Right*, 297, and Wheeler-Bennett, *The Nemesis of Power*.

[27] See Samuel Hynes, *The Auden Generation: Literature and Politics in England in the 1930s* (London: Faber & Faber, 1976), 368–9; Robyn Marsack, *The Cave of Making: The Poetry of Louis MacNeice* (Oxford: Oxford University Press, 1982), 48; Edna Longley, *Louis MacNeice: A Study* (London: Faber & Faber, 1988), 64; Julian Symons, *The Thirties and the Nineties* (Manchester: Carcanet, 1990), 120–2; Peter McDonald, *Louis MacNeice: The Poet in his Contexts* (Oxford: Oxford University Press, 1991), 89; O'Neill and Reeves, *Auden, MacNeice, Spender*, 199.

and to the encouragement it gave to the French leaders Bonnet and Daladier to abandon their treaty obligations to Czechoslovakia.[28] Any 'issue | Involving principle' must be 'bound in fact', for an issue is just that: a fact-shaped situation in which principles are conflictually involved. The disturbing of 'in fact' by the enjambment works to ruin the balance of this statement, to upset the integrity of the line. The phrase 'Accessories after the act' indicates, with its rhyming recall of the judicial phrase 'after the fact', that those who wish to appease may be offering as a principle what is, in fact, 'panic and self-deception'. The poet ambiguously includes himself by writing 'all we foresee', but his opening, 'one— meaning I—is bored, am bored', offers a guiding viewpoint for the lines. MacNeice hints here at a disjunction between the versions of the crisis with which he is surrounded and his own view of an 'issue | Involving principle but bound in fact', which will be lost in misconceptions and fear, a fear of 'drowning hands' and 'men like dead frogs'. Boredom and fear express MacNeice's being both a part of the crisis and isolated, detached from it by his own views. Such combinations of involvement in a situation and distance from it are at the ambivalent heart of MacNeice's *Autumn Journal*.

   Yet the mixtures of involvement and detachment are unstable, preventing the poetry from settling into a single view of the crisis. The next eight lines introduce a further response to the public debate:

> And we who have been brought up to think of 'Gallant Belgium'
>   As so much blague
> Are now preparing again to essay good through evil
>   For the sake of Prague;
> And must, we suppose, become uncritical, vindictive,
>   And must, in order to beat
> The enemy, model ourselves upon the enemy,
>   A howling radio for our paraclete.   (p. 114)

Edna Longley cites this passage to suggest that MacNeice 'makes the poem a warning against the two "musts" in that passage, thus acting as Grigson's "critical moralist"'.[29] This is undoubtedly part of the passage's meaning: we must preserve ourselves from irrational hate, even if it is in the interests of saving ourselves and defeating Hitler. The reference to the First World War's 'issue | Involving principle' (Britain declared war in

---

[28]   See Churchill, *Second World War*, 266–7.
[29]   Longley, *Louis MacNeice*, 72.

1914 when Belgian neutrality was violated) carries ov\
aversion to becoming 'uncritical, vindictive'. Such feeli\
duced the wartime anti-German hysteria and contribute\
ously punitive reparation clauses in the Versailles Treaty.

Yet another way of reading the passage would find th\
adopting the stance of the detached 'critical moralist', th\
appeasement may also derive from memories of the Great \   ..nd the
wish, hardly an evil one, that such wars should never happen again.
MacNeice's passage may even be responding to Hitler's speech at the
Nuremburg rally on 12 September, or that of 26 September at the Berlin
Sportpalast, 'a masterpiece of invective which even he never surpassed'.[30]
In it, Hitler contrasted his own war service with the life of President
Beneš, and stated that 'there marches a different people from that of
1918'.[31] This aligns the passage with Chamberlain's appeasement policy.
It assumes that if war comes we will have to model ourselves on the
enemy, as, for instance, in the style of Bomber Harris's reaping 'the whirl-
wind'. We will have to be uncritical and vindictive. We will have to 'essay
good through evil | For the sake of Prague'. Thus, the detachment indi-
cated by the 'we suppose' in MacNeice's lines produces a double
significance in the 'warning against the two "musts"'. Caught up in the
situation of the Munich crisis, these lines can sound like appeals for peace
at any price, so as to avoid the need to become brutalized. They can also
imply that if fight we must, then it is the task of detached intellectuals like
MacNeice to preserve us from having to 'model ourselves upon the
enemy'.

It is crucial to *Autumn Journal* that intellectual high-mindedness, that's
to say, in more generous parlance, being a 'critical moralist', has to remain
in contact with its subject matter, the actual, ordinary conflicts of emotion and desire which people felt at the time. Thus, similarly, in the page
on Munich from *The Strings are False*, MacNeice writes of a George
Formby show that 'His pawky Lancashire charm was just what we
wanted',[32] the word 'pawky' nevertheless giving an evaluative detachment to the phrase. The occasion also finds its way into *Autumn Journal*:

> And I go to the Birmingham Hippodrome
> Packed to the roof and primed for laughter
> And beautifully at home
> With the ukelele and the comic chestnuts ...   (p. 116)

[30] Bullock, *Hitler*, 461.   [31] Cited in Bullock, *Hitler*, 463.   [32] *The Strings are False*, 174.

. hat phrase 'beautifully at home' is a reminder that MacNeice in his isolation also needed to belong. However detached from situations by his upbringing and education, MacNeice strove to be *in situ*, and that involved accepting that his work would contain the ordinary sensations he shared with those around him.

The conclusion of section VIII coincides with those events in Munich at the end of September:

> The crisis is put off and things look better
> And we feel negotiation is not in vain—
> Save my skin and damn my conscience.
> And negotiation wins,
> If you can call it winning,
> And here we are—just as before—safe in our skins;
> Glory to God for Munich.
> And stocks go up and wrecks
> Are salved and politicians reputations
> Go up like Jack-on-the-Beanstalk; only the Czechs
> Go down and without fighting.   (p. 117)

The benefit of MacNeice's expansive style lies in its ability to move quickly through a series of interrelated feelings: relief, high hopes, low motives, disgust, bitter mockery, underlying self-interest,[33] and, finally, shame. Richard Griffiths summarized responses to Munich as 'either disgust or relief'; MacNeice combines both of these in the passage where the European leaders sacrifice Beněs and Masaryk's country, and produces from the combination of these feelings the further one of shame. We feel relief, but intuit that our motives for feeling it are poor, and are then disgusted with ourselves for feeling it, and so feel ashamed. MacNeice's own italicized pronoun in the following lines may contain tonally all these sensations:

> *We* are safe though others have crashed the railings
> Over the river ravine; their wheel-tracks carve the bank
> But after the event all we can do is argue
> And count the widening ripples where they sank.   (Ibid.)

At this point the Munich situation appears to fade from the poem. Nevertheless, in section XII MacNeice evokes a pre-war mood, a recognition, if any were still needed, that war is inevitable despite the agreement: 'People have not recovered from the crisis' (p. 123) and 'Those who are

---

[33] See T. S. Eliot, *The Idea of a Christian Society* (London: Faber & Faber, 1939).

about to die try out their paces' (p. 124). Yet the atmosphere of Munich lingers over the entire poem, as a matter of 'Principle . . . bound in fact'. First, though, there is a by-election.

Robyn Marsack spells out the precise relation of this event to the Munich situation. 'Quinton Hogg, son of the Lord Chancellor and a university contemporary of MacNeice's, was defending the seat specifically on the issue of foreign policy and the Munich Agreement; against him stood A. D. Lindsay, the Master of Balliol. Hogg's majority was almost halved but he retained the seat.'[34] In section XIV, MacNeice writes about his involvement in the election, once again emphasizing mixed emotions and motives:

> And what am I doing it for?
>   Mainly for fun, partly for a half-believed-in
> Principle, a core
>   Of fact in a pulp of verbiage . . .   (p. 128)

Again there is the conjunction of those two words 'Principle' and 'fact'. Yet because MacNeice writes with such honesty about his misgivings, his sense that there are 'only too many who say' that '["]To turn the stream of history will take | More than a by-election"' (ibid.), because MacNeice is trying to resist the pull of political illusion, again in the light of Munich, he may have been, and may still be, taken to be absenting himself in isolation and detachment. Samuel Hynes, who grants MacNeice's honesty, sees the poem as an expression of helplessness:

It has no personal momentum, no important decisions are made; the most positive thing that MacNeice does is to work in an Oxford by-election (which his candidate loses). Nor does it propose any positive values, any programme for confronting the future[35]

I can't say I recognize MacNeice's poem in these opinions, certainly not its 'principle bound in fact' or its 'Principle, a core | Of fact'. *Autumn Journal* summarizes the election result as follows:

> So Thursday came and Oxford went to the polls
>   And made its coward vote and the streets resounded
> To the triumphant cheers of the lost souls—
>   The profiteers, the dunderheads, the smarties.   (pp. 128–9)

Yet MacNeice's poem states why it is important to take part in the politi-

---

[34] Marsack, *Cave of Making*, 50.
[35] Hynes, *Auden Generation*, 372.

cal process, even if you lose, and reserves the right to castigate even the winners if he does not believe in their values. The phrase 'coward vote', for instance, comes into sharp relief when read in the light of Hogg's defence of Chamberlain's appeasement policy.

In his Clark Lectures of twenty-five years later MacNeice forged a false distinction when he noted that 'the cruder kind of allegory . . . can be used to cover subjects from which the inner life is excluded—such things as General Elections'.[36] The inner life in *Autumn Journal* is not excluded from a by-election, at least. Hynes then accurately answers his own question ('what have politicians to do with a man's loneliness?'). He refers to passages of the poem about MacNeice's broken marriage: 'the private loss is an analogue of public loss, and the poet's helpless misery is an appropriate response to the public situation as well as to the private one'.[37] How odd, and how common, that writers on poetry fail to register the significance of the poem's mere existence in their comments on the state of mind supposedly revealed by it. By being 'a way of happening', the completed poem makes something happen for the poet doing things with words too. Hynes refers to the 'poet's helpless misery'. Yet anyone who could, as early as 22 November 1938, outline to T. S. Eliot at Faber & Faber so clear an image of *Autumn Journal* ('A long poem from 2,000 to 3,000 lines written from August to December 1938') should not, I think, be described as 'helpless'.

MacNeice concludes by calling his poem 'a confession of faith'—one in which 'There is a constant interrelation of abstract and concrete'.[38] In poems, the confessions of faith are best located in the nature of the poem itself, often counterpointing, and counteracting, the expressions of overt feeling, such as 'helpless misery' or 'boredom', which the poem includes. This is to contradict Hynes's belief that *Autumn Journal* 'has no alternatives to offer, beyond a vague solidarity of resistance against the common enemy'. It is not true that of MacNeice's past in the poem, each element is treated 'with the ironic knowledge that it is irrelevant to the present crisis'.[39] The achievement of *Autumn Journal* is partly to articulate the interrelated relevance of these things to the experiences of people in crises, while acknowledging the ordinary appearance of irrelevance in relations between one person's life and a public crisis gripping Europe.

---

[36] Louis MacNeice, *Varieties of Parable* (Cambridge: Cambridge University Press, 1965), 76.
[37] Hynes, *Auden Generation*, 368 (twice).
[38] Cited in Marsack, *Cave of Making*, 43 (twice).
[39] Hynes, *Auden Generation*, 372, 370; but see also 369.

III

Reviewing Gilbert Murray's translation of *The Seven Against Thebes* on 10 May 1935 MacNeice argued for the preservation of the integrity of the original's verse lines wherever possible: 'I think a translation should start from the Greek, preferably line for line.' A good translator should also be able to 'see what the English looks like just as English'.[40] The integral rhythmic structure of a poetic line is at the heart of MacNeice's poetics. In the whole of *Autumn Journal* there are only fifteen lines that have full stops or question marks syntactically dividing them. MacNeice noted in the letter to T. S. Eliot that *Autumn Journal* 'is written throughout in an elastic kind of quatrain. This form (a) gives the whole poem a formal unity but (b) saves it from monotony by allowing it a great range of appropriate variations'.[41] Yet clearly these variations are ones of line length, enjambment, syntactical extension, and of rhyme. They serve to confirm syntactic closure or chime against the movement of the sentence. MacNeice is sparing in his use of the strong medial caesura created by a full stop. There is a relation between the integrity of verse lines, whether enjambed or end-stopped, and the philosophy of self and other in *Autumn Journal*.

Section XVII dramatizes a debate between the virtue in self-coherent autonomy and the virtue in relationship, in interdependence:

> And Aristotle was right to posit the Alter Ego
> > But wrong to make it only a halfway house:
> Who could expect—or want—to be spiritually self-supporting,
> > Eternal self-abuse?
> Why not admit that other people are always
> > Organic to the self, that a monologue
> Is the death of language and that a single lion
> > Is less himself, or alive, than a dog and another dog?   (p. 135)

MacNeice's deployment of verse lines here dramatizes the issue for him. So 'Who could expect—or want—to be spiritually self-supporting,' and 'Eternal self-abuse?' are both end-stopped, both isolated within their lines. In the following quatrain the first three enjambed line-endings point to isolations. They counteract them, though, by linking the sense to the following line: 'other people are always | Organic to the self', 'a

---

[40] *Selected Literary Criticism of Louis MacNeice*, ed. A. Heuser (Oxford: Oxford University Press, 1987), 9–10.
[41] Cited in Marsack, *Cave of Making*, 43.

monologue | Is the death of language', and 'a single lion | Is less himself,
or alive, than a dog and another dog'. Still, it must be noted that MacNeice
is not advocating a blurring of differences. His enjambments are significant exactly because his sense of lineal rhythm emphasizes the lines as
units even when they form parts of long syntactic chains:

> A point here and a point there: the current
>   Jumps the gap, the ego cannot live
> Without becoming other for the Other
>   Has got yourself to give.   (Ibid.)

What MacNeice is dramatizing, then, in the syntax and rhythm of his
lines, is a belief in the virtue of autonomy, of lines having their own rhythmic coherence and integrity, but that this virtue is only valuable when
brought into relation with other such autonomous entities. MacNeice is
appealing for the interrelation of the distinct, as a core value, and the form
of *Autumn Journal* is a sustained hymn, not quite to what Peter McDonald
calls 'the self being realized in the other, the other in the self',[42] for just as
I cannot presume upon another's self-realization in me, so too I can't presume to lodge my self-realization in another. The two selves have to be
realizing in themselves, each in the situation of its relation with the other.

   The poem's linear movement, its concern, as indicated not least by the
title, with time and the passage of time, an issue again dramatized by
the enjambing of longer syntactic units, also contributes to this belief in
the value of interrelation, of involvement:

> Aristotle was right to think of man-in-action
>   As the essential and really existent man
> And man means men in action; try and confine your
>   Self to yourself if you can.
> Nothing is self-sufficient, pleasure implies hunger
>   But hunger implies hope:
> I cannot lie in this bath for ever, clouding
>   The cooling water with rose geranium soap.   (p. 136)

The formal intelligence in such lineation has the ambivalence of an internal debate. He is drawn to the idea of virtue in internal coherence, the self
as virtuous in so far as it can separate itself from the contingencies and
accidents in situations. He is attracted to the soothing detachment and
isolation of staying in the bath. Yet he has experienced how limiting and

---

[42] McDonald, *Louis MacNeice*, 89. See, for an example of MacNeice's self-analysis in this
regard, his letter to Eleanor Clark of 21 May 1940, cited in Stallworthy, *Louis MacNeice*, 273–7.

partial such a virtue would inevitably prove. Thus, 'try and confine your |
Self to yourself if you can' is, for MacNeice, an impossible dare. You
can't. Nevertheless, this false isolation, something distinct from independence, is an attractive illusion that the poet will acknowledge, even as
he recognizes how he must, sooner or later, get out of the bath.

An enforced isolation is identified in the next section: 'This England is
tight and narrow, teeming with unwanted | Children who are so many,
each is alone' (p. 137) and McDonald[43] links the passage in section XVII
to the previous section's account of Ireland: 'Ourselves alone! Let the
round tower stand aloof | In a world of bursting mortar!' (p. 133). Thus,
the remarks in the poem that seem to concern MacNeice's ideas about
relations between individuals are also to be understood as comments on
nations and foreign affairs. MacNeice was not to be impressed by the
Republic's policy during the war, a note which may be detected in his
reporting a comment made in Dublin on hearing that Chamberlain had
declared war: 'A young man in sports clothes said to us: "Eire of course
will stay neutral. But I hope the English knock hell out of Hitler." '[44]
MacNeice's remarks about translation are again relevant. You must begin
with a respect for the integrity of the foreign original ('start from the
Greek, preferably line for line'), and you must also appreciate the language of the translation for itself ('what the English looks like just as
English'), but the act of translating itself, by which 'Diction and rhythm
will . . . differentiate',[45] instances a necessary involvement of one with
another, exemplifying McDonald's phrase 'the self being realized in the
other', or, perhaps, of one work of art being re-realized in the textures of
another language.

The relation of these principles to the Munich crisis is not straight-
forward. MacNeice's views of translation appear to suggest that the
integrity of countries needs to be respected. This indicates a belief that
Czechoslovakia should be left to determine her own affairs. However,
the issue is complicated by the situation of the ethnic minorities in the
country, and by the Wilsonian principle of self-determination. Hitler was
good at exploiting this principle. Speaking at Saarbrucken on 9 October
1938 he announced that 'inquiries of British politicians concerning the
fate of Germans within the frontiers of the Reich—or of others belonging to the Reich are not in place . . . We would like to give these gentlemen

---

[43] See McDonald, *Louis MacNeice*, 88–9.
[44] *The Strings are False*, 212.
[45] MacNeice, *Selected Literary Criticism*, ed. Heuser, 9–10.

the advice that they should busy themselves with their own affairs and leave us in peace.'[46] The *Kristallnacht* pogrom took place just over a month later, on 9–10 November, again raising the issue of when persecution of minorities in a country justifies the active involvement of neighbours in their domestic politics.

Is it then right to wish to preserve the principle of non-intervention in another nation's affairs by remaining aloof? Does it protect the principle of sovereignty to maintain peace and non-intervention by sacrificing the Sudetenlands? MacNeice's poem is shaped upon the principle, and it seems a direct response to the problems of acting rightly over Czecho-slovakia, that the integrity and value of someone's self-sufficiency, a state's independence, can only exist and be maintained by involvement with and from others. Similarly, you respect the identity of a foreign text not by leaving it alone, but by translating it in as accurate and vital a way as possible. Once Hitler has violated the principle of not meddling in the internal affairs of a country, non-intervention cannot protect the princi-ple. To follow the principle of non-intervention is to sacrifice that very principle, or, as MacNeice puts it, 'the issue | Involving principle' is 'bound in fact | To squander principle in panic and self-deception' (p. 114).

In the letter to Eliot, MacNeice stated that 'There is constant inter-relation of abstract and concrete'. In the March 1939 note to *Autumn Journal*, he announced that 'I have certain beliefs which, I hope, emerge in the course of it but which I have refused to abstract from their context' (p. 101). One reason why the Munich crisis demanded 'principle . . . bound in fact' and not principle which is 'bound in fact | To squander principle' is that the principles involved only had their specific signifi-cance in that situation. This interrelation of principle and context is one plank in MacNeice's anti-Platonic stance, so that when 'reading Plato talking about his Forms | To damn the artist touting round his mirror' the poet counters:

> no one Tuesday is another and you destroy it
> If you subtract the difference and relate
> It merely to the Form of Tuesday. This is Tuesday
> The 25th of October, 1938. (p. 124)

The interrelation also finds an echo in MacNeice's ideas about poetic form. He notes in *Modern Poetry* that 'My object in writing this essay is

---

[46] Cited in Bullock, *Hitler*, 472.

partly to show that one and the same poetic activity produces different forms in adaptation to circumstances.'[47]

This is not the same as Chamberlain's 'we must adjust our foreign policy to our circumstances'. The difference is that the Prime Minister is explaining appeasement as necessary because we are not in a position to mobilize: our straitened circumstances provide him with an excuse. In MacNeice's remark the circumstances offer a resistance with which the poetic activity, in adapting itself, works to produce a particular formal solution: the circumstances help to generate the effects and qualities of the specific form. The flexibility of *Autumn Journal*'s quatrains, in relation to the Munich crisis, generates literary occasions in which ordinary utterances can express the anxiety and anguish of the moment, while simultaneously discovering a shape that counteracts that 'chattering terror'. MacNeice had lost his dog:[48]

> But found the police had got her at St. John's Wood station
>   And fetched her in the rain and went for a cup
> Of coffee to an all-night shelter and heard a taxi-driver
>   Say 'It turns me up
> When I see these soldiers in lorries'—tumble of tumbrils
>   Drums in the trees
> Breaking the eardrums of the ravished dryads—
>   It turns me up; a coffee, please.   (pp. 113–14)

He also observes in *Modern Poetry* that 'the Poet's first business is *mentioning* things. Whatever musical or other harmonies he may incidentally evoke, the fact will remain that such and such things—and not others—have been mentioned in his poem.' This assertion would be ingenuous about formal contributions to poems if MacNeice did not qualify it with a parenthesis: '(on analysis even this selection [of materials] will be found to come under the question of Form)'.[49] Among the pleasures of *Autumn Journal* is the discovery of an improvised rhythmic ordering and an alternation of rhymed lines and non-rhymed feminine endings, this discovery occurring often amid the narration of unpromisingly mundane incidents, such as saying 'a coffee, please'—banal details which in times of crisis

[47] MacNeice, *Modern Poetry*, 33.
[48] In *Zoo*, published during November 1938, MacNeice describes keeping a dog: 'When I am alone with my dog, there are not two of us. There is myself—and something Other. It gives me a pleasant feeling of power, even of black magic, to be able to order this Other about and give it food which it actually eats' (*Selected Prose of Louis MacNeice*, ed. A. Heuser (Oxford: Oxford University Press, 1990), 49; see also 58).
[49] MacNeice, *Modern Poetry*, 5.

have a valuable solidity just because the ordinary transactions of life are themselves under threat.

Such shaping is self-referentially focused upon the beliefs involved at the close of several parts. Section IV, for instance, concludes:

> And though I have suffered from your special strength
>   Who never flatter for points nor fake responses
> I should be proud if I could evolve at length
>   An equal thrust and pattern.   (p. 108)

Thrust and pattern in *Autumn Journal* are provided by the variations of paratactic and hypotactic syntax, and the 'elastic kind of quatrain'. Again in *Modern Poetry*, MacNeice notes that in the poets of his generation 'history is recognized as something having a shape and still alive, something more than a mere accumulation of random and dead facts'.[50] Yet *Autumn Journal*, I think, does not believe in 'the stream of history', as MacNeice calls it in the by-election section, not in history's having a definite course, but in its being shaped, like syntax, by the constrained choices of particular people. If the politicians and leaders are making mad or foolish moves, others may notice, respond, and criticize. This, MacNeice's poem affirms, is vitally important to all our futures. Thus, the 'something more' is what is provided in a poem by the rhythmic and syntactic ordering. Composition finds such pattern through the shaping of situation in poetic form, and the adaptations of such form to the recalcitrant conditions of mentioned things. MacNeice attributes 'shape' and vitality to the days of crisis in which history may seem arbitrarily chaotic, shaped by nothing to which value could be ascribed. At the close of section XVII the poet associates his creative activity not with the 'musical or other harmonies he may incidentally evoke' but with the discovery of meaning and choice, something not incidental to music or harmonies, but the music of the poetry itself:

> Still there are still the seeds of energy and choice
>   Still alive even if forbidden, hidden,
> And while a man has choice
>   He may recover music.   (p. 139)

Through such pattern-making MacNeice is able to signal relations between the political, personal, and philosophical issues of freedom, choice, fulfilment, and responsibility.

---

[50] MacNeice, *Modern Poetry*, 17.

IV

On his way to Spain in December 1938 MacNeice spent Christmas in Paris. As he describes the visit in his autobiography, 'Paris was under snow and very beautiful. We ate and drank a great deal'.[51] In *Autumn Journal* XXII, MacNeice makes of his time there a debate between what he calls in his letter to Eliot 'the sensual man, the philosopher, the would-be good citizen'.[52] The sensual man gets his say, but his headlong tone and catalogue of needs are prefaced by 'So here where tourist values are the only | Values, where we pretend'. Among the things they pretend is:

> [']that gossip
> Is the characteristic of art
> And that the sensible man must keep his aesthetic
> And his moral standards apart—'   (p. 147)

I think MacNeice's values are travestied here, but the ideas directly expressed are ones that he could contemplate. In 'Letter to W. H. Auden' of 21 October 1937 he states that 'Poetry is related to the sermon and you have your penchant for preaching, but it is more closely related to conversation and you, my dear, if any, are a born gossip.'[53] MacNeice's method is to affirm what a philosopher and would-be good citizen might think, namely, that aesthetic and moral standards are neither clearly distinguishable nor ever wholly dissociable. He expresses this as the implied opposite of what the sensual man would prefer to think, which is that if it's beauty you want, forget about morality—as in the jaded jest about translations and women: the more beautiful the more unfaithful.

In 'A Statement' for the *New Verse* 'Commitments' double number of Autumn 1938 MacNeice noted that 'The poet at the moment will tend to be moralist rather than aesthete.' He prefaced this remark, however, by observing that though 'I have been asked to commit myself about poetry', 'I have committed myself already so much *in* poetry that this seems almost superfluous.'[54] While not an aesthete, the poet as 'critical moralist' is also necessarily committing himself in poetry, his poem 'cannot live by

<hr/>

[51] MacNeice, *The Strings are False*, 176.
[52] Cited in Marsack, *Cave of Making*, 43.
[53] MacNeice, *Selected Literary Criticism*, ed. Heuser, 86. Heuser's footnote refers to Auden's 'In Defence of Gossip', in which he states that 'All art is based on gossip' (W. H. Auden, *Prose and Travel Books in Prose and Verse, i. 1926–1938*, ed. E. Mendelson (Princeton, NJ: Princeton University Press, 1996), 425–30, and see p. 428).
[54] MacNeice, *Selected Literary Criticism*, 98.

morals alone',[55] and to this end the formal principles of *Autumn Journal* are an aspect of its ethical principles regarding personal relations and foreign affairs. At the end of the poem, we sleep—

> On the banks of Rubicon—the die is cast;
>   There will be time to audit
> The accounts later, there will be sunlight later
>   And the equation will come out at last.   (p. 153)

Here the deferring of the final rhyme to one line later than expected performs the deferral of auditing accounts, of sunlight, and the equation's coming out. The expressions of the future in the final three lines, whether predictions or hopes, are affirmed by that final rhyme. The rhyme sound comes round, though later than you thought, and the poem's formal equation does come out at last. *Autumn Journal* ends by promising that in nurturing the seeds of 'energy and choice' (p. 139) we can face the future arising from our bungled past.

After citing some criticism of the poem Edna Longley concludes: 'not every commentator has found *Autumn Journal* psychologically or politically adequate to its task'.[56] MacNeice himself lost confidence in the shape that he had made. Fifteen years later, in *Autumn Sequel* (1953), he wrote:

> An autumn journal—or journey. The clocks tick
> Just as they did but that was a slice of life
> And there is no such thing.   (p. 331)

MacNeice is right, 'there is no such thing'; the poet has forgotten what he wrote in *Modern Poetry*. The 'slice' is his selection of material 'which will be found to come under the question of Form'. What's happening is being done not by the psychological or political adequacy but by the relationship between the mentionings of things, in all their various inadequacies, and the formal shaping of these things in and by the poem. MacNeice had written in his letter to T. S. Eliot that he thought *Autumn Journal* his 'best work to date'. Looking back over sixty-odd years, I'm inclined not only to agree with him, but to think it his best work, full stop.

---

[55] MacNeice had criticized the Auden–Isherwood collaboration *On the Frontier* in these words on 18 Nov. 1938: 'But a play cannot live by morals alone' (*Selected Literary Criticism*, 103).
[56] Longley, *Louis MacNeice*, 61.

CHAPTER 5

Dependence in the Poetry of
W. S. Graham

I

Reviewing *The Nightfishing* in 1956, James Dickey wrote that W. S. Graham was 'the most individual and important young poet now writing in English'.[1] Graham was then thirty-eight years old. His poetry and literary life would seem to have been an expression of independence. In a review of *The White Threshold* from 1950 Edwin Morgan saw Graham as remaining 'undistracted and unwooed',[2] while Calvin Bedient in 1974 assumed that 'His cultivated eccentricity argues the right to stand alone.'[3] But independence had its price. Others have seen Graham's—at least up to *The Nightfishing* (1955)—as only too dependent on the voice of Dylan Thomas. Kenneth Allott, on the basis of that volume, grudgingly accepted that 'W. S. Graham is probably a poet, although one who cherishes some bad poetic habits and is excessively literary'.[4] Edward Lucie-Smith was not much warmer, putting Graham's independence, which he implies is mere isolation, down to unfortunate coincidences of publishing: 'W. S. Graham is a poet who has been somewhat unlucky in his timing. His best-known volume was *The Nightfishing*, which appeared in the same year as Philip Larkin's *The Less Deceived*.'[5] Lucie-Smith makes

---

[1] James Dickey, *Babel To Byzantium: Poets and Poetry Now* (New York: Grosset and Dunlap, 1971), 45.

[2] Edwin Morgan, cited by Damian Grant, 'Walls of Glass: The Poetry of W. S. Graham' in M. Schmidt and P. Jones (eds.), *British Poetry since 1970* (Manchester: Carcanet, 1980), 22.

[3] Calvin Bedient, *Eight Contemporary Poets* (Oxford: Oxford University Press, 1974), 166.

[4] Kenneth Allott (ed.), *The Penguin Book of Contemporary Verse*, 2nd edn. (Harmondsworth: Penguin, 1962), 309.

[5] Edward Lucie-Smith, *British Poetry since 1945* (Harmondsworth: Penguin, 1970), 103. Donald Davie reviewed *The Nightfishing* in 1955, saying of the title poem that 'Mr Graham's quality is apparent at once, when we see that instead of improvising line by line, he has obviously planned his long poem, "The Nightfishing", precisely as an artefact, as one whole thing in itself.' Davie was criticized by Tony Lopez for deliberately obscuring Graham's qualities when he objected to

Graham's reputation painfully dependent on the tides of literary fashion. So when Morgan wrote of Graham's 'undeviating and dangerous single-mindedness',[6] was it challengingly 'dangerous' for the reader, or damagingly thus for the poet and his poetry's reception?

The solitude of independence can be bracing, but also chilly. Damian Grant describes Graham as 'concerned with putting into words those sudden desolations and happiness that descend on us uninvited there where we each are within our lonely rooms never really entered by anybody else and from which we never emerge'.[7] For Graham life appears an imposed independence, from which freedom may be sought in poetry. His brief manifesto, published in 1946, is called 'Notes on a Poetry of Release'. In this aloneness and isolation of the self Graham's poetry finds an irreducible condition, but the actions of his poems—recognizing and speaking from that solitude—form messages that are emblems of aloneness potentially relieved.

Independence has its price, and, in the case of W. S. Graham, who dedicated himself single-mindedly to his poetry, it was one that others would also have to pay, not least the devoted Nessie Dunsmuir, his wife. Here is one form of dependence in independence, and Graham's letters exemplify it in detail. Writing to Sven Berlin on 12 March 1949 he reported that 'Things are at their worst ever financially and it will be a fight to keep out of a job of some kind'. Later in the letter he added that 'After this I write to London to try to borrow £10 to pay the back rent here.'[8] Things never got much better, though mitigated by supporters like the painters John Minton, Roger Hilton, and Bryan Wynter, by Harold Pinter, and the poet Robin Skelton, who arranged to buy manuscripts for the University of Victoria (BC) library on a regular basis. On his 1974 reading tour of Canada Graham offended his supporter, with temporarily difficult results, as is made clear in a letter to Bill and Gail Featherston:

I think I've fucked myself with Robin and he has stopped the money. (Say nothing to Robin. He will probably tell you.) I think all along the line I was compelled to be 'agin' and I couldn't help it. Bill, I've written him and said that I would

---

'the hieratic solemnity with which he takes his own poetic vocation' and 'the solemnity of the tone' (Lopez, *The Poetry of W. S. Graham* (Edinburgh: Edinburgh University Press, 1989), 12–19, citing Davie at 16. For the source of Lopez's idea see Andrew Crozier, 'Thrills and Frills', in A. Sinfield (ed.), *Society and Literature 1945–1970* (New York: Holmes and Meier,1984), 199–233).

[6] Morgan, cited by Grant, in Schmidt and Jones (eds.), *British Poetry since 1970*, 22.
[7] Ibid. 28.
[8] W. S. Graham, *The Nightfisherman: Selected Letters*, ed. M. and M. Snow (Manchester: Carcanet, 1999), 87.

like to do our MALAHAT and I hope his anger doesn't extend to stopping that. Now, Bill, do not broach the money subject with Robin. I mean the £25 a month he has been paying me for the last year for MSS and all the notebooks. I must have been daft, Ness says. Why didn't I just keep my trap shut. OK OK OK[9]

Here a person who *is* fiercely independent, but whose chosen course has forced him inevitably to depend upon patrons and friends, has experienced embarrassing ambivalences and conflicts—which may well have emerged on his Canadian tour. Graham's letters are frequently exercises in managing the shame of having to cadge and maintaining the self-esteem that is being attacked by the need to borrow.

In a letter that begins by informing Skelton of the death of the poet's friend Brian Wynter, and in which he admits to having been drunk in the morning, Graham concludes with a characteristic attempt to express a connective feeling and to reserve an autonomous toughness:

Rob, I go to the funeral on Saturday. Who shall I be? Shall I put on the intense face or the concealing face or the interesting face? Did I like him? Did I love him? Were you in Canada when I was there? Give me a hug across the sea. Sylvia, give me a wee kiss. I am not really sentimental. I am as hard as Greenock shipbuilding nails.[10]

The role-playing in this, messy as it is, can be assumed from the series of questions about the kind of face he will wear at Wynter's funeral. Yet more vulnerably exposed, in a letter of 27 June 1972 from Cornwall to his wife in Scotland Graham wrote: 'I miss you more than I can tell you. To be without you here is some experience of something. It is not that I am a weak man. I have my strong side somewhere if only I could find it.'[11] What makes this more convincingly self-descriptive is that it contrasts 'weak' and 'strong' qualities of the self, rather than 'sentimental' and 'hard' aspects of a social performance. The poet's dependent vulnerability is revealed in the letter to his wife. He frequently copes with it by travesty and denial in his correspondence with others.

Graham's idiom for addressing interlocutors in the poems, his first-name terms, his 'my boy' and 'my dear', is similarly touched with a gauche instability—an instability which stands in self-critical relation both to his recorded social behaviour and his epistolary style. Julian MacLaren-Ross rather coldly reports that 'Graham in some way contrived to promote

[9] Ibid. 269–70.
[10] Ibid. 288.
[11] Ibid. 262.

unpleasantness around him. Unpleasant things tended to happen in his vicinity.'[12] One of the most dramatic instances of a stylistic instability, its oscillation between a piercingly overdone tenderness and a cold-faced denial, is in a letter of 15 April 1973 to the Duncans:

> Here I am. Alone in this place and I write to you across the night shires of England. Do I like you both because I am alone awake in my night-surrounded house? I dont know. You might be something. Who knows? At least I make you to myself something now. Tall shy Ronnie. Compact, easy to love, Henriette. My dears, here I am sitting at my great creative typewriter typing my life away for some reason. Dont be so daft. I am only trying to speak 'from one aloneness to another'.
>
> I have a tenor singing the best aria from Turandot and it is turning my brain to slush. So sweet, so good. That is all right. Hold me in your four arms, you two. Come my dearest dears. Enough. Finis.

Vertically up the margin beside this passage Graham wrote: 'Do not read this letter as a softness. I am as hard as fucking nails.'[13] Yet there is a soft-ness, weakness, a vulnerability, not about the letter itself, but about the felt need to annotate it with the cliché 'hard as nails' illustrated by the expletive intensifier. Citing another letter to Bill Featherston, in which Graham touches on his class origins, Tony Lopez observes that 'Graham's uneasiness at what he took to be his rather humble social position explains a good deal about him.'[14] Yet, while the 'uneasiness' is incontestably present, is it the class origins that are causing the problem? Many who have come from similar backgrounds do not demonstrate such radically unstable modes of address in their correspondence.

As the letters suggest, there are evidently weaker and stronger con-ditions of dependence. The weaker exists where bodily life is compelled by reliance upon something—drink, for example—whose effect on the desiring body when received can be largely predicted. There is a causal relationship between the stimulant and its effects. The word's second meaning the *OED* gives as 'the relation of having existence conditioned

---

[12] Julian MacLaren-Ross, *Memoirs of the Forties* (1965), cited in Lopez, *Poetry of W. S. Graham*, 4.

[13] '"Dear Pen Pal in the distance": A Selection of W. S. Graham's Letters', ed. R. Grogan, *PN Review*, 73, 16/5 (1990), 16. This letter does not appear in *The Nightfisherman*.

[14] Lopez, *Poetry of W. S. Graham*, 7. In 'Remembering the Movement' Davie describes 'the unforgivable literary sin of going much further than halfway to meet our readers, forestalling their objections, trying to keep in their good books' (Donald Davie, *The Poet in the Imaginary Museum*, ed. B. Alpert (Manchester: Carcanet, 1977), 72). A study of this period's poetry might see the 'uneasiness' in Graham's modes of address and what Davie calls the Movement's 'craven defensiveness' as different responses to similar problems of class tone and poetic style.

by the existence of something else'. A baby has such a dependence on its mother's body; it is in 'The condition of being a dependent', which is the *OED*'s third meaning and extends to 'subjection' or 'subordination'. A prisoner is in an enforced dependence on his guards. If the word is used to express relations between autonomous adults in society, dependence will involve greater risk, for the effect of others upon whom we depend is less predictable than mother's milk, a prisoner's food, or the drinker's bottle. Whether or not the provision of these needs can be relied on is another matter. 'You can depend on me' also implies a sense that the undependability of others is ever present and must be fended off by an assurance that a promise, for example, will be kept.

That life repeatedly involves depending and being dependent on others implies that the word can describe relations where the effect of that upon which we depend is uncertain. The *OED*'s fifth meaning takes this condition of dependence within uncertainty to an extreme limit: 'the condition of resting in faith or expectation (upon something)' and it then cites Jowett: 'Living . . . in dependence on the will of God'. The ways of God are not revealed to us and can't be presumed upon even by the most faithful of the faithful. This fifth sense is crucial to Graham's poetry, for that lonely room 'never really entered by anybody else and from which we never emerge' leaves relations with other people dependent on hope, trust, and varying degrees of a necessarily risk-laden confidence. Graham's letters exemplify an acute awareness of the dangers involved in the expression of relationship on almost every page.

In a notebook of 1949 Graham wrote: 'To show you *need* something from another person destroys any chance of receiving it. People love him who does not *need* love.'[15] The first sentence acknowledges a need and gives advice about self-esteem and its relation to receiving what you do need. The second suggests why many love a God who does not need their love. In the second sentence Graham is making '*need*' into a sign of weak dependence. A strong dependence is implied in his first sentence. There are three main related areas of dependence in Graham's work: dependence upon words; dependence upon an interlocutor; and dependence upon a reader. Yet with his poetry the direction of dependence may equally be reversed: language dependent upon its users; the listeners dependent upon what they are in the process of hearing; readers dependent upon the poet. Dependence in his poetry is strong for two reasons. It

15 W. S. Graham, 'From a 1949 Notebook . . .', in *Edinburgh Review*, 75 (1987), 36.

does not rely upon knowing or assuming the nature or effects of that upon which it depends. Moreover, since the direction of dependence can be reversed, the interdependence of both on each presupposes not the subjection or subordination of the *OED*'s third meaning, but an equality of trust and reliance upon the other in uncertainty.

Graham's work explores a ranging awareness of weak dependence: there are poems which include childhood and parental relations, more than one which inhabit or refer to prisons and asylums, while there are many that touch on drinking.[16] His poetry seeks the creation of a strong dependence out of those weak relationships. Graham's explorations of mutual dependence locate his 'right to stand alone', his 'individual liberty of thought or action' (*OED*), in a literary situation strengthened by the acknowledgement of a primary human need for relationship. These explorations are all the more necessary and bracing because they occur in poems attentive to the chill conditions that isolate us from each other. In maturity, weak dependence may be an indication of damage or unmitigated vulnerability. Graham's poems work to transform the weak into the strong.

II

The poet's dependence on the sound of words can appear shameful and demeaning. In Tennyson's lines from *The Princess* 'The moan of doves in immemorial elms, | And murmuring of innumerable bees',[17] readers are to imagine the bees humming and to cherish the skill with which the poet has collocated 'immemorial', 'murmuring', and 'innumerable'. These words have nothing in themselves to do with bees, and it is this gratuitousness in the sound patterns of poems that can be thought demeaning. In his 'Conversation about Dante' (1933–4) Osip Mandelstam describes the sound of *Inferno* 32 as having a 'deliberately shameless, intentionally infantile orchestration'.[18] It includes the line: 'né da lingua che chiami mamma e babbo'[19] (nor for a tongue that cries mamma and papa). Mandelstam thinks the canto imitates the sound of a baby calling without

---

[16] See e.g. 'To Alexander Graham', 'Clusters Travelling Out', and 'Letter III', in W. S. Graham, *Collected Poems 1942–1977* (London: Faber & Faber, 1979), 215–16, 184–8, 113–15. Page references to poems cited from this volume will be given in the text.

[17] *The Poems of Tennyson*, 3 vols., ed. C. Ricks (London: Longmans, 1987) ii. 288.

[18] Osip Mandelstam, *Selected Essays*, trans. S. Monas (Austin, Tex.: University of Texas Press, 1977), 34.

[19] Dante Alighieri, *Inferno* can. 32, l. 9.

shame—it appearing shameful for a grown man to make sounds like 'chiami mamma'. Rather than bees, Tennyson's lines might echo 'Seventeen-months-old Christine', as reported in Dorothy Burlingham and Anna Freud's *Young Children in Wartime* (1942), 'who said: "Mum, mum, mum, mum, mum" . . . continually in a deep voice for at least three days'.[20] The extent of a poet's dependence on the sound of words (and it is this which, to differing degrees, marks the poet out from all other writers) may express a preserved residuum of feeling related to the complete dependence on a mother for food and well being. Poets are fed by the nature of their mother tongue.

The revulsion that some readers experience from Dylan Thomas's music may be explained by the poet's dependence on the sounds of words. Thomas's poetry can be felt to reveal a weak subjection to verbal music, a helplessness that depends on auditory power alone to restore the bliss of a satisfied infant. The more the poem appears to coordinate sounds for their own sake, at the expense, or in excess, of purposeful conceptual speech, the worse embarrassment may become. Perhaps this is because an overt verbal music relies so much upon the poet assuming the compositional and affective efficacy of the sound of his or her own voice. At the receiving end, it depends upon the reader succumbing to a music whose effect is believed to be certainly determined; that is, can be depended on to work in the same way each time.

Ortega Y Gasset has contrasted the pleasure of being drunk with that of winning in a sweepstake, so as to illustrate that 'An aesthetic pleasure must be a seeing pleasure':

The drunken man's happiness is blind. Like everything in the world it has a cause, the alcohol; but it has no motive. A man who has won a sweepstake is happy, too, but in a different manner; he is happy 'about' something.[21]

Commenting on this remark in his chapter on 'Aesthetic Explanation and Perplexity', Frank Cioffi proposes that when Wittgenstein writes that 'There is a "Why?" to aesthetic discomfort, not a "cause" to it'[22] he is calling attention to 'the difference between a blind pleasure and a seeing one—between a drunkard's euphoria and the gambler's, between so

[20] Cited by Adrian Stokes in the preface to *Inside Out*, in *The Critical Writings*, 3 vols. ed. L. Gowing (London: Thames & Hudson, 1978) ii. 141.

[21] José Ortega Y Gasset, *The Dehumanization of Art* (New York: Doubleday, 1956), 25.

[22] Ludwig Wittgenstein, *Lectures and Conversations on Aesthetics, Psychology and Religious Belief*, ed. C. Barrett (Oxford: Blackwell, 1966), 14.

many units of alcohol in the blood and a royal flush'.[23] Though this distinction is well taken, a further one may be worth making. There are socially debilitating conditions of compulsive gambling and dependence on alcohol, but, whatever the consequences of devoting a life to writing poetry, no one, I think, would be inclined to put a person into rehab so as to wean them from a compulsive dependence on metrical composition.

Graham's poem 'Press Button to Hold Desired Symbol' from *Malcolm Mooney's Land* interweaves all three of these human habits. It describes Garfield Strick playing the fruit machine in his pub, the King William the Fourth in Madron, Cornwall:

> King William the Fourth's electric One
> Armed Bandit rolls its eyes to Heaven.
> Churchtown Madron's Garfield Strick
> Stands at the moment less than even.[24]

The poem encourages him to keep on trying although he's losing, and although while the pictures of fruit expensively whirl his 'wife is stirring jam at home'. Graham's quatrains rhyme on second and fourth lines, and the 'chances of rhyme',[25] as Charles Tomlinson has called them, are brought into analogous relation to the chances of the machine paying up. The poem sketches a sense of Strick's dependence on these wheels of fortune with its reference to 'the worship of his eye', to 'the orchard of magic seed', and the 'oracle' which 'rolls | Its eyes too fast for him to read'. The poem ends with the flush of drinkers in the pub being surprised by Strick's flush of success:

> King William the Fourth pays out
> With a line of clattering oranges.
> Garfield turns. His glass shatters
> Its shape in our astonished gaze.
>
> In the high air on thin sticks
> The blanched rags in the wind blow.
> The brass cylinder turns round
> Saying I know I know I know.   (p. 168)

---

[23] Frank Cioffi, *Wittgenstein on Freud and Frazer* (Cambridge: Cambridge University Press, 1998), 56.

[24] Graham's *Collected Poems 1942–1977* has no full stop at the end of this verse. It has been silently corrected in W. S. Graham, *New Collected Poems*, ed. M. Francis (London: Faber & Faber, 2004), 176.

[25] Charles Tomlinson, 'The Chances of Rhyme', in *Collected Poems* (Oxford: Oxford University Press, 1985), 194–5.

Unlike the drink in the glass, whose alcohol has a cause-and-effect relation with brain chemistry, the flush of the gambler's success has a relation
to skill, as is underlined by Graham's imperative title: 'Press Button to
Hold Desired Symbol'. Thus, the gambler's winning can be a seeing
pleasure, despite not being able to read the fruit because it spins too fast,
because the luck of the pay-out is interwoven with Strick's best efforts at
judgement and the speed of hand that the fruit machine player develops.

Writing to Mary Harris from Yaddo on 14 July 1948 Graham commented that he had 'been on the drink quite a bit', adding: 'What cocktails
here, Manhattans, Martinis, Tom Collins, and all calculated to "disarrange
the senses".'[26] If his allusion to Rimbaud's attempt to arrive 'à *l'inconnu*' by
means of the '*dérèglement* de *tous les sens*' gestures at an artistic justification
for the drink, his 'calculated to' reveals the difference between drink or
drugs and poetry. Graham's 'Press Button to Hold Desired Symbol'
draws attention to the element of luck and chance in its composition by
aligning the paying out of the fruit machine with the poem's coming
round to a rhyme. It is as if the knowledge of the brass cylinder was what
had made the final stanza felicitously close with a row, not of oranges, but
of 'I know'. Yet poetic devices cannot be mixed like a cocktail. They
cannot be 'calculated to' produce any definite effects. Wittgenstein con-
tended that no causal relation may be discerned between an aesthetic
phenomenon and a perceived response.[27]

Why did Graham choose to have the winning 'line' as a row of oranges,
rather than plums or bells? It's much easier to rhyme on 'plums' and 'bells'
than it is on 'oranges'. The difficulty of finding rhymes in English is sometimes illustrated in the handbooks by citing the notion that there is no full
rhyme in the language for the word 'orange'.[28] Graham's closing rhyme in
that penultimate quatrain ('oranges'/'gaze') is barely even an assonance.
The relationships between freedom and constraint in creative choice (and
between cause and effect in produced aesthetic effects) are so much more
open to opportunity, variation, unpredictability, invention, and the like.
Consequently, the flush of success when a poem comes right is that much

[26] *Nightfisherman*, 76. Graham's allusion is to the phrase in a letter from Rimbaud to Paul
Demeny, 15 May 1871 (Arthur Rimbaud, *Oeuvres Complètes*, ed. A. Adam (Paris: Gallimard, 1972),
251).
[27] Cioffi attempts to demonstrate that Wittgenstein is mistaken in this belief. See *Wittgenstein
on Freud and Frazer*, 47–79, and, for a discussion of related issues, P. M. S. Hacker, *Wittgenstein:
Connections and Controversies* (Oxford: Oxford University Press, 2001), ch. 3.
[28] Graham rhymes 'orange' with 'courage' at the close of 'The Visit' (*Uncollected Poems*
(Warwick: Greville, 1990), 17).

more 'seeing' than in the case of gambling. The number of elements that have been brought into concord, and significant discord, by human skill is incalculably greater. There is, as it were, so much more to see in the seeing pleasure.

Even with the so-called 'chances of rhyme' the fact that concepts and ideas are linked by homophonic associations is not, at the level of a poet's creative life, a matter of chance at all. As Wittgenstein observed: 'It is an accident that "last" rhymes with "fast". But it is a lucky accident, & you can *discover* this lucky accident.'[29] Similarly, it is, for a serious poet in French, an unlucky accident that 'amour' rhymes so well with 'toujours', or, looked at as opportunity rather than constraint, a lucky one in English that (outside the stock-in-trade of popular-song-lyric writing) there are no usable full rhymes for 'love'. Yet such relations of sound and sense are not matters of luck, but judgement. Wittgenstein's word in the original German for 'lucky' is, in fact, 'glücklicher', which could as felicitously be translated as 'happy': a 'happy accident'. The happiness or luck involved here all depends on the poet's having a vast repertoire of competence in the relationships offered by the sounds and meanings of words. Thus, dependence of the poet on the medium, words, is a mutual dependence, for the words are entirely dependent on the medium of the poet for finding their happiest and most memorable auditory and semantic combinations.

III

The complexities of interdependence in the field of composition are matched by ones in the field of reading and its aesthetic pleasures. The experience of discussing a poem's auditory components (and attributing meaning to them) suggests that the fluidity of pronunciation, accent, stress, pitch, and tone makes it dangerous for poet and critic alike to depend too confidently upon how the poem will sound in another's ear. Nor can the responses that this hearing may or may not prompt be assumed. Michael Schmidt has noticed in Graham's work that 'From an early attitude of complete trust in words . . . he grew more cautious with them, introducing discipline and distance between them.'[30] Later work contains numerous poems that explore the poet's dependence on words,

---

[29] Ludwig Wittgenstein, *Culture and Value*, rev. 2nd edn., trans. P. Winch, ed. G. H. Von Wright et. al. (Oxford: Blackwell, 1998), 93e.
[30] Michael Schmidt, *An Introduction to Fifty British Poets* (London: Pan, 1979), 299.

which assume that words are not to be relied on like so many units of alcohol. Part 8 of 'Approaches to How They Behave' from *Malcolm Mooney's Land* (1970) begins: 'And what are you supposed to say | I asked a new word but it kept mum' (p. 172). Dependence on words that have life independently of the writer is an irreducible difficulty and condition of writing poetry.

The temptation to retreat from this fact is referred to in 'Notes on a Poetry of Release', where, reminding himself of Mallarmé's advice to the painter and amateur sonneteer Edgar Degas ('Mais, Degas, ce n'est point avec des idées que l'on fait des vers ... *C'est avec des mots*',[31]) Graham states:

The most difficult thing for me to remember is that a poem is made of words and not of the expanding heart, the overflowing soul, or the sensitive observer. A poem is made of words.[32]

In the 1949 notebook Graham enters beside the heading 'words—' a close paraphrase of T. S. Eliot's remarks on allusiveness in his essay 'The Music of Poetry' (1942). Graham's version reads:

rich connected and poor connected. The poet should dispose the richer among the poorer at the right points. He cannot afford to load a poem too heavily with the richer—for it is only at certain moments that a word can be made to insinuate the whole history of language and a civilization. This is an *ALLUSIVENESS*, the concern of every kind of poet.[33]

Graham was developing the mature style of his 1949 and 1955 volumes, where richness of association is tempered by the interspersing of simple words, the language of work and daily experience. The critical self-consciousness, restraint and control implied in Eliot's remark helped shape Graham's poems from this period.

Damian Grant wrote that the poet's early work shows 'Graham drunk with words'.[34] Grant may have this from Schmidt, who describes early Graham as 'word-drunk' and 'in the thrall of Dylan Thomas'.[35] With these descriptions, Graham is likened to a drinker and a prisoner, going to words as to a bottle of whisky and to Thomas's poetry as to a plate of food

[31] See Paul Valéry, *Degas Danse Dessin* (Paris: Gallimard, 1938), 92.
[32] W. S. Graham, 'Notes on a Poetry of Release', *Poetry Scotland*, 3 (July 1946), 56. The essay has been reprinted as an appendix in *The Nightfisherman*, 379–83.
[33] W. S. Graham, 'From a 1949 Notebook...' 31. For the passage in T. S. Eliot's 'The Music of Poetry' see *On Poetry and Poets* (London: Faber & Faber, 1957), 32–3.
[34] Grant, in Schmidt and Jones (eds.), *British Poetry since 1970*, 23.
[35] Schmidt, *Fifty British Poets*, 298.

pushed under a door, weakly dependent on them. 'Explanation of a Map' is in *2ND Poems* (1945):

> My word
> Knows mister and missus, measure and live feature,
> So fume and jet of the floor and all its towns
> Wording the world awake and all its suns.   (pp. 29–30)

Graham was trained as an engineer, and many of his poems have the separateness of made objects. Yet it is the construction of these lines from 'Explanation of a Map' that causes dissatisfaction. A large claim is voiced in 'My word | Knows' and it is not substantiated by the analogical sound effects standing in for the substance of the world, as in 'mister and missus, measure and live feature'; the alliteration and internal part-rhyme feel like words snatched at and settled for. Not 'Wording the world awake', they lull to enchant with a gesture at wholeness: 'and all its towns', 'and all its suns'.

The much-reiterated comparison with Dylan Thomas is partly mistaken. Thomas's word music is frequently occasioned by a well-signalled, if vague, theme: innocence, mortality, the continuum of nature and human life. 'Poem in October' enthrals with simple words and cadences:

> These were the woods the river and sea
>   Where a boy
>   In the listening
> Summertime of the dead whispered the truth of his joy
> To the trees and the stones and the fish in the tide.[36]

The last line of anapaests demonstrates a simple dependence on rhythmic predictability. Graham tends not to give readers the purchase of a general thematic concern, though the poet did once list his major themes:

The difficulty of communication; the difficulty of speaking from a fluid identity; the lessons in physical phenomena; the mystery and adequacy of aesthetic experience; the elation of being alive in the language.[37]

Helpful about his concerns and approaches to the art of poetry, this gives nothing away about the character of particular poems.

'Here next the Chair I was when Winter Went' is from *Cage Without Grievance* (1942) and touches the traditional themes of love and death:

---

[36] Dylan Thomas, *Collected Poems 1934–1952* (London: J. M. Dent, 1952), 96.
[37] W. S. Graham in J. Vinson and D. L. Kirkpatrick (eds.), *Contemporary Poets* (London and New York: St Martin's Press, 1975), 575.

> So still going out in the morning of ash and air
> My shovel swings. My tongue is a sick device.
> Fear evening my boot says. The chair sees iceward
> In the bitter hour so visible to death.   (p. 19)

Graham's best mature work has a similarly discrete movement in short sentences between particulars, as here from 'My shovel' to 'My tongue', 'my boot' and 'The chair'. These lines depend far less than 'Poem in October' on overt sound effects to give form. The things are not bound up into an incantatory unity that would rob them of their separate existences. The 'device'/'iceward' rhyme of a final and a penultimate syllable hints that every act of speech moves the speaker nearer to the grave. The poet speaks and walks towards the end of the day; the disappearance of light; cold darkness in which death can still see to snatch at him. The movement of the poem announces a thread of being: quiet, undemonstrative, and with plenty of space for thought to live between the sentences, as between the words, allowing the reader's mind into a process of pondering, moving on, and returning. This is one value in a poem's resistance to ready thematic absorption, as Graham wrote in 'Notes on a Poetry of Release':

The meaning of a poem is itself, not less a comma. But then to each man it comes into new life. It is brought to life by the reader and takes part in the reader's change. Even the poet as a man who searches continually is a new searcher with his direction changing at every step.[38]

For there to be 'change at every step' recognized and performed in a poem there must be memory of previous states, and a memory for the sounds of words which have come before.

Thomas and Graham are also distinguishable by their rhythms. Thomas's are deft and flexible, but also firmly determined, as in the close of 'Fern Hill':

> Oh as I was young and easy in the mercy of his means,
> Time held me green and dying
> Though I sang in my chains like the sea.[39]

Security is again found in a line of anapaests. Their chant is firm-footed. Graham's rhythm moves with a lighter, exploratory tread. Here is the first sentence of 'Since all my steps taken', the opening poem of *The White Threshold* (1949):

---

[38] 'Notes on a Poetry of Release', 58.   [39] Thomas, *Collected Poems*, 151.

> Since all my steps taken
> Are audience of my last
> With hobnail on Ben Narnain
> Or mind on the word's crest
> I'll walk the kyleside shingle
> With scarcely a hark back
> To the step dying from my heel
> Or the creak of the rucksack.   (p. 47)

The poet's steps, Bedient notes, 'listen to themselves' and he adds: 'even as the venturer resolves not to hark back, he yet does, perhaps must'.[40] The poem moves to touch on 'All journey, since the first | Step from my father and mother', and depends upon its auditory process. It is attending to its own past. Yet in the lightness of Graham's rhythmic tread there is a dependence which is neither shameful nor demeaning, because each note walks apart as it is sounded together with the others. The eight lines of the first sentence are delicately rhymed: taken/Narnain, last/crest, shingle/heel, hark back/rucksack. The extent to which a reader harks back is carefully modulated, though increasingly heard, as the rhymes culminate in the slightly askew stresses on 'hark back' and 'rucksack'.

A speaking, not a chanting, voice lets the stresses fall irregularly, though the poem is sure-footed enough. Graham said of his rhythms:

Although I love the ever-present metronome in verse, I am greedy for my rhythmic say. The gesture of speech often exists, moving seemingly counter to the abstract structure it is in. The three-accent line, not specially common in the body of English poetry, even a kind of strait-jacket, interested me enough for me to keep to it for a bit and try to ring the changes within.[41]

The measure of 'Since all my steps taken' is the iambic trimeter, the 'three-accent line'. In shorter measures the placing of individual syllables becomes even more crucial to rhythmic poise, and it has been noted that 'monosyllables . . . have an isolated verbal integrity'.[42] In the second line of this poem ('Are audience of my last') should the stress fall on the final syllable of 'audience' or on 'of' or 'my'? This is Graham's 'gesture of speech', and only two stresses are clearly determined, those on 'last' and the first syllable of 'audience'. In the first line ('Since all my steps taken') the word 'taken' wrong-foots the final, expected iamb—becoming a trochee.

---

[40] Bedient, *Eight Contemporary Poets*, 164.
[41] Vinson and Kirkpatrick (eds.), *Contemporary Poets*, 575.
[42] Schmidt, *Fifty British Poets*, 299.

The rhythm derives not so much from an 'abstract structure' with words 'moving seemingly counter', not a sensed underlying pattern with variations. It is achieved by a ranging voice which, for the guidance of the reader, refers to a pattern whenever there might appear to be none. Thus, after 'taken' the iambic returns at the beginning of the next line, is lost again, and resumes with 'my last'. The reader cannot depend upon Graham's most characteristic rhythms as upon a metronome. His rhythms depend to that extent upon trust. Through its rhythmic vicissitudes the poem bears voices 'walking towards that other'; harking back and hoping forward animates its form with a living process—'the elation of being alive in the language'.

In the fifth part of 'The Nightfishing' Graham returns to the poem as a thread of being:

> At this place
> The eye reads forward as the memory reads back.
> At this last word all words change.
> All words change in acknowledgement of the last.
> Here is their mingling element.
> This is myself (who but ill resembles me).   (p. 104)

Morgan wrote that by the early 1970s in Graham's poetry a 'growing lucidity humanizes the verse, but without removing its obsessional preoccupation with the endless dyings and metamorphoses of the self'.[43] Experience of the self as it changes is a main concern of 'The Nightfishing', and a trace of that theme, bearing upon the processes of reading, can be heard in the lines above. It is an idea of grammar which could have been drawn from T. S. Eliot's observation about the literature of Europe: 'for order to persist after the supervention of novelty, the *whole* existing order must be, if ever so slightly, altered'.[44] Graham puts this similarly in 'Notes on a Poetry of Release': 'when, after all . . . I am at the last word and look back I find the first word changed and a new word there, for it is part of the whole poem and its particular life depends on the rest of the poem'.[45] Eliot's idea about cultural order is true of sentences, especially in poems. 'All words change in acknowledgement of the last': the words in a line of verse depend for their meaning both forward and backward. As Eliot says, 'the past should be altered by the present as much as the

---

[43] Edwin Morgan, cited in Vinson and Kirkpatrick (eds.), *Contemporary Poets*, 576.
[44] T. S. Eliot, 'Tradition and the Individual Talent', in *The Sacred Wood* (London: Methuen, 1920), 50.
[45] 'Notes on a Poetry of Release', 58.

present is directed by the past'.[46] To feel this in the smallest additions of words in writing or reading is again to experience a vital process, a consciousness of being moving in the movement of the verse.

In the last section of 'The Nightfishing', his body thrown into the sea, the speaker re-enacts a Shakespearean and then Eliotic metamorphosis through drowning:

> My dead in the crew
> Have mixed all qualities
> That I have been and,
> Though ghosted behind
> My sides spurred by the spray,
> Endure by a further gaze
> Pearled behind my eyes.   (pp. 106–7)

The casual allusion to 'Those are pearls that were his eyes'[47] compacts together grammatical, personal, and cultural processes of change and renewal. It lightly shows dependence on the literary past as well as, in Eliot's terms, its dependence on him. This is one reason, to adopt section sixty-three of 'Implements in their Places', why 'Feeding the dead is necessary' (p. 252). Allott complained that Graham 'is excessively literary'; yet, as with what has been called 'his own peculiar, evasive metres', so too Graham has a delicate way with allusion. The poem does not depend helplessly on a reader's picking up the source. There is an allusion to Feste's song in 'It raineth now | Across the hedges and beneath the bough' (p. 229) from 'How are the Children Robin'. Not feeding off the literary past, with 'scarcely a hark back', Graham's words neither quite touch nor quite renounce the famous words they half-hear: 'For the rain it raineth every day.'

Though 'The Nightfishing' approaches a close with 'So I spoke and died' (p. 107), Morgan's idea of 'the dyings and metamorphoses of the self' is easier said than done. Graham's remarking 'the difficulty of speaking from a fluid identity' acknowledges this, as do many of his poems. The problem with 'So I spoke and died' is that the 'I' stays alive in uttering its own death, and the poem rights that contradiction as the verse continues to this end:

---

[46] Eliot, *Sacred Wood*, 50.
[47] *The Tempest*, I. ii. 401; T. S. Eliot, *Collected Poems 1909–1962* (London: Faber & Faber, 1963), 67.

> So within the dead
> Of night and the dead
> Of all my life those
> Words died and awoke.   (Ibid.)

Similarly, the 'metamorphoses' cannot be complete, because the poems are harking back, are a memory cumulatively reading, to imply a tenuous continuity of self that is recording these changes of self. In 'Letter II' from the 1955 volume Graham intensifies alteration by using the third-person pronoun for his youthful self, yet, though changed, he is still the same and will continue:

> Then in a welding flash
> He found his poetry arm
> And turned the coat of his trade.
> From where I am I hear
> Clearly his heart beat over
> Clydeside's far hammers
> And the nightshipping firth.
> What's he to me? Only
> Myself I died from into
> These present words that move.   (p. 110)

'What's Hecuba to him, or he to Hecuba'?[48] The strong dependence of the present on the past and of the past on the present both creates and itself depends on a double consciousness of the self in time: the 'I' furthers its continuity by rendering the discontinuities it experiences. The continuous self, harking back to part 5 of 'The Nightfishing', is associated by Graham with the sea and with the poem itself: 'Here is their mingling element'. The discontinuities are marked in every finite statement which refers to the self, outgrown as soon as it is uttered: 'This is myself (who but ill resembles me).' The discontinuous stations of selfhood alter backwards as they develop forwards: 'All words change in acknowledgement of the last' or, as Graham, puts it in 'Letter II':

> My musing love lie down
> Within his arms. He dies
> Word by each word into
> Myself now at this last
> Word I die in. This last.   (p. 112)

---

[48] *Hamlet*, II. ii. 561.

A further importance of Graham's 'Letter II' is that, alongside concerns with the vicissitudes and processes of the self, it addresses a loved one, 'My musing love'. Of Graham's development it has been noted that 'The would-be magical language of the early poems has devolved into a tenuous, distrustful dependence on words'. It happened partly because, as Graham writes in his transitional sequence, 'The Dark Dialogues', from *Malcolm Mooney's Land*: 'always language | Is where the people are' (p. 159).

IV

Graham's development into the moving poet of the later collections itself depended upon his courage in articulating 'the elation of being alive' and 'of being alive in the language'.[49] The dependencies of life are accommodated into the relative autonomy of his completed poems, as here in four more lines from 'Letter II' in *The Nightfishing*:

> Tonight in sadly need
> Of you I move inhuman
> Across this space of dread
> And silence in my mind.   (p. 111)

James Dickey saw that: 'There are all kinds of violence to syntax, like "tonight in sadly need," but you feel you do not need to forgive these, since many of the poet's best effects depend directly upon such wrenchings.'[50] Yet if that line 'tonight in sadly need' depends upon the peculiarity of the adverb of manner placed as if it were an adjective, the words themselves signify a dependence which is sad, and unfortunate, and a pity. It's as if to be in need of someone were itself a sorry state, or again: 'To show you *need* something from another person destroys any chance of receiving it.' Does the condition of need in 'Letter II' render the speaker 'inhuman'? Or is it because this is a poem speaking? Or does the speaker feel inhuman because of the evident isolation from which he seeks release? The poem calls upon the addressed figure to come into the poem by responding, but no words return:

> O offer some way tonight
> To make your love take place
> In every word. Reply.

[49]   Graham in Vinson and Kirkpatrick (eds.), *Contemporary Poets*, 575.
[50]   Dickey, *Babel and Byzantium*, 42.

A few lines later other imperatives ring with an unrelieved isolation:

> Break
> Break me out of this night,
> This silence where you are not,
> Nor any within earshot.
> Break break me from this high
> Helmet of idiocy.

Graham's first enjambment and his penultimate line respond to a prompt from Tennyson's desolating poem of human isolation and time's passing, 'Break, Break, Break'. In the second part of 'Malcolm Mooney's Land' he similarly harks back to the same poet's lyric from *The Princess*, 'The splendour falls on castle walls | And snowy summits old in story'[51] with 'The new ice falls from canvas walls' (p. 143). In the lines above, his rhyme of 'are not' and 'earshot' sounds a hollow echoing note, as does 'high' and 'idiocy'. These words imply a sharp dissatisfaction of the writer's with his orientation towards other people through his poems. The urgent calling upon another, who is later revealed as a love and muse, suggests a need for renewal which depends upon the at least tacit existence of an interlocutor.

The original distinction was between a weak, subservient dependence on a known and craved-for stimulus, and the strong dependence upon something that involves a 'condition of resting in faith or expectation'. In 'About an Interlocutor' (1913) Mandelstam argues that addressing living interlocutors, the poet's friends and relations as it might be, 'takes the wings off the verse, deprives it of air, of flight. The air of a poem is the unexpected. Addressing someone known, we can only say what is known.'[52] Yet even those to whom we are closest remain distinctly unknowable. Just as we cannot know the future, so we can never guarantee how another person will behave. As a result, speaking, a projection into the future, necessarily involves a risk which, while it can be reduced through familiarity, cannot be absolutely removed. This element of risk keeps the air and life in a poem. Graham's lyrics to his wife Nessie Dunsmuir would be cases to contrast with Mandelstam's idea.

In a letter dated 11 October 1950 Graham wrote from the orthopedic ward of the Royal Cornwall Infirmary:

All Art is the result of trying to say to an other one *exactly* what you mean. Because we are all each so different from each other inside (different even from good

---

[51] *The Poems of Tennyson*, ed. Ricks, ii. 231.
[52] Mandelstam, *Selected Essays*, 59.

friends we think we are extremely sympathetic to), one of the things we try again and again is to establish communication. What a stuffy pompous lecture. FINIS.[53]

Again Graham's point is hedged about by come-off-it second thoughts. Located 'within our lonely rooms never really entered by anybody else and from which we never emerge', Graham's mature and later poems ever more directly come to express the need to achieve relationship within conditions that assume other people will remain 'all each so different from each other inside'. Other people's differences and their being unknowable increase with Graham's consciousness of identity's fluidity. His poems do not presume upon the existence or nature of the person addressed, or, if they do, they acknowledge that presumption as a danger in dependence, a dependence that more usually in his poems rests upon the insecurities of hope and expectation.

A tone to invoke an interlocutor appeared early. 'No, listen, for this I tell' from *Cage Without Grievance* doesn't let on who is being addressed; a second person implied in the 'your mind' of line eight is repeated in the poem's close when speaker and listener are combined in the last line:

> The sky holds stars and lice
> In the disk of the chimney eye.
> They have no prophecy
> To hatch or harass your mind.
>
> We fall down darkness in a line of words.   (p. 23)

That final line succinctly describes the experience of its own printed self. Yet since this poem is not addressed to friends or relations, it hardly tests Mandelstam's proposition; and the uncertainty of addressee allows the poem its distinct 'air of . . . the unexpected'. Advance is marked in *The White Threshold* by the poems to inscribed interlocutors, the concluding 'Three Letters'. They are addressed, one each, to Graham's brother, his father, and his mother. All three are dedicated to the memory of his mother. Many of Graham's interlocutors are the recently dead. They sustain a separation between speaker and addressee that creates dependence within and through inevitable isolation. Here is the conclusion of 'To my Mother':

[53] Cited in *Edinburgh Review*, 75 (1987), 5. This fragment of a letter is not in *The Nightfisherman*, but another one (no. 70), written on the same day to Montcrieff Williamson, indicates what Graham was doing in the orthopedic ward: 'on a wild rainy night 3 weeks ago I walked 5 miles into St Ives to attend a birthday party and coming home I managed (don't ask me how) to fall off a roof 30 feet and land on concrete' (p. 124).

> Sometimes like loneliness
> Memory's crowds increase.
> Suddenly some man I am
> So finds himself endless stream
>
> Of stepping away from his
> Last home, I crave my ease
> Stopped for a second dead
> Out of the speaking flood.
>
> Under (not ground but the words)
> You rest with speaking hordes.   (p. 87)

The delicate reliance on a past is heard in the faint consonantal chiming of Graham's near rhymes. And the past, in memory, urges a continuity of speech upon the poet through his 'endless stream | Of stepping away' or 'the speaking flood' from which he finds himself momentarily separated: 'Stopped for a second dead'. Loneliness itself corresponds to that continuity, memory stimulated to populate a past in proportion to the self's isolation from its personal history.

The poem is not out to describe Graham's mother. Though she is known and addressed, the poet does not 'only say what is known' because it's the mother's absence which is present in the poem. Graham, like Wordsworth's poet in the preface to *Lyrical Ballads*, has a 'disposition to be affected more than other men by absent things as if they were present'.[54] The address to an interlocutor can affectingly answer to that disposition by invoking the present absence of a figure, such as a mother, once weakly and subordinately, but later more strongly and separately, depended upon: 'I crave my ease', he acknowledges. Not to offer confidences about her, Graham's 'letter' finds his dead mother at rest in the continuum of language, in the word horde which the poet inherits as his mother tongue: 'Under (not ground but the words) | You rest with speaking hordes.' She is lain with the other dead who mumble to us still by means of learnt language that reverberates upon the inner ear.

'The Thermal Stair', from *Malcolm Mooney's Land*, is an elegy addressed to the painter Peter Lanyon, killed in a gliding accident in 1964. Lopez has seen such poems as concerned with 'the awkwardness of outliving friends', and among the most moving are those to Lanyon, Hilton, and Wynter.[55] 'The Thermal Stair' begins directly: 'I called today, Peter, and

---

[54] William Wordsworth, *The Poems*, 2 vols. ed. J. O. Hayden (Harmondsworth: Penguin, 1977) i. 877–8.

[55] Tony Lopez, 'On "Malcolm Mooney's Land" by W. S. Graham', *Ideas and Production*, 4

you were away' (p. 154). A romantic artist who depends on weakness as the source of strength,

> The poet or painter steers his life to maim
>
> Himself somehow for the job. His job is Love
> Imagined into words or paint to make
> An object that will stand and will not move.
>
> Peter, I called and you were away, speaking
> Only through what you made and at your best.   (p. 155)

Graham clearly liked this phrase 'to maim | Himself somehow for the job', applying it to himself and others on various occasions. His poem 'The Thermal Stair' depends on its power to summon the presence of a dead man, a dependence whose strength resides in the poem's simultaneous awareness of its powerlessness. It moves towards a conclusion by inviting Peter Lanyon down to the pub as two lighthouses 'Godrevy and the Wolf | Are calling Opening Time' (p. 156). The elegy's final lines find Graham asking the painter to help him stagger home, and make it to the end of the poem:

> Uneasy, loveable man, give me your painting
> Hand to steady me taking the word-road home.
> Lanyon, why is it you're earlier away?
> Remember me wherever you listen from.
> Lanyon, dingdong dingdong from carn to carn.
> It seems tonight all Closing bells are tolling
> Across the Dutchy shire wherever I turn.   (p. 157)

There's a good deal of Graham's sense of human community in the paired adjectives 'Uneasy, loveable'—as if people's being difficult made their value as objects of love that much more authentic for him. If the dead offer less resistance to our love, it is a love all the more unrequited. Graham's lyric voice resounds here because it calls into a silence from whence no reply, no help can come. No hand steadies Graham to the end of the poem but his own writing hand.

There are further elegies for painters in *Implements in their Places*. Roger Hilton's friendship had received its tribute in the brusquely exasperated

---

(Dec. 1985), 61. Two other essays by Tony Lopez have been informative: 'Reading W. S. Graham's "Implements"', *Swansea Review*, 1 (Apr. 1986), 57–76, and 'W. S. Graham: An Introduction', *Edinburgh Review*, 75 (1987), 7–23. Most of this material appears in the same author's *The Poetry of W. S. Graham*.

'Hilton Abstract' from *Malcolm Mooney's Land*. That poem is on first-name
terms with its interlocutor in the opening line, and strikes a characteristic
note at the end of the first verse ('It is the longed-for, loved event, | To be
by another aloneness loved') but veers off into an extraordinary display of
uneasiness:

> Hell with this and hell with that
> And hell with all the scunnering lot.
> This can go and that can go ...   (p. 169)

The poem then justifies its outburst by claiming that 'the great humili-
ties | Keep us always ill at ease'. Graham's letters of advice and encour-
agement to Hilton when in jail for drunken driving or in psychotherapy
and treatment for alcoholism provide support for the literal truth of the
opening and close of his elegy. 'Lines on Roger Hilton's Watch' is a poem
both about and partly spoken by the watch 'Which I was given because |
I loved him and we had | Terrible times together' (p. 230). 'Dear Bryan
Wynter' begins similarly with a plain address:

> This is only a note
> To say how sorry I am
> You died. You will realise
> What a position it puts
> Me in.   (p. 255)

Graham's dependence on Wynter's friendship can be heard in the letters
he wrote in the early months of 1975, the months after the painter's
sudden death on 11 January of that year.[56] Into a silence of no replying
Graham asks 'Are you still somewhere ... ?' The poet wonders if he's just
'greedy to make you up | Again out of memory'. He realizes that in lyric
poems the unanswering dead upon whom the poet calls are no different
in their silence from the living in their unspeaking, perhaps unhearing,
absence:

> Speaking to you and not
> Knowing if you are there
> Is not too difficult,
> My words are used to that.
> Do you want anything?
> Where shall I send something?
> Rice-wine, meanders, paintings
> By your contemporaries?   (pp. 255–6)

[56] See *The Nightfisherman*, letters 181, 184.

Graham's work has inhabited and explored the isolation of the voice within its own realm. Its aloneness sounds in the fictive question forms of 'Dear Bryan Wynter': they are not rhetorical because answers are not presumed in their structure, tone, or context, and they are not functional questions because they could not conceivably be answered. Yet how distinctly they invoke the interlocutor's present absence, expressing a need which is answered to only by the calling itself, only by the still poem speaking.

These recognitions in Graham's later work appear in the deepening solitude of his love poems for Nessie Dunsmuir. The first of these, 'Except Nessie Dunsmuir' from *2ND Poems*, is not addressed to her:

> Call what the earth is quiet on her equal face
> That has a mouth of flowers for the naked grave
> Sucking my thumb and the mill of my pinched words
> In the dumb snecked room chiming dead in my ear.
> Now time sooner than love grows up so high
> Is now my warfare wife locked round with making.   (p. 43)

The second-person address would be crucial to Graham's development, for the experimental confidence of these lines banishes from the poem's texture much of a feeling for the situation which it strains to voice. 'Is now my warfare wife locked round with making' may imply some trouble and strife for a woman married to a poet, but the assurance of 'making' turns 'warfare' and 'locked round' into instances of its own inspirational force and self-importance. There is reflexivity in 'locked round with making', for while the phrase may suggest the domestic situation of a poet's wife, it also describes the woman in the poem itself. Yet 'her equal face' and 'a mouth of flowers' appear to issue from need.

The second-person address of 'I leave this at your ear' from *Malcolm Mooney's Land* creates a notional space where the poet's wife rests, and, because in a lyric poem the 'you' addressed does not usually answer, this supposed place is also a landscape that the poet cannot enter. The lyric voice of a second-person address calls into life another unheard voice that it can never be. Graham's poems of this kind, like his questions that do not presume or imply an answer, depend not on describing or prescribing what the addressee should be like, but on finding her inviolable and inscrutable:

> I leave this at your ear for when you wake,
> A creature in its abstract cage asleep.
> Your dreams blindfold you by the light they make.

> The owl called from the naked-women tree
> As I came down by the kyle farm to hear
> Your house silent by the speaking sea.
>
> I have come late but I have come before
> Later with slaked steps from stone to stone
> To hope to find you listening for the door.
>
> I stand in the ticking room. My dear, I take
> A moth kiss from your breath. The shore gulls cry.
> I leave this at your ear for when you wake.   (p. 157)

The second line, 'A creature in its abstract cage asleep', relates ambiguously to two possible antecedents: it could refer to 'you', who then are 'A creature'; or it could refer to 'this', the poem. Forming a self-contained object with its enclosing rhymes on first and third lines, its repetition of first and last lines, the poem attributes wholeness to the sleeping wife. There is neglect in Graham's apologetic 'I have come late but I have come before | Later with slaked steps'. The word 'slaked' might hint at drinking into the small hours on an earlier occasion, while in this instance the poet may only have neglected her because he has been devoting himself to his art, producing the poem that he now leaves at her ear. 'To hope to find you listening for the door', he writes, a man resting in faith or expectation, dependent upon a known but unknowable other person.

Collected Poems 1942–1977 closes with 'To my Wife at Midnight', another second-person address, thriving on a childlike, but not a childish, questioning of silence:

> Where we each reach,
> Sleeping alone together,
> Nobody can touch.
>
> Is the cat's window open?
> Shall I turn into your back?
> And what is to happen?
>
> What is to happen to us
> And what is to happen to each
> Of us asleep in our places?   (p. 261)

Once again the enclosing rhymes of the three-line stanza (reach/touch, open/happen) separate the figures in the poem, give them wholeness. The price for this integrity is isolation. To be alive is to be alone, yet the poet's words depend upon being brought to life in readers. So long as they live within others, they make the bed in which the poet and his wife lie singularly together and inseparably apart.

V

W. S. Graham's winning tone in 'Dear Bryan Wynter' or 'To my Wife at Midnight' is a hard-won simplicity. Does this quality of directness achieved by calling upon an intimate but isolate interlocutor carry as far as the unknown reader? Can the poet's voice also invite the reader into a form of interdependent relationship? Schmidt didn't see it that way when he wrote: 'Graham feels a strange hostility towards the reader, the "you" he addresses; he watches us warily, at the same time watching himself.'[57] The title given to the posthumous *Poems from Notebooks* volume edited by Margaret Blackwood and Robin Skelton sounds, in isolation, an aggressively non-commercial note. The poet's widow felt inclined to mitigate with a joke the chosen title in her preface: 'the work of the notebooks survived his rigorous judgment and *Aimed at Nobody* affords an opportunity for "somebody" (or "nobody!") to encounter it'.[58] The poet's anonymous reader is indeed like a child's Mr Nobody, but in the context of the 'Proem' from which the phrase was borrowed Graham's words are making an issue of the 'aimed' rather more than the 'nobody', because he too qualifies its chillingly apparent indifference to readers:

> It is aimed at nobody at all.
>
> It is now left just as an object by me
> to be encountered by somebody else.[59]

Aiming poems at specific people risks straitjacketing their aesthetic trajectories, and, as we have seen, Graham's sense of another's unknowability saves his addressed poems from a presuming to know that would diminish them. Being by definition unknown, the anonymous reader offers a more severe danger to the poet presupposing an audience and its nature. Here the poem's dependence on a reader is set within a necessary unknowing, a necessarily bracing independence.

Yet Graham's tone is frequently more quizzical and entertained than hostile or blankly matter-of-fact, as in these two stanzas from 'Untidy Dreadful Table' in *Implements in their Places*:

[57] Schmidt, *Fifty British Poets*, 302.
[58] W. S. Graham, *Aimed at Nobody: Poems from Notebooks*, ed. M. Blackwood and R. Skelton (London: Faber & Faber, 1993), p. vii.
[59] Ibid. p. xi.

I sit here late and I hammer myself
On to the other side of the paper.
There I jump through all surprises.
The reader and I are making faces.

I am not complaining. Some of the faces
I see are interesting indeed.
Take your own, for example, a fine
Grimace of vessels over the bone.   (p. 198)

And in the fifth part of 'A Private Poem to Norman Macleod' the grandeur and humility of isolation can be heard in Graham's changing tone:

Remember the title. A PRIVATE
POEM TO NORMAN MACLEOD.
But this, my boy, is the poem
You paid me five pounds for.
The idea of me making
Those words fly together
In seemingly a private
Letter is just me choosing
An attitude to make a poem.   (p. 221)

The grandeur is in the dated, upper-class idiom, 'my boy'; the humility in the childlike 'just me'. Graham is watching himself: this is neither a truly private poem that happens to have been published, nor is it aimed at a known readership. Graham brings the poem nearer to whoever reads it by speaking for a few sentences at the magazine editor who wrote inviting a contribution. Within a possible context of weak dependence, the 'five pounds', the poem gains strength from the candour with which Graham speaks to himself as to a possible listener or reader in 'Remember the title' and 'The idea of me making | Those words fly together'.

The letter of 15 April 1973 to the Duncans which I commented on earlier oscillates between a piercingly overdone tenderness and a cold-faced denial. It isn't so much a try-out for the modes of the poems, as their careering parody—a point indicated by the very allusion to his poetry of trial communications from isolation. The tonal weaknesses in the letter are wrapped up with the attempt to hold the projected natures of the interlocutors in the style: 'Tall shy Ronnie. Compact, easy to love, Henriette. My dears . . .'. Graham's 'my boy' in 'But this, my boy, is the poem | You paid me five pounds for' does not fail the poem's precarious tonal balance, because no intimacy of address is being claimed. The 'my boy' expresses an edgy distance, an 'uneasiness', not a seeing eye to eye. By contrast with the 'my dearest dears' of the letter, the 'My dear' of 'My dear, I take | A moth kiss from your breath' in 'I leave this at your ear for when you wake' has identified a tender familiarity. The feeling is strengthened by his wife's not hearing what the poet has written until she wakes and inhabits the 'creature in its abstract cage' herself. Comparing Graham's verse addressed to interlocutors with his expressively idiosyncratic letters reveals just how much creative control of both pitch and tone the poems winningly demonstrate.

'Notes on a Poetry of Release' is much concerned with the role of the reader. 'The poem is itself dumb', Graham writes, 'but has the power of release. Its purpose is that it can be used by the reader to find something out about himself' and then:

> The poem is not a handing out of the same packet to everyone, as it is not a thrown-down heap of words for us to choose the bonniest. The poem is the replying chord to the reader. It is the reader's involuntary reply.[60]

What these last two, themselves rather inscrutable, sentences suggest is that the poem is composed as a reply to, and somehow from, an imaginary reader. This might be the case when the imaginary reader is a single interlocutor. 'I called today, Peter, and you were away'—which opens 'The Thermal Stair'—rises upon the air of however many previous exchanges between the two men, one of whom is now truly an imaginary reader because dead. This 'replying chord to the reader' might indicate that the poem creates its ideal reader, but Graham's 'The poem is not a handing out of the same packet to everyone' suggests rather that it is aimed at our actual, incomprehensible variousnesses—rather than a never-to-be-encountered ideal type:

> Meanwhile surely there must be something to say,
> Maybe not suitable but at least happy
> In a sense here between us two whoever
> We are. Anyhow here we are and never
> Before have we two faced each other who face
> Each other now across this abstract scene
> Stretched between us. This is a public place
> Achieved against subjective odds and then
> Mainly an obstacle to what I mean.   (p. 152)

---

[60] This and the next three are from 'Notes on a Poetry of Release', 57, 56, 58, 57 and 58 (sentences appear twice).

The complex relations of reader and poet are multiplied when, reading a lyric out loud which someone else has written, you the reader temporarily borrow the poet's pronoun and, as I, address yourself. Thus spoken, the poem becomes your involuntary reply.

Yet interpreting Graham's poems is not a free-for-all. Section 40 of 'Implements in Their Places' is a hollow taunt to the reader. The poem leads up to this joke with:

> I leave you this space
> To use as your own.
> I think you will find
> That using it is more
> Impossible than making it.   (p. 246)

This is true because the spaces left to fill in are part of Graham's poem. The reader depends on the poet to complete his own lines, and Graham confesses that he has been playing low tricks when he concludes the section: 'Try. Try. No offence meant.' Reading cannot be a free-for-all. The poet wrote in 1946 that 'The poem is the replying chord to the reader. It is the reader's involuntary reply'. Reading a poem, we are not free to decide what words are used. The uttered words are involuntary in this sense. Yet, free to put down the book, each reads and pronounces the poem with natural variousnesses inviolably intact. Every reply will have its legitimate differences. As Graham also wrote in 'Notes on a Poetry of Release': 'Each word is touched by and filled with the activity of each speaker.'

Each Graham poem depends on readers for vitality and significance. Yet readers in turn depend on the poem itself, which is their involuntary reply. They are invited to use it to find out something about themselves, for the poem, as Graham said, 'is brought to life by the reader and takes part in the reader's change'. Readers are in a position to do this because the poet has, by not defining or prescribing who they are or should be, left them with the chance to achieve what he requests for himself in the second part of 'What is the language using us for?':

> I want to be able to speak
> And sing and make my soul occur
>
> In front of the best and be respected
> For that and even be understood
> By the ones I like who are dead.

> I would like to speak in front
> Of myself with all ears alive
> And find out what it is I want.   (pp. 192–3)

My arguing for a strong dependence on the language, on interlocutors, and on readers in Graham's poetry has depended upon an attentive reader. Both of us have been dependent upon the strength with which the poet followed out a direction outlined in 'Notes on a Poetry of Release' and which, in the body of his work, he fulfilled:

It is a good direction to believe that this language which is so scored and impressed by the commotion of all of us since its birth can be arranged to in its turn impress significantly for the benefit of each individual. Let us endure the sudden affection of the language.

To 'endure the sudden affection of the language' he writes, and the pleasure of unexpectedly receiving warmth is characteristically tempered by its being sensed as an imposition upon us. Finally, then, this is the ambivalence towards dependence that, over more than forty years, vivified the poetry which W. S. Graham 'left just as an object' and which has here been 'encountered by somebody else'.

CHAPTER 6

Elizabeth Bishop's Art

I

The words 'One Art' appear both at the head of a villanelle by Elizabeth Bishop and on the title page of her selected letters. Their editor, Robert Giroux, explains that the title of this book 'stands for the art of poetry, to which she devoted her life' and that '*One Art* also stands for the art of letter writing, which she practiced more casually and with more prolific results'.[1] Bishop's devotion, though, involved keeping poetry at a certain unbiddable distance. During 1967 she writes, worrying about Lowell's recent production rate: 'He has so much better things to give the world (as his wife said) than hasty reactions to all the pressures here in N.Y.'. Bishop herself could not be hurried. Soon after the beginning of their relationship, Lota Costellat de Macedo Soares writes to Arthur Gold and Robert Fitzdale: 'You should see the mail she gets asking, begging, etc. and nope, she is cooking a cake! Like now!'[2] Bishop's villanelle in fact addresses another art, one which lies behind the arts of poetry, letter writing, the memoir, short fiction, and literary translation, all of which she practised: 'The art of losing'.[3] The word 'art' appears without inverted commas in my title because I want to address an issue suggested by Colm Tóibín in his review of her correspondence:

the book is important for two main reasons, the first of which is the fact that some of the letters, in themselves, are written with wonderful wit and skill; secondly, they tell a great and tragic lesbian love story, documenting, along the way, in tentative tones, a quintessential gay sensibility.[4]

---

[1] Elizabeth Bishop, *One Art: Selected Letters* ed. R. Giroux (New York: Farrar, Straus and Giroux, 1994), p. viii.

[2] Ibid. 481, 264.

[3] Elizabeth Bishop, *Complete Poems 1927–1979* (New York: Farrar, Straus and Giroux, 1983), 178.

[4] Colm Tóibín, 'The South', *London Review of Books*, 16/15, 4 Aug. 1994, 8.

This gendering and object-preferencing implicitly asks if her gay sensibility was also documented in the poems. It also asks, given the Bishop industry's commitment to reading her works for their contribution to the developments of American women's and lesbian poetry, what sense there is in referring, as Robert Giroux does, to 'the art of poetry'. This was an art to which Bishop couldn't help returning, as she wrote to May Swenson on 16 November 1968: 'I really haven't written a poem since I can't remember when. However—one always does start again, it seems.'[5]

Elizabeth Bishop's is poetry written by a gay woman orphan with an alcohol problem. Her editor is inclined to play down the last of these: 'When depressed she had trouble with drinking, but in all our years I never once saw her drunk.'[6] Bishop, it seems, did not imbibe excessively and behave badly in public, as was the pattern with a number of her contemporaries. Rather, she would have crises when alone (in borrowed apartments, for example) and then write sometimes excruciatingly embarrassed apologies about the mess or trouble caused.[7] The additional strain which this put on her longest relationship, that with Lota, can be sensed in these last cited words, again to Gold and Fitzdale on 18 March 1967:

Dearest boys: just a billet-doux to tell you how much I liked your letter. Can not write more than that because still shaky and [out?] of the sanitorio 10 days. E. B. is undertaking a cure for all the nonsenses and alcoholism she had this horrible year of '66. Affectueusement, Lota.[8]

Something of Bishop's love life can be traced in the dedications to volumes and poems. Of her four books, *North & South* (1946) is not 'for' or 'to' anyone. *A Cold Spring* (1955) is 'To Dr. Anny Baumann', her doctor and epistolary confessor. *Questions of Travel* (1965) and *Geography III* (1976) are respectively 'For Lota de Macedo Soares' and 'For Alice Methfessel', both lovers and long-term companions. There is also 'Quai d'Orléans', a poem '*for Margaret Miller*' whom she appears to have had a crush on. 'Anaphora' is '*In memory of Marjorie Carr Stevens*' with whom she lived for some years at Key West. 'Under the Window: Ouro Prêto' is '*For Lilli Correia de Araújo*', with whom she had an affair when her life with Lota Soares was collapsing. There are also poems dedicated to women friends, poets, men, and an aunt.

---

[5] Bishop, *Selected Letters*, 501.
[6] Ibid. p. ix.
[7] See ibid. 176–7, 479–80.
[8] Ibid. 461.

As it did during the twentieth century, 'gay' shifts meaning in her poetry. 'A Cold Spring', written in 1953, describes a new-born calf which 'got up promptly | and seemed inclined to feel gay'; here, the word means much the same as it had done when Yeats in 'Lapis Lazuli' (1938) announced 'that Hamlet and Lear are gay'.[9] Bishop's last poem, 'Sonnet', written twenty-six years later, and published in *The New Yorker* three weeks after her death, enacts one of its tacit themes not least by being an inverted quasi-sonnet, the sestet preceding the octave:

Caught—the bubble
in the spirit-level,
a creature divided;
and the compass needle
wobbling and wavering,
undecided.
Freed—the broken
thermometer's mercury
running away;
and the rainbow-bird
from the narrow bevel
of the empty mirror,
flying wherever
it feels like, gay![10]

Bishop's 'gay!' here adds the contemporary implication into a context where the earlier meanings of 'cheerful' or 'brightly coloured' are relevant and present. Though the form of Bishop's dividedness involved her lesbianism, any of her readers will probably have felt divided in one way or another, since object choice depends for everyone on there being at least a notional option in the, more or less, two sexes. Self-division is directly addressed in 'The Weed', her early poem modelled on George Herbert's 'Love Unknown':

The weed stood in the severed heart.
'What are you doing there?' I asked.
It lifted its head all dripping wet
(with my own thoughts?)
and answered then 'I grow,' it said,
'but to divide your heart again.'[11]

[9] W. B. Yeats, *The Collected Poems*, 2nd edn., ed. R. J. Finneran (Basingstoke: Macmillan, 1991), 294.
[10] Bishop, *Poems*, 192.   [11] Ibid. 21.

Much later in life Bishop was able to imagine such division lifted away. In 'Santarém' (1978) she remembers the 'conflux of two great rivers' and seems to see the structuring oppositions of 'literary interpretations | such as: life/death, right/wrong, male/female' being 'resolved, dissolved, straight off | in that watery, dazzling dialectic'.[12] There is, perhaps, a wishful strain in these late evocations of freedom and undividedness, to be sensed in the exclamation mark that concludes 'Sonnet', or her calling these massive binary oppositions in 'Santarém' just 'literary interpretations'.

In early work it is rather a mysterious unhappiness that finds form and voice. 'Chemin de Fer', the sense of whose 'iron road' needs no belabouring, finds the speaker unable to get into stride:

> Alone on the railroad track
> I walked with pounding heart.
> The ties were too close together
> or maybe too far apart.

These 'ties' could also be of family and love, suffocation or loneliness. She comes across a 'little pond | where the dirty hermit lives', and sees it 'lie like an old tear | holding onto its injuries | lucidly year after year'. The young woman with heart troubles finds in the hermit an image of a life used up in keeping people at bay, and like many an isolate prophet, he is possessed by the needs and the need of some community:

> 'Love should be put into action!'
> screamed the old hermit.
> Across the pond an echo
> tried and tried to confirm it.[13]

Across the pond of 'injuries' the call to have love 'put into action' is echoed, is responded to, by a weak return of an echo, of the same again. The myth of Narcissus may also be echoing here. The quatrain's closing rhyme does, though, achieve what the echo only attempts—and the hint of same-sex love in 'Chemin de Fer' hardly precludes interpretations that can apply, like Shakespeare's *Twelfth Night*, to anyone with love-object problems caused by damage that is clung to like a necessary self-definition.

The matter of her sexual orientation is a subtextual theme in Bishop's 'Efforts of Affection: A Memoir of Marianne Moore'. As if merely to

---

[12] Bishop, *Poems*, 185.   [13] Ibid. 8.

illustrate how, though she could be 'over-fastidious', 'Marianne . . . was capable of calling a spade a spade, or at least calling it by its archaic name', Bishop recalls her mentor

worrying about the fate of a mutual friend whose sexual tastes had always seemed quite obvious to me: 'What are we going to do about X . . .? Why, sometimes I think he may even be in the clutches of a *sodomite . . .!*'

The theme recurs in a page devoted to curiosity on Bishop's part about writers Moore has met or might have been expected to admire. She asks 'what Djuna Barnes was "like"', only to receive the reply: '"Well . . . she looked very smart, and her shoes were *beautifully* polished."' Then follows a clutch of poets who just happen to have been bisexual or gay men:

we were on a street associated with the *Brooklyn Eagle*, and I said fatuously, 'Marianne, isn't it odd to think of you and Walt Whitman walking this same street over and over?' She exclaimed in her mock-ferocious tone 'E*liz*abeth, don't speak to me about that man!' So I never did again. Another time, when she had been talking about her days on *The Dial*, I asked how she had liked Hart Crane when he had come into her office there. Her response was equally unexpected. 'Oh, I *liked* Hart! I always liked him very much—he was so *erudite.*'

This paragraph closes by recalling that 'She was devoted to W. H. Auden, and the very cat he had patted in the Brooklyn tearoom was produced for me to admire and pat too.' The entire memoir ends with reflections on Gerard Manley Hopkins's remarks in a letter of 3–10 February 1883 to Bridges about 'the "artist" versus the "gentlemen"'. Hopkins's words include the thought that 'As a fact poets and men of art are, I am sorry to say, by no means necessarily or commonly gentlemen. For gentlemen do not pander to lust or other basenesses'. Thus, the gentleman 'is in the position to despise the poet . . . for anything that showed him *not* to be a gentleman . . . but if he is a gentleman perhaps this is what he will not do'. Bishop uses this remark to affirm that Moore would have vehemently agreed that 'to be a poet was not the be-all, end-all of existence'.[14] Yet doesn't it also discreetly imply that had Moore as a lady or gentlewoman been able to despise Bishop for 'lust or other basenesses', this is what she would not have done?

Lota's psychiatrist in Rio had been trained by Melanie Klein. In a letter to Lowell of 30 March 1959 Bishop refers to the object-relations theorist

---

[14] Elizabeth Bishop, *Collected Prose*, ed. R. Giroux (New York: Farrar, Straus and Giroux, 1984), 130, 143, 155, 155–6, 156.

in the context of literary rivalry: 'I am delighted to hear that Elizabeth [Lowell's wife] has been writing so much—although envious, too, I suppose. (See a grim little book by Melanie Klein, *Envy and Gratitude*—superb in its horrid way.)'.[15] The horrid grimness of Klein's superb theories appears in a recent account of relations between Moore and Bishop that illuminatingly overinterprets 'Efforts of Affection':

> What silently echoes throughout Bishop's memoir is the apprehension that if Moore knew the complete truth about Bishop she would greet it with disdain. And it is this censoriousness that Bishop incrementally presents in her descriptions of Moore's response to any sign of sexual 'aberration.'[16]

Yet, as I've already said, the memoir's author consciously elaborated such an apprehension. After all, some fourteen years earlier Bishop had published 'The Shampoo', the final poem in *A Cold Spring*, which comes immediately after the playfully teasing 'Invitation to Miss Marianne Moore', the poem a New York friend thought '"mean,"'—which Bishop 'found rather upsetting because it wasn't meant to be'.[17] It is likely that some readers have had difficulty with Bishop's tone there not because it is 'deeply ambivalent',[18] but because it is so evidently able, within the peculiar manners of their friendship, to be warmly amused at its subject's eccentricities. Perhaps Moore, like Queen Victoria, didn't believe women could do such things. She shows no sign in these letters of having been offended by the poem. The reported anecdotes and Hopkins quotation in 'Efforts of Affection' suggest, if anything, that Moore *did* know the truth about Bishop's sexuality, but saw no reason either to commend her for or comment upon it.

Moore's relations with the poet are given an 'anxiety of influence' treatment by Joanne Feit Diehl, except that instead of Bloom's Freudian Oedipal struggle between fathers and sons we have a Kleinian mother–daughter conflict:

> One can, in this context, understand Bishop's characterization of Moore as a split, fragmented, repressed, somewhat antiquated 'other' as a way of insuring difference, a means of rationing Moore's verbal gifts so as not to be consumed by them (and reciprocally destroying the mother's breast—the very source of those gifts).[19]

---

[15] Bishop, *Selected Letters*, 371.

[16] Joanne Feit Diehl, *Elizabeth Bishop and Marianne Moore: The Psychodynamics of Creativity* (Princeton, NJ: Princeton University Press, 1993), 41.

[17] Bishop, *Selected Letters*, 160.

[18] Feit Diehl, *Elizabeth Bishop and Marianne Moore*, 50.

[19] Ibid. 44.

This account presents Moore as a shattered internal object, a paranoid-schizoid part-object, her creativity reduced. It sharply summarizes Melanie Klein's horrid grimness in action, and while it may possibly account for something of the relationship between these poets of different generations, it does so by underreading Bishop's tone in 'Efforts of Affection'. The critic herself appears to reduce the creative value of Bishop's constructive effort, in favour of a diagnostic account of the conflicts it is supposed to have been prompted by.

Bishop was only too aware of a real damaged mother and the real damage it had caused her. The poet's first letter to Moore is dated 19 March 1934; on 4 June she writes to Frani Blough, a Vassar friend: 'I guess I should tell you that Mother died a week ago today. After eighteen years, of course, it is the happiest thing that could have happened.'[20] The eighteen years are those that Mrs Bishop had spent in mental institutions. The poet's father had died when she was eight months old, and her mother, whose psychological health never recovered from this loss, was last seen by Elizabeth in 1916 when she was five. One of the almost immediate consequences of her deciding to live in Brazil was that she discovered a home in which both lovers could also mother each other. Lota's nickname for Bishop, whose baking has already been mentioned, was 'Cookie'. One result of this happiness was that Bishop began to write prose about her childhood. During 1953 she completed 'In the Village', a story dramatizing her mother's absence in the form of an inaudible scream hanging over the seaboard settlement, echoed, like the voice across the pond in 'Chemin de Fer', by the ring of blacksmith Nate's anvil:

All those other things—clothes, crumbling postcards, broken china; things damaged and lost, sickened or destroyed; even the frail almost-lost scream—are they too frail for us to hear their voices long, too mortal?
Nate!
Oh, beautiful sound, strike again![21]

In this moving close some complexities in recovery are glanced at: it is as if the writer were to recover from the effect on her life of 'things damaged and lost, sickened or destroyed' by imaginatively recovering, evoking and invoking, 'clothes, crumbling postcards, broken china . . . even the frail, almost-lost scream'. Nevertheless, at the story's end comes not the sound of Nate's anvil but, following her exclamatory appeal, the silence of a

---

[20] Bishop, *Selected Letters*, 24.
[21] Bishop, *Prose*, 274.

close: her 'recovery from' is dependent on a symbolic 'recovery of', which itself depends upon a recognition that all 'those other things' are, in fact, gone.

II

'The art of losing isn't hard to master': by the opening line of the villanelle 'One Art' Bishop doesn't mean (what someone once patiently explained to me) that the art of *coping with loss* isn't hard to master. Her poem's 'joking voice' depends on the fact that there cannot, strictly, be arts of the involuntary. Even the most automatically inspired, aleatory surrealist still has to use a writing implement, and, after recovering from a broken wrist, Bishop herself 'found I couldn't write verse at all without a pen in my hand'.[22] Just as there is no art of yawning or having the hiccups, so the art of falling only exists for stuntmen or parachutists, who in each case are not really falling, for the first pretends to fall and the second jumps. Most art followers can tell you that grasping the creative intention is not the *summum bonum* of appreciation or criticism, but artists nevertheless need at least a minimal element of intention to practise doing what they do.

Bishop's poem continues its inversion of the expected by attributing intention to the lost objects:

> The art of losing isn't hard to master;
> so many things seem filled with the intent
> to be lost that their loss is no disaster.[23]

'All small jokes must be labeled JOKE, I see', Bishop wrote, and here too she underlines it by writing that the things just 'seem filled'. Still, having granted her readers that hint, she returns to the notion of making losses controllable by being intended:

> Lose something every day. Accept the fluster
> of lost door keys, the hour badly spent.
> The art of losing isn't hard to master.

But how can you lose your door keys on purpose? Getting blind drunk is a way of increasing the chances that you might lose them, but the losing itself just can't be consciously done. In the three lines above, 'One Art' wavers between an impossible control in the imperative 'Lose something' and an impossible resignation in 'Accept'. Commenting on the advice to

---

[22] Bishop, *Selected Letters*, 495.   [23] Bishop, *Poems*, 178.

stop feeling guilty about the loss of Lota, Bishop observes: 'But if only one weren't just human.'[24]

The first extant draft of 'One Art' includes the lines:

> —This is by way of introduction. I really
> want to introduce myself—I am such a
> fantastic lly good at losing things
> I think everyone shd. profit from my experiences.[25]

The poem's final version remains more openly autobiographical than most of Bishop's completed and published work. In stanzas three to five it sustains the joke of 'intending to lose' by enlarging upon what the experiences were that 'everyone shd. profit from':

> Then practice losing farther, losing faster:
> places, and names, and where it was you meant
> to travel. None of these will bring disaster.

> I lost my mother's watch, And look! my last, or
> next-to-last, of three loved houses went.
> The art of losing isn't hard to master.

> I lost two cities, lovely ones. And, vaster,
> some realms I owned, two rivers, a continent.
> I miss them but it wasn't a disaster.

Bishop *was* something of a serial loser. While working at the Library of Congress in 1949 she finds her pen has gone missing: 'I wonder if by any chance Mr. Matisse found it—black with a gold band & a white spot, answers to the name of "Schaefer."' Flying down to Rio in July 1952 'we remembered everything like our gift orchids and quarts of milk—and left Lota's prize purchase, two trays, on the plane'. To Joseph and U. T. Summers eighteen months later she 'can't find your last letter' and 'my beautiful new Herbert was one of the books that got lost coming here'. None of these would bring disaster, but to Kit and Ilse Barker she strikes a grimmer note: 'Please write me again—but be sure, if you can't do that right away, to give me your various addresses—or one that will reach you in England. I hate to keep losing people.'[26]

On Sunday 17 September 1967 Lota, whom by then Bishop had lived with more or less continuously for the previous fifteen years and ten months, flew to New York. There the poet met her:

---

[24] Bishop, *Selected Letters*, 504, 490.

[25] Transcribed in Brett C. Millier, *Elizabeth Bishop: Life and the Memory of It* (Berkeley and Los Angeles, Calif: University of California Press, 1993), 508.

[26] Bishop, *Selected Letters*, 194, 240, 282, 250.

the plane was three hours late, and the minute I saw her I knew she shouldn't have been allowed to come—in fact I think I'll go back to Brazil and shoot her doctor. Anyway—she was exhausted—we passed a quiet afternoon, *no cross words or anything like that*—but I could see she was in a very bad state of depression and [I] didn't know what to do, really, except try to get her to rest. Well—sometime toward dawn she got up and tried to commit suicide—

These lines from a letter of 23 September were written after Lota had been in a coma for a week, having taken an overdose of Valium, a coma from which she never came round, dying of heart failure two days later. Writing on 2 October, Bishop returned to that last afternoon:

I think perhaps she felt some miracle would take place and she'd feel better the minute she got to New York. I'll really never know—and of course can't help blaming myself. I tried to cheer her up—had lots of lovely plans for her—promised we'd take an apartment in Venice next spring for a month or so

Venice was not the only place they 'meant | to travel'. Bishop's letters return to plans that have had to be postponed because of the weakness of the cruzeiro against the dollar, the lack of recent literary earnings or grants, or, in later years, because of Lota's destructively exhausting commitment to a recreational-park development whose construction she organized in Rio.

The deterioration of their love and Lota's death meant the immediate or painfully long-drawn-out loss of almost everything listed in stanzas three to five of 'One Art', the exception perhaps being 'my mother's watch'. Bishop describes her return to Brazil for six weeks at the end of 1967 as 'the very worst stretch I remember ever having gone through'. 'Can you imagine', she writes, 'arriving at the only home (forgive me for being corny, but it is true) I have ever really had in this world and finding it not only not mine—I had agreed to that—but almost stripped bare?' She discovered that most of Lota's relatives and friends blamed Bishop for the suicide, and people whom she had imagined also her friends were turning away. Mary Morse, a previous lover of Lota's, was bequeathed the house mentioned above: 'Mary never seemed to see for one moment that anything I asked for was for its associations, pure & simple—I don't give a damn about THINGS'.[27] Bishop also found that, not for the first time, her letters to a companion had been lost:[28]

[27] Bishop, *Selected Letters*, 468, 471, 488, 490, 489.
[28] Those to Marjorie Carr Stevens were also destroyed (see ibid. 99).

I learned in Rio that everyone had tried to keep Lota from going to New York—and that she had spent most of her time in bed, writing me letters. This breaks my heart. I wrote her, thank god, almost every day—my letters had been burnt, however. ALL my letters, from the past, too, which seems a bit excessive.[29]

This is why Lorrie Goldensohn[30] is not wrong to read 'One Art' as reworking her loss of the person who 'went to sleep in my arms the night of September 17th'. As Bishop wrote, 'There will never be anyone like her in this world or in my life, and I'll never stop missing her—but of course there is that business of "going on living" . . .'.[31]

Brett Millier's biography points out that a lifetime of losses, including the end of her Brazilian period, are interleaved with a later crisis.[32] Her villanelle was not directly inspired by the loss of Lota, the sexually neutral 'you' addressed in the final verse being a different woman:

> —Even losing you (the joking voice, a gesture
> I love) I shan't have lied. It's evident
> the art of losing's not too hard to master
> though it may look like (*Write* it!) like disaster.

'One Art' was composed in the autumn of 1975, during a temporary separation between the poet and her last companion, now executor, Alice Methfessel. However, this simply underlines that when it comes to losing people they are all one. Every loss, and the subsequent crises associated with it, re-enacts earlier losses, reawakens earlier fears of abandonment, loneliness, and the old unsatisfactory means of coping with them. Bishop's final line with its bracketed self-commandment '(*Write* it!)' redeploys for her own end the inserted parentheses in her favourite Herbert poem, 'Love Unknown', and in the close of Hopkins's 'Carrion Comfort'. Its order to write, to complete the poem's set form, given Bishop's lifelong creative reluctance hints at another source, William Empson's villanelle 'Missing Dates', whose final stanza begins: 'It is the poems you have lost, the ills | From missing dates, at which the heart expires.'[33]

A common critical turn in discussing Bishop's poem is to emphasize as Millier does that 'This is all, perhaps, "one art"—writing elegies,

[29] Ibid. 492.
[30] Lorrie Goldensohn, *Elizabeth Bishop: The Biography of a Poetry* (New York, Columbia University Press, 1992), 261–2.
[31] Bishop, *Selected Letters*, 491.
[32] Millier, *Elizabeth Bishop*, 513.
[33] William Empson, *The Complete Poems* ed. J. Haffenden (London: Allen Lane, 2000), 79.

mastering loss, mastering grief, self-mastery.'[34] Wrestling with the angel of the villanelle gives a way to achieving both aesthetic and psychic equilibrium, but Bishop's close does not boast so glib a triumph. In earlier stanzas she pretends to be the clown who overcomes helpless indignities like slipping on banana skins by placing them in her way before the show. Yet her final words add an extra twist by admitting, under self-applied pressure, that she was only pretending to lose things on purpose, so as to gain a false mastery. Loss does look like disaster. The poem, then, achieves equilibrium at the point where the speaker relinquishes the need for a denial-like control. Study of the drafts[35] indicates that this resolution was discovered during composition, not placed there before the show, though the choice of the villanelle form suggests some intuition of a structural requirement that would have to repeat a predicament only to reaffirm and transform it in the poem's close. The line Bishop liked best of her own was 'awful but cheerful', which ends 'The Bight'.[36] Kleinian 'reparation' for earlier psychic damage has understandably been proposed as a way of reading Bishop's work,[37] but her favourite line knows that reparations are not recoveries, and in 'One Art' the cheerful measure of balance is to be had only in accepting the truth of the awful losses.

III

If Bishop was wary of bringing her sexual orientation into the foreground of her published poetry, she also preferred to distance herself from limitations she found in some women's writing, and from being pigeon-holed as a woman poet. Robert Lowell, reviewing her first book in 1946, called 'Roosters' and 'The Fish' 'outside of Marianne Moore, the best poems that I know of written by a woman in this century'.[38] Over twenty-five years later, in a letter to Lowell of 28 January 1972, Bishop told him it would be better to 'be called "the 16th poet" with no reference to my sex, than one of 4 women—even if the other three are pretty good'.[39] When in 1953 she appeared in *Vogue*, her response was 'Oh dear I hate that picture

---

[34]   Millier, *Elizabeth Bishop*, 513.

[35]   There are transcriptions and accounts of the 'One Art' drafts in Millier, *Elizabeth Bishop*, 506–13, and Victoria Harrison, *Elizabeth Bishop's Poetics of Intimacy* (Cambridge: Cambridge University Press, 1993), 193–7.

[36]   Bishop, *Poems*, 61.

[37]   Feit Diehl, *Elizabeth Bishop and Marianne Moore*, 104–5.

[38]   Robert Lowell, *Collected Prose*, ed. R. Giroux (New York: Farrar, Straus and Giroux, 1987), 78.

[39]   Cited in Harrison, *Poetics of Intimacy*, 33.

of myself, and that insistence on my "coldness and precision," etc. I think that's just some sort of cliché always used of women poets'.[40] She thought that some of the social role-playing in women's writing was damaging, fundamentally because it limited the material, restricted the outlook, and tempted the authors to upholster the truth:

That Anne Sexton I think still has a bit too much romanticism and what I think of as the 'our beautiful old silver' school of female writing, which is really boasting about how 'nice' *we* were. V. Woolf, E. Bowen, R. West, etc.—they are all full of it. They have to make quite sure that the reader is not going to misplace them socially, first—and that nervousness interferes constantly with what they think they'd like to say.[41]

Bishop's literary and cultural instincts in the mid-century were urging her to repudiate the gender marker because submitting to its pressures would threaten her commitment to represented truth. Such gender-marking appeared a form of, at best, unconscious condescension. She hated working on the book about Brazil with *Life* magazine not least because of her editors' patronizing mendacity: 'they keep paying lip service to "distinguished writing," "your own opinions," "your fine reputation," and blah blah blah—*lying* like RUGS'.[42]

With the development of the women's and gay liberation movements in the 1960s and 1970s Bishop's just-call-me-a-poet stance came in for some criticism from, for example, Adrienne Rich.[43] Her work was seen as barely a blush away from Marianne Moore's supposed prudery. If there was to be a poetry which could address directly issues of gender and sexuality Bishop's would have to be repudiated. More recently academic feminism and gender studies have sought to reveal how her poetry can sometimes 'elude the social consequence of difficulties inherent in her position as lesbian and as lover'. Of 'It is marvellous to wake up together', an unpublished poem she had found, Lorrie Goldensohn writes: 'Bishop puts in place the imprisoned lover who will in future poems break her bonds and assume an openly female body, if only for the most part a child's. As her female identity emerged in print, so did the contours of her

[40] Bishop, *Selected Letters*, 262.
[41] Ibid. 386–7. A transcription of the letter with some variants, such as the appearance of 'K. A. P' (Katherine Anne Porter) in the list of writers, can be found in Harrison, *Poetics of Intimacy*, 32.
[42] Ibid. 400.
[43] See Adrienne Rich, *On Lies, Secrets, and Silence: Selected Prose 1966–1978* (New York: Norton, 1979) 33–49, 247–58.

identity as a poet.'[44] One of Bishop's best sources of income from writing was *The New Yorker*, which in 1951 was 'quibbling' with her 'over an indelicacy in a poem'.[45] This was also the McCarthy era, as a number of Bishop's letters indignantly record. Nevertheless, perhaps a woman's body and a lesbian identity can be sensed in poems without a literalistic reliance on the 'openly female body', a notion helplessly sabotaged anyway by Goldensohn in her concession 'if only for the most part a child's'.

Bishop appears, if discreetly, as a poet with a body and gay sensibility in 'The Map', the first poem in her first book. Its second stanza contains this identifying diction and tone:

> We can stroke these lovely bays,
> under a glass as if they were expected to blossom,
> or as if to provide a clean cage for invisible fish.[46]

Stroking the 'lovely bays' does it. Auden[47] has some similarly camp-sounding adjectives in work that brackets Bishop's use of 'lovely'—a word also adopted in 'One Art'. Her stanza closes with a simile drawn from a curiously distanced yet intimate picture of women shopping: 'These peninsulars take the water between thumb and finger | like women feeling for the smoothness of yard-goods.' 'The Map' is an attempted metaphysical love poem. Christopher Reid, writing an extended reference-book entry on the poet without any mention of her sexuality, notes nevertheless that in early poems like this 'the inadequacy or misleading suggestiveness of certain images stands figuratively for the broader perils of intercourse with the perceived world'.[48] John Donne had used geography to figure the intimate plights of the body: 'Whilst my physicians by their love are grown | Cosmographers, and I their map'.[49] Bishop describes a map to half reveal and half conceal what was probably an unreciprocated passion. The poem was written during 1934–5, the period of her crush on a Vassar contemporary, Margaret Miller:

---

[44] Goldensohn, *Elizabeth Bishop*, p. xii (the poem appears on pp. 27–8).

[45] Bishop, *Selected Letters*, 222.

[46] Bishop, *Poems*, 3.

[47] W. H. Auden has 'sexy airs' in 'A Summer Night' (1933) and 'doggy life' in 'Musée des Beaux Arts' (1938), see *The English Auden: Poems, Essays and Dramatic Writings 1927–1939* ed. E. Mendelson (London: Faber & Faber, 1977), 136, 237.

[48] Christopher Reid, 'Elizabeth Bishop', in I. Hamilton (ed.), *The Oxford Companion to Twentieth-Century Poetry in English* (Oxford: Oxford University Press, 1994), 48.

[49] John Donne, 'Hymn to God my God, in my Sickness', in *The Complete English Poems*, ed. A. J. Smith (Harmondsworth: Penguin, 1971), 347.

> The names of seashore towns run out to sea,
> the names of cities cross the neighboring mountains
> —the printer here experiencing the same excitement
> as when emotion too far exceeds its cause.

That fourth line is the one strong hint that this is not just a poem about a map. The mention of Newfoundland 'flat and still' in the same stanza may prompt thoughts of her orphan childhood, but this line also invites reflection on how bereavement and unrequited love share the characteristic of being objectless emotion, emotion which 'too far exceeds its cause'. Donne used the very same place name in 'To His Mistress Going to Bed': 'Licence my roving hands, and let them go | Before, behind, between, above, below. | O my America, My new found land'.[50] It seems likely that this famous poem was in the back of Bishop's mind as she composed hers.

Reviewing *North & South*, Lowell also remarked that in a few poems, including 'The Map', 'she is self-indulgent, and strings a whimsical commentary on an almost nonexistent subject'.[51] He probably didn't know, and understandably couldn't intuit, what some of its subject might be. Almost fifty years later Victoria Harrison is in little doubt:

> To envision relationship as a haven where partners 'spread [...] out,' 'lie [...] in,' 'hang,' 'lean down to lift,' 'draw [...] around,' 'tug [...] at from under,' 'run out,' 'lend [. . .]' is to constitute sexuality as an intimacy of shared and exchanged subject positions. Bishop's move is radical precisely because she posits intimacy without a phallus. Her images do not define a sexuality of contrast, female to male, passive to active or aggressive, receiving to penetrating, dependent to independent.[52]

Where Lowell couldn't see the body in the map, Harrison (though she later reinstates them) asks readers to substitute the nouns of a lesbian love scene for those of a topography. Further, her representation of heterosexual partnering is schematic and stereotyped. The praise of a lesbian tenderness, said to be radical because 'Her images do not define a sexuality of contrast', is itself dependent upon a clichéd sexuality of contrast, not least that of same-sex with two-sex relationships. It thus offers an idealized picture of girl-girl intimacy, as if it were free of the negative relational dynamics of power which supposedly characterize heterosexuality

---

[50] Ibid. 125.
[51] Lowell, *Collected Prose*, 78.
[52] Harrison, *Poetics of Intimacy*, 45.

alone. Pondering on a buried allusion to Donne's 'To His Mistress Going to Bed' serves broadly to sexualize Bishop's poem without recourse to sentimentalized gender differences. This is not to mention what gay men are supposed to feel about the radicalism of a non-phallic intimacy. Her reading of the couplet about the printer 'experiencing the same excite-ment | as when emotion too far exceeds its cause' is cheerfully reminis-cent of the late poem 'Santarém': 'these names serve . . . to dissolve distinction, thanks to the excitement of the printer'.[53] Yet Bishop wrote 'as when emotion too far exceeds'; the excitement is dangerous because it is in excess of what causes it, like unrequited infatuation. 'The Map' is not a modish hymn to would-be radical lesbianism, but a poem giving shape and expression to feelings for which there may well have been no other responsive subject or object.

The experience of having emotions which excite because too far in excess of their cause is, like that of loss, something independent of gender or sexual orientation. Bishop's poems are good when their technique, their unrepeatable specificity of verbal design, is identical with the explo-ration of precisely, but not necessarily directly, recounted events, ideas, and feelings. The events, ideas, feelings, and the verbal designs, because 'precise', are saturated with the poet's history and character. Elizabeth Bishop's poems do not document her gay sensibility, just as they don't confess it, or make a stand for it. They are suffused with it.

However, being gay is no guarantee of sensibility, nor sensibility of becoming a poet. David Kalstone's posthumously published book[54] explores this process of how a sensibility is turned into an oeuvre. James Buchan in his review of Bishop's letters claimed that their chief interest lies in showing 'the stages through which great verse is made'. Then 'it's quite simple', he adds: 'You read every poet you can find in four or five languages, and his or her letters, and work till you drop'.[55] Bishop's letters, as is already clear, frequently bemoan the fact of not being able to work, and the effort required, I think, deserves better than *that* joking voice. Pigeon-holes are really best avoided:

'Woman' poet—no, what I like to be called now is *poetress*. I was at a friend's house here the other day and he introduced me to a Brazilian lady—he murmured to her in Portuguese that this was the American poet, etc., and the lady, determined to

[53] Harrison, *Poetics of Intimacy*, 46.
[54] David Kalstone, *Becoming a Poet: Elizabeth Bishop with Marianne Moore and Robert Lowell*, ed. R. Hemenway (London: Chatto & Windus, 1989).
[55] James Buchan, 'The Great Letters of a Great Poet', *Spectator*, 7 May 1994, 26.

show off her English, shook my hand enthusiastically and said, 'You are the famous American poetress?' So I allowed I was. I think it's a nice mixture of poet and mistress.[56]

Such boxes are to be eschewed because they serve to turn attention away. Bishop insists that playing second fiddle ('best woman poet' to Lowell's 'best poet') is just not good enough: she wants to play and be judged on the same terms. My impression of their relative standing among younger poets in the mid-1990s, despite Buchan's calling her 'grossly overrated',[57] is that time has vindicated Bishop's quietly firm ambition for her art.[58] Her wish to be considered a poet without qualifying adjectives is the more radical move. It refuses to accept that her situation as it shaped and was shaped by writing could be marginalized as not relevant to ordinary human experience, and not belonging in an ordinary way to world culture. After her death James Merrill memorably described the poet's 'instinctive, modest, lifelong impersonations of an ordinary woman',[59] and while the point of such a remark seeks tacitly to underline her extraordinary differences, she, rightly, would perhaps have refused the implication. Elizabeth Bishop's work will continue to be read and her life and writings studied not because she was an exemplary woman, or representative lesbian, but because she wrote some memorable, moving poems. That is why I think everyone shd. profit from her experiences.

[56] Bishop, *Selected Letters*, 333.
[57] Buchan, 'Great Letters', 26.
[58] Christopher Reid notes, for example, that 'her standing has, if anything, risen since her death, and it is not uncommon to hear her placed among the greatest of American poets', ('Elizabeth Bishop', in Hamilton (ed.), *Oxford Companion*, 49).
[59] Cited by Giroux (*Selected Letters*, p. vii).

CHAPTER 7

'The bliss of what?': Bishop's Crusoe

I

Elizabeth Bishop didn't much like England. In March 1936 she sent a
postcard of Piccadilly Circus to Frani Blough: 'Since last week your fond-
ness for England has made me feel a little suspicious of you.'[1] Twenty-
eight years later, writing on 19 June from the Hotel Pastoria, London,
Bishop describes some Crusoe-in-England-like experiences to her doctor, Anny Baumann. Her companion Lota Costellat de Macedo Soares
had recently returned to Rio de Janeiro after their visit to Italy:

I did want her to see a bit of England, too—but she was finally so depressed by
the high state of agricultural cultivation in Italy, the advanced 'civilization,' the
huge trees in the parks, etc.—as compared to Brazil—that perhaps it's just as well
she didn't come. They're all even bigger and better here. (I really prefer something a bit harsher, I confess.)

Then there's the weather in June: 'It is terribly cold—or else my blood is
thinned by the tropics—and raining, naturally. Although I like the tea
very much, I'm already beginning to feel hysterical when I see those
biscuits.'[2] Her 'my blood' and 'I like the tea' echo towards the close of
'Crusoe in England':

> Now I live here, another island,
> that doesn't seem like one, but who decides?
> My blood was full of them; my brain
> bred islands. But that archipelago
> has petered out. I'm old.
> I'm bored, too, drinking my real tea,
> surrounded by uninteresting lumber.

---

[1] Elizabeth Bishop, *One Art: Selected Letters*, ed. R. Giroux (New York: Farrar, Straus and
Giroux, 1994), 39.
[2] Ibid. 426.

> The knife there on the shelf—
> it reeked of meaning...   (p. 166)[3]

Iain Crichton Smith's Robinson foresees his return from the island as an emergence 'from the world of sparse iron into the vast cinema of sensation'.[4] Similarly, when interviewed by Edward Lucie-Smith on that same 1964 visit for the London *Times*, Bishop joked that 'being in England is rather like going to the movies after you've read the book'.[5]

Practising poets have to like their own company. A familiar dilemma in the poetic calling is that the solitude it requires is frequently just what the poet engaged in trying to write can barely endure. Frank O'Hara, one of the most sociable of poets, touches on such a conflict of impulses more than once. He has a 'weekend coming up | at excitement-prone Kenneth Koch's', though

> I wish I were staying in town and working on my poems
> at Joan's studio for a new book by Grove Press
> which they will probably not print
> but it is good to be several floors up in the dead of night
> wondering whether you are any good or not

Elsewhere he writes 'but I didn't really care for conversation that day | I wanted to be alone' and a line later 'now I am alone and hate it'.[6] Furthermore, the solitary devotion to writing is often consciously associated for the writer with an indirect self-therapy. The solitude of someone engaged in writing is then an aspect of the illness and a necessary context for its treatment. Trying to effect a cure can aggravate the disease. Adam Phillips has observed that 'turning pain into meaning... is usually itself construed as a painful and often ascetic process. Like crime and punishment, that is to say, the cure can seem a mirror-image of the disease.'[7] A fix of this order lies close to the heart of Elizabeth Bishop's life and writing.

---

[3] Citations of Elizabeth Bishop's poetry are given as page numbers from *The Complete Poems 1927–1979* (New York: Farrar, Straus and Giroux, 1983).

[4] Iain Crichton Smith, *The Notebooks of Robinson Crusoe* (London: Gollancz, 1975), 91.

[5] *Conversations with Elizabeth Bishop*, ed. G. Monteiro (Jackson, Miss.: University of Mississippi Press, 1996), 13.

[6] Frank O'Hara, *The Collected Poems*, ed. D. Allen (Berkeley and Los Angeles, Calif.: University of California Press, 1995), 328, 429. Bishop thought his poetry 'mostly bad in the surrealist way—but I think he's improving' (*Selected Letters*, 371). As for his sociability, Robert Fitzdale reports: 'Frank called in the morning after the party and wanted to see Elizabeth again, and she said, "I think we've had enough of Frank O'Hara."' (see Gary Fountain and Peter Brazeau, *Remembering Elizabeth Bishop: An Oral Biography* (Amherst, Mass.: University of Massachusetts Press, 1994), 155–6).

[7] Adam Phillips, 'Guilt', in *On Flirtation* (London: Faber & Faber, 1994), 144. For philo-

II

Bishop would never have allowed herself to describe the situation of her art in these terms. However, when asked late in life the inevitable question ('Why do you write poetry?'), she did say: 'I was very isolated as a child and perhaps poetry was my way of making familiar what I saw around me.' Bishop also made a number of comments on the relation of solitude to writing which suggest her awareness of the dilemma outlined above. In the same 1978 interview Alexandra Johnson commented: 'A luxuriant romanticism has grown up around how a poet should live and work.' Then she asked: 'How necessary is that quiet, circumscribed life?' To which Bishop replied:

Well, you get a place all set up, as I've done only one time in my life, which was in Brazil. You have your books and pencils and papers ready. Then you find yourself writing some of your best lines standing up in the kitchen putting them on the back of an envelope.

Interviewed twelve years earlier in that study she had made fun of its suitability for a poet: 'Everybody who comes here asks about the view; is it inspiring? I think I'll put a little sign saying "Inspiration" on those bamboos! Ideally, I suppose any writer prefers a hotel room completely shut away from distractions.' Well, perhaps 'Ideally' they do. In practice, though, it seems likely that what was so beneficial about her 'place all set up' with Lota Soares was, at best, not only that she had a separate study, but also that there were other people around for company and support, though not too often. 'I was able to work in Brazil', she writes, 'because I had no distractions. For the first time in my life I had a study of my own, one that was peaceful, holding all my books, in the middle of a grove. Only on weekends did we have visitors.'[8]

The relation of solitude to writing also involves the negotiation between the private and public in a poem's behaviour. In a letter to Robert Lowell about a typescript of *For the Union Dead* she addressed the problem in the light of an obligation to tell the truth. She has two 'minor questions but, as usual, they have to do with my George Washington handicap—I can't tell a lie even for art, apparently; it takes an awful effort

sophical reflections on privacy, solitude, and isolation see Julie C. Innes, *Privacy, Intimacy, and Isolation* (New York: Oxford University Press, 1992) and Philip Koch, *Solitude: A Philosophical Encounter* (Chicago and La Salle, Ill.: Open Court, 1994).

[8]   *Conversations with Elizabeth Bishop*, 98, 104, 18, 79.

or a sudden jolt to make me alter facts'.[9] Yet can there be art if you don't alter the facts? Quite rightly, Bishop made a great thing of her devotion to accurate detail: 'For "Crusoe in England" . . . Miss Bishop had a friend visit a goat farm to find out how goats open their eyes'. Yet when George Starbuck enthused about the same poem ('I suppose Crusoe was a city kid. It's such fun, the accuracy with which you borrow flora and fauna for his little island'), Bishop replied: 'It's a mixture of several islands.'[10] This implies both the condensation of experience needed for art, and Bishop's reluctance to allow such inner processes supremacy.

She hated Lowell's use of others' words, writing most forcefully about *The Dolphin* on 21 March 1972:

I'm sure my point is only too plain. Lizzie is not dead, etc.—but there is a 'mixture of fact & fiction,' and you have *changed* her letters. That is 'infinite mischief,' I think . . . One can use one's life as material—one does, anyway—but these letters—aren't you violating a trust? IF you were given permission—IF you hadn't changed them . . . etc. But *art just isn't worth that much.*[11]

Lowell responded that it was his way of telling the truth, though George Oppen points to how such an aim can itself underline a poet's social isolation: 'Not, perhaps I should add, that I take truthfulness to be a social virtue. I think very probably it is not. But I think it is poetic: I think really that nothing else is.'[12] Bishop was perfectly able to see the comic possibilities in a dependence on social conventions, as in 'Manners', subtitled '*For a Child of 1918*':

> When automobiles went by,
> the dust hid people's faces,
> but we shouted 'Good day! Good day!
> Fine day!' at the top of our voices.   (p. 121)

Nevertheless, manners and discretion, whatever else they may be, are social filters for the ghastly truth. This social filter—like the 'joking voice, a gesture | I love' (p. 178) in 'One Art'—is a form of respect for others and a defence of the self. Defences, for Bishop, are not to be scorned or

[9] *Selected Letters*, 408.
[10] *Conversations with Elizabeth Bishop*, 73, 86.
[11] *Selected Letters*, 562. For further exploration of the issues involved here see David Kalstone, *Becoming a Poet: Elizabeth Bishop with Marianne Moore and Robert Lowell*, ed. R. Hemenway (London: Chatto & Windus, 1989), 239–47, and my *In the Circumstances: About Poems and Poets* (Oxford: Oxford University Press, 1992), 83–104.
[12] Letter to Charles Tomlinson, 5 May 1963, in George Oppen, *The Selected Letters*, ed. R. Blau DuPlessis (Durham, NC: Duke University Press, 1990), 82.

dismissed. 'Do I have too many defences?' Wesley Wehr asked her; she answered: 'Too *many?* Can one ever have *enough* defences?'[13] This fundamental conflict in poetry, and not only poetry, between a need for truth telling and for respectful social presentation adds to the difficulties involved in completing poems and publishing them. It focuses the dilemmas of the solitary imagination and how it is to survive in the 'relation of the state | To the individual',[14] in the self and its situations. Bishop's criticism of *The Dolphin* has Lowell's relations to both in mind: 'I don't want you to appear in that light, to anyone—Elizabeth, Caroline—me—your public! And most of all to yourself.'[15]

Bishop didn't appreciate the young Anne Stevenson's attempt to offer a philosophical reading for her work. Speaking to Wehr in 1966, she said: 'Some of our critics can find something in common between just about anything. Comparing me with Wittgenstein! I've never even read him. I don't know *anything* about his philosophy.'[16] However, as reported by Regina Colônia in 1970, she gives an account of poetry which, whether influenced by Wittgenstein or not, describes something of what could be meant by the art as a 'form of life'. Needless to say, she uses a less claim-making phrase:

Writing poetry is a *way of life*, not a matter of testifying but of experiencing. It is not the way in which one goes about interpreting the world, but the very process of sensing it. When one is 'on the move,' one obviously *discovers* things, but that is merely part of the process. That's why poetry can eventually transmit some sort of experience to the reader, but that is far from being its purpose.

Bishop is commenting on the role poetry plays in a person's life. The 'process of sensing' involved finding moments in which objects and events became outward criteria for the isolated and unspeakable inner

---

[13] *Conversations with Elizabeth Bishop*, 44.

[14] Ezra Pound, *Personae: The Shorter Poems*, rev. edn. ed. L. Baechler and A. Walton Litz (New York: New Directions, 1990), 199.

[15] *Selected Letters*, 562.

[16] *Conversations with Elizabeth Bishop*, 43, and, similarly, 65. Millier gives a context for these remarks: 'Anne Stevenson had sent the manuscript of the Twayne Series book for approval, and even though Elizabeth carried it with her everywhere she went, it was six months before she could bring herself to comment on it and grant her permission. Stevenson had remarked on some similarity of Bishop's philosophy to Wittgenstein's, and Elizabeth took pleasure in the idea that like M. Jourdain, who found he had been speaking prose all his life, she had "a philosophy" despite her inability to describe it. Stevenson sent her a copy of one of Wittgenstein's books, which Elizabeth read haltingly but faithfully' (Brett C. Millier, *Elizabeth Bishop: Life and the Memory of It* (Berkeley and Los Angeles, Calif.: University of California Press, 1993), 366).

life. Here, too, is an aspect to Bishop's art that echoes Wittgenstein. Her being loath to 'put her feelings' into poetry meant that reading her involves an understanding of the works' surfaces as alive with implication for a consciousness experiencing life. Nevertheless, this is a consciousness that can only be understood in the terms of art, the terms of the poem itself. Bishop's poetic strategies require readers to be tipped off about the realm 'Whereof one cannot speak . . .'—as the famous last words in Wittgenstein's *Tractatus* have it. So in 'The Bight', subtitled for this purpose '[*On my birthday*]', the abandoned and stove in boats are 'like torn-open, unanswered letters', while an earlier reference to Baudelaire is picked up by 'The bight is littered with old correspondences' (p. 60). Like a good symbolist poet, she doesn't allude to what the littering of the bight corresponds to in the poem. Yet her liking for its closing phrase speaks volumes: 'awful but cheerful'.

Later in the same interview Bishop turns to the place of poetry in the life of a reader. She has been expressing a fear that the 'age we live in, with its terrible *boom* in mass communications, has things about it that endanger poetry as we know it'. Then she reflects that it is the marginal place of the art in life that may help to ensure its untainted survival:

Down through the ages, poetry has been expressly spared for two good reasons. First, writing poetry does not pay, or when it does pay, it pays little. (The result is that only those who want to write poetry for its own sake continue with the genre.) Secondly, very few people read poetry, something which has enabled it to escape popularity and vulgarization. Thus poetry has evaded the distortions that it might have undergone.

And even in the event that the modes of mass communication were to spread poetry as widely as they have popular music, there would emerge in all probability an underground—as in the seventeenth century—in which poems would once again be written on single sheets of paper to be distributed to a limited number of readers.[17]

Bishop's account of poetry as a '*way of life*' is like Wittgenstein's not because she knows something about his philosophy. His later work is an attempt to describe better how language, including the language of the arts and art appreciation, ordinarily functions in the lives of those who are taking part in the relevant 'games'. He is, for example, recorded as saying: 'What belongs to a language game is a whole culture. In describing musical taste you have to describe whether children give concerts, whether

[17] *Conversations with Elizabeth Bishop*, 51–2.

women do or whether men only give them, etc., etc.'[18] Richard Wollheim observed that 'Art is, in Wittgenstein's sense, a form of life'.[19] Elizabeth Bishop's 'Crusoe in England' is a late retrospect on poetry as a '*way of life*'. The young Anne Stevenson was perfectly justified in alluding to her father's championing of Wittgenstein as a way of illuminating Bishop's work.

III

The situation of Robinson Crusoe was an occasion and theme that Bishop meditated on intermittently through much of her writing life. As early as July 1934, on the island of Cuttyhunk, she wrote in a notebook:

> On an island you live all the time in this Robinson Crusoe atmosphere; making this do for that, and contriving and inventing . . . A poem should be made about making things in a pinch—& how it looks sad when the emergency is over.[20]

The sad look of things 'when the emergency is over' foreshadows exactly the mood of her 'Crusoe in England'. It also succinctly describes a series of prose poems written in 1904 that she may then have known: Saint-John Perse's 'Images à Crusoé'. Twenty-two years later, in a letter from Brazil to Pearl Kazin on 30 November 1956, Bishop wrote:

> We've had a terrific four-day storm here and there wasn't a scrap of airmail at the P.O.—perhaps the planes have been held up. Lota was away in Rio and I was all alone with the servants and the toucan (who has a sore foot) & the cat (who was being wormed) and the *roaring* waterfall. I feel as if I'd undergone a sort of Robinson Crusoe experience.[21]

Victoria Harrison reports that her poem was begun in 1963. Brett Millier writes that a draft called 'Crusoe at Home' was close to being included in *Questions of Travel* (1965). The uncompleted poem was 'granted new life when she visited Darwin's house in Kent, took on considerable depth of feeling in the next six years and became "Crusoe in

[18] Ludwig Wittgenstein, *Lectures and Conversations on Aesthetics, Psychology and Religious Belief*, ed. C. Barrett (Oxford: Blackwell, 1966), 8.

[19] Richard Wollheim, *Art and its Objects*, 2nd edn. (Cambridge: Cambridge University Press, 1980), 104. For another treatment of Bishop's poetry in relation to Wittgenstein's philosophy see Barbara Page, 'Elizabeth Bishop: Stops, Starts, and Dreamy Divagations', in L. Anderson and J. Shapcott (eds.), *Elizabeth Bishop: Poet of the Periphery* (Newcastle upon Tyne: Bloodaxe, 2002), 12–30.

[20] Cited in Victoria Harrison, *Elizabeth Bishop's Poetics of Intimacy* (Cambridge: Cambridge University Press, 1993), 190.

[21] Bishop, *Selected Letters*, 332.

England." '[22] This 'considerable depth of feeling' foreshadows the death of Lota, the end of another relationship through mental instability, and the break-up of Bishop's life in Brazil. The poet seems to have returned to the drafts in the spring of 1970, and completed 'Crusoe in England' during the summer of the following year.

Bishop described herself in a 1951 letter to Lowell as a 'minor female Wordsworth', but the allusion to 'Daffodils' in 'Crusoe in England', far from suggesting that it is a Wordsworthian poem of the imagination,[23] indicates a quarrel with such a view of her as a blithe poet of nature:

> the poems—well, I tried
> reciting to my iris-beds,
> 'They flash upon that inward eye,
> which is the bliss . . .' The bliss of what?
> One of the first things that I did
> when I got back was look it up. (p. 164)

Lorrie Goldensohn notes: 'What else does the insertion of that anachronism do for the poem but once again illustrate how exactly limited is the medicinal value of art . . . Crusoe cannot verify that *solitude* is bliss until he returns to human society.'[24] 'Crusoe in England' has more affinity with Coleridge, as David Kalstone proposed, it being 'a kind of "Dejection Ode" countered by the force and energy that memory has mustered for the rest of the poem'.[25] In her 30 November 1956 letter Bishop moves from 'the *roaring* waterfall' to 'a sort of Robinson Crusoe experience' and immediately to 'I kept reading Coleridge's letters'. The '*roaring* waterfall' is also an S. T. Coleridge experience, combining the 'mighty fountain' that 'momently was forced' in 'Kubla Khan' with its 'woman wailing for her demon-lover!' and the storm with its 'little child | Upon a lonesome wild' evoked in part VII of 'Dejection: an Ode'.[26] Bishop's habitual

[22] Millier, *Elizabeth Bishop*, 366–7.

[23] See Bonnie Costello, *Elizabeth Bishop: Questions of Mastery* (Cambridge, Mass.: Harvard University Press, 1993), 203–5.

[24] Lorrie Goldensohn, *Elizabeth Bishop: The Biography of a Poetry* (New York: Columbia University Press, 1992), 251. See also Christopher Ricks, 'Loneliness and Poetry', in *Allusion to the Poets* (Oxford: Oxford University Press, 2002), 261–81, with discussion of 'Daffodils' and 'Crusoe in England' at 270–3. For Wordsworth on Crusoe see his 1822 poem 'To Enterprise', and 'Reminiscences of the Rev. R. P. Graves, M.A.', in *The Prose Works of William Wordsworth*, ed. A. B. Grosart (London: Moxon, 1876), iii. 468.

[25] David Kalstone, *Five Temperaments* (New York: Oxford University Press, 1977), citing H. Bloom (ed.), *Elizabeth Bishop: Modern Critical Views* (New York: Chelsea House, 1985), 71.

[26] S. T. Coleridge, *The Complete Poems*, ed. W. Keach (Harmondsworth: Penguin, 1997), 251, 310. For Coleridge on Crusoe see *Coleridge's Miscellaneous Criticism*, ed. T. M. Raysor (Cambridge, Mass.: Harvard University Press, 1936), 299–300.

self-denigrations are also present in the letter, when she concludes 'I feel as if I could scarcely be said to exist, beside C.' Kalstone's evoking Coleridge aptly isolates two strands in the poem. Yet I doubt that 'Crusoe in England' has this 'force and energy that memory has mustered', for it also deploys a Coleridgean irony by which its power and failure are inextricably intertwined.

In her conversation with George Starbuck, Bishop underlines the divergences between her poem and the original narrative:

GS: I forget the end of *Robinson Crusoe*. Does the poem converge on the book?
EB: No. I've forgotten the facts, there, exactly. I reread it all one night. And I had forgotten it was so moral. All that Christianity. So I think I wanted to re-see it with all that left out.[27]

'Crusoe in England' ends with an interjected aside: '—And Friday, my dear Friday, died of measles | seventeen years ago come March.' Starbuck could have easily found out that Friday doesn't die at the end of the first *Robinson Crusoe*. Nor does he die of measles. He is killed by a force of 'warlike savages' when trying to mediate between them and Robinson's ship in *The Farther Adventures of Robinson Crusoe*.[28]

Differences such as these make it difficult to credit the assertions of those, like David Lehman, who would read the poem as neither more nor less than a monologue dramatizing Crusoe himself. In 1966 Ashley Brown asked the poet: 'What do you think about the dramatic monologue as a form—you know, when the poet assumes a role?' Bishop replied:

I suppose it should act as a sort of release. You can say all kinds of things you couldn't in a lyric. If you have scenery and costumes, you can get away with a lot. I'm writing one right now.[29]

'Crusoe in England' begins with memories of scenery and comes towards its close with bits of costume. It's likely that the dramatic monologue she alluded to in 1966 is the early draft, 'Crusoe at Home', which almost went into *Questions of Travel*. Bishop discusses the benefits of the form not as

---

[27] *Conversations with Elizabeth Bishop*, 88.

[28] Crusoe orders his man on deck to speak to the savages: 'Friday cried out they were going to shoot; and unhappily for him, poor fellow, they let fly about three hundred of their arrows, and to my inexpressible grief killed poor Friday'; and Crusoe observes: 'I was so enraged with the loss of my old servant, the companion of all my sorrows and solitudes, that I immediately ordered five guns to be loaded' (Daniel Defoe, *The Life and Strange Adventures of Robinson Crusoe*, (1719), part II (Boston, Mass.: David Nickerson, 1903), 179. It seems likely that Bishop was unaware of this, and the *Robinson Crusoe* she read in a night is almost certainly the first volume only.

[29] *Conversations with Elizabeth Bishop*, 26.

allowing the poet, playwright-like, to dramatize the life of a character, but, rather, to extend the possibilities, or escape the limits, of lyric. The ventriloquizing of Robinson in her poem is a transparent device. 'Crusoe in England' *is* readable as a retelling of the Crusoe story. However, as a mode of indirection for Bishop to meditate upon her own experience without the burdens of supposed truthfulness and inevitable exposure entailed by the then fashionable 'confessional' poem, it comes into focus. Like William Cowper's 'Verses, Supposed to be Written by Alexander Selkirk', one of whose printings is attributed to Crusoe, it is a double-aspect text. We read it as Robinson, but understand it, metaphorically, as a commentary on Bishop's own creative life: 'And this is how it is,' wrote Wittgenstein of another poem that tells the story of a life, 'if only you do not try to utter what is unutterable then *nothing* gets lost. But the unutterable will be—unutterably—*contained* in what has been uttered!'[30]

IV

Bishop's 'In Prison' is a short story driven by the assumption that solitude and isolation, when not chosen by their sufferer, could prove to be the makings of a person, a person curiously like a writer. The speaker begins: 'I can scarcely wait for the day of my imprisonment. It is then that my life, my real life, will begin.' Towards the story's close there is a long paragraph devoted to 'Writing on the Wall':

I have thought of attempting a short, but immortal, poem, but I am afraid this is beyond me; I may rise to the occasion, however, once I am confronted with that stained, smeared, scribbled-on wall and feel the stub of pencil or rusty nail between my fingers. Perhaps I shall arrange my 'works' in a series of neat inscriptions in a clear, Roman print[31]

The treatment of solitude in *Robinson Crusoe* has an autobiographical source in Defoe's living in hiding so as to escape his creditors and an experience of imprisonment for debt. Paul Valéry imagines his Crusoe as an author with an 'Oeuvres complètes de Robinson'.[32] David Lehman

---

[30] Paul Engelmann, *Letters from Ludwig Wittgenstein with a Memoir*, ed. B. F. McGuinness, trans. L. Furtmüller (Oxford: Blackwell, 1967), 7. The poem is 'Graf Eberhards Weissdorn' by Ludwig Uhland, cited and translated at pp. 83–4. For more on 'aspect-seeing' and Bishop see Page, 'Elizabeth Bishop', in Anderson and Shapcott (eds.), *Elizabeth Bishop*, 19–21, and chapter 1 of my *Poetry, Poets, Readers: Making Things Happen* (Oxford: Oxford University Press, 2002).

[31] Elizabeth Bishop, *Collected Prose*, ed. R. Giroux (New York: Farrar, Straus and Giroux, 1984), 188–9.

[32] Paul Valéry, 'Histoires Brisées', in *Oeuvres*, ii, ed. J. Hytier (Paris: Gallimard, 1960), 414.

draws upon a likely similarity between Bishop's story 'In Prison' and her later poem: 'like Crusoe on his island, he will attempt to convert an alien landscape into one that responds to his humanity'.[33] Yet Bishop's account of life on the island in 'Crusoe in England' is a return upon the insouciance of this assuming that all a writer needs for self-realization is the condition of doing time. Her poem is a demonstration of how the imagination cannot be sufficient unto itself.

'Crusoe in England' begins with the appearance of a new volcano, and 'an island being born'. Yet this quickly leads to a jaded nostalgia—similar to that of Saint-John Perse's 'Images à Crusoé'—for the lost island, a jadedness sharpened by resentment at the inaccuracy of other accounts, of other books. Like a latecomer to the Crusoe theme, Bishop's imagination lives in a conflictual world of earlier imaginings:

> They named it. But my poor old island's still
> un-rediscovered, un-renamable.
> None of the books has ever got it right.   (p. 162)

This note returns towards the end of the poem when the relationship between Robinson and Friday is touched upon: '(Accounts of that have everything all wrong.)'. Thus, Bishop's Crusoe is not only isolated by his experience of solitude on the island and his sense of not fitting when he returns to 'another island, | that doesn't seem like one'. He is islanded from the start by the sense that his version of this pastoral exclusion is at odds with those of others that take it upon themselves to retell or interpret events. Bishop's poem can be read as an indirect account of her life in Brazil and with Lota de Macedo Soares. Those remarks in the poem seem at least partly shaped by such experiences as the conflict over her *Brazil* for the *Life* World Library, described at her insistence on the title page as 'by Elizabeth Bishop and The Editors of LIFE'. They may echo difficulties of mutual understanding between herself and Lota's relatives and friends after her death in New York. The young Anne Stevenson's writing to her while researching the first book devoted to Bishop's work may also have contributed to a sense of embattled interpretations.

Similarly, the treatment of Robinson's imaginative activities on the island hardly adds up to an endorsement of Andrew Marvell's remark in

---

[33] David Lehman, '"In Prison": A Paradox Regained', citing Bloom (ed.), *Elizabeth Bishop: Modern Critical Views*, 142.

'The Garden' that 'Two Paradises 'twere in one | To live in Paradise alone'.[34] The waterspouts on the island are imagined as

> Glass chimneys, flexible, attenuated,
> sacerdotal beings of glass . . . I watched
> the water spiral up in them like smoke.
> Beautiful, yes, but not much company.   (p. 163)

What kind of a writer would be satisfied with reading his or her own work in place of any communication with others? The sense of creation with no social end reaches terrifying proportions just before the arrival of Friday. Robinson has 'nightmares of other islands' and these 'infinities | of islands, islands spawning islands' are particularly fearful because he knows

>   that I had to live
> on each and every one, eventually,
> for ages, registering their flora,
> their fauna, their geography.   (p. 165)

The mention of geography, Bishop's admiration for Darwin's prose, and her own visit to the Galápagos Islands would be enough to suggest that this nightmare is interwoven with the poet's own creative temperament. The registering of natural details, for which she was praised in her lifetime, could also be viewed as a burdensome obligation, especially if such description were not freighted with a humanly communicative purpose. Interviewed for the *Christian Science Monitor* in 1978, Bishop admitted that there was 'a certain self-mockery' in this passage that suggested to the interviewer, Alexandra Johnson, 'the poet's duty or his burden'.[35] Thomas Travisano makes a similar point, calling this 'a nightmare version of her life of observations: a career of infinite but barren travel'.[36]

Much the same can be said about time, solitude, and what Marianne Moore famously calls 'things that are important beyond all this fiddle'.[37] Bishop's Crusoe attempts to capture the ambiguous emotions of his situation in puns:

[34] Andrew Marvell, *The Poems*, ed. H. MacDonald (London: Routledge & Kegan Paul, 1952), 53.
[35] Cited in Marilyn May Lombardi, *The Body and the Song: Elizabeth Bishop's Poetics* (Carbondale and Edwardsville, Ill.: Southern Illinois University Press, 1995), 140.
[36] Thomas J. Travisano, *Elizabeth Bishop: Her Artistic Development* (Charlottesville, Va.: University of Virginia Press, 1988), 181.
[37] Marianne Moore, *The Complete Poems*, ed. C. Driver (Harmondsworth: Penguin, 1982), 226.

> I'd heard of cattle getting island-sick.
> I thought the goats were.
> One billy-goat would stand on the volcano
> I'd christened *Mont d'Espoir* or *Mount Despair*
> (I'd time enough to play with names),
> and bleat and bleat, and sniff the air.   (Ibid.)

The hill has only the one name in Defoe. This is an instance of poetic technique appearing to lack purpose without communicative urgency—prompting wit for its own sake, but a wit that doesn't come over as funny, or helpfully playful, merely as a futile pastime. Yet the underlying communicative purpose of the lines is to register precisely this problem. 'Crusoe in England' explores the damaging consequences of thinking that the imagination will naturally thrive in the purity of isolation from society. Bishop's Robinson, like Valéry's, attempts the transition from achieved practical well-being to spiritual self-sufficiency, but it doesn't appear to work:

> Home-made, home-made! But aren't we all?
> I felt a deep affection for
> the smallest of my island industries.
> No, not exactly, since the smallest was
> a miserable philosophy.   (p. 164)

This self-correction, a characteristic of the Bishop style, leads into a stanza of self-criticism that sounds like a poet's account of agonizing over the possible causes of writers' block:

> Because I didn't know enough.
> Why didn't I know enough of something?
> Greek drama or astronomy? The books
> I'd read were full of blanks . . .   (Ibid.)

Bishop's biographer notes that such questioning 'does not occur to Defoe's Crusoe, whose great island discovery is the utter sufficiency of the Bible; his books are not "full of blanks." '[38]

V

In recent years many have been tempted to see 'Crusoe in England' as a poem about Bishop's lesbianism, and, more particularly, about her

---

[38] Millier, *Elizabeth Bishop*, 448.

relationship with Lota de Macedo Soares.[39] The editors of *Remembering Elizabeth Bishop*, for example, locate a completion date for the poem as spring 1970, after the departure from Ouro Prêto of the poet's 'secretary', a native of Seattle: 'she found herself suddenly writing again, for the first time in months, and finished "Crusoe in England", her lengthy auto-biographical poem about the loss of Lota'.[40] Elsewhere in the same volume Frank Bidart speculates that 'she was able to cut off parts of her mind in order to make the poem. For example, someone once said something to her about how "Crusoe in England" is a kind of autobiographical metaphor for Brazil and Lota. She was horrified about the suggestion. And obviously the poem is.'[41] Leaving aside Brazil for the moment, I imagine Bishop might have had reasons other than self-repression for being horrified at the suggestion. After all, the poem is 182 lines long; of these, only 13 are about Friday.

James Merrill, by contrast, notes that 'the poem must have been written off and on in Brazil. A 1965 letter to Howard Moss says that it needs "a good dusting."'[42] Merrill later goes on to speculate:

Was Friday then neither soulmate nor servant, lover nor cannibal—just another teenager cavorting on the beach at Rio? I once idiotically asked the author, on being shown this poem before publication, if there couldn't be a bit more about Friday? She rolled her eyes and threw up her hands: Oh, there used to be—*lots* more! But then it seemed . . . And wasn't the poem already long enough?

Despite its concluding lines, 'Crusoe in England' is an elegy less for Friday than for the young imagination that running wild sustained itself alone. Friday's role is to put an end to the monologue. Until he appears it is chiefly resourcefulness and bravado . . . that keep Crusoe going in his solitary realm.[43]

This is a good suggestion. It vaunts the possibility of 'Crusoe in England' being a gay poem. Then, after suggesting that such an idea is not far off wishful thinking on his own part, Merrill points his readers to what

[39] See e.g. Joanne Feit Diehl, *Elizabeth Bishop and Marianne Moore: The Psychodynamics of Creativity* (Princeton, NJ: Princeton University Press, 1993), 104–5; Goldensohn, *Elizabeth Bishop*, 250–1; Harrison, *Poetics of Intimacy*, 191–3; Lombardi, *The Body and the Song*, 37; Travisano, *Elizabeth Bishop*, 182.
[40] Fountain and Brazeau, *Remembering Elizabeth Bishop*, 265. See also *Selected Letters*, 527: 'in spite of the awful people here, I am feeling more myself than I have in 4 or 5 years, I think, and it is very pleasant. I have finished a long poem and have four more going'.
[41] Fountain and Brazeau, *Remembering Elizabeth Bishop*, 333.
[42] Kalstone, *Becoming a Poet*, 255.
[43] Ibid. 257. The exchange of letters between Bishop and Merrill is cited and discussed in Harrison, *Poetics of Intimacy*, 191–2.

the greater part of the poem may be about: the 'young imagination' sustaining 'itself alone'. However, I suspect there is some idealizing going into this version of the Crusoe imagination—which more resembles that of the young Arthur Rimbaud's poem 'Roman', in which he invents a verb from the given name of Defoe's hero: 'coeur fou Robinsonne à travers les romans'.[44] In Bishop's poem imaginative autonomy has stagnated and got Robinson into a terrible pickle before Friday comes along 'to put an end to the monologue'. 'Just when I thought I couldn't stand it | another minute longer, Friday came': this is how the poem's tenth verse begins. What has come before is the history of a solitary, self-reliant creativity; but it is hard not to feel that the story has ended in failure some time before the arrival of company.

Here is the section of the poem devoted to Friday, who also reappears in its closing pair of lines:

> Just when I thought I couldn't stand it
> another minute longer, Friday came.
> (Accounts of that have everything all wrong.)
> Friday was nice.
> Friday was nice, and we were friends.
> If only he had been a woman!
> I wanted to propagate my kind,
> and so did he, I think, poor boy.
> He'd pet the baby goats sometimes,
> and race with them, or carry one around.
> —Pretty to watch; he had a pretty body.
>
> And then one day they came and took us off.   (pp. 165–6)

Bishop's line 'If only he had been a woman!' has a foreshadowing in Valéry's 'Histoires Brisées':

> Tentation de Robinson.
> Le pied marqué au sable lui fait croire à une femme.
> Il imagine un Autre. Serait-ce un homme ou une
> femme?
> Robinson divisé—poème.[45]

This thought about Friday's gender does not even appear to cross the mind of Defoe's Robinson:

---

[44] Arthur Rimbaud 'Roman', in *Oeuvres Complètes*, ed. A. Adam (Paris: Gallimard, 1972), 29.

[45] Valéry, 'Histoires Brisées', in *Oeuvres*, ii. 415.

It happen'd one Day about Noon going towards my Boat, I was exceedingly
surpriz'd with the Print of a Man's naked Foot on the Shore, which was very plain
to be seen in the Sand: I stood like one Thunder-struck, or as if I had seen an
Apparition[46]

The original Robinson is too concerned about his physical safety to find
it in his mind to wonder if it might be a large-footed woman. Both
Valéry's and Bishop's figures inhabit physically safe places in which it is
their mental security that most concerns their creators. This is how the
narrative of a castaway and the story of his physical and spiritual survival
would be adapted by a small crowd of solitary-feeling poets during the last
century.[47]

Perhaps there is also an allusion in Bishop's poem to John Donne's
'We kill ourselves to propagate our kind.'[48] What this prompts is the
thought that her passage about Friday is also alive with half-suppressed
reflections on the non-reproductive nature of gay sexuality. After all, if
there is an echo of Donne here it starts thoughts about ambivalence
towards heterosexual coupling embedded in the curious phrasing with
which Bishop's Crusoe expresses the desire to have children. There
might even be an ambiguity in the phrase 'my kind' (as in the Isherwood
title *Christopher and his Kind*), which would underline the contradiction in
homosexuality—one that contemporary mores and medical possibilities
have worked to overcome. You used to need heterosexual desire to
propagate gays. Numerous critics have taken 'Crusoe in England' to be an
implicitly lesbian poem, yet it is perhaps worth bearing in mind that
Bishop was hardly the poet to produce an anthem, however discreetly or
indirectly. Her George Washington handicap would oblige her to look
more squarely at the case than such a piece of counter-cultural propaganda would allow. She had, after all, lived during the previous twenty
years through two important lesbian relationships both of which had
ended painfully, and, as already noted, 'Crusoe in England' seems to have
been completed in a lull after her 'secretary' had returned to North
America from Ouro Prêto for psychiatric treatment.

---

[46] Daniel Defoe, *Robinson Crusoe*, ed. M. Shinagel (New York: Norton, 1994), 112.

[47] See e.g. Bishop's translation of 'Infancy' by Carlos Drummond de Andrade, in which the
poet reads 'the story of Robinson Crusoe, | the long story that never comes to an end' (*The
Complete Poems 1927–1979* (New York: Farrar, Straus and Giroux, 1983), 258).

[48] John Donne, 'An Anatomy of the World: The First Anniversary', l.110. Travisano notes:
'Images of frustrated or meaningless propagation have cycled through the poem, and they reach
their culmination here' (*Elizabeth Bishop*, 182).

VI

In her reading of 'Crusoe in England' Joanne Feit Diehl addresses by means of Melanie Klein's writings and object-relations theory the issue of Bishop's art as one of reparation. She contrasts the poem with Bishop's Nova Scotian memoir: 'If "In the Village" sketches a psychically successful journey from mourning to reparation, "Crusoe in England" delineates a similar trajectory with a more somber outcome.' She goes on to outline what produces this 'somber outcome':

> Friday's loss proves irreparable because in this poem of unreconciled mourning, no other object comes to take his place. The haunting singularity that marks Crusoe's island speaks to Friday's reality as well, for he can neither be forgotten nor replaced. Reparation here would mean the internalization of Friday into the self and substitution for him in the external world.[49]

This account confuses the narration in the poem with the poem as a psychic narrative about the poet herself. As I have suggested elsewhere, the poetry of reparation, so as not to be merely wishful, is obliged to include an account of actual damage as irreparable. What is required for reparation is not the replacement of the object lost, or the undoing of the damage done, but an emblematic action that makes a reparative gesture even as it narrates the damage. This work is achieved, if it is achieved, by the completed poem in its figuration as an art object. In this light, there is no need for a happy ending to a work to perform a reparation.[50] In the conclusion to her book, though, Feit Diehl offers a way of viewing 'Crusoe in England' as nonetheless a reparative action:

> Thus, a text such as 'Crusoe in England' can be understood as the delineation of an insufficient holding environment and the narrator's attempts to create his own idiom of care against a background of wondrous depletion. Indeed, the compensatory nature of object-relations aesthetics gestures towards a fundamental theory of art: namely, that creativity springs from the desire to make reparation to the limited mother, to return to the holding environment reconceived by the daughter-poet, an environment that through its reformulation attempts to make up the deficit of the original, infantile relation.

This outlines in psychoanalytic terms what a reparative poetic text might be doing. It remains uncommitted about whether 'Crusoe in England' is

---

[49] Feit Diehl, *Elizabeth Bishop and Marianne Moore*, 104.
[50] See my *In the Circumstances*, 1–23.

such a text, for, as she had earlier concluded: 'If, as in Bishop's case, the relationship [with the mother] is marked by disruption and abandonment, is it any wonder that all the inventiveness in Crusoe's possession cannot redress his subsequent loss?'[51] No, I suppose not; but more difficult questions might be: Can all the poetic inventiveness in Bishop's possession redress, or offer an emblematic reparation for, her subsequent loss? Is 'Crusoe in England' an attempt to do this? Feit Diel's account seems to conclude that the poem is an attempted reparation, one that fails at the narrative level. My version of reparative poetry would *expect* it to fail at the narrative level, but allow for its achieving something in its diction, tone, and form—if read as working in contrapuntal relation to the narrative of loss.

As we know, Lota's psychiatrist had been trained by Melanie Klein. In the letter to Robert Lowell of 30 March 1959 she refers to the 'grim little book by Melanie Klein, *Envy and Gratitude*—superb in its horrid way'.[52] Bishop's response to the theory appears both divided and uncommitted. Moreover, there is another possibility beyond Joanne Feit Diehl's, which is that 'Crusoe in England' is a refusal of reparation, an account of someone who, however in need of repair, prefers, for the sake of loyalty to loss, the harder way of doing without it. Thus, for 'Crusoe in England' the exploration of solitude and imagination is not a separate issue from isolation and sexual orientation; the isolation is also an instance of a sensibility suffused with its experiences, sexual or otherwise.

One last reason why the poem seems to turn its back on consolations of whatever kind is that in this poem's view the art of poetry is not to be idealized as an unequivocal good. It cannot be made to stand off from the accidents and incoherences of experiences in and of the world. It cannot be made, like a distantly patronizing Lady Bountiful, to bring to bear upon narrations of suffering its healing balms of technique. For Bishop, the benefits of poetry were only to be had in relation to itself:

People seem to think that doing something like writing a poem makes one happier in life. It doesn't solve anything. Perhaps it does at least give one the satisfaction of having done a thing well or having put in a good day's work.[53]

Poetry as a life of writing, the solitude and devotion that it requires, is inextricably interwoven with the suffering and the damage experienced. 'I

---

[51] Feit Diehl, *Elizabeth Bishop and Marianne Moore*, 108, 105.

[52] Bishop, *Selected Letters*, 371.

[53] *Conversations with Elizabeth Bishop*, 41.

wanted to study medicine,' Bishop recalled in 1976, 'But when I'd gotten out of college I'd already published several things and—and I think Miss Moore discouraged me'.[54] In her practice of poetry, to recall Adam Phillips's terms, it is not that 'the cure can seem a mirror-image of the disease', but rather that the seeming cure is an aspect of the apparent sickness. For those of us who, like John Keats, have put faith in the healing powers of poetry, this is the hardest lesson to be experienced when reading 'Crusoe in England'.

---

[54] *Conversations with Elizabeth Bishop*, 57.

CHAPTER 8

Allen Curnow Travels

I

'I'm a stranger here myself' expresses a solidarity between people from somewhere else who meet on the grounds of a similarity in different foreignnesses. Allen Curnow likes the phrase, employing a variation in 'Friendship Heights' from 1972, 'I am absently walking in another summer | a stranger here myself' (p. 156),[1] and he teases out further senses by halving it over a line break ten years later for 'Impromptu in a Low Key': 'I'm a stranger | here myself' (p. 89). The phrase echoes beyond the situation of the overseas traveller. Curnow from about 1973, a little like W. B. Yeats some fifty years before, had found himself detached from his personal contributions to 'the anti-myth about New Zealand'. He commented on that situation in 1982: 'we have heard enough of "national identity", but this doesn't mean that it will go away'.[2] The beginning of his second career coincides more or less with the moment Britain 'entered Europe' and weakened its links to the Commonwealth. Looking back in 1990 the poet observed that 'As years went by, I began to feel that I'd done the best I could for this country, and it had done it's best for me—recognition and that kind of thing—and that this wasn't quite enough, either for me *or* the country.'[3] Seven years later Elizabeth Lowry struck a familiar note when praising him for being 'one of the country's cultural pioneers', but she added that 'his role in promoting a distinctive New Zealand poetic won't perhaps be fully appreciated for some generations to come'.[4] A stranger here myself, I attempt to

---

[1] References to Allen Curnow's poetry in the text are from *Early Days Yet: New and Collected Poems 1941–1997* (Manchester: Carcanet, 1997).

[2] Allen Curnow, 'Author's Note', in *Selected Poems* (Harmondsworth: Penguin, 1982), p. x.

[3] 'Allen Curnow Talks to Peter Simpson', *Landfall*, 175 (Sept. 1990), 301–2, repr. in Elizabeth Alley and Mark Williams (eds.), *In the Same Room: Conversations with New Zealand Writers* (Auckland: Auckland University Press, 1992).

[4] Elizabeth Lowry, 'Belonging Down There' (review of *Early Days Yet*), *Times Literary Supplement*, 4929, 19 Sept. 1997, 12.

sketch the significance in Curnow's work of a more than national context by looking at how this 'distinctive New Zealand poetic' responded to the larger world.

How does local detail come to have more than local significance? Can an outsider's view be other than a superficial glossing of such detail? Donald Davie has asserted that Curnow 'is a well-travelled poet, but not at all a cosmopolitan'.[5] The New Zealander had qualified Yeats's 'One can only reach out to the universe with a gloved hand—that glove is one's nation' by asking: 'If a poet can't know his country, which he has seen, what can he do about the universe, which he hasn't?'[6] There is at least one intermediate point between these two extremes: places poets have seen, but ones that aren't their own country. Travelling means encountering cultures where the tight fit of your glove is brought home by the fact that few, if any, are wearing the same style in the new landscape. Such encounters present poets, and others, with the challenge of recognizing both what we irremovably are, and what we can never be. They bring into sharpened contrast both what separates us, and what we share.[7]

Even in English-speaking countries the glove, though wearable, is never a perfect fit. Of some months spent in Washington DC during 'the euphoric spring months' of 1961, Curnow said: 'My poem "A Framed Photograph", for one, dates from this time—it records in part a most agreeable visit to—or "with" as Americans say—Mr and Mrs William P. Bundy.'[8] Just such differences of usage, a 'with' for a 'to', position the perspectival angles through which, experiencing phenomena, we find identities challenged and reinforced, as, for example, in his poem's sardonic reporting of the colloquialism 'I guess':

> What, exactly,
> did he do at the Pentagon? He guessed he was
> a deputy assistant secretary of defence,
> *a political appointment*, modestly confided.   (p. 165)

[5] Donald Davie, 'Postmodernism and Allen Curnow', *PN Review*, 77, 17/3 (1991), 33.

[6] 'Conversation with Allen Curnow', in *Look Back Harder: Critical Writings 1935–1984*, ed. Peter Simpson (Auckland: Auckland University Press, 1987), 254.

[7] On the basis of poems, other writings, and advice, I have Curnow's overseas experience as: in London, crossing America, and returning to New Zealand through the Panama Canal during 1949–50; in Washington DC and New York in 1961; giving a reading tour of the US East Coast in 1966; in Washington again and in Venice during 1974; visiting Venice, Rome, Naples, and, perhaps, Sicily in 1978; in London, the South of France, and Liguria during 1983; at the Cambridge Poetry Festival, England, in June 1985, and the International Festival of Authors in Toronto the following October. After that date he made three visits to England and Italy, went at least once to Australia, and made holiday visits to Pacific Islands.

[8] 'Curnow Talks to Simpson', 300.

Curnow's 'modestly' acknowledges the elocutory force of 'I guess' in American speech. It's an implicature lost in the third-person singular past tense. We might then suppose that the host doesn't quite know what he does at the Pentagon. Yet the phrase also implies that Bundy is having the poet on—hinting through the modesty that he is closer to the President than a career civil servant might be.

More haplessly, Bill Manhire's poem 'Wingatui', the name of a South Island racecourse, with its 'yellow moon' that 'floats silks across the bird-cage',[9] had been taken for 'a bit of surrealist waffle' by the editor of 'Pseuds Corner', who reprinted it from an issue of the *TLS*. Its poet, amused by the entire business, remarked that 'Poems sometimes need more translation than we initially realize when they move from one English-speaking country to another' and added:

> the area where horses parade before a race, which we call the bird cage, is known as the paddock in England. Of course, that means something else again here. Someone said to me the other day that if Rupert Brooke had been a New Zealander, instead of 'some corner of a foreign field', he would have written 'some corner of an overseas paddock'.[10]

If the poet is translated to another place, the resulting poems' locations will be doubled by the superimposition of the native language culture, the 'overseas paddock', upon the context of the 'foreign field'. One conclusion from the 'Wingatui' incident might be that understanding international varieties of English as situation determines them is part of what must be assumed in a claim to know the language now.

'Interesting' is how 'Impromptu in a Low Key' describes 'the way | the English say | *round the corner* and the | Romans *cento* | *metri*' (p. 88). Translation problems increase as poetry draws upon a language universe overseas, beyond the pale of the English-speaking. One response to this situation (as in, for example, *The Pisan Cantos*) was the development of a far-fetched, impure diction made up of snatches from many languages and cultures. Curnow's early sonnet exploring the chances of introducing 'the landscape to the language' had imagined 'Latin skies' daubed 'upon Chinese lagoons' and concluded that you won't get anywhere 'without some word that will have lied' (p. 199). His later poems live with that

---

[9] Bill Manhire, *Zoetropes: Poems 1972–82* (North Sydney: Allen & Unwin, 1984), 43.
[10] 'Bill Manhire Interviewed by Iain Sharp', in Alley and Williams (eds.), *In the Same Room*, 24. For further comments on this poem and its relation to the situation of New Zealand poetry see Ian Wedde, 'Introduction', in Ian Wedde and Harvey McQueen (eds.), *The Penguin Book of New Zealand Verse* (Auckland: Penguin, 1985), 26.

verbal moral crisis and accommodate themselves to overlap and discrepancy, incorporating terms and phrases borrowed from such diverse contexts as a Japanese tidal-wave warning, Verlaine's 'Clair de Lune',[11] and an Italian railway carriage: '*tsunami! tsunami!* splintering deadwood of the boat' (p. 16), '*jets* | *d'eau* the fire brigade pumps' (p. 31), and 'our family motto . . . | *è pericoloso sporgersi*' (p. 45). Alongside this linguistic travelling is the frequent placing of Maori terms, such as 'Ngai-tahu | *kainga* and excavated *paa*' (p. 27), with the same italic tweezers, and sometimes combining them, as in the vertiginous 'Karekare doppelgänger' (p. 118). Curnow's later poetry alerts readers to the histories of relations between language and world, interwoven with the experience of human movement across the globe,[12] and which, as he puts it in 'A Passion for Travel', result in '*pakeha* thistles in the wrong forest' (p. 81). The Maori loanword, meaning here 'introduced' or 'not indigenous',[13] underlines the verbal transplanting of Curnow's second career. His later poems take it for granted that travel is in the species' blood, and that the local contains the foreign.

The importance of elsewhere for this New Zealand poet has little in common with the 'customs and establishments | it would be much more serious to refuse' of Philip Larkin's poem, three quatrains that acknowledge 'the salt rebuff of speech, | Insisting so on difference',[14] but which remain decidedly monoglot. Larkin felt able to behave as if nowhere mattered outside England. However important it may have been for Curnow to establish a poetry suited to his New Zealand experience, it would have been difficult to succumb to a Larkin-like view of cultural centrality—one which has come to seem defensively and indefensibly marginal when looked at from anywhere else.[15] Larkin's three mature

---

[11] Ezra Pound alludes to this third quatrain of the poem in the close to Canto LXXIV, the first of *The Pisan Cantos*, in *The Cantos of Ezra Pound*, 4th coll. edn. (London: Faber & Faber, 1987), 449.

[12] When, for example, 'relaxing in a divan on the veranda of your bungalow', you have borrowed your 'relaxing' from Italy, your 'bungalow' from Bengal, its 'veranda' from Portugal via India, and your 'divan' from ancient Persia. Thus, it is not only that English is 'pakeha' in New Zealand; it is 'foreign' in England too.

[13] Curnow explains that 'pakeha' usually means simply 'not Maori' (*Selected Poems*, (Auckland: Auckland University Press, 1982), 200), but the fact that the Maori are themselves not 'indigenous' to New Zealand, or Aotearoa, is a reminder that if you take a long enough perspective few have roots which are not 'pakeha'.

[14] Philip Larkin, 'The Importance of Elsewhere', in *Collected Poems*, ed. A. Thwaite (London/Hessle: Faber & Faber/Marvell, 1988), 104.

[15] Manhire noted, when commenting on difficulties in understanding 'Wingatui', that the problem of translation is 'especially true with the Poms, who have become parochial and provin-

collections consist of poems which rarely let fall any awareness of other pieces by the same poet whose company they are keeping in their respective or in previous volumes. This may be one result of Larkin's outwardly rejecting Yeats as model, after *The North Ship*. Curnow's poems, like Yeats's, are alive with their being part of a book, a sequence, or an oeuvre: phrases echo between texts; place names with associations and talismanic words frequently recur. As a result, and increasingly with later collections, each group of poems bears the textual history and cultural outlook of its author's writings as a whole. Thus, works prompted by experiences of travel, such as 'Moro Assassinato', are not just poems located overseas; they are Curnow poems set there, and ones in which the author's presence is carefully inscribed.

By 1990 Davie was able to pitch discussion of *Selected Poems 1940–1989* on a high plane of regard:

If we ask, as Foden does, where Curnow stands in relation to modernism and postmodernism, we see him no longer as one of a specially endangered species, but as a voice that vies with other poets' voices, speaking many languages, on an international stage. It is a status that Curnow earned many years ago.[16]

Poets such as Attilio Bertolucci, Elizabeth Bishop, and Czeslaw Milosz, also born in 1911, began writing when the technical developments of the first-generation modernists were a *fait accompli*, yet long before the term 'postmodern' became current. Bishop and Curnow, in their earlier work, also exemplify an initial reaction from free verse, both writing sestinas in the 1930s ('A Miracle for Breakfast'[17] and 'Statement'[18]) which take a hint from Auden, only five years their senior, and his: 'Hearing of harvests rotting in the valleys'.[19] They are latecomers and forerunners at the same time.

Writing in 1984, when Curnow's poetry was becoming better known overseas, Elizabeth Smither emphasized the continuing importance of his home place for the work:

cial without noticing it' ('Manhire Interviewed by Sharp', in Alley and Williams (eds.), *In the Same Room*, 24).

[16] Davie, 'Postmodernism and Allen Curnow', 31. He is referring to Giles Foden's 'Seriously Substantial' (a review of *Selected Poems 1940–1989*), *Times Literary Supplement*, 14–20 Sept. 1990, 978. In 'Allen Curnow as Post-Modern Metaphysical', *PN Review*, 105, 21/7 (1995), 35–41, Chris Miller takes up the debate.

[17] Elizabeth Bishop, *The Complete Poems 1927–1979* (New York: Farrar, Straus and Giroux, 1983), 18–19.

[18] Curnow, *Selected Poems*, 5–6. The poem is not collected in *Early Days Yet*.

[19] W. H. Auden, *The English Auden: Poems, Essays and Dramatic Writings 1927–1939*, ed. E. Mendelson (London: Faber & Faber, 1977), 135–6.

You would think that international recognition would be the time for Allen Curnow to drop all the local literals or littorals out of his work and go as the lark goes for the ether over New York or London or wherever the centre of poetry is—but not at all—he stubbornly insists on putting his own street name, his climate, his turn of phrase into the thing. If he travels or an international incident stirs a chord, though the international thing may get caught up with fishing, that goes in too. But with complete unaffectedness and no sense of incongruity[20]

Her prose adverts to the poet's creative freedom, yet sketches a context of constraints. International fame offers the temptation to become groundless, but Curnow is not drawn: 'he stubbornly insists'. If he is inspired by a foreign place or world news, there is 'unaffectedness and no sense of incongruity'. Why should there be? J. G. A. Pocock has remarked that 'the insecurity and self-dispraise which mark new societies as strongly as does self-assertiveness lasted through the second period of New Zealand history . . . and may have disappeared only in the third'.[21] Are Smithers's comments perhaps shadowed by a trace of 'cultural cringe', of 'self-dispraise' in the possibility of 'incongruity', and the Larkinesque defensive-assertive in her thought that references to elsewhere might fail to avoid 'unaffectedness'?

Remarking that though Curnow is 'a well-travelled poet' he is 'not at all a cosmopolitan', Davie reveals himself as a troubled patriot of Larkin's generation. Smithers's observation that Curnow's localisms have survived the growth of the poet's international recognition has, in common with Davie's comment, a qualm about poetry unauthenticated by relation to a home language, by a relation to a home place, and by *its* relation to a national history. Curnow as a New Zealand poet has evidently shaped his work in relation to such coordinates. However, by 1973 there was no need to create what already existed. Curnow's travel poems look back towards and away from this recently found cultural autonomy and self-esteem. In thus pointing away, they intimate a poetry that no longer needs to harp on national identity. It might by a world poetry of the future, like the culture for which Osip Mandelstam felt the 'nostalgia' of a homesick traveller. Yet, being in a capacious English, or in one of the Englishes, it would be a poetry taking its place among other such world poetries.

---

[20] Elizabeth Smither, 'New Zealand: Pocket of Poetry', *PN Review*, 41, 11/3 (1984), 32.

[21] J. G. A. Pocock, 'Removal from the Wings' (a review of *Making Peoples: A History of the New Zealanders from Polynesian Settlement to the End of the 19th Century* by James Belich), *London Review of Books*, 19/6, 20 Mar. 1997, 13. He is referring to the Dominion period and the one that began when Britain entered the Common Market.

II

Though Curnow had made early contact with two powerful elsewheres of poetry in English,[22] Robyn Marsack notes that 'Until 1949 he had not travelled outside New Zealand—unlike the majority of his literary contemporaries'.[23] Talking to MacDonald P. Jackson over the turn of 1972–3, Curnow explained how he first came to leave the country:

> Well, the idea was really Holcroft's and Brasch's and J. H. E. Schroder's and I forget who else, that when the State Literary Fund was first set up, some money should be spent on sending Curnow abroad. The idea was, I suppose, to export me for a year and see what happened.[24]

What happened, among many things,[25] is that he worked in Fleet Street, got to know DylanThomas,[26] and, back in New Zealand, his father died. 'Elegy on my Father' is dated 'London, November 1949'. The poem wears its indebtedness on its sleeve:

> Spring in his death abounds among the lily islands,
> There to bathe him for the grave antipodean snows
> Fall floodlong, rivermouths all in bloom, and those
> Fragile church timbers quiver
> By the bourne of his burial where robed he goes
> No journey at all.   (p. 187)

The two-hemisphere seasonal perspective on a clergyman's death, the spring and autumn in November, provides Curnow with a geographically double occasion to deploy Thomas's rhetoric of organic process inflected with a Christian symbolism, but also with a measure of doubt. The churchman is buried in his workplace, but his 'going beyond' is described

---

[22] In the late 1930s John Lehmann published him in *Penguin New Writing*, and *Poetry* (Chicago) printed some poems during the 1940s.

[23] Robyn Marsack, 'A Home in Thought: Three New Zealand Poets', *PN Review*, 46, Cambridge Poetry Festival Special Issue, 12/2 (1985), 56. As is indicated on the back flap of *Selected Poems 1940–1989* (London: Viking, 1990), Curnow attended the festival of 14–16 June 1985, gave a reading on the Friday night with Clampitt, Heaney, and Hébert, and contributed to a presentation of poems by Pound with Tomlinson the following afternoon.

[24] 'Conversation with Allen Curnow', in *Look Back Harder*, 255.

[25] His work also came to the attention of the young Donald Davie: 'Curnow and I have been aware of each other since appearing in the dear damned *Poetry London* more than forty years ago; I have always respected his work; and he and his wife stayed with us, briefly but memorably, some seven years ago' ('Postmodernism and Allen Curnow', 31). Davie's essay was written in 1990; he is remembering back to 1949 and recalling 1983.

[26] See 'About Dylan Thomas', in *Look Back Harder*, 319–25.

as 'No journey at all'. 'Elegy on my Father' would not have had this sound without Curnow's travelling an extra mile towards the Dylanesque.[27] Like its models, the poem builds full-mouthed stanzas of alliterated vowel music, larded with internal and end rhyme, compounded nouns, and neologisms. However, Curnow's art required a larger conceptual canvas than those that sponsored it. This is not because it is possible to outdo Thomas's descants on the theme of 'womb' and 'tomb', but because here a larger imaginative geography of the real is required:

> One sheet's enough to cover
> My end of the world and his, and the same silence.
>
> While in Paddington autumn is air-borne, earth-given,
> Day's nimbus nearer staring, colder smoulders;
> Breath of a death not my own bewilders
> Dead calm with breathless choirs
> O bird-creation singing where the world moulders!   (p. 187)

An inconsistency of style allows Curnow's true tone and subject to appear: 'One sheet's enough to cover | My end of the world and his'—the 'sheet' being a shroud, a world map, and a piece of paper with a poem written on it. The contrasting seasons in northern and southern hemispheres, and the distances (spiritual, geographical, and mortal) separating father and son, give to Curnow's poem a concrete situation and informational burden not common in Thomas's work. Thus, 'Elegy on my Father' implies the poet's 'own street name, his climate'. The poem shows a Curnow who has travelled far to come into his own, but it is a journey that has cost him in guilt at having had the opportunity. The poem closes by calling upon the '*sweet relic*' to set the separated at one, to '*atone | To our earth's Lord for the pride of all our voyages*' (p. 188).

A similar shadow of guilt in travelling, back home this time, falls across 'When the Hulk of the World':

> Oh then, sweet claustrophobe
> I leave among the lost leaves of a London wood
> (So dark, we missed the middle of our road)
>   Can spring condone, redeem
> One treachery of departure from that life,
> Shiftless to fetch this love?   (p. 193)

---

[27] Given the lilt of this poem, it is surprising to read that Curnow 'hadn't read him with what I'd call a poet's intensity or close attention at the time I met him. I did know the better part of his work at that time, the book called Deaths and Entrances in particular, but he was not one of the poets I felt most impressionable about' (ibid. 255).

The poem's guilty feeling again leans upon a Christian vocabulary, and an allusion to the opening of Dante's spiritual travel poem, *La divina commedia*. Here too it is autumn in London, spring in New Zealand, and there is a farewell taking place which looks to all the world like a romantic one. By contrast, the two parts of 'Idylls in Colour Film', about the Panama Canal zone in 1950, read as equivocal justifications for the pleasure of journeying and the sharp but fleeting acquaintance with places experienced by someone passing through:

> Avid the traveller slums the shops,
> Tickling a vein which no blood leads
>
> That street where one was knifed last night.
> Home and abroad is where to be,
> With a mast-high moon, eyes crackling bright.
> The Caribbean's the next sea.   (p. 186)

The second part asks: 'Have we lived | Anywhere if not here…?' (p. 187). This 'lived' must imply 'intensely', as contrasted with the quotidian existence of home, which is, however, safer than the violent streets of that strip of Latin America, with its 'dollar shadows' where 'The Zone Troops | Strike MacArthurian attitudes' (p. 186)—a sardonic collocation of 'Idylls' and the '. . . Arthurian'. Qualifying the guilts and separations of other poems from this period overseas, 'Idylls in Colour Film' prefigures works more at home in the world at large. It points towards a poetry ready to accept what 'Impromptu in a Low Key' describes as the *'essential | onceness'* of such mixed experiences as seeing 'a sign in | Sicily GROTTA DI POLIFEMO', though 'when you get there you see | why Homer was | blind as a bat' (p. 88).[28]

'An Oppressive Climate, a Populous Neighbourhood', set in a July 1961 New York City, presents a variation on the theme of Alfred Hitchcock's *Rear Window* to fend off various temptations. 'I pan to the flight above', he writes, underlining the cinematic allusion, where 'a hand shifts a pot-plant | From the sill, one hand, the perfection of anonymity'. The poet then turns to comment, but, unlike James Stewart in the film, resists making inferences or deductions about the people in the view:

> What we cherish is our own business, this hand innocently
> Withdraws its treasure. Put it simply that the owner may be stripped

---

[28] 'Homer … | blind as a bat' echoes Ezra Pound's 'poor old Homer blind, | blind as a bat' (Canto VII, in *The Cantos*, 24).

Naked for the heat and has nothing to hide but himself.
Satisfied, I put no impertinent question to myself

Concerning these companions, least of all any literary question.

Curnow does, nevertheless, raise some religious and literary issues by concluding this part of the poem with a long open-ended question, one which starts by alluding to the thermometer shots that punctuate the film while artfully giving back to the American colloquial exclamation its religious referent:

Hell, let's face it, is horribly hot and overcrowded,
But where else do you find the niceties of neighbourly regard
Better observed and the mitigable nuisance of neighbourly love
Better understood than in this City we have been building so long?   (p. 179)

'You don't know the meaning of the word "neighbours"!' shouts the woman on the balcony whose dog is killed by Raymond Burr—an incident which prompts and helps explain the descant on the barking dog in the poem's second part. As Grace Kelly says in response to Stewart's doubts about the morality of his spying: 'I'm not much on rear window ethics.' Curnow's phrase 'neighbourly regard' worries at the interweaving of voyeurism, fantasy, human solidarity, self-righteous busybodying, and deductive logic in *Rear Window*.

Like the grieving dog owner who addresses a sermon to the surrounding apartments, Curnow's poem is aware of the Christian duties in 'regard' for one's neighbours. The pithiness and complexity of Christ's teachings on the subject ('Thou shalt love thy neighbour as thyself', Matthew 22: 39) are shaping the entire poem. In *Rear Window* the spies will also come to be espied. Similarly, the poet is looking 'from this back window' at 'A grey-headed man' who looks 'from that back window' at the poet himself, 'A brown-headed man', in the first two stanzas. Whether we can love ourselves enough to be able to love our neighbours, and how precisely we are to do this without trespassing on their privacy is glanced at in Curnow's 'mitigable nuisance of neighbourly love'. Is the 'City we have been building' the Pandemonium of *Paradise Lost*, whose architect had 'built in heaven high towers . . . but was headlong sent | With his industrious crew to build in hell'?[29] Is it the product of repression and exploitation required for the building of human civilization as described in William Blake's lyric, 'The Mental Traveller', where

---

[29] John Milton, *Paradise Lost*, ed. A. Fowler (London: Longmans, 1971), bk 1, ll. 749–51.

The trees bring forth sweet Extacy
To all who in the desart roam
Till many a City there is Built
And many a pleasant Shepherds home[30]

Is it even, in its observings and understandings of neighbourly regard and love, a human attempt at the Just one? Curnow's poem, through its looking into others' apartments and its inclusion of his own body, is an experiment in the mutual respect and understanding involved in approaching (and maintaining a decent distance from) another culture. The summer climate and population density of New York City are underlined as experiences of otherness through implicit differences with, say, the North Island coast at the same time of year. The poet's New Zealand perspective is essential because appreciating the distinctive characteristics of another culture requires a consciously articulated grasp of one's own.

III

Curnow's presence in 'An Oppressive Climate, a Populous Neighbourhood' reminds readers of a New Zealand perspective on the world. Other poems, like 'Elegy on my Father' and 'When the Hulk of the World', recall the continuing existence of the country when the speaker is not there. Manhire has remarked of his 'Zoetropes' that it

is a poem which most New Zealanders 'get' immediately, but which other readers find baffling. It takes its life from the fact that New Zealand vanishes if you leave it. All New Zealanders who travel know that small moment of inward twitching when you catch sight of a capital Z in the newspaper, and the subsequent disappointment when the word turns out to be Zaire or Zoo or Zoetrope. A little burst of hope replaced by an extended sense of loss—it's the Kiwi way.[31]

Curnow's 'An Excellent Memory' is differently exercised by verbal recognitions that reinforce for the traveller a sense of identity through place.[32] An acquaintance of the poet's, who knew 'by heart the whole sonnet', recites Charles Brasch's 'The Islands (ii)' at least as far as its penultimate line:

---

[30] William Blake, *The Complete Poems*, ed. A. Ostriker (Harmondsworth: Penguin, 1977), 502.

[31] Bill Manhire, 'Note' to a self-selection of poems, *A Calendar of Modern Poetry*, *PN Review*, 100, 21/2 (1994), 125.

[32] The second and third verse paragraphs of 'An Excellent Memory', from 'The cartographer . . .' to ' . . . a puzzling globe', may recall Elizabeth Bishop's 'The Map', in *Complete Poems 1927–1979*, 3.

> all the way down to 'distance
> looks our way' and it did,
> over the martinis in Observatory Circle,
> Washington D. C., demanding by way
> of an answering look nothing more
> than an excellent memory.   (p. 86)

This perspective of recall, from America towards home, by means of recited lines where 'in these islands, meeting and parting | Shake us', is reversed in the poem's close. It excellently remembers the Washington evening from years later in New Zealand: 'That was | 8 November 1974, just about | midnight, give or take a few minutes' (ibid.). The casual lack of specificity in the last phrase echoes, perhaps, Pat Laking's not having recited Brasch's last line: 'And none knows where he will lie down at night.'[33]

In two key sequences, *Trees, Effigies, Moving Objects* and 'Moro Assassinato', such reversible perspectives (what 'An Excellent Memory' calls 'a there for a here') are placed side by side. The first part of the latter, 'The Traveller', interweaves them into as close to a simultaneity as is consistent with the presence of memory, chronology, and narration:

> Paratohi rock, the bell-tower
> of San Giorgio recompose
> the mixture's moment;
>
> the tales are all one tale
> dead men tell, the minor
> characters the living.   (p. 119)

Though we leave behind Karekare beach and Paratohi rock in the rest of this sequence about 1970s Italian political violence and conspiracy, the New Zealand viewpoint has been established for the entire work. It is one that readers are reminded of later: 'You're a guest, in a stricken house, | eavesdropper, easy tourist.' (p. 130). Nor is this any old outsider, but a particular New Zealand poet looking on. Curnow was at pains to emphasize such particularity when defending the earlier *Trees, Effigies, Moving Objects*:

Anyone can be sixty-one, and almost anyone can live in New Zealand and visit Washington. But it's personal when all this happens in one man's poems. Anyone

---

[33] Charles Brasch's sonnet was anthologized in Allen Curnow (ed.), *The Penguin Book of New Zealand Verse* (Harmondsworth: Penguin, 1960), 179.

can be a vicarage child and remember Nebuchadnezzar's band and his image very distinctly. Anyone can go to a rock party at sixty. Anyone can be a poet—but the coincidence of all three is an unlikely one. That's what I mean by personal. But if the poem succeeds it must seem inevitable.[34]

Accepting the necessity of personal pressure, and taking responsibility for how that element must become something inevitable, Curnow may leave his work vulnerable to the charge of being overconcerned with his limiting perspective, 'his own street name, his climate'. This particularity, however, has the benefit of protecting the poems from damage caused by the assumption of an impossible objectivity, or access to special knowledge and insight. *An Incorrigible Music* addresses the matter of, in Goethe's words, 'Dichtung und Warheit', poetic imagination and truth, when confronted with the world's incorrigible violence. It is an issue tested in Curnow's century by Ezra Pound, throughout his long attempt to understand and take part in Italian history.[35] The detachment in Curnow's poetic stance both constitutes the source of a limit in the sequence, a limit he directly addresses, and simultaneously outlines the terms of its success.

Commenting on *Trees, Effigies, Moving Objects* in 1973, Curnow observed:

there are other pressures—they may go back to the childhood I was trying to describe—which have more to do with being a New Zealander than being sixty. I mean the pressure of the *here* where one is, and the *there* which is all the world. I don't know that I understand them better, but I think I have now contained them in better poems. I chose a particular *there*, which is Washington, D. C., and a particular *here*, which is somewhere between Lone Kauri Road, Hobson Bay, and the Waipoua Forest.[36]

The 'there' poems in this sequence come from his visit to America twelve years earlier—as Curnow was at pains to recall, so as to counteract the assumption that he had been entirely inactive as a poet during the sixties. 'Some of the drafts or work-sheets go back to 1961', he commented: 'I was in Washington D. C. through the euphoric spring months of that year, after John Kennedy's inauguration as President, not a little clouded

---

[34] 'Conversation with Allen Curnow', in *Look Back Harder*, 265.

[35] For more on Pound's involvement with Italian cultural and political history see my 'Ezra Pound and Italian Art', in R. Humphries (ed.), *Pound's Artists: Ezra Pound and the Visual Arts in London, Paris and Italy* (London: Tate Gallery, 1985), 121–76, and 'Ezra Pound: Translation and Betrayal', in *In the Circumstances: About Poems and Poets* (Oxford: Oxford University Press, 1992), 173–97.

[36] 'Conversation with Allen Curnow', in *Look Back Harder*, 264.

by the adventurist Bay of Pigs attack on Cuba and the forebodings over Vietnam.'[37] 'A Framed Photograph' begins:

> The renaissance was six months old.
> All the Kennedys were living at that time.
> Jackie was hanging pictures in the White House.
> *I figured he could use the experience,* Jack hornered,
> *when he starts in legal practice,* naming Bobby
> for Attorney-General.   (p. 164)

Family pride and backstage goings-on are hinted at behind the allusion to Jack Horner pulling out a plum and giving it to his brother. The 'cuckold-maker' sense or 'horner', as in the main character of William Wycherley's *The Country Wife*, also infects the word '*experience*', the name of Jimi Hendrix's band, tingeing it with a sexual colouring redolent of the 1960s. A decade of hindsight has tarnished that brief flush of 'renaissance':

> Act one, scene one,
> of the bloody melodrama. Everyone listened
> while everyone read his poems. BANG! BANG!
> and we cried all the way to My Lai.   (p. 164)

The colloquial 'cried all the way to' invites reflections on the self-serving convenience of national weeping over the fate of the Kennedy brothers. Their deaths removed two suspiciously liberal characters from the stage, better facilitating, under the President Johnson of Robert Lowell's 'Waking Early Sunday Morning',[38] the intensified build-up of the US military in Vietnam, an involvement begun by Kennedy which was to inflict itself on Australasia too. Punctuating this are the many assassinations and killings signified by the exclamations in capitals, echoing (as it might be) the chorus of a sixties hit by Sonny and Cher: 'bang bang, I shot you down | bang bang, you hit the ground'. This 'BANG! BANG!', with its grimly hollow ironies, is a technical gesture which adverts, perhaps inadvertently, to the poem's own weakness and acknowledgement of an ambivalent culpability, its 'we cried . . .'.

Elizabeth Bishop has a poem set in Washington with a curiously similar device for needling the military. 'View of the Capitol from the Library of Congress' describes how

---

[37] 'Curnow Talks to Simpson', 300.
[38] For some observations upon this poem's final stanza in relation to issues of the poetic impulse and violence see my *In the Circumstances*, 8–9.

> On the east steps the Air Force Band
> in uniforms of Air Force blue
> is playing hard and loud, but—queer—
> the music doesn't quite come through.

She then fancies that 'the trees must intervene, | catching the music in their leaves', which allows her deadpan conclusion, punning on brass instruments and the 'top brass' of the military:

> Great shades, edge over,
> give the music room.
> The gathered brasses want to go
> *boom—boom*.[39]

Her lines indirectly respond to the Korean War, to the possibility that nuclear weapons would be used there. Bishop's '*boom—boom*' has this in common with Curnow's 'BANG! BANG!'—for his poem looks indignantly back to the real and possible atomic bombings of Hiroshima, Nagasaki, North Korea, and the Cuba missile crisis by bringing together a Jamaican girl dusting a Bechstein and the chemical dust of President Truman and (Bundy's wife's father) Dean Acheson, that

> jaunty pair
> smiling the air
> that flutters their trousers on Capitol Hill?
> Why Hiroshima Harry and the dandy Dean,
> dust free.   (pp. 164–5)

Bishop's poem cutely pretends to be describing a scene. Curnow's sarcastically insinuates its political points. Bishop's poem, as its title hints, is all but silently caught in the ironies of her situation as a discreetly lesbian, liberal-minded poet in residence at the Library of Congress during the McCarthy era: her word 'queer' means no more than arrestingly peculiar. Curnow's poem displays the greater freedom of its detachment in both time and place. Such a distancing may also give it the appearance of being retrospectively calculated.

Here I seem to disagree with Manhire, who, reviewing *An Incorrigible Music*, felt that the book had 'an air of slight contrivance, a flavour not so much of pre- as of post-meditation', an air which '*Trees, Effigies, Moving*

---

[39] Bishop, *Complete Poems 1927–1979*, 69. Bishop's comments in letters on the poem don't suggest an overwhelming conviction of its quality or power (see *One Art: Selected Letters*, ed. R. Giroux (New York: Farrar, Straus and Giroux, 1994), 210, 307).

Objects, did not'.[40] He, however, is comparing the echoes that rebound from poem to poem within the two sequences. I am identifying a perspective of retroactive insightfulness in 'A Framed Photograph'. What Bishop's and Curnow's poems have in common, marked by their similar reductions to the double iterating of aggressive noise, is that each expresses, and suffers from, an impotence in the face of massive institutional power. In Bishop's the weakness is partly a result of her vulnerability to the forces sustaining Cold War politics. She was part of a persecuted minority (though could never have publicly presented herself in this light), and, through her having American nationality and being a temporary government employee, associated with those forces of persecution. In 'A Framed Photograph' the equivalent of Bishop's situatedness is the poet's equivocal position as a guest enjoying 'a most agreeable visit' with the Bundys in Friendship Heights. The play on 'I guess' in 'He guessed he was | a deputy assistant secretary of defence' implies the remembering writer's evasion of a guest's politeness requirement, as does:

> Hospitably home at cocktail time he took
> one careful gin and tonic, excused himself
> to mind State papers.   (p. 165)

The release of the writing from the constraints of its circumstance allows the sharply implied critical perspective on American foreign policy to emerge, though at the expense of sounding blankly well rid of it. The poem grimly twists the sense of the Bundy's Washington suburb 'Friendship Heights', leaving readers to intuit a less crushing sense of these decades in 'the one that didn't get written'[41] among the interstices of this sequence's lines and spaces.

Thomas Nagel's extension of moral luck to contexts of national political shame suggests a reason for Bishop's technical problem and Curnow's:

it is nearly impossible to view the crimes of one's own country in the same way that one views the crimes of another country, no matter how equal one's lack of power to stop them in the two cases. One *is* a citizen of one of them, and has a connexion with its actions (even if only through taxes that cannot be withheld)— that one does not have with the other's. This makes it possible to be ashamed of

---

[40] Bill Manhire, 'Blood in the Blood', *NZ Listener*, 29 Sept. 1979, 80.
[41] Allen Curnow, 1972 note to *Trees, Effigies, Moving Objects*, in *Selected Poems*, 241. The equivalent note in *Early Days Yet* appears to have been shortened for this edition.

one's country, and to feel a victim of moral bad luck that one was an American in the 1960s.[42]

Bishop's 'A View of the Capitol from the Library of Congress' was written at a time when composing a poem critical of the military could well have been taken for an 'unAmerican activity'.[43] Its discretion is characteristic of the poet, but also understandable given the situation. Curnow's 'A Framed Photograph' was shaped in less pressing circumstances, and the calibrating of its power, its sarcasm, in the context of its writer's indignant powerlessness is, as a result, not quite so understatedly fine.

IV

Curnow has let it be known that the murderous kidnap and shooting of Aldo Moro did not provide him with the spur for *An Incorrigible Music*, rather, it coincided with his working on the sequence and insisted that its example ramify the theme.[44] The dust jacket to the 1979 first edition notes that 'the greater part was written and arranged as a sequence during a period of intense activity in 1977 and the New Zealand summer of 1977–78, when the terrible events which are the subject for its completion had yet to occur'. To this, Curnow's own note adds that the character of *An Incorrigible Music*

was decided, and most of the poems written, some months earlier than the kidnapping of Aldo Moro in the Via Fani, Rome, with the death of his five guards, on 16 March 1978. It was impossible to live in Italy from early April through June, reading the newspapers, catching the mood from chance remarks or no remarks at all, and not to be affected.[45]

Moro, a leading Christian Democrat and five times Prime Minister, had been in negotiations to bring about a compromise by which his party, the DC, and the Communists, the PCI, who had gained 34.4 per cent of the votes in the 20 June 1976 elections, could form a coalition government:

[42] Thomas Nagel, *Mortal Questions* (Cambridge: Cambridge University Press, 1979), 34.

[43] Bishop held the post of consultant at the Library of Congress during the year 1949–50, during which time Curnow recorded some poems for her. William Carlos Williams, appointed to the same position in 1952, did not serve as a result of false accusations of his being a 'communist' (see Bishop, *Selected Letters*, 298, 300 n).

[44] For a succinct account of the Moro assassination see Paul Ginsborg, *A History of Contemporary Italy: Politics and Society 1943–1988* (Harmondsworth: Penguin, 1990), 383–7.

[45] Allen Curnow, *An Incorrigible Music: A Sequence of Poems* (Auckland: Auckland University Press, 1979), front dust-jacket flap and p. 6.

> Two hours on his feet that day,
>   talking the Catholics round
> to live with the Communists' power
>   in the parliament of the land   (p. 122)

The strategy may have held little appeal to either political side. During what was left of Moro's life in captivity Italians were not surprised that the police proved unable to find him. Curnow's poem shows itself inflected by such 'chance remarks' when it mentions that the entire forces of the state were unable to discover where Moro was being held: 'in the Prison of the People | which 30,000 police, etc., could never locate' (p. 125). Moro's letters to his wife and political allies produced no compromises or attempts to negotiate him free. It was claimed that the letters were inauthentic because produced under duress. Once kidnapped, he appeared to have been consigned to oblivion by all sides:

> Silence in Jesus Square, his Demo-Christians
> denied him by protocol, *il vero Moro è morto
> il 16 Marzo, ultimo suo giorno di libertà.*
>
> Consenting silence in the house of the Left,
> Christ's communist other woman, three in a bed
> with Rome, last word of his long clever speeches,
> *grosso orchestratore.*   (p. 125)

The reference to '*il vero Moro*' is drawn from the disowning of Moro's letters by his party's and some Church leaders, who insisted that they had not been written by 'the real Moro'.[46] Curnow's poem suggests that the Communists went along with the DC decision to deny their leader, and he uses the analogy with Peter denying Christ to give an ethical slant to his account.[47] This decision, with its probable death sentence, is protested against in the snatch of a Moro letter to the DC party secretary which the poem translates as follows: 'I do not accept | the unjust, ungrateful judgment of the party' and 'I request that at my funeral, nobody | representing the State, nor men of the Party, | take part' (p. 128). In his account of events Paul Ginsborg concludes that the Communists, whom he

---

[46] In 'Non è lui' (Franco Fortini, *Insistenze: Cinquanta scritti 1976–1984* (Milan: Garzanti, 1985)) the Italian poet and critic denounces this strategy and gives an account of why Moro's letters may have seemed unlike him, an account which also invokes the parallel between Moro and Christ (p. 202). The article is mistakenly dated 'April 1977'. See also Leonardo Sciascia, *L'affaire Moro* (Palermo: Sellerio, 1978).

[47] For a different version of the parties' attitudes to negotiating with terrorists see Ginsborg, *Contemporary Italy*, 385.

describes as having first insisted on standing firmly against the Red Brigades, took the best line: 'The crisis of Italian terrorism, as is generally recognized, dates from the death of Moro. With hindsight, it would thus seem correct to argue that those who advocated intransigence were in the right.'[48] 'Moro Assassinato' is nearer to the events than this, and has (unlike 'A Framed Photograph') barely any political hindsight. It presents a more local understanding not entirely born out by Ginsborg's researches.

The sequence has its moments of Swiftian 'savage indignation', as if responding to Yeats's challenge: 'Imitate him if you dare, | World-besotted traveller',[49] and devotes many more lines to the kidnappers and life in the Prison of the People than to the complicity of the Christian Democrats. The second poem, 'An Urban Guerrilla', does not employ indirection in its treatment of the sex and violence theme:

> it was cleaning your gun ten times
> a day, taking time
> washing your cock, no love
> lost, aimlessly fondling
> the things that think faster than fingers,
> trigger friggers, gunsuckers.   (p. 121)

Curnow's concern is with these events as exemplifications of the species' compulsion to butcher sacrificial victims on the grounds of belief, or with a general human collusion in such killing. Moro's murder on 9 May 1978 is represented at close range: 'the Beretta 7.65s | had to hit the left hunch-breasts | eleven times, the grey head | whiplashed, nodding to the shots' (p. 129). The head's imagined movements are then made to make eleven affirmative gestures, like a Moro agreeing to his death, his sacrifice for the continuance of the Republic, or a consummation of his political career. Moro is thus represented as if he were repeating the agony in the garden, when Jesus

> was withdrawn from them about a stone's cast, and kneeled down, and prayed,
> Saying, Father, if you be willing, remove this cup from me: nevertheless not my
> will, but thine, be done.   (Luke 22: 41–2)

Yet the '*yes yes yes yes* | *yes yes yes* | *yes yes yes yes*' (p. 129) is a gross travesty of Jesus's sacrificial acceptance of the divine will, and it is this perspective of

---

[48] Ibid.

[49] W. B. Yeats, 'Swift's Epitaph', in *The Collected Poems*, 2nd edn., ed. R. J. Finneran (Basingstoke: Macmillan, 1991), 246.

travesty which opens up the poem's distance from the Christian Demo-
crats, the Communists, and the Church—all of whom were, reluctantly
at best, ready to sacrifice Moro.[50] A last letter to the politician's wife,
Noretta, which is rendered in excerpt by Curnow, makes it clear enough
that Moro is not embracing his fate as a martyr for the Italian state: 'no
time to think | how incredible it is, this punishment | for my mildness
and moderation' (p. 127). In 'Bring Your Own Victim' Curnow distinguishes between Isaac, for whom Abraham could substitute a ram, and
the fact that 'Caiaphas and Pilate found | no proxy for Jesus' (p. 115).
However, as the poet also knows, the New Testament sacrifice of son by
father is transformed by Jesus' acceptance, and it is the absence of anything resembling it which makes talk of Moro's sacrifice appear both
opportunistic and callous.

In the next section Curnow reinscribes his internal viewpoint: 'a guest,
in a stricken house, | eavesdropper, easy tourist.' (p. 130). Nagel's moral
luck distinction could again apply. The hosts are suffering from the moral
bad luck of being Italians during the 1970s. The guest poet dramatizes a
foreign situation, one that happens, as if by a ghastly coincidence, to
resemble the theme of his new sequence of poems. Though indignant at
the nihilistic violence of the extreme left during the *anni di piombo*, 'Moro
Assassinato' takes no political sides, alluding to the complicity in Moro's
death of left and right, 'three in a bed | with Rome' (p. 125). Giles Foden
believes that 'it is certainly Pound who appears to be the most enduring
influence on Curnow',[51] and the quoting of politically significant letters
in poems was first tried in the 'post-bag' section of his Canto IX. Yet
Pound's attempts at literary involvement with Italian history came to grief
because the American poet felt wishfully and yet hatefully compelled to
defend the politics of an Italy he barely understood. In his poetry Pound
neither visualizes the reality of bloody violence with Curnow's horrified
clarity nor deploys the politically detached viewpoint of, for example,
'Moro Assassinato' and 'In the Duomo'. Even when presenting events
from the early Renaissance, as in the Malatesta Cantos, Pound paints over
the violence with a literary varnish ('One year floods rose | One year they

---

[50] This distinction, between 'being sacrificed by others' and 'offering yourself as a sacrifice for
others', is not raised in the two essays on Curnow's poetry and sacrifice I have looked at: Edward
Burman, 'The Culminating Sacrifice: An Interpretation of Allen Curnow's "Moro
Assassinato"', *Landfall*, 153, 39/1 (Mar. 1985); Alex Calder, 'Sacrifice and Signification in the
Poetry of Allen Curnow', in Mark Williams and Michele Leggott (eds.), *Opening the Book: New
Essays on New Zealand Writing* (Auckland: Auckland University Press, 1995).

[51] Foden, 'Seriously Substantial', 978.

fought in the snows'). He also has an interpretative axe to grind: 'So they burnt our brother in effigy . . . I. N. R. I. Sigismund'.[52]

The wartime Canto LXXIII casually drops the fact that the girl in the Romagna, who sacrifices herself by leading some Canadian soldiers into a minefield, has previously been raped by some of their compatriots. Thanks to her heroic fascist exploit, as the poem sees it, she kills twenty men—a revenge for sexual violence which is double the customary reprisal rate against civilians during 1943–45. Her action also frees some German prisoners, in the interests of ultimate Axis victory. This ghastly passage is attributed to the spirit of Cavalcanti, but it is an antique ghost who is not unfamiliar with the broadcasting of crude propaganda:

> Tozza un po' ma non troppo
>> raggiunse lo scopo.
>>> Che splendore!
> All'inferno 'l nemico,
>> furon venti morti,
> Morta la ragazza
>> fra quella canaglia,
> Salvi i prigionieri.[53]

[A bit plump but not too much | she gained her end. | What splendour! | The enemy to hell, | there were twenty dead, | the girl dead | amongst those scum, | the prisoners saved.]

Foden commented that such 'typographical adventures' are 'classic modernist stances that poets less brave than Curnow have now abandoned' and Davie objected that this 'is a left-handed compliment: "less brave" may mean "not so dumb"'.[54] Yet both remarks fail to register that the crisis of such modernist poetry occurred in its unfounded assumption of a special access to transhistorical understanding. Curnow, however much he adapts Poundian techniques to his purposes, avoids grounding a claim to significance for his poems on tendentious beliefs about the true understanding of a foreign history or politics.

In his review of *An Incorrigible Music* Manhire notes that Curnow describes himself (somewhere in Naples, reading the newspaper headline that gives the poem its title) as 'a guest, in a stricken house, | eavesdropper, easy tourist'. He further observes that this 'may have been how he felt at that time, as a New Zealander in Italy, but it is not how one senses his

[52] Pound, *The Cantos*, 34, 54–6.
[53] Ibid. 813.
[54] Davie, 'Postmodernism and Allen Curnow', 32–3.

presence in the poems'.[55] Edward Burman is more overtly critical of '9 May 1978', the section in which these lines occur. 'It clearly represents an important moment in Curnow's experience of Moro's kidnapping and murder,' he notes, 'but again demonstrates how the poetic transformation of vague or imagined facts is on the whole more satisfactory than simple statements of fact.'[56] This poem, in concert with the opening section, is essential in locating the sequence's viewpoint, the historical presence of the poet-figure in the poem. What Manhire detects and Burman reinforces is that the poetic authority of the writing does not fit the limiting embarrassment of the poet as tourist voyeur. No, it doesn't; but it is because the poem contains the latter that the cold power of the former is located as a perspectivally restricted response, and not as an especially true or privileged presentation of how it was. What could be felt as a shamelessly dramatic appropriation of such 'vague or imagined facts' by the composing poet is avoided through this acknowledgement of the experiencing self's happening to have been there at the time. The telling details are the result of, and are focused by, a representative subjectivity.

Earlier in his essay Burman had commented that '"Moro Assassinato" is not a New Zealand poem, and neither is it an Italian poem'; he then notes that 'it is precisely in superseding these artificial limitations . . . that Curnow has made his masterpiece'.[57] 'Moro Assassinato' is a sequence written by a professional poet in his late sixties. Its style is that of the well-known Allen Curnow. The poet indicates his New Zealand context in the first part, and his being in Italy during the events narrated in the eighth. Neither 'a New Zealand poem' nor 'an Italian poem' are 'artificial limitations': the latter is a neutral, descriptive category, the former a self-conscious cultural notion. 'Moro Assassinato' is a poem largely in English by a New Zealander. That he was so immediately able to render these grim events as a 'culminating' example of his book's themes suggests a detachment from the tangled political implications of the events in Italian and European Cold War history which no Italian, and probably no European, could have managed. After all, it is true only at a certain level of generality, or with a very deep perspective, that

> All the seas are one sea,
> the blood one blood
> and the hands one hand.   (p. 119)[58]

---

[55] Manhire, 'Blood in the Blood', 81.   [56] Burman, 'Culminating Sacrifice', 34.
[57] Ibid. 22.
[58] These lines echo the much earlier traveller poem, 'When the Hulk of the World' in which

Smither has observed that 'The greatest gift in New Zealand poetry remains the 12,000 miles',[59] not least in that it provides a sometimes disorientating but almost immediate imaginative distance. Manhire's need to detach the apologetic tourist note from the poem's hardness of vision, or Burman's to separate the sequence from the idea of 'a New Zealand poem' both testify to the desire to claim Curnow's work as not merely a good local product by a 'World-besotted traveller'. They would see it as a piece of art on a level with works written in English anywhere. Curnow has achieved this by writing a sequence that would have been different if written by anyone else. Not by superseding artificial limitations, he does this by operating at full stretch within the limits of his historical and cultural situation.

In the poem's final section Curnow collocates the commemoration of Aldo Moro's death with a customary Italian way of announcing deaths in the family: having small black-edged posters printed with the name of the dead person, which are then pasted to walls. Attilio Bertolucci refers to such posters in his native town of Parma:

Mai

come ora la morte appare amara
a chi ne legge gli avvisi
sui muri intiepiditi dal volgere
calmo ma inevitabile delle ore
verso un meriggio ardente e la sosta
del pasto che il vino fa fervida e tanto più loquace
se era, il nome abbrunato, familiare.[60]

[Never | so much as now does death seem bitter | to whoever reads the posters | on walls warmed by the calm | but inevitable turning of the hours | towards a burning afternoon and the pause | of a meal made fervid, more talkative | by wine if the darkened name was familiar.]

Bertolucci's poem makes its point by alluding to a common sight that registers especially at this particular moment of an ordinary day. Curnow's describes as foreign a custom with which Bertolucci assumes familiarity.

'Seas will be seas, the same; | Thick as our blood may flood' (p. 193). The *Early Days Yet* text of 'Moro Assassinato' has line 2 as 'The blood one blood'; the capital 'T' is probably a proof-reading slip.

[59] Smither, 'New Zealand', 31.

[60] 'Un'esortazione ai poeti della mia città' (Attilio Bertolucci, *Viaggio d'inverno* (Milan: Garzanti, 1984), 44).

This implies a perspective formed by an expectation of the readers' cultural knowledge:

> The poor publish their grief
> on doors and doorways,
>
> the black bar printed above
> and below the name of the dead   (p. 130)

A few lines later he describes a very old grandmother, a memento mori in a 'dark doorway', sitting underneath the poster **'Per Aldo Moro'**: 'Dreamlessly nonna nods | into her ninetieth year, | where she sits, catching the sun' (pp. 130–1). Curnow's line ending, 'nods | into', momentarily pictures the ancient woman seeming to give an affirmative gesture in the dark mouth of death (the doorway). It is an apparent 'yes' that recalls, and underlines, the enforced affirmation of Moro's 'grey head | . . . nodding to the shots' (p. 129).

Burman fairly objects to Rob Jackaman's description of the grandma as 'a mysterious and rather sinister figure—an ancient crone', sensing rather a 'simplicity and tenderness'.[61] Is he right, though, to praise the passage for showing 'exemplary use of local colour'?[62] Would he use that tell-tale phrase to describe a New Zealand detail like 'the old man' who 'fumbles | at his fob' (p. 27) from the close of 'An Evening Light'? While 'local colour' is a phrase that catches the tourist using the unfamiliar to add spice to a life of routine, 'Moro Assassinato' is the work, rather, of a traveller. The poem acknowledges that people who travel may have to play the tourist now and then, if only to please their hosts. Moreover, significant detail is not colouring for the outline on a ground in poems, not exploited as the means to some end. The detail forms the ground and the end or it is not significant in itself and for the poem. The echo of Moro's 'nodding' with nonna's 'nods' demonstrates that the imagination which found poetic meaning in the events of the politician's kidnapping and death is far from that of someone who makes 'use of' the dozing grandma for 'local colour'.

V

Though Curnow, like Blake before him, has done his share of mental travelling, his equivocal elegy for Wallace Stevens keeps its distance from that stay-at-home cosmopolitan. The American poet has finally had to go

---

[61] Burman, 'Culminating Sacrifice', 34.   [62] Ibid.

abroad. Not on what the 'Elegy on my Father' calls 'No journey' (p. 187),
he has taken off for the beyond:

> And what comparisons with your style when crossing
> Composedly the blue thresholds to sit down
> Oceans away (because all airs bore alike
> And Indian-wise an alien offshore fragrance)—
> Or mulch with moist real hands the seedy words
> To bear in season as fresh-cut coxcomb blooms
> As anyone else's green and god-sown country
> Whose natives, planting and watering botany books,
> Had their disappointments?

Curnow teases the reduction of all foreignness to the imagined exotic in
Stevens, a climate fed by his correspondence, his books, and pictures.[63]
The New Zealand poet asks him whether the dead can be 'less alien | Or
more at home . . .?'(p. 201). If coming to terms with poets from other
countries is a form of mental travelling, it also requires such a keeping of
distances. Discussing Stevens with MacDonald P. Jackson, Curnow
found himself touching on poetic contamination: 'the philosophy in
Stevens's writing . . . may have affected me in recent work, without fear of
what I call being contaminated by his style. It's contamination by style
that one dreads most.'[64] In a sense Stevens's travels in imagination are
close to what any poet inspired by travel is likely to be doing: the poems
set elsewhere are frequently not written in the overseas place, but back
home. The poetic composition of travel poems is often, in this respect as
much as Stevens's, an imaginative journey.

Smithers's reference to 'literals or littorals' is a collaged realigning of 'A
Passion for Travel' and 'Do Not Touch the Exhibits'. In Curnow's
Rapallo poem the 'littorals' are not his Pacific beaches; they are 'the native
littoral | cultivations' beside 'the Ligurian blue, too much of it'(p. 44). The
former poem unpacks its title by picturing a proof-reader at work:

> According to copy
> the word is exotic. He cancels
> the literal r and writes an x.   (p. 80)

[63] For an account of how much Stevens relied on the overseas experience of others for his
poetry see Alan Filreis, *Wallace Stevens and the Actual World* (Princeton, NJ: Princeton University
Press, 1991).

[64] 'Conversation with Allen Curnow', in *Look Back Harder*, 259. For a trenchant distancing
from an overseas, geography-inflected poetics, see 'Olson as Oracle: "Projective Verse" Thirty
Years On', in *Look Back Harder*, 305–18.

It uses this association of words through a typesetter's slip to explore the attraction of being transposed, and of finding transposed phenomena, whether it be 'at Palermo the palm lily *ti australis*' or 'The tall German | blonde' with 'pudenda awash' (p. 81). Composed on a broader canvas, 'Organo ad Libitum' is a musical-erotic fantasia in which memories of travel are swept up into the poem's meditative process. For part II finds him disappointed in France:

> Paris having the rottenest
> summer for years the crowds
> packed in out of the rain to the
> Cinéma Paramount leaving
> Montparnasse to the web-footed tourists   (p. 91)

The ninth has him in Italy: 'Tiziano's | rapt airborne virgin in the Frari | was an assumption removed *per* | *restauro* in '74'. The section collages this art-historical let-down in Venice with a travel anecdote about attitudes to disappointment from the other end of the country: 'Domenico's | mother said and he quoted "life | is bitter we must sweeten the coffee"'. (p. 96). Curnow's note reports that: 'One day we (my wife and I) drove with him [Domenico Parrani] along the north Sicilian coast from Capo Skino to Capo d'Orlando, where it amazed him that we took our *espressi* without the usual sugar' (p. 246). These lines appreciate a local custom, cherish a folk wisdom, and do so by including the fact of their different (and, in the context, strange) habits. For travellers and host the enlarging of perspective is mutual.

The speed of Curnow's mental travelling in these late works gives a verve and appetite for life to overseas poems set in more or less one place. 'Do Not Touch the Exhibits', for example, has him experiencing the series of tunnels through cliffs along the Ligurian coastline, with intermittent beaches, bays, and villages:

> A gulp of sea air, the train
> bites off a beach, re-enters the rock.
> A window, a blind cathode, greyly reflects,
> Plato sits opposite, his nose in a map.

Nine lines later 'Daylight chips in again, with cypresses, | olives, loquat' (p. 44). This oscillation of light and dark starts the thought of Plato's cave, followed by reflections on inside and out of the carriage, and the mind. These in turn prompt a sense of experience's fleeting possession, and thoughts on whether indeed it is possessed. Curnow's enclosure in the carriage and the family motto '*è pericoloso sporgersi*' (it is dangerous to lean out), suggest that 'Do Not Touch the Exhibits' is also grazed by thoughts of love and death. There is a 'brace of NATO frigates' with their 'unmuzzled guns, "optional extras"' and Botticelli's 'Venus . . . paroled from the Uffizi'. The reproduction of the well-known painting is also both inside and out, being 'screwed | to the wall under the baggage rack' and 'space reserved in the mind' (pp. 44–5). It is reproduced on the wall as a visual experience, in the mind as a memory, and in the poem as words— which is why the punning 'paroled' seems such a *mot juste*. Just as the reproduction is behind glass, so is (depending on which side you are on) the Ligurian scene through which the train passes, or the poet inside the carriage. Many poems have been inspired by this coastline,[65] yet, despite the noise, 'Do Not Touch the Exhibits' adds its note to the chorus, being amusedly alive to the passing scene, drawing the reader towards the multiplicity in experienced life, while its title reminds us that, like the works in the Uffizi, 'tactile values' are for the imagination and we must keep our hands to ourselves.

Manhire suggested of *An Incorrigible Music* that 'these poems suffer from what I think has always been Curnow's most serious limitation as a poet: a reluctance to risk lines that might sound as if they were naively forged or uttered'.[66] Curnow's lines feel composedly written, not simply said. A cool calculation, a post-meditation, is purposefully shaping their emotional heat. Yet it is characteristic of important writers that their real limits are inextricably interwoven with their sources of greatest power. This is because their work is the expression of an entire cultural situation, a personal and a communal historical moment, or series of such moments, and, as such, articulates the best that can be done with what is available at the time. Curnow's 'reluctance to risk', as Manhire puts it, and the air of calculation are a part of his effort to achieve a language for his surroundings not helplessly indebted to the vocabularies of someone or somewhere else. They are likewise inflected with English's being *pakeha* in New Zealand, or a more recent arrival than the Maori languages.

In his review Foden felt that while 'Putting words in inverted commas . . . can sometimes make for a powerful line of poetry . . . one begins to feel that even a collection with the scope of this one cannot usefully sustain

---

[65] The final chapter in Charles Tomlinson, *Some Americans: A Personal Record* (Berkeley and Los Angeles, Calif.: University of California Press, 1981) refers to numerous poets who have found inspiration in Liguria.

[66] Manhire, 'Blood in the Blood', 80–1.

the practice more than a few times.' He derives Curnow's use of the technique from Pound's *Mauberley*, and takes it to be a means for producing 'an ironical charge', reviving 'an out-moded meaning' or breathing '"new life" into a debased usage'.[67] While Curnow can deploy these devices (as in the frigates with their 'optional extras'), the frequency and variety of occasions in which they occur, and other similar emphases too, suggests not so much a Poundian control of nuance for purposes of linguistic renewal or cultural commentary, as the indication of a verbal situation. For Curnow inverted commas tease local significances from the words' not fitting the world. This non-fit is not caused by a dissociation of sensibility, by the decline of the West, or by some other Jeremiad explain-all. It is an ordinary, natural condition of human language, a condition that came about partly through innumerable migrations of populations and which, in the last quarter of the twentieth century, was intensified and underlined by rapid global travel and communication. Nor is this separation incompatible with the daily workings of a natural language, with all its lived attachments and associations, spoken, thanks to whatever entanglements of history, in a particular place.

Back to back in the *Selected Poems 1940–1989*, 'A Time of Day' remembers Curnow's first flight and 'Narita' imagines a last. The poet and his wife briefly passed through Japan on their return from Cambridge in 1985:

Narita was Tokyo's very new airport, 'small green hills with ginkgo trees': only a week before we flew out, a JAL Boeing 747 on an internal flight crashed, killing 500; only a few weeks earlier, as many died when another 747 went down west of Ireland; Narita was a memento mori for anybody presenting a boarding pass that week & Changi (Singapore's) is the most hateful big airport I can think of—did you ever have to read Vathek? In those places I think of the Halls of Eblis.[68]

There is hubris in transit lounges, as 'What Was That?' baldly reminds us: 'the Boeing crashed' (p. 140). In the fifth part of 'Organo ad Libitum' the memento mori of air travel recurs when Curnow recalls the 'antarctic volcano' of 'Mt Erebus, on which an Air New Zealand DC 10 crashed on a sightseeing flight, killing nearly 300 passengers and crew' (p. 246). The pilot 'sits with his | back to you "busier than God" his | instrument flashes the crash is | programmed' (p. 93). Later still, in 'Narita', a jumbo

---

[67] Foden, 'Seriously Substantial', 978. There is an acute account of Pound's use of the strategy in Geoffrey Hill's 'Our Word Is Our Bond', in *The Lords of Limit: Essays on Literature and Ideas* (London: André Deutsch, 1984),141–3.

[68] Allen Curnow, unpublished letter to Peter Robinson, 28 May 1996.

jet's 'tail section | ruptures' and 'the sky inhales heavily' sucking the passengers and crew into the heavens:

> all four hundred, some gifted or beautiful
> or with greedy heirs, have to die now,
> only to make sure of you
>
> this instant sooner or later than you think.
> The prettiest accessories, like
> silk scarf, matching lipstick, badge
>
> of rank are brightness fallen from the air   (p. 32)

Remembering James Dickey's poem 'Falling', about a stewardess who fell through an emergency exit,[69] and a hint from Auden's 'Consider this and in our time' ('It is later than you think'[70]), 'Narita' may also remember and reverse the close to Eugenio Montale's 'Dora Markus', part I, in which 'forse | ti salva un amuleto che tu tieni | vicino alla matita delle labbra' (perhaps | an amulet saves you which you keep | near to your lipstick). The woman of Montale's poem is entrusted to life by means of these personal possessions ('e così esisti!'[71] (and thus you exist!)). In Curnow's the stewardess's accessories are signs of her dying. 'Narita' certainly recalls Thomas Nashe's 'Brightness falls from the air', in the one lyric for which he is usually remembered ('Adieu, farewell earth's bliss . . .'). This phrase may be the result of a misprint. In a stanza where 'Beauty is but a flower, | Which wrinkles will devour', a conjectural 'Brightness falls from the hair' would make plainer sense.[72] Curnow's touch is to reuse the perhaps misprinted line in a grimly apt situation where it fits better than in its original context. To recall Smither's remark, he does this 'with complete unaffectedness and no sense of incongruity'. No insinuation is being made about cultural decline or traditions of value, as in poets who patented the device of overt citation early in his century. The technique has taken its place as part of an established repertoire, and Nashe's phrase is simply plucked from the air, an air to which Allen Curnow's poems now themselves belong.

---

[69] James Dickey, *Poems 1957–1967* (New York: Collier, 1967), 49–55.

[70] Auden, *The English Auden*, 47.

[71] Eugenio Montale, *Le occasioni*, ed. D. Isella (Turin: Einaudi, 1996), 58–9.

[72] The song appears in *Summer's Last Will and Testament*, in Thomas Nashe, *The Unfortunate Traveller and Other Works*, ed. J. B. Steane (Harmondsworth: Penguin, 1972), 195. The misprint conjecture was first advanced by R. B. McKerrow in his 1958 edition of Nashe's works.

CHAPTER 9

Charles Tomlinson in the
Golfo dei Poeti

I

Charles Tomlinson first went to Italy in the autumn of 1951. He had gone
there as a secretary to Percy Lubbock, the author of *The Craft of Fiction*.
Lubbock lived in a villa between Lerici and Fiascherino. It is a literary
coastline, with many poetic associations. Across the bay from Lerici, at
Portovenere, is Byron's Grotto. Shelley lived in a villa at San Terenzo, up
the coast towards La Spezia. D. H. Lawrence was staying in Fiascherino
in 1914, reading *I Poeti Futuristi* (1912).[1] Travel northward up the Ligurian
coast and there is Monterosso, where you can walk along the Lungomare
Eugenio Montale, and further up towards Genoa is Rapallo, where Yeats
and Pound had homes. Go southward down the coast to Bocca di Magra.
There, Vittorio Sereni's family rented a holiday house. Across the river, at
Fiumaretta, Franco Fortini spent his summers. Inland is Sarzana, the
town where Guido Cavalcanti was exiled from Florence, where he was
thought to have written the *ballata* whose opening, 'Perch' i' no spero di
tornar giammai',[2] was rendered into English as 'Because I do not hope to
turn again'.[3]

Tomlinson had not been at Lubbock's villa *Gli scafari*[4] for a month
when he was sacked because of his accent. The incident with its explanation is given in the memoir *Some Americans*. Percy Lubbock

had been legislating on the pronunciation of the English *a* as in *past* and *castle*,
insisting that it should be long also in *ants*. Clearly he had not revisited the island

---

[1] See D. H. Lawrence, *The Complete Poems*, ed. V. de Sola Pinto and W. Roberts (Harmondsworth: Penguin, 1977), 9.
[2] Guido Cavalcanti, *Rime*, ed. G. Cattaneo (Turin: Einaudi, 1967), 61.
[3] T. S. Eliot, *Collected Poems 1909–1962* (London: Faber & Faber, 1963), 95.
[4] See Charles Tomlinson, *Collected Poems* (Oxford: Oxford University Press, 1985), 26–7, and,
for his 'Fiascherino', 12–13. Page numbers in parentheses refer to this volume.

for a long time, for even the English aristocracy would hesitate to lengthen the *a* of *ants*. But what he was evidently indicating—as far, that is, as good manners permitted—was that our Midland *a*'s sounded displeasing to him. But what of that? One could hardly feel wounded by a man who imagined *ants* should be pronounced *aunts*. Two weeks later I received my dismissal. It was most mysterious.

Lubbock had returned to Florence with Lady Dick-Lauder. The letter came from his step daughter, Iris Origo: he no longer wanted a secretary. Could one be dismissed for an accent? It hardly seemed plausible, but we could imagine no other cause for offence.[5]

Tomlinson, however, may have received a lasting mark from this episode, and at an early stage in his life as an artist. He was twenty-four, having been born at Stoke-on-Trent in 1927. The English class system is complex, involving infinitesimal degrees of definition by contrast and comparison. In an interview honouring his sixtieth year the poet answered the question 'Did you feel your education drew you away from your home background?' with these remarks:

My parents believed in education and so what successes I had were a pleasure to them. We must have been a more sensible lot in Stoke than that lot up in Leeds, to judge from the way the poet Tony Harrison writes. We were virtually all working-class children—I hardly knew what the middle classes were till I got to Cambridge—and no teacher ever tried, as in Harrison's case, to change my accent—and this was a grammar school, mind you, nothing experimental about it. Also, you'd never have used a term like 'working class' to describe yourself. You might have spoken of working people or ordinary people. Working class is one of those labels dear to the theoretical and it covers up immense differences. I notice that Harrison's father had a telephone and used to spit in the fire. My father never rose to the first and he'd never have descended to the second.[6]

It is one thing to be at ease with your origins when you are a sixty-year-old who has made his literary mark, another when a struggling and winded twenty-four. A wound delivered by Lubbock's dismissal may have been the more painful because of the family pride in Tomlinson's account of his father's possessions and habits. The poet is saying that he comes from good, respectable people. The wounding memory lasted long enough

    [5] Charles Tomlinson, *Some Americans: A Personal Record* (Berkeley and Los Angeles, Calif.: University of California Press, 1981), 98.

    [6] 'Charles Tomlinson at Sixty: In Conversation with Richard Swigg', in *PN Review*, 59, 14/3 (1987), 58. However, in 'The Unison: A Retrospect', from *Renga: A Chain of Poems by Octavio Paz, Jacques Roubaud, Edoardo Sanguinetti, and Charles Tomlinson* (Harmondsworth: Penguin, 1979), 37, Tomlinson observes of himself that 'one belonged, oneself, to a country where, at school, children are taught, in their writings (or were up to a generation ago), "Never say *I*" '

to show in a poem called 'Class', about the Midland pronunciation of the first letter of the alphabet, first collected in *The Way In* (1974). In 'Class' Tomlinson says that he tried to pronounce the *ah* of proper English, but couldn't, and the short, hard, regional *a* 'too visibly shredded his [Lubbock's] fineness' (p. 249). The poem is more openly dismissive of his one-time employer than the memoir, though the latter's image of the dead Lubbock being mummified for transportation back to England has a touch of revenge about it.[7] Tomlinson

> always thought him an ass
> which he pronounced arse.   (p. 249)

With the exception of one sentence, 'Class' is written in the first person. Referring to the title of Lubbock's *The Craft of Fiction* with its tricky-to-pronounce second word, Tomlinson introduces a sense of 'class' meaning 'quality'. This sense is also socially complex and ambiguous, given its application to people or to works of art, or the assumption that the one meaning might or should inform the other. He writes: 'that title was full of class' and goes on:

> You had only to open your mouth on it
> to show where you were born
> and where you belonged.   (pp. 248–9)

Tomlinson's lineation divides the statements linked by 'and' to suggest that you don't necessarily and permanently belong where you happened to be born. If you don't remain there, but retain some of your native characteristics—your accent, for example—then your identity may be partially defined by ambiguous relations between places, class positions, and the sounds of your own voices. Many English people's speech is unstable in this way.

These changes of place, these fluctuating pronunciations, are cases of translation. Donald Davie's poem 'Housekeeping' has a fine stanza in which the verb appears:

> From homestead Autumns in the vale of Chard
> Translated in youth past any hope of returning,
> She toiled, my father a baby, through the hard
> Fellside winters, to Barnsley, soused in the Dearne.[8]

Davie is doing some translating himself here: 'Autumns', with its capital

---

[7] Tomlinson, *Some Americans*, 125.
[8] Donald Davie, *Collected Poems 1950–1970* (London: Routledge & Kegan Paul, 1972), 136.

letter, and 'winters' without indicates that the poet's grandmother has moved between literary eras as well as English landscapes. She has been translated from a golden rural past into the nineteenth-century industrial north. When the poet writes 'She toiled', deferring the indirect object 'to Barnsley' for a line and a half, he effects such a translation: the simple past 'toiled' means 'worked' and begins life in the poem as a conventional Augustan loco-descriptive term used without an object to describe field labourers. When it gains the indirect object and northern place name it means 'walked with effort', and, reinforced by the mention of a baby, pictures a vagrant displaced mother as from one of Wordsworth's encounter poems. Davie's grandmother is 'Translated in youth' from one literary period into another, from one age to another. She is defined in the poem by where she has come from and where she has got to at one and the same time. The participle 'Translated', meaning 'moved from one place to another', has an Augustan tang about its etymological literalness.

Tomlinson, in the first of his Clark Lectures, discusses Dryden's use of 'translated' as a synonym for 'metamorphosed' in his version of Ovid's *Metamorphosis*, book XV. Tomlinson is commenting on how 'All Things are alter'd' and 'Translated grow, have Sence, or can Discourse':

The audacity, the *sprezzatura*, with which Dryden throws in the word 'Translated' here—he who *translated* Chaucer into modern English and who said he expected someone to do the same for him one day—wittily incorporates the notion of literary translation into the conception of an ongoing world empowered by the metamorphoses of its own elements[9]

Tomlinson cites another instance of the word's use in the Ceyx and Alcyone story: 'The Gods their Shapes to Winter-Birds translate'.[10] In the second lecture he extends his ideas of metamorphosis to include 'a sense of the provisional nature of personality',[11] and translation too can concern itself with the flowing natures of selves. It can focus on what goes and what stays, as Eliot observed in 'The Dry Salvages': 'People change, and smile: but the agony abides.'[12] Charles Tomlinson's poetry itself explores the overlayerings in a life of changes of place, of social mobility, stylistic development, and human identity—all of which are themselves influenced by and achieved through the poet's commitment to other cultures and the activity of literary translation.

---

[9] Charles Tomlinson, *Poetry and Metamorphosis* (Cambridge: Cambridge University Press, 1983), 3.
[10] Ibid. 5.   [11] Ibid. 26.   [12] Eliot, *Collected Poems 1909–1962*, 209.

II

Relations between accent and identity involve, among many things, the use of pronouns. Imagine the three lines from 'Class' translated into the first-person singular: 'I had only to open my mouth on it to show where I was born and where I belonged.' Having these lines in the second person (and they are the only part of the poem that is) allows a general point to be made: it would be the same for anyone pronouncing *The Craft of Fiction*. The lines can also sound self-addressed, the poet using 'you' to talk about himself indeterminately. Another poem, 'Tramontana at Lerici', written in the same decade as the Lubbock incident, begins in the second person:

> Today, should you let fall a glass it would
>   Disintegrate, played off with such keenness
> Against the cold's resonance (the sounds
>   Hard, separate and distinct, dropping away
> In a diminishing cadence) that you might swear
>   This was the imitation of glass falling.   (p. 27)

This 'you', with 'should' and 'might' rendering conditional its relation to active verbs, effects a concatenation of experiences which anyone might conceivably have. The imagined experience of 'sounds | Hard, separate and distinct', which forms part of a poetic idea in development, is elaborated around the simple likelihood that if I drop a glass . . . I will swear. The poem's opening stanza places its reader in the midst of sensory events and at a remove from experiences like breaking glasses and swearing—faux pas at a dinner party given by Percy Lubbock. In the third stanza the poem introduces a perceiver to which sensations are attached:

> At evening, one is alarmed by such definition
>   In as many lost greens as one will give glances to recover,
> As many again which the landscape
>   Absorbing into the steady dusk, condenses
> From aquamarine to that slow indigo-pitch
>   Where the light and twilight abandon themselves.   (p. 27)

'At evening, one is alarmed': this sounds rather posh. The impersonal pronoun—which can be used as a first person pronoun with the intent to exclude others not hearable in 'you' when it indicates a first person—this 'one' cannot easily express warmth between people. 'Tramontana at Lerici' moves into its final stanza with a distinct drop in temperature:

And the chill grows. In this air
  Unfit for politicians and romantics
Dark hardens from blue, effacing the windows:
  A tangible block, it will be no accessory
To that which does not concern it. One is ignored
  By so much cold suspended in so much night.   (p. 27)

The 'Tramontana' is a north wind, and Tomlinson has also punningly situated his poem at sunset, *il tramonto*. In its final lines, the pronoun's social tone, the wind, and the sunset's effects are working in concert to exclude the perceiver: 'One is ignored'. Yet to think of wind and pronoun as acting concertedly would be to miss the presence of a voice saying the poem. This voice is the sign of a body's presence but also of a self's, the body defined as having identity, and of that self in the pronoun 'one' turning itself away, under the constraints of a politeness code, from the threshold of its own self. The disembodied voice is a ventriloquism of a class accent delivering a body blow to the poet.

The poem performs the combined coldnesses—the wind, the dusk, a social rejection—from which its speaker appears to suffer. Yet this performance has had its influence on how Tomlinson has been received. Michael Schmidt summed this up in his review of the *Collected Poems*: 'The case against the poems is quite simply that they are *cold*.'[13] This is to say that not only is 'one' ignored by 'so much cold', but so are reviewers and readers who have, in their turn, the poet ignored a third time around: in experience, in the composition, and in its reception. Kenneth Allott admitted to feeling put off by the fineness of 'Tramontana at Lerici' when anthologizing the poem in 1962. Understandably, though mistakenly, he wrote that 'human beings and their awkwardnesses have been squeezed out'.[14] Yet there is a world of human awkwardness in Charles Tomlinson's uneasy pronouns. When Allott added that Tomlinson was 'an aristocratic "*mutilé*" of the aesthetic war' he mistook Tomlinson's 'one' for the thing itself. Tomlinson is not an aristocrat—rather, in 'Tramontana at Lerici' he shows the consequences of damage inflicted by the feeling that one had better sound like one.

I once thought that Tomlinson's uses of 'you', 'we', and 'one', and of impersonal abstractions such as 'the eye' and 'the mind', were conscious tactics for foisting assent on readers without obliging the poet to become

---

[13] Michael Schmidt, 'Charles Tomlinson', *PN Review*, 52, 13/2 (1986), 71.
[14] For this and the following citation, see Kenneth Allott (ed.), *The Penguin Book of Contemporary Verse*, 2nd edn. (Harmondsworth: Penguin, 1962), 363.

fully embroiled in the poem's matter. That was ungenerous and untrue, because the self in his poems is not exactly the source of perceptual and moral insight that it might appear. 'Against Portraits' and 'A Self-Portrait: David', both from later collections, make such insecurity their theme. The poet prefers here 'a face half-hesitant, | face at a threshold' (p. 230). Still, his poems remain preserved, for reasons given in 'Against Extremity', from more threatening instabilities of the self. Tomlinson's pronouns are also less stable than I had granted. He acknowledges in 'Over Elizabeth Bridge . . .': 'that uncertainty | And restless counterpointing of a verse | "So wary of its I", Iván, is me' (p. 226). In 'The Scream', from his 1978 collection, the poet is dragged out of sleep by just such a piercing noise. It proves to come from a hedgehog which a badger has mortally hurt but failed to finish off. The poet, going outside with a torch and discovering it, dramatizes the altering condition of the perceiver. The poem begins 'A dream so drowned my mind,' and seems secure in the first-person singular. Yet within a dozen lines a sound meets 'the ear' and the narrative slips for a sentence into the second person. 'I struck uphill,' it continues, but as the enigma of the scream grows more intense, another shift occurs: 'A dream | Had delivered me to this, and a dream | Once more seemed to possess one's mind', and soon thoughts 'crowded together | To appal the mind with dream uncertainties' (p. 310). The more abstracted, impersonal ways of speaking tend to appear when mental confidence is under greatest threat.

III

The collection in which 'Tramontana at Lerici' appeared, *Seeing is Believing* (1960), was widely praised—praise, though, qualified by many with criticism that the book lacked a human dimension, that it had no people in it. John Rathmell, in the magazine *Prospect*, wrote:

in the face of the very considerable achievement represented by *Seeing is Believing* it would be perhaps disingenuous to ask for more than the very great deal he has in fact done; yet in the final analysis one cannot help feeling that the implied defence:

> There are portraits and still-lifes
> And the first, because 'human'
> Does not excel the second . . .

is specious.[15]

[15] John Rathmell, 'Charles Tomlinson', *Prospect* (winter 1960), 38.

Kenneth Allott confessed: 'I happen to prefer Larkin's "human" poetry, but the quality of the better poems in *Seeing is Believing* cannot be denied by any honest judge.'[16] Fifteen years after the book's appearance Tom Paulin, commenting on 'Winter Encounters', reiterated the objection:

Though Tomlinson means that there is an energising quality, a sense of true communion and encounter, behind both the people's casual conversation and the 'changing light' and 'responsive stone', the effect is one of detachment and distance—the 'intensity' seems located beyond the human, not within the people who are talking to each other.[17]

Whether in response to criticism or not, Tomlinson's next book, *A Peopled Landscape*, seemed designed as an answer to such complaints. One of its poems is just such a peopled landscape drawn from the hillsides above Lerici. 'Up at La Serra' has been described by Vittorio Sereni in a Festschrift to celebrate Tomlinson's fiftieth birthday as 'insieme una situazione poetica e un piccolo studio sociologico'[18] (at once a poetic situation and a small sociological study). This poem was composed with the aid of overlayered acts of translation. A problem to explore in it is succinctly stated by Schmidt when he says of the entire volume: 'First, Tomlinson's critics said he was cold because there were not any people in his poems. When he published *A Peopled Landscape* they were not satisfied. His people joined the rocks and stones and trees on an equal footing, as objects.'[19]

In the year that Tomlinson published *A Peopled Landscape* Oxford University Press issued his translations of the Spanish poet Antonio Machado, *Castilian Ilexes: Versions from Machado*, which he had made in collaboration with his colleague at Bristol University Henry Gifford. The word 'Versions' in their title is a signal, for even at first glance many of the poems look more like works by Tomlinson than Machado. They are written in the 'three-ply', stepped-down line that Tomlinson adapted for his purposes from William Carlos Williams's later works. One of these, a version of 'Poema de un día' (Poem of a Day), prefigures 'Up at La Serra', and is indicated as a source in Tomlinson's poem:

[16] Allott (ed.), *The Penguin Book of Contemporary Verse*, 362.
[17] Tom Paulin, *Thomas Hardy: The Poetry of Perception* (Oxford: Oxford University Press, 1975), 9.
[18] 'A Letter from Vittorio Sereni', in *PN Review*, 5, 5/1 (1977), 42.
[19] Schmidt, 'Charles Tomlinson', 71.

> This was the Day
>   which began all reckonings
>   she heard them say
>   with a woman's ears;
>   she liked
>   the music from the wireless.
>   The padre
>   pulled
>   at his unheeded angelus
>   and the Day went down behind
>   the town in the bay below   (pp. 81–2)

The capital letter for 'Day' in the two cases it occurs seems a discreet acknowledgement of a debt to 'Poem of a Day'. 'Poema de un día', subtitled 'meditationes rurales' (rural meditations), is a monologue spoken by the poet from his isolation at Baeza in 1913, where he taught French in a country school. He situates himself in this obscure province, and this mundane job, at the beginning of the poem:

> Behold me
>   here—the nightingales'
>   apprentice, master
>   of *la gaya scienza*
>   formerly:
>   I teach
>   the living tongues
>   to a damp and bleak
>   sombre and straggling
>   village that belongs
>   half to La Mancha, half
>   to Andalucia.[20]

Machado's masterpiece is a self-consciously philosophical poem. It speaks with colloquial force to Miguel de Unamuno in the year that he published *Del Sentimiento Trágico de la Vida* (1913) about the relative merits of Immanuel Kant and Henri Bergson. Tomlinson, translating with guidance from his colleague Henry Gifford, chose to render Machado's 'maestro de gay-saber' as 'master | of *la gaya scienza*'. Footnoting the reference in his book of translations, Alan S. Trueblood correctly refers the phrase to the poetic art of the Provençal troubadours. Tomlinson's rendering includes this sense, but adds a further allusion to Nietzsche's

---

[20] Charles Tomlinson, *Translations* (Oxford: Oxford University Press, 1983), 34.

Die Fröhliche Wissenschaft, whose title in the second edition of 1887 was glossed with exactly the phrase used here: 'La gaya scienza'. The spirit of Nietzsche's volume, which included samples of his own poetry, is more than likely to have influenced Machado's oddly genial, even jocular, treatment of his predicament in a town of extreme provincial obscurity. In section 78 of *The Gay Science*, for instance, Nietzsche praises an art without which 'we would be nothing but foreground, and would live entirely under the spell of that perspective which makes the nearest and most vulgar appear tremendously big and as reality itself'. In 'Poema de un día' Machado is practising exactly what Nietzsche describes as 'the art of "putting oneself on stage" before oneself'.[21]

Machado moved to Baeza from Soria in Old Castille after his wife, to whom he had only been married for a few years, died. This tragic event of his life comes into the first of three passages I want to look at with an eye on the Spanish poem:

> En estos pueblos, ¿se escucha
> el latir del tiempo? No.
> En estos pueblos se lucha
> sin tregua con el reló,
> con esa monotonía
> que mide un tiempo vacío.
> Pero ¿tu hora es la mía?
> ¿Tu tiempo, reloj, el mío?
> (Tic-tic, tic-tic . . .) Era un día
> (Tic-tic, tic-tic) que pasó,
> y lo que yo más quería
> la muerte se lo llevó.[22]

The poem asks if in places like this you can catch the Bergsonian 'durée réelle', the sense of homogeneous time. No, it says, you can only struggle with the dessication of mechanically divided clock time. Into this desolate idea of a day split into so many seconds Machado works a brief allusion to the death of his nineteen-year-old wife, Leonor, on 1 August 1912. She had been in Paris with him when he had attended Bergson's lectures in that same year. Here is Tomlinson's rendering of the lines:

---

[21] Friedrich Nietzsche, *The Gay Science*, ed. B. Williams (Cambridge: Cambridge University Press, 2001), 79. *Castilian Ilexes: Versions from Antonio Machado* (Oxford: Oxford University Press, 1963) includes an introduction by Henry Gifford. Trueblood's rendering of the poem into an American idiom can be read in Antonio Machado, *Selected Poems*, trans. Alan S. Trueblood (Cambridge, Mass.: Harvard University Press, 1982), 125–35, 286–7 nn.

[22] Antonio Machado, *Poesías completas*, 10th edn. (Madrid: Espasa-Calpe, 1984), 204–5.

> in villages like these
>> does one catch
> the pulse of time?
>> Truceless
>>> before the clock
> one, rather, fights
>> against monotony
>>> that, in these villages
> alights
>> to measure
>>> the passage of their vacancies.
> But, clock, is yours
>> this time of mine—
>>> are mine your hours?
> (Tick, tick)
>> There was a day
>>> (tick, tick) that passed
> and that which I
>> most loved
>>> death made away.[23]

The rhythms and lineations of Tomlinson's version hold a reader's
attention focused, at the price of a certain preciosity in the isolation and
placing of words: the technical self-consciousness of 'alights | to measure
| the passage . . .', in comparison with Machado's one line 'que mide un
tiempo vacío', or Tomlinson's commitment to the 'three-ply' line dis-
membering Machado's two plain lines of lament ('y lo que yo más quería
| la muerte se lo llevó'), adding a touch of melodrama or sentimentality
with the catch in the breath where the line breaks on the first-person
singular: 'and that which I | most loved | death made away'. A related
nicety, this time tonal, may be noted in the way the passage is made to shift
from impersonal questioning to Machado's own situation. Tomlinson's
use of the pronoun 'one' with third-person-singular verbs imitates this
change from 'se escucha' and 'se lucha' to 'tu hora es la mía'. Yet, again,
there seems a class tone and detachment that sits uneasily with the opening of Tomlinson's translation, or of the original: not least because the
tone is distinctly English, and its engrafting on to a Spanish location
appears askew. With the 'rather' in 'one, rather, fights | against mono-
tony', the word is sanctioned by the 'No' in Machado's text. Yet the char-

23 Tomlinson, *Translations*, 36.

acter of these turns in the meditation is different. The Spanish feels like a confrontation with a flat contradiction:

> In these villages, do you hear
> the beat of time? No.
> In these villages you struggle
> Without let-up with the clock,
> With this monotony

Tomlinson's 'one, rather, fights | against monotony' articulates a moralized preference. It resembles this clause from the long last sentence of *The Stones of Venice*, chapter 1: 'or whether, rather, we shall not behold in the brightness of her accumulated marble pages on which the sentence of her luxury was to be written'.[24] Tomlinson's tonal engrafting momentarily lifts the speaking self from his constricting situation and lets him contemplate as an alternative what appears to be a necessity.

How is this speaking self situated within and with regard to its own situation? There are passing verbal echoes of Tomlinson's translation in other poems from *A Peopled Landscape*. In 'The Picture of J. T. in a Prospect of Stone' an internal dialogue includes: 'Say, rather | it resists' (p. 74). In 'John Maydew *or* The Allotment' the figure delineated is last seen eyeing a toad which breathes 'in the assuagement | of his truce' (p. 67)—a compromise with post-war English history, fixed by Tomlinson in a word that may derive from the 'tregua' of Machado's poem. The 'dispossessed | and half-tamed Englishman' (p. 66) of 'John Maydew *or* The Allotment' returns from war to find that he must choose between 'an England, profitlessly green' and a landscape where 'slag in lavafolds rolls | beneath him' (p. 67). The first part of the poem seems to be spoken to the man in his allotment, but, immediately after remarking on a bitterness 'rooted in your silence' (p. 66), the second-person address gives out in a row of dots. The man does not reply, and the rest of the piece describes him in the third person. Within this poem's fluency there is an absence of encounter, and a suggestion of its impossibility.

These instances catch a dilemma in Tomlinson's outlook. John Maydew is caught good and proper by his situation, and this 'truce' is part of his entrapment, while the 'rather' in 'The Picture of J. T. . . . .' is mental play, conjuring possibilities with which to meditate on a glimpse of the

---

[24] John Ruskin, *Works*, ed. E. T. Cook and A. Wedderburn, Library Edition, 39 vols. (London: George Allen et al., 1903–12) 9, 59. Tomlinson acknowledged a debt to Ruskin in Peter Orr (ed.), *The Poet Speaks: Interviews with Contemporary Poets* (London: Routledge & Kegan Paul, 1966), 250 and see, for examples, *Collected Poems*, 35, 101–2.

poet's own daughter. The thinking and speaking self is situated outside the context in which the object of its meditation lives. This gain in freedom from the entrapping location, a need at the heart of Tomlinson's aesthetic project, incurs a consequent loss of purchase. The mind and the speaking self in Tomlinson's poems frequently display a disembodiment, and this is not quite what appears in the conclusion to 'Poema de un día':

> Sobre mi mesa *Los datos*
> *de la conciencia*, immediatos.
> No está mal
> este yo fundamental,
> contingente y libre, a ratos,
> creativo, original;
> este yo que vive y siente
> dentro la carne mortal
> ¡ay! por saltar impaciente
> las bardas de su corral.[25]

The concept of a homogeneously experienced 'durée réelle' in Bergson's book is linked directly to 'Les deux aspects du moi'. There's 'le moi superficiel' and, ever in danger of being lost from view by the exigencies of social life, 'le moi fondamental'—'le moi intérieur, celui qui sent et se passione, celui qui délibère e se décide, est une force dont les états et modifications se pénètrent intimement . . .' (the inner me, the one which feels and enthuses, the one which deliberates and decides, is a force whose states and modifications are intimately impregnated . . .).[26] Yet, in the spirit of 'la gaya scienza', Machado treats 'este yo fundamental' with first a genial scepticism ('no este mal': it's not bad) and then a decisive qualification ('dentro la carne mortal | ¡ay! por saltar . . .'). This turn has been prepared for earlier in the poem, when Machado contrasts Bergson's theory of a free self in embodied experience with a Kantian self-transcendence. Machado's movement from 'carne mortal' to 'saltar' in the poem's closing lines echoes the passage on Kant in the first chapter of Unamuno's *Del Sentimiento Trágico de la Vida*, in which the philosopher poet plays on the expression 'salto mortal', a somersault, in the phrase 'salto inmortal'.[27] Here's how Tomlinson handles the poem's end:

---

[25] Machado, *Poesías completas*, 208.

[26] Henri Bergson, *Oeuvres*, ed. A. Robinet (Paris: Presses Universitaires de France, 1970), 83. For a useful introduction to Machado's poem and its various contexts see Arthur Terry, *Antonio Machado: Campos de Castilla* (London: Grant and Cutler, 1973), chs. 4–6, esp. pp. 84–91.

[27] The translator draws attention to this wordplay in a footnote (see Miguel de Unamuno, *The Tragic Sense of Life*, trans. J. E. Crawford-Flitch (New York: Dover, 1954), 4).

My table bears
—*les données de la conscience*
immédiates.
It's adequate
this I
that's fundamental
and at times
creative and original, that
mingling in mortality
its freedom and contingency,
can feel
can see, and yet
must overleap the confines
of its narrow keep.[28]

Tomlinson's version earns respect and admiration for its fluid rhyming of conceptually weighty but relatively textureless abstractions. He has created his own technical problem in part, though, and found an impressive solution. The Spanish states the conditions of an embodied and constrained existence. Machado's 'yo' is not 'mingling in mortality', like an individual in a crowd, but 'dentro la carne mortal' (within mortal flesh). Also, it does not mingle 'its freedom and contingency', like possessed qualities, but *is* contingent and free.

In the original there is the statement of the self's being subject to conditions of time and space, being an organic entity inseparable from its situation on the earth. From this situation the self gains some conceptual independence through speaking and writing. The English translation, though, appears to acknowledge that this 'I', the speaking self of the poem, only derives from a body that is situated in contingency and mortality. What a reader mainly experiences is its freedom, its ability to 'overleap the confines' of a situation. It's as if the voice of the Tomlinson translation faintly condescends to its own body, and to the pronoun with which it identifies itself as the subject of sentences. This is the difference between saying in two lines 'No está mal | este yo fundamental' and saying in three 'It's adequate | this I | that's fundamental'. Similarly, different senses of embodiment appear in the grammars of the final lines. In Machado's poem the 'yo' 'vive y siente . . . por saltar impaciente' (lives and feels . . . to overleap, impatient). In the Tomlinson it is not incorporated so as to grow larger than its confines, but rather is required to turn against its physical limits in order to fulfil the obligation to be impersonal, so the self will not be restricted to its own small situation. Yet the vast bulk of Machado's poem acknowledges, while accommodating itself to, just such a restricted situation by means of its insistently joking rhymes (adapted from Jorge Manrique's *coplas* on the death of his father) and qualified tones of ironic detachment. Tomlinson's 'I' 'can feel | can see, and yet | must overleap . . .'. His 'and yet' interprets Machado's '¡ay!'. An ambiguous exclamation becomes the measured explanation of a further responsibility. The English version dramatizes a self that is socially and morally, in diction and syntax, faintly superior to the material limits of its own body.

IV

In both Machado's 'Poema de un día' and Tomlinson's 'Up at La Serra' poets are represented as living in obscure provincial villages. In both too they are attempting to give themselves the confidence to make significant art within their constrained situations. In Machado's case he is achieving it by asking if it can be done. The poet in 'Up at La Serra' is Paolo Bertolani, and La Serra is his village, on the hillside above Lerici. He was born there in 1931, and so was twenty years old when Tomlinson's poem described him as one 'who had no more to offer | than a sheaf of verse | in the style of Quasimodo' (p. 78). Tomlinson is a mere four years older than his subject. Bertolani continued writing too, and went on to achieve a style of his own—much of his work being written in the dialect of his home village.

Before looking in detail at what 'Up at La Serra' achieves and the problem it contains I should quote Tomlinson's own trepidations, on discovering, twenty years later, that the person he had put in his poem had continued to write poetry and fiction. In *Some Americans* he describes how Paolo Bertolani

discovered from Vittorio Sereni, who coincidentally owned a holiday house nearby, that I had long ago written a poem called 'Up at La Serra.' This work was something of an embarrassment to me, for in it I had tried to imagine the life of a young poet 'up at La Serra' who

> knew, at twenty
> all the deprivations such a place
> stored for the man
> who had no more to offer
> than a sheaf of verse
> in the style of Quasimodo . . .

I wrote the poem at a time when I was experimenting in the use of Williams's three-ply cadences. It was the first of a series in which people are trapped by political or historic situations. Without La Serra—and without Williams—I might not have got these poems under way, so once more Italy and America had combined for me. By the seventies, however, and by the time I resumed contact with Paolo, I came to wonder whether I had not been tactless in using names—his name in particular—and presumptuous, even, in venturing to imagine what had been in his mind in the 1950s.[29]

I much admire Tomlinson's readiness to acknowledge debts incurred. Just as Williams helped him with his own poems, so also with his rendering of Machado's poetry. He translates Machado into a form translated from America, in order to translate into English poetry the experience of a small village in Italy. This also helped him write about the English provinces in poems such as 'John Maydew *or* The Allotment'. The possibilities for disorientation and mismatching are extreme, and it is largely a measure of Tomlinson's skill that objection was not made nor offence taken by those involved. Sereni translated the poem to read at a launch for Bertolani's second book *Incertezza dei bersagli* at Vicenza in 1976. The translation has never been published. Following the passage Tomlinson cites above, 'a sheaf of verse | in the style of Quasimodo', these lines appear:

> Came the moment,
> he would tell it
>   in a poem
>   without rancour, a lucid
> testament above his name
>   —*Paolo*
>   *Bertolani*
> —*Ciao, Paolo!*
>   —*Ciao*
>   *Giorgino!*
> He would put them
>   all in it—   (p. 79)

Tomlinson has done just this: he has put them all in. Yet what about himself? The difference between 'Up at La Serra' and 'Poema de un día' is that

[29] Tomlinson, *Some Americans*, 120–1. For a characteristic view of Tomlinson's achievement in 'Up at La Serra', described as 'the most significantly connective' of his 1960s poems, see Richard Swigg, *Charles Tomlinson and the Objectivist Tradition* (Lewisberg, Pa.: Bucknell University Press, 1994), 108–12.

in the latter Machado is present and speaking. He is experiencing and conveying the feeling of being trapped by political and historic situations.

Tomlinson presents dialogue between Bertolani and others, including tourists, foreigners such as the poet will have appeared to be:

> and you told
> the visitors:
> — *We are not communists*
> *although we call ourselves communists*
> *we are what you English*
> *would call . . . socialists.*   (p. 80)

Is this being said to the poet Charles Tomlinson? It sounds as if he had translated it from Bertolani's Italian, remembered or imagined. Yet, unlike Machado's poem upon which it is modelled, 'Up at La Serra' doesn't at any point contain the poet as a physical entity in the imagined space of the writing, receiving the experience he relates to readers. An election is taking place, and, in the evening, news arrives of the results:

> — *We have won*
> *the election.*
> — *At the café*
> *the red flag is up.*
> He turned back
> quickly beneath the tower.
> Giorgino
> who wanted to be a waiter
> wanted to be a commissar
> piling *sassi*
> into the dentist's wall.   (p. 81)

The word *sassi* means 'stones' or 'pebbles'; it stands out from the passage not only because in a foreign language, but because it follows a group of lines which might have sounded something like: 'Abbiamo vinto l'elezione. La bandiera rossa è lassù al bar!' If this snatch of conversation has made it into English italics, why has the Italian word for stones been left in the original? This is a mark, among many others, of the poet's presence writing the poem. Yet, unlike the indications that derive from the practically innumerable instances of conscious technique which could be pointed to, the presence of the Italian word does not indicate the poet absorbed into the form of his words, but the occluded presence of an Englishman abroad.

Tomlinson's final chapter in *Some Americans* is sprinkled with short phrases in Italian and in italics. There is 'the old, luxuriantly white-moustached peasant who offered a whole history of the modern world through his account of the growth and decline of *i baffi*, the moustache',[30] and the man who 'never married and, having bought the land that had belonged to a local count, was known for the rest of his life as *il conte*', and there are 'those who *in tempo di guerra* had hidden in holes in the ground to avoid the conscription'. These people 'like Paolo, were faced with the prospect of unemployment and looked to the communists—they had just won the elections hereabouts—to put things to rights'. Tomlinson's tone here is nostalgic and affectionate. It too has wanted to, and has, put things to rights.

By comparison 'Up at La Serra' treats the situation with a faintly knowing, possibly helpless condescension. Here is a passage about Bertolani at twenty, and what he, perhaps, had said to Tomlinson of his hopes

He believed
that God was a hypothesis,
that the party would bring in
a synthesis, that he
would edit the local paper for them,
or perhaps
go northward to Milan   (p. 80)

By saying 'He believed' the English poet distances his own voice from the hopes or fears that his Italian acquaintance experiences, mediating them to the England of the Conservative Prime Minister Harold Macmillan and his election slogan 'You've never had it so good'. Tomlinson's use of occasionally dropped Italian substantives like *sassi* or *baffi* gives his writing set in foreign places a smack of the local tongue, as any good travel writer might. Yet that is exactly the moment when the poet situates his voice outside the concerns that he reports. This may be thought honest of him, and more judicious than Ezra Pound's attempt to read everywhere as instancing his polemical vision. Yet Tomlinson's detachment nevertheless implies an authority which derives from not being situated and defined in a relation to the occasion composed. The poet's line-endings in 'He believed | that God was a hypothesis | that the party would bring in | a synthesis' sceptically weigh the Italian's hopes, pausing before what he believes in each case. The effect is similar to a crafty sentence of James

---

[30] For this and the following three citations see Tomlinson, *Some Americans*, 108.

Joyce's from 'Eveline'. Frank, Eveline's sailor sweetheart is telling her about the life he will take her away to: 'He had fallen on his feet in Buenos Ayres, he said, and had come over to the old country just for a holiday.'[31] Joyce's 'he said' is designed (as Hugh Kenner first over-emphatically pointed out) to open questions about what the significantly named Frank is saying. Tomlinson may not be deliberately doing the same with the 'He believed', but it serves to make English readers doubt the acuity of young Italians believing in the PCI, the Italian Communist Party.

There is also talk of elections in Machado's 'Poema de un día':

> Es de noche. Se platica
> al fondo de una botica.
> —Yo no sé,
> don José,
> cómo son los liberales
> tan perros, tan inmorales.
> —¡Oh, tranquilícese usté!
> Pasados los carnavales,
> vendran los conservadores,
> buenos administradores
> de su casa.[32]

Machado has no need to express directly his views on this conversation. His rhymes and the reiterative mention of time ticking by offer all the comment needed. It is just another part of the rural situation that he is able to distance, but by no means to escape, in his meditation on a day. Tomlinson paraphrases this scene in his version:

> Night:
> the talk is on
> in the rear room
> at the apothecary's
> where they define
> what makes the liberals such swine
> and Don José
> scents consolation
> in the return (predicted)
> of the conservative administration[33]

---

[31] James Joyce, *Dubliners* (Harmondsworth: Penguin, 1956), 37.
[32] Machado, *Poesías completas*, 207.
[33] Tomlinson, *Translations*, 40.

A detail the translation doesn't contain is the local landowner's being sucked up to by the other voice speaking at the apothecary's: 'Yo no sé, | don José'. And this allows Don José to respond with some home-grown political wisdom about the party of his personal interests. Machado is outside the village shop where such talk goes on, both in that he is not taking part, and that the opinions expressed are not his own, so that he feels himself, as poet and citizen, removed from the locals' outlook. However, his exclusion is a part of his unavoidable belonging. It is part of his situation, like the expression of support for Italian communist intellectuals in Sereni's 'Un posto di vacanza' (A Holiday Place) set at Bocca di Magra, a few miles down the coast from La Serra, and in the election year when Tomlinson first visited Liguria:

> e nel '51 la lagna di un raro fuoribordo su per il fiume
> era ancora sottilmente allarmante,
> qualunque cosa andasse sul filo della corrente
> passava per testa mozza di trucidato.
> Ancora balordo di guerra, di quella guerra
> solo questo mi univa a quei parlanti parlanti
> e ancora parlanti sull'onda della libertà . . .[34]

[and in '51 a rare outboard motor's whine upriver | was insidiously alarming still, | whatever was floating on the line of the current | passed for a slaughtered man's lopped head. | Still benumbed with war, with that war, | this only united me to those speakers speaking | and still speaking on the wave of liberty . . .]

It is Sereni's sense of being cauterized by the war, of sharing a historic fate, even in the division and exclusion of his imprisonment in North Africa during 1943–5, which unites him with the theoreticians of liberty whom he brushes against on holiday. Such a lack of attachment, such exclusion or equivocation, these form part of the writer's situation within the world experienced and mediated. Tomlinson's position on the fringes of 'Up at La Serra' is more marginal. Yet in excluding himself from the picture he risks being tactless by not seeming to have experienced the facts, the very situation, in which he places his protagonists, nor even to have experienced his own apparent cultural marginality and irrelevance.

---

[34] Vittorio Sereni, *Poesie*, ed. D. Isella (Milan: Mondadori, 1995), 224–5. 'Un posto di vacanza' was first published in its entirety in *Almanacco dello Specchio*, 1 (1972), 105–12, in an issue which included twenty-one poems by Tomlinson and a selection of Paolo Bertolani's work.

V

In his published letter to Tomlinson, Sereni concluded with these warmly generous words:

Ebbene, caro Tomlinson, la spregiudicatezza nel vedere e nell'ascoltare con cui la sua poesia affronta le cose conferma questa qualità per cui la poesia è davvero un mezzo di conoscenza. Ma in lei tale qualità è doppiata e rafforzata da questa caratteristica: non c'è in lei (per questo parlavo di spregiudicatezza) alcuna conoscenza precostuita. In lei la conoscenza è un risultato, un coronamento dell'esperimento specifico, si forma col formarsi della poesia. Questa lezione è per noi importante, mi induce ad avvertire una affinità con lei e col suo lavoro, accende fiducia in me verso me stesso.[35]

[Well, dear Tomlinson, the lack of prejudgement in seeing and hearing with which your poetry confronts things confirms this quality by which poetry is truly a means for understanding. But in you, such quality is doubled and reinforced by this characteristic: in you there is not (it's why I mentioned lack of prejudgement) any preconstituted understanding. In you understanding is an outcome, a crowning of the specific experiment, it forms with the formation of the poem. This lesson is important for us, induces me to notice an affinity with you and your work, it kindles fidelity in me towards myself.]

The open-mindedness with which the poet, in Sereni's formulation, sees and hears is a quality to which Tomlinson has committed himself, and it is a means for understanding the world. Reservations about the degree to which Tomlinson has conducted specific experiments in sense perception free from preconceived understandings are prompted by strategies in which an 'I' is withheld, but a detached source of knowledge and judgement implied. This is why Tomlinson was afraid that 'Up at La Serra' might have appeared tactless and presumptuous.

The gift of an affinity with Tomlinson in Sereni's letter involves the English poet's including himself within the process of understanding that the Italian poet sees as a prerequisite of poetic knowledge. When he says that Tomlinson's work 'accende fiducia in me verso me stesso', he finds in his response to it a quality different to the sense in 'Tramontana at Lerici' that the pronoun 'One' in 'One is ignored' turns the poet away at the door of his own self. Sereni discovers, in reading Tomlinson's poems, that his own self, as a contingent and free locus of poetic perception, is reinvigorated. 'Up at La Serra' concludes with the twenty-year-old Italian poet's confidence in his powers:

[35] 'A Letter from Vittorio Sereni', 42.

> *—Salve, Giorgino*
>   *—Salve*
>   *Paolo, have you*
> *heard*
>   *that we have won the election?*
>   *—I am writing*
>   *a poem about it:*
>   *it will begin*
>   *here, with the cliff and with the sea*
> *following its morning shadow in.*   (p. 82)

Since the poem Bertolani is writing will begin at the point where 'Up at La Serra' does in fact start, 'The shadow | ran before it lengthening' (p. 78), it's as if Tomlinson's poem is a translation in imagination, a shadowing in another language, of the poem Bertolani might have written. Tomlinson's impressive, ambitious poem pits itself against received English styles of verse. Resisting a native environment, its provincial styles and attitudes, 'Up at La Serra' (a poem about being trapped in a province with a borrowed poetic style) survives an air of having been willed into existence.

Two poems form afterwords to 'Up at La Serra'. The first, from Bertolani's *Incertezza dei bersagli*, is called 'La Casa di Charles'. It concludes:

> Non tornare, se tornare
> non puoi sopra un uccello marino
> e in un punto da cui—anche volendo—
> tu non possa vedere lo scempio che hanno fatto
> uomini e anni su quel gioco che era la vita.[36]

[If you return do not | return unless riding astride | a seabird's back from the same spot | where even in flight the eye | can't seize on this scape that men | and the years have unshaped from the play that was life.[37]]

The thought of a seabird's flying is picked up in 'Graziella', the third part of 'The Return', the title poem (dedicated to Paolo Bertolani) of Tomlinson's 1987 collection. Graziella was the Italian poet's wife, who had died after a painful illness:

> The dead do not return, and nor shall we
> To pry and prompt the living or rehearse
> The luxuries of self-debating verse.

---

[36] Paolo Bertolani, *Incertezza dei bersagli* (Milan: Guanda, 1976), 35–6.
[37] Tomlinson, *Some Americans*, 122.

Their silence we inhabit now they've gone
And like a garment drawn the darkness on
Beyond all hurt. This quiet we must bear:
Put words into their mouths, you fail to hear
What once they said. I can recall the day
She imitated my clipped, foreign way
Of saying *Shakespeare*. English, long unheard,
Came flying back, some unfamiliar bird
Cutting a wing-gust through the weight of air
As she repeated it—*Shakespeare Shakespeare*—
Voice-prints of a season that belongs
To the cicadas and the heat, their song
Shrill, simmering and continuous.[38]

Tomlinson's work between 1951 and 1963 has an instructive uneasiness in the poet's articulation of his self and his 'I'. Antonio Machado was able to take strength, however sceptically, from Bergson's 'moi fondamental': 'No está mal | este yo fundamental, | contingente y libre'. It is a necessary locus of poetic knowledge, heard in the reciprocity of Bertolani's and Tomlinson's poems, the echoing of 'Non tornare' in 'do not return' and the 'uccello marino', in 'some unfamiliar bird'. 'I can recall the day', Tomlinson writes, the locus of a poetic knowledge, one situated in the world, an 'I' revitalized for Vittorio Sereni by some of the English poet's earlier work, helping him kindle a 'fidelity in me towards myself'.

[38] Charles Tomlinson, *The Return* (Oxford: Oxford University Press, 1987), 10.

CHAPTER 10

'Absolute circumstance':
Mairi MacInnes

I

'But then I understood something very simple: to make things happen,
you have to go away.'[1] The last words of Mairi MacInnes's memoir
Clearances echo back down her family's generations. Her mother left
Australia, where she had been born to English emigrants, to serve as a
nurse in Gallipoli. There she met the writer's father, a doctor from the Isle
of Skye. MacInnes's title—while it most directly evokes ideas of mental
spring-cleaning (each chapter being a clear out of long-gathered memories and reflections)—plainly harks back to the treatment of the Scottish
Highlands after the The Forty-Five. Her parents made their home first in
County Durham, then in Windsor. She herself married an American of
Irish and French-Canadian descent. He took her first to post-war West
Berlin. Then she lived in Maine while he commuted to a teaching post in
New Jersey. There followed a New Jersey sojourn sometimes together
and sometimes not. These various arrangements were interspersed with
years in Vermont, Mexico City, and Madrid. Finally, after her husband's
retirement, MacInnes returned first to the north Yorkshire countryside,
and then, in old age, to the city of York.

Yet it's not her own or her parents' departures that prompt this concluding epigram reminiscent of what the young Joyce wrote about his
Dublin. Rather, her husband would leave MacInnes alone with their three
children for months on end while he held academic fellowships in
Europe. She would be left to cope with nostalgia for the British Isles in an
America that seems to have remained a foreign country. The subtlety and
tact of MacInnes's writing is revealed by the fact that she leaves it to the
reader to link this insight into her husband's motivation with her own

[1] Mairi MacInnes, *Clearances: A Memoir* (New York: Pantheon, 2002), 275.

impulse in marrying him. What kept driving them apart during their middle years was the very thing that had bound them together in the first place. Yet the strains and obligations of marriage and parenthood all but silenced MacInnes as a writer for the best part of thirty years—from her mid-1950s début to her re-emergence and consolidation during the last two decades of the twentieth century.

Mairi MacInnes was born in 1925 and began to emerge, if that's the word, in the mid-1950s when the Movement was figuring as an event in the history of literary journalism. However, the index to Blake Morrison's *The Movement: English Poetry and Fiction of the 1950s* reveals how faint a mark she made—one passing reference in a 1956 retrospect by John Wain: 'the present literary generation is the first one in the history of English literature, and quite possibly the last, to have made its *début* by means of broadcasting . . . Some representative names would be: A. Alvarez, Kingsley Amis, Anthony Hartley, Philip Larkin, Mairi MacInnes'.[2] This list resembles one Amis made some three years before, writing to Wain on 6 November 1953: 'In a list of 28 white hopes of English letters were featured you, of course, me, of course, Al, Philip L., Mairi'.[3] Her place in these roll-calls was based on a 'pamphlet of novice poetry',[4] *Splinters* (1953), published by subscription through Wain himself and William McCance at Reading University. The poet's present view of that *'début'* can be judged from the inclusion of just one poem, 'Theomachy', in *The Pebble: Old and New Poems* (2000) from the University of Illinois Press. During the same decade her first novel, *Admit One* (1957), appeared from Putnam. The novel, somewhat like Larkin's *A Girl in Winter*, follows the life of a Katharine from thirties forebodings through to post-war austerity. Despite this promising start, the writer then disappeared entirely from sight. What happened? The short answer, as her memoirs make abundantly clear, is that Mairi MacInnes became Mairi McCormick and began a period of expatriation that lasted for over thirty years.

In 'Why Poetry: An Essay', the afterword to *The Ghostwriter* (1999), MacInnes sketches the absolute circumstance of this drift from literary view which happened almost fifty years earlier:

[2] Blake Morrison, *The Movement: English Poetry and Fiction of the 1950s* (Oxford: Oxford University Press, 1980), 43.
[3] Zachary Leader, 'Raising Ron Cain: How Amis and Larkin mocked their own Movement', *Times Literary Supplement*, 5066, 5 May 2000, 15.
[4] Mairi MacInnes, *The Pebble: Old and New Poems* (Urbana and Chicago, Ill.: University of Illinois Press, 2000), 158 (also in *The Ghostwriter* (Newcastle upon Tyne: Bloodaxe, 1999), 71).

No more inclusion in anthologies, reduced publication in journals, no more invitations to write reviews, no invitations to read at the old ICA off Piccadilly, no poetry evenings with competent poets at George and Paddy Frazer's in Chelsea; no literary parties where William Empson and Kathleen Raine and Janet Adam Smith are kind to the young; no lunch with Kingsley and Hilly Amis at which they pump me for information about the man I am living with. My novel has been published and Olivia Manning and others have reviewed it generously. But that is that. The baby keeps me at home and prevents me from getting to know German society well enough to use it in a second novel. I do not publish another for forty years. But this is life, I think. My husband has forced me to live.[5]

Nearly two decades later, in *Thomas Hardy and British Poetry* (1973), Donald Davie quoted her poem 'Hardly Anything Bears Watching' entire. A footnote indicates that it had appeared in *The Spectator* on 16 August 1963. Though an uncharacteristically plain-speaking lament in six quatrains, 'Hardly Anything Bears Watching' has no apparent agenda beyond the need to register its sense of loss:

> No comfort from the boy who draws
> upon my memory of bombs.
> The man recalls
> brave days on a far-off sea.
>
> Picture after picture fails.
> When I was young
> the pavement curbs were made of stone,
> a substance like my fingernails.
>
> It is not like that any more.
> I do not see
> the essential life of inorganic things.
> Humanity has covered all.[6]

The 'curiously level tone of voice which can carry off the big blunt words' in what Davie also calls 'this surely admirable poem' struck me too. Once more though, the critic, with an only too evident agenda, precipitately tacked on the moral: 'Miss MacInnes's poem says that to buy sympathy with the human, at the price of alienation from the nonhuman, is a hard bargain at best.'[7] Yet this slogan is only partially in tune with, for instance,

[5] *The Pebble*, 158–9; *The Ghostwriter*, 72.
[6] *The Pebble*, 13–14; first collected in *Herring, Oatmeal, Milk & Salt*, in T. and R. Weiss (eds.), *Quarterly Review of Literature*, poetry series, iii (Princeton, NJ, 1981), 17.
[7] Donald Davie, *Thomas Hardy and British Poetry* (London: Routledge & Kegan Paul, 1973), 67, 68. Davie's other response to MacInnes's work is the poem 'Love-Poems: for Mairi MacInnes', in *Collected Poems*, ed. N. Powell (Manchester: Carcanet, 2002), 39.

the evocative and ambivalent simile clinched by a rhyme which makes the 'curbs' of the pavement 'like my fingernails'. The poet herself, like others written about in that book, thought Davie's attention 'occasionally very clever and acute, and occasionally wilfully unjustifiable'.[8] That old-style polite 'Miss MacInnes' also indicates that Davie knew little about the poet's situation in the early 1970s.

Attempting to read more of the poetry described as of interest in Davie's book produced, in the case of Mairi MacInnes, absolutely nothing. And it was only in the mid-1990s that I came across *The House on the Ridge Road* (1988) published by a small press in Boston, Massachusetts; *Elsewhere & Back: New & Selected Poems* (1993) published by Bloodaxe; and a novel, *The Quondam Wives* (1993), from Louisiana State University Press. As the acknowledgements to the Bloodaxe volume indicate, MacInnes had published a collection called *Herring, Oatmeal, Milk & Salt* (1981) in Princeton. This proved to be in a series from the *Quarterly Review of Literature*, a multiple author sampler containing five separate books. *Herring, Oatmeal, Milk & Salt* is, then, MacInnes's first mature collection of poems, while the 1993 volume from Bloodaxe is her first poetry book published in the UK for forty years. Though John Ashbery, in a lecture called 'The Invisible Avant-Garde', thought that for such artists the period of neglect has got ever shorter 'so that it now seems to be something like a minute',[9] there are still many ways for writers of eventual distinction to remain for the best part of a lifetime almost entirely invisible.

II

For certain casts of mind, circumstance is 'purely arbitrary', or 'merely contingent'. It is as if the fact that the world happened to be just so at a particular time on a certain day is an accident, quite meaningless, and there is no reason why everything could not have been entirely different. Yet for others the word 'occasion' points, via its root in the verb 'to fall', towards the fact of everything having undeniably happened in this and in no other possible way. For such writers, seeing the situation as art is more a process for recognizing how things had to be and of finding what value can be attached to that, less a practice for making meaning out of selected

---

[8] Mairi MacInnes, postcard to the present writer in an envelope postmarked 25 Apr. 2001.
[9] John Ashbery, cited in John Palattella, 'Heavy Lifting', *London Review of Books*, 23/11, 7 June 2001, 36.

bits in a supposedly chaotic welter. Perhaps it was a leaning on my part towards the first way of seeing things that produced a start at MacInnes's phrase 'absolute circumstance' and the thought that it was not an oxymoron but a perceived insight.

Those words can be found in the third and final verse to her 'Evening on the Estuary, Noon at Sea', a poem dedicated to the painter Estéban Vicente on his eightieth birthday:

> Here, as darkness fills out,
> absolute circumstance also
> begins to bloom.
> The colors of land and water
> grow deep in reflected light.
> Here and in your painting, master,
> what's allowed will happen.
> The eye arrives alone at its center,
> its eventual passion.[10]

Immediately appealing in this stanza is its unemphatic, interwoven music. We can hear how 'out' at the first line-end exfoliates into the 'absolute', with its echoing last syllable. Similarly, the word's first five letters, shuffled and minus the 'b', generate 'also'. That dropped 'b' is then picked up by the alliteration of the third line whose 'n' and 'm' consonants reverse those of 'circumstance'. Similarly, the last syllable of 'happen' is taken into the first of 'center', and the second of 'eventual', while 'alone' in the middle of the penultimate line prepares for the hidden almost-rhyme with 'passion' at the poem's close. There is also muted part-rhyming in the interspersed sequence of 'water . . . master . . . center' and in 'happen . . . passion'. On 3 February 1818 Keats wrote praising poetry which 'does not startle' one's soul 'or amaze it with itself—but with its subject. How beautiful are the retired flowers!—how would they lose their beauty were they to throng into the highway, crying out, "Admire me, I am a violet! Dote upon me, I am a primrose!"'[11] MacInnes's music blooms like Keats's thankfully retired flowers. Her style instances 'absolute circumstance', too, for the way it sounds like a fait accompli appears to be happening as the occasion befalls.

---

[10] Mairi MacInnes, *The House on the Ridge Road* (Boston, Mass.: Rowan Tree, 1988), 32; repr. with alternate lines indented in *Elsewhere & Back: New & Selected Poems* (Newcastle upon Tyne: Bloodaxe, 1993), 20.

[11] John Keats, letter to J. H. Reynolds, 3 Feb. 1818, in *Letters of John Keats to his Family and Friends* ed. S. Colvin (London: Macmillan, 1935), 68.

The first two verses of 'Evening on the Estuary, Noon at Sea' prepare for this conclusion by essaying similarities and differences between the composition of an art work and of a natural scene. In the estuary, as 'Ash drifts thick in mile-wide smears | far out at sea' this process is 'emptying content'—something a painting stops time precisely to avoid; in the second stanza, where the poet remembers 'riding out of Orkney | on the ferry to Scrabster',

> It was midsummer in the far north,
> the air very bright,
> the wind hard at work—
> so much haled out of the fabric of matter
> and tuned like matter, luminous,
> excited by present arrival in Caithness.

The 'so much' MacInnes's poem evokes may also be 'absolute circumstance' in which the 'fabric of matter' is 'tuned like matter'. Her poetry's idea of art appears a texture and attunement learned from the ordering of the natural world itself. It can be found as meaning, though, only when experienced as the 'present arrival' of a self, a human 'circumstance'; for that word also implies a present—and necessarily included—point of attention around which everything else is taken to stand. This is another reason why Davie's moral is rendered partial through the implication that human sympathy could ever be had at the expense of the non-human, or the non-human have significance without a human presence.

During a rare venture into academic prose MacInnes underlines how the absolute circumstance in a human perspective also contributes to the occasion of meaning. 'The idea of alcoholism,' she notes, 'like the idea of a city, has grown up complicated by our needs as witnesses, quite apart from variation in the thing itself.'[12] Her poems are especially sensitive to the complicating variations of 'our needs as witnesses' in a questioning relation to 'variation in the thing itself'. She achieves this by doing without over-insistences of incantation or interpretation—as in 'Among the Sea Islands, Georgia', where change and dereliction leave just a few stone markers of human effort: 'Only milestones in woods are left, | pointing to lost plantations, | and the gravestones of "Lotty," "Tib."' The feeling she then announces is still not 'sympathy with the human', for the poet's exclamation is produced by the absence of occasion for human solidarity:

---

[12] Mairi McCormick, 'First Representations of the Gamma Alcoholic in the English Novel', *Quarterly Journal of Studies on Alcohol*, 30/4 (Dec. 1969), 957.

'How sad, somehow, it is, | this scrupulous lack of consequence!' Whatever the expressed needs of the poet as witness, her articulated desire to have the scene religiously transformed through spring's arrival is rebuked by the qualifying situation in what follows:

> What if the spring lets fall
> its present like a canticle,
> and snakes coil warming in the path,
> and that painted bunting
> like a pentecostal flame
> flickers in the bush?
> The boatman does not care.
> He checks his fine gold watch
> and says it's time to go.
> A squall is coming. We cannot wait.
> Nothing to be done about this.
> Nothing matters now.[13]

The boatman represents a different relationship between humanity and circumstance. He has his weather eye open. He beckons the visitors back to the boat as if to underline the lack of consequence narrated, while the poem renders that desolating recognition as of consequence. If such meaning is inevitably a human addition to the scene, it aspires to the condition of those stone markers, not an inscription that has overwhelmed the scene's condition of truth, but one that acknowledges the landscape's contribution to what the human meaning could possibly be. It is as if you can't have one without the other—usually the case with poets whose work is prompted by ambivalence about lived occasions.

III

'Welcome to Mendocino', among MacInnes's most sustained perform-ances, is described by Richard Wilbur on the back cover of *The House on the Ridge Road* as a 'delectable poem' whose author is 'amusedly objective'. This complex of authorial attitude and readerly pleasure also touches on her invitations toward, and withdrawals from, environment. This com-pleted poem in six parts opens with some non-human stuff, which the poet seems neither alienated from nor sympathetic towards:

---

[13] *The Pebble*, 40–1.

> A tremendous sea, covered with experienced waves.
> Crumbling sandstone cliffs, their rock lodes,
> their lofty citadels, cut out and marooned.
> Seaweed, sea lions, and a set of pelicans
> assumed, and the sea passing them by,
> the mastering element, the present controller.

The opening line sees the 'tremor' in 'tremendous' and knows that the place is near the San Andreas Fault, being 'some ninety miles, half a day from San Francisco'. Beauty and fear are again not far apart. For development, it interleaves this account of the Pacific coastline with an attention to the human dimensions of the historic place: 'They went home to add a superfluous fret | of wooden filigrees to eaves and rails, | . . . an outside staircase twined like morning glory.'[14] Her poem similarly twines together the perpetual presence of the indifferent sea with the vicinity's comic or sad human dimensions. MacInnes describes 'the tourist, touched with fire' whose 'eyes prickle' and whose 'wallet's heavy' as he 'muses from shop to shop and buys expensively, | the sea at his back, the malign neglected sea'. After a description of some 'amaryllis as in Greek Sicily', she adds: '"Naked Ladies," | frowns the prim innkeeper, and slashes off their heads.'

Her third section begins: 'Unionised labor's gone inland, | gone to the back country, | where the sea is musing and gentle'. Yet MacInnes is most exercised by that 'tremendous sea, covered with experienced waves'. But 'experienced' waves? The epithet implies a bargaining with the non-human. She strikes this note again in part II with 'the experienced sea' and 'the malign neglected sea', and it is the theme she returns to at her poem's close:

> The sea grumbles far away, the sea devoid of honor,
> gobbling, dangerous, cold, forever
> missing something, it doesn't know what.
> 'Oh, for God's sake!' it cries, and bellows all night
> through the lace curtains of the famous Mendocino inn.
> What if the only thing wrong is the moon?
> The sea wants its words too, to declare that
> it is various and detailed and craves to be looked at,
> and gives of itself for ever. It only imagines it is hungry,
> full as it must be with continent wolfed.

---

[14] This and subsequent citations are to *The Pebble*, 46–51; for the five-part version see *The House on the Ridge Road*, 36–42; the revised version is also in *Elsewhere & Back*, 68–72.

'The sea wants its words too', perhaps because this final section does end the poem properly, as the five-part version printed in *The House on the Ridge Road* fails to do. The earlier text stops with the 'perfectly round stones of Mendocino' that 'the two Marys' have gathered as souvenirs. The stones are doubtless smoothed by the action of the sea, but seem to have been gathered into the trinket sphere of human sympathy, and their power as symbols combining the non-human with a human function is muffled. MacInnes seems, in revising, to have acknowledged the sea's need to be both first and last.

Naturally, the poem too wants its words—as MacInnes makes clear enough in 'I Object, Said the Object', an important piece for her develop-ment which 'Why Poetry' comments on at length. In its final verse what must be new poems come 'uttering sounds unchosen, spontaneous, not | chidden, flocking'.[15] Yet what comes flocking in the 'Welcome to Mendocino' is a personifying of the sea which sounds appropriate and chosen. This descriptive anthropomorphism is rendered benign by a Bishop-like 'joking voice, a gesture | I love'[16] that recalls the older writer's poem 'The Bight': 'the water in the bight doesn't wet anything, | the color of a gas flame turned as low as possible. | One can smell it turning to gas; if one were Baudelaire | one could probably hear it turning to marim-ba music.'[17] MacInnes's joking style ('So what's the sea been up to?') acknowledges that you can't describe anything without turning it into the terms of the human. However, doing so in a knowingly whimsical style makes the helplessness of the gesture quite evident, which in turn allows the elemental forces their vast and indifferent autonomy.

'Not wanting to be there where you are is the beginning of all this busi-ness', the poet John Welch has written, and 'In imagination you had to be somewhere else.'[18] MacInnes presents such relationships of imagination to resistance and displacement as a familial conflict in the memoir-essay that gives *Herring, Oatmeal, Milk & Salt* its title. The poet's father, a Hebridean doctor who spent his working life in County Durham, experi-enced the immediate surroundings of the North-East as an exile:

So did he offer me only the famous Scottish sentiment, filletted of fact and analy-sis? My mother, who'd come from Australia, scoffed. Her past was long ago and

[15] *The Pebble*, 25; for her discussion of the poem see 160–3; *Elsewhere & Back*, 57, and *The Ghostwriter*, 73–5.
[16] Elizabeth Bishop, *Complete Poems 1927–1979* (New York: Farrar, Straus and Giroux, 1983), 178.   [17] Ibid. 60.
[18] John Welch, 'The Life of It', *PN Review*, 138, 27/4 (2001), 12.

far away—nearly out of sight. But he was more bound to his place of origin than she was. He had a message to pass on. She not only kept quiet about the past, but saw no value in it.[19]

So the mother, who put her earlier life behind her to live the present as fully as possible, demonstrates less attachment to place than the father, who, because of his longing for elsewhere, has an ambivalent relationship to present circumstance. It is as if in order fully to register the immediate surroundings you have to be both tied to them by obligations and resistant to them because of a prior sense of loyalty to other absent places. The father's exile generates a vividly unhappy relationship to location— where the mother's expatriation and amnesia produce a toughly indifferent acceptance.

Such conflictual themes come through in many of MacInnes's poems, especially those set in the USA, where, despite a nearly three-decade residence, she was never able to feel entirely at home. 'The Scots in America' takes this as its subject. It begins with a memory of the poet's aunt in Scotland who had said, providing a refrain-like opening for each of three verses, 'The Scots is a proud people,' and, offering a contrast which appears at the opening and near the close, 'The English is an ignorant people.' MacInnes's poem notes that she speaks the tongue of the ignorant ones and is only part Scots—such an identity, with a border running through it like disputed terrain, being common in the British Isles. Her sense of not quite fitting at a 'Highland Service' in Doylestown, Pennsylvania, is a nuanced one:

> and I was surprised to hear the minister,
> Mr. Vanderboost, wore borrowed kilts
> and the ten pipers in full Highland fig
> were costumed by Canadian mail order.
> None of them had set foot in Scotland,
> and it didn't matter, for when they played
> the ancient airs of the Covenanters
> as on a sequestered moor, no eye was dry,
> and a summer storm whipped up outside
> to rip the soft leaves from the churchyard trees
> and drench the church's plain glass windows
> with an almost familiar rain.[20]

[19] *Herring, Oatmeal, Milk & Salt*, 40.
[20] *The Pebble*, 7–8; first published in *Herring, Oatmeal, Milk & Salt* (the lines with capitalized initial letters), 9.

In MacInnes's case resistance to environment is produced by an under-stated detachment in the description, a style which serves to let the character of individual words make their contributions to the quiet build-up of this turn from a faintly superior reserve to a shared sense of belong-ing in displacement. But what seems to finesse this turn is not the pipers' airs producing tears, but the natural event of the summer storm which comes to recall rain drenching the face on a sequestered moor.

IV

MacInnes's views of marriage, nature, culture, and displacement seem at least partly rooted in her mother's having met her father at Gallipoli, where she served as a nurse. The poet's admiration for the mother's war service is warmly explored in 'Why Poetry'.[21] The couple met in a field hospital and after the end of hostilities her mother abandoned life in Australia and came to the British Isles. 'The Caul', dedicated to her, evokes the young Australian on a ship docking at Tilbury in February 1919. Seeing her husband-to-be again, away from the 'deaths and chaos' of the 'bitter Greek winters under canvas', she finds 'a stranger | in shab-biest tweeds, whom she felt nothing for' and so: 'while cranes hoisted kit in great nets | and orderlies toted her trunk ashore, panic | struck her'.[22] The Americanism 'toted' appears to inter-thread the poet's experiences of marriage and emigration with those of her parent before her. This episode from how her mother was 'cut | into the pack after all, and dealt' is returned to in '1919':

> Repeat it, however: in that wintry Bloomsbury room
>   in the run-up to marriage, she dreams
> malarial dreams; dreams and drowns in grief,
>   cries out for company, oranges,
> clean sheets, aspirin, tea, her bevies
>   of sisters, the Murray River, past lovers[23]

The poem sounds out the traces of a life as echoing through the 'bevies' that grew up by a 'river' where 'lovers' were known. Do poetic effects like this produce an arbitrary illusion of inevitability, or pay tribute to the exactness of things being precisely thus as they unfolded? By not under-

---

[21] *The Pebble*, 154–6; *The Ghostwriter*, 68–9.
[22] *The Pebble*, 103; *The Ghostwriter*, 41.
[23] *The Pebble*, 140.

lining such confluences of sound, but letting them make their momentary points, the poem demonstrates an affinity with the second possibility.

In 'The Old Naval Airfield' MacInnes approaches the circumstance of her own past love, but not without reluctance:

> I looked out Henstridge lately,
> somewhere where it always was,
> even then, without maps or signs,
> and thought of Philip, chief flying instructor,
> brave Philip, who soon was dead;
> long ago, though, many years ago.[24]

An earlier version called 'The Old Naval Airfield at Henstridge, Dorset', first collected in 1988, shows how reluctant MacInnes was to approach this matter. The lines from 'and thought of Philip' to 'many years ago' do not appear. Her poem runs straight to 'Pretty old, bosky old, footpath | country' and takes the reader on a walk to the airfield, discovers 'the rusted roof of a hangar | half-fallen in' and then 'look, | the old control tower, a tall wreck | marooned in breaking waves of grass!' In revision this becomes 'Philip's control tower'. The earlier text has just two verses, the second pulling back from the rendered scene to exemplify, mysteriously, what the airfield meant:

> Survival is a form of murder.
> My father ran round the garden in the dark
> shouting, 'She's dead, and I could've done more
> for her. I could have, and I didn't.'
> She'd said earlier, 'He couldn't do more,
> that man, best man who ever lived.'
> Truth is, you can always do more.
> You have to survive, that too, but it's murder.
> He lived on, as you do if you can.[25]

The one change to this verse for later printings is that 'done more' moves to the next line, an improvement in the enjambed deploying of sense, which lets the line-end repetitions of 'murder' (with first apparently literal, then idiomatic usages) and the 'do more' echo more clearly because not overplayed. In 'The Old Naval Airfield at Henstridge, Dorset' a reader assumes a link between the story of her father's grief and the visit to the old airfield. This prompts those intensely articulated

[24] *The Pebble*, 35; *Elsewhere & Back*, 21 (as two verses with alternate lines indented).
[25] *The House on the Ridge Road*, 26.

lessons from experience in the final three lines. Yet what has produced them can only be guessed from the remains of the wartime scene. The mysteriousness sends the reader back to the airfield, trying to decipher its relevance to what comes later. The problem is, though, that in the absence of maps or signs the reader will probably fictionalize a pilot-and-sweetheart story that may, in the absence of detail, confuse the poem's absolute circumstance. The later version of the poem appreciates that the narration of scene alone does not make the experience intelligible enough to readers as they encounter the surroundings. Here the flowering of the meaning's occasion has been more difficult, and part of what that involved only a later poem reveals.

The flying instructor who is first implicity remembered in 'The Old Naval Airfield at Henstridge, Dorset' and then at least named and made part of the circumstance in 'The Old Naval Airfield' appears to have been a wartime love, someone rather differently mourned in 'Passion' from *The Ghostwriter*:

> I said at home: 'I heard he was killed.'
> My mother barely paused. 'Perhaps it's just as well.'
>
> 'But only twenty-eight, and after five years of war,
> accidentally killed? That's not unfair
>
> for a real hero, one of the best,
> as everyone said? Don't you think it's a waste?'

These jarringly rhymed, ambivalent couplets are mended with the full chime of the poem's end: 'his birdwing smile, and enchanting air of belief | in me—too soon at odds with grief'.[26] With this close, the things at odds are set more nearly at one. 'Passion' sets to rest what 'The Old Naval Airfield' timorously approaches and veers away from. It overlays upon the story of her wartime love the difficult matter of her mother's death and her own mourning for the person who had made that somewhat resented and still puzzling remark about the young man's death being 'just as well'. Perhaps the mother, habituated to dismissal of the past, thought the airman somehow not suitable for her daughter—or that anyway pining wouldn't bring him back. The young woman's view was different, as can be sensed from her early poem 'Lament' where she writes of how the heart would 'Leap to see the wings of his brows | Softly inclined towards me' and ends: 'Through the empty stations of the night

<hr>

[26] *The Pebble*, 107; *The Ghostwriter*, 44–5.

| My love is passed and gone.'[27] If those 'stations' are on the railway lines of young people's assignations, they may also be the 'air stations' of a flight instructor, with other wings than his eyebrows.

'Looking for Heroes', the chapter of her memoir set during the Second World War, concludes with an account of how early loss provides you with 'a new yardstick'. This 'causes you to doubt and confuse both the things you have known and the things you come on for the first time'. Then MacInnes adds: 'I am a skeptic about myself'. It's a useful quality in a writer. Elsewhere she notes that trying to write a poem meant trying to be honest. Her doubting and questioning of responses to people and things is part of trying to see them clearly, and for such work what she calls 'the low road' is demonstrably the best one to take. 'I often think that your despair is *voulu*,' one of MacInnes's friends remarks—presumably about this lingering addiction to the early loss and sense of bereavement, and the poet herself describes this as an 'unsolicited opinion' that 'verifies your suspicion'. Yet here it is possible to detect a divergence between the memoir of the lived life and of the writing life. Holding on to feelings, solidifying them, regarding them from different points of view so as to understand them is exactly what a writer might do, even when the person herself had been wise, and wisely advised, to move on.

Clearances is also a companion volume to MacInnes's poetry. It situates pieces such as 'The Old Naval Airfield'—which brings together the matter of her lost pilot, the deaths of parents, the problem of survivors' guilt, and, something less clear in the poem but now elucidated by the memoir, the idealizing in memory of the lost. The memoir calls by the nickname of Freddy the young flying instructor whom MacInnes met when a Wren driver in the latter stages of the war, but the poem gives him his baptismal name Philip. Her chapter 'Looking for Heroes' collocates a chance return to the airfield where she had been stationed with an equally casual visit to the home of the Pembroke family at Wilton. In her poem MacInnes has echoed the real name of her lost fiancé in that of Sir Philip Sidney. She also remarks that the story of the dying poet giving his water to a wounded soldier at Zutphen is apocryphal.[28] Here too a subtly self-sceptical intelligence is at work. The account of this part of her life is among the most gripping in the memoir, one which most fulfils the promise of the book's title; for here something seems well and truly cleared out—as appears less so of her poems on the subject.

[27] *Splinters* (Reading: University of Reading Printing School, 1953), 7.
[28] *Clearances*, 74 (three times), 75 (twice), 71.

V

MacInnes's fiction represents marriage as setting women at odds with their situations and then finds them inclined to take revenge for displacement by hitting out at the environment. The theme feels as if it is being discovered in the process of writing *Admit One*. Towards the book's close Katharine, now an MP's wife, attempts some amateur social work in her husband's constituency and half-haplessly risks wrecking his career by involving the press—vitiating the jejune attempt to do some good as well. The book's blurb says her husband 'is forced to take Katharine more seriously' while 'in terror, she in turn finds a comfortable protector'. Yet its closing pages, in which the young wife's misjudgements are smoothed over by the MP, feel like a capitulation, a loss. MacInnes's prose leaves the issues more dispiritingly open than the blurb would seem to like: 'On the gleaming roadway she paused a while, the blue white glare of the street lamps turning her lips a livid purple and her hair ashen, and then she decided, and began to walk homewards.' That detail of the 'street lamps turning her lips a livid purple' echoes the description of an unknown woman's sexual encounter with a stranger some twenty pages earlier: 'We were standing under those livid lights that turn lipstick purple'.[29] The identity of the woman as Katharine is thus confirmed at the point where she appears with 'livid' lips and 'ashen' hair to commit herself to 'walk homewards'.

In *The Quondam Wives* a similar theme is consciously and more fully evolved. In a convincing rewrite of the *Lear* plot, the two elder sisters attempt to revitalize a country house and bankrupt estate by turning it into a tourist trap while at the same time planning to let an extraction company excavate for gravel to build a motorway. This rape of the countryside is headed off by a reshaping of the tragic end in which revenge is enacted by the circumstance of '*A storm, with thunder and lightning.*' The consequences are that the ghastly plans are abandoned. The resistant environment itself has taken revenge on the vengeful plot of the elder daughters, killing the culpable father and the opting-out daughter into the bargain: 'Dark clouds congregated over the high wood. The green of the parkland was livid.'[30] That same word 'livid', used with muted ambiguity at the close of *Admit One*, now more overtly focuses the entire

[29]   Mairi MacInnes, *Admit One* (London: Putnam, 1956), 1, 199, 223.
[30]   Mairi MacInnes, *The Quondam Wives* (London and Baton Rouge, La.: Louisiana State University Press, 1993), 113.

book's theme: the parkland may be a strange stormy colour, but this time it's clearly furious too. MacInnes's novel includes two characters who have no equivalents in Shakespeare's play: the Lear character's ex-wife and mother of the elder daughters, Alice, an American businesswoman; and Esmé, his much younger second wife and mother of the Cordelia character. The plans to wreck the countryside are thus intimately connected with the motives of the elder daughters, who have been shaped by a failed marriage with an American who was living in England.

So the event which most troublingly links the non-human and the human for MacInnes is, perhaps not surprisingly, marriage—because she also appreciates that the human is part of the non-human in so far as natural forces are driving through us all. That early love which came to grief makes the young poet's heart leap like an 'Exulting dolphin'.[31] But, as Richard Wollheim has aptly noted, 'the parallel in the sexual sphere to talking of an artistic instinct would be to postulate a "matrimonial" instinct'.[32] The natural forces driving through us have to be organized by culturally possible forms if they are to result in the beneficial creation of children or art. Naturally, for a mother who is also a writer, these mediated desires to create may appear in conflict, and themselves the occasion for painful displacements and losses.

VI

The epigraph to *Clearances* is from 'Poem' by Elizabeth Bishop: 'Life and the memory of it so compressed | they've turned into each other.'[33] Bishop is an exemplary figure here. Of composing poetry again in her fourth decade when pregnant and living in New England, MacInnes writes: 'Maine led me to take the low road in writing a poem.'[34] The poet explains: 'Bishop's voice spoke in the night, not Robert Lowell's. He took the stage, she stayed in the wings. He had bravura, she disliked it. Even now, long after his rhetoric has dated, her voice continues to speak its everyday speech.'[35] MacInnes has already described in the post-war chapter, 'Cutting Loose', her encounter with Lowell ('an unappealing figure at odds with his poems') at a Salzburg summer school. He called

[31] MacInnes, *Splinters*, 7.
[32] Richard Wollheim, *Art and its Objects*, 2nd edn. (Cambridge: Cambridge University Press, 1980), 106.
[33] Bishop, *Complete Poems*, 177.
[34] *Clearances*, 224.
[35] Ibid.

her experiments with the style of Wallace Stevens 'distinguished verse', which, she adds, 'conveyed his disapproval unambiguously in perfectly polite form'. A few lines later, when she agrees to have her palm read, 'Lowell snapped to me, "You're no poet!"' This is the Cal Lowell who was soon after 'taken away in an ambulance to a Munich hospital'—a sequence of events from which his poem 'A Mad Negro Soldier Confined at Munich' derives.[36]

MacInnes had happened into what seems to have been a sexual hothouse. Another Lothario makes a clumsy pass at her: 'I thought he was helping me to my feet when I felt his mouth close to my ear whispering, "Miriam, be mine!" and understood I was part of a farce.'[37] Yet Salzburg was also where she first met her husband, the American scholar and writer John McCormick—though it was not until some years later that he made his far more successful advances to someone who clearly likes her first name, and evidently dislikes people making a mess of it. In Mexico City at the start of the sixties, her husband becomes obsessed with bullfighting ('The book he wrote . . . was called *The Complete Aficionado* and has become a classic'[38]). MacInnes does not hide her hatred of the sport, and her resistance to her husband's interest—which didn't extend, though, to preventing him from fighting a bull in the interests of research. Their Mexican acquaintances weren't exactly understanding of her point of view either: 'So did I feel excluded, was I hostile, was I jealous? "Tell me, Maria," he asked me in his grandee fashion . . . "what do you think of John's *afición?*"'[39] On her book's first page she describes being rung up by a woman anthologizing Irish women poets who (I imagine) mistakes her birthplace in County Durham for County Down, and assumes her name is Irish. MacInnes then describes how she is of Highland descent, and that her name is Scots Gaelic. 'I pronounced it for her. "Mahri." . . . "Too bad," she said, and rang off.' Then comes a remark which locates MacInnes firmly in the tradition of poets who happen to be women, rather than of women poets: 'Obviously the nature of the poems—their worth, damn it—did not concern her'.[40]

The story she tells in *Clearances* bears a number of resemblances to Bishop's—as so well told in Brett C. Millier's *Elizabeth Bishop: Life and the*

---

[36] Ibid. 95–6. For 'A Mad Negro Soldier Confined at Munich' see Robert Lowell, *Selected Poems* rev. edn. (New York: Farrar, Straus and Giroux, 1977), 58.

[37] *Clearances*, 94.

[38] Ibid. 181.

[39] Ibid. 161.

[40] Ibid. 3–4.

8

Memory of It (1993). There are the shared aesthetic tendencies, the loved and lost houses, a South American sojourn, a New England seaboard period, an encounter with a moose, and, most importantly, a long-running relationship with someone from another culture that is both profoundly enabling and complexly difficult. There is even the coincidence that MacInnes worked on a research programme in alcoholism at Rutgers, and, as is well known, Bishop suffered from it. Yet here, really, the similarities end, for MacInnes, after a few not-very-satisfactory relationships, married and, despite it all, stayed married to her John. *Clearances* also makes perfectly clear that her husband is a person of extraordinary resilience and adaptability—one who, unsurprisingly, seems to have expected others to be as able to cope, make do, and thrive.

Her description of his life before they met is awe-inspiring in both its sweep and understatement. His mother died when he was an infant and he was left with first grandparents then aunts by his father, so 'John saw that he was in effect on his own'. He financed his education through public high school during the Depression with a succession of odd jobs:

> the one that influenced him most, was as a deckhand on a freighter sailing out of New Orleans to the Mediterranean. At the outbreak of war in Europe he was a student in the University of Minnesota, where hand supported head in the same way, the possessor of hand and head often suffering great hardships. After Pearl Harbor John joined the navy, and spent more than four years commanding escort vessels or acting as navigator on larger ships on the Atlantic or Pacific. On demobilization he entered Harvard Graduate School on the GI Bill, to study comparative literature. He was already married, and had a child, Jonathan. The family went to Salzburg as soon as his thesis was accepted.[41]

As well as providing a succinct picture of her husband's early life, these crisp sentences offer a portrait of MacInnes the prose writer. The story she tells in the sustained narrative of her memoir explains and elaborates feelings that were first brought to light in poems such as 'I Object, Said the Object' and in 'Why Poetry'. (*Clearances* also revisits her conflictually familial sense of place essayed in the prose study 'Herring, Oatmeal, Milk & Salt'). Like the friend who accused her of wilfully sustaining her despair, a reader might feel that the long-brooded-over sense of her marriage is a little *voulu*, but this would be to misappreciate the compulsions of poet and writer.

In the final paragraph of 'Why Poetry' MacInnes throws down a chal-

[41] *Clearances*, 125.

lenge: 'Writing about the conflict, I put in jeopardy what I have been at great pains to preserve, and for this reason, I suspect: that literature itself is about fidelity and the efforts to escape it, with all the accompanying pains and joys.'[42] The word 'escape' upsets expectations here by describing writing as an ambivalent attachment to and attempted freedom from the circumstances of a life. Yet the terms for this irreducible ambivalence are always in need of resolutions, achieved on a once-only basis in works like MacInnes's 'Learning Another Language':

> In another part of the forest
> The thrushes sing in different phrases.
> In each part, the melodies are distinct.
> Castaway on the massive body of the earth
> (Sky overhead pale and empty as a page),
> You, poor fool, feel flints puncture your skin.
> O self! O drench of meaning![43]

The 'Castaway' circumstances of a life have bloomed as the absolute circumstance of art. Those decades of invisibility were the condition in which, for better or worse, her impressively independent loco-descriptive poetry has demonstrated how the conflict of fidelity with escape can result in a fine responsiveness over the distances. Relationship to person and landscape is, after all, MacInnes's key subject, her yardstick, and she has to give it a shape in thought, has to make 'Life and the memory of it' turn 'into each other'.[44] Her writings in both poetry and prose achieve this literary transformation with such understated skill, such feeling for the subtleties of the low road taken, that her writing itself comes to exemplify the only apparently simple understanding that 'to make things happen, you have to go away'.[45]

---

[42] *The Pebble*, 165.
[43] *Herring, Oatmeal, Milk & Salt*, 16; repr. with alternately indented lines in *The Pebble*, 11–12.
[44] Bishop, *Complete Poems*, 177.
[45] *Clearances*, 275.

CHAPTER 11

Tom Raworth and the Pop Art Explosion

I

Difficulties for advanced artists in the middle of the pop-art explosion were outlined by Hal Foster in a *London Review of Books* article called 'Pop Eye':

It is possible to conclude from this commingling of Modernist art and comic strip that by the early 1960s most devices of the avant-garde had become little more than gadgets of commercial design. And certainly this is one dilemma of the postwar or 'neo' avant-garde: some of the anti-art measures of the prewar or 'historical' avant-garde had become the stuff not only of established taste but also of the spectacle industries.[1]

These remarks cut so sharply across the 'high'- and 'mass'-art divide that you might be forgiven for thinking artists such as Robert Rauchenberg or Andy Warhol (both of whom earned a living at first by doing commercial design work) were, however ambivalently, involved in the preservation of the distinction between fine and commercial, high and mass art, even as they benefitted from crossover and juxtaposition. Certainly Arthur C. Danto found the challenge of the Warhol Brillo Boxes a prompt in that direction, being enabled to see them as art in 1964 thanks to his dawning idea of 'an artworld'.[2] T. J. Clark too implied as much when contrasting pop with abstract expressionism: 'The "popular" was easier to handle than the vulgar—it has more of a smell of art about it.'[3] Foster's reference to the 'spectacle industries' equally recalls the ways in which Clark has

<hr/>

[1] Hal Foster, 'Pop Eye', *London Review of Books*, 24/16, 22 Aug. 2002, 7. See also comments on the use of Jackson Pollock drip paintings by Cecil Beaton in a 1 Mar. 1951 *Vogue* fashion shoot in T. J. Clark, *Farewell to an Idea: Episodes from a History of Modernism* (New Haven, Conn., and London: Yale University Press, 1999), 302–4, or remarks on the designer takeover of her op art in Bridget Riley, *Dialogues on Art* (London: Zwemmer, 1995), 66–70.

[2] Arthur C. Danto, 'The Art World', *Journal of Philosophy*, 61/19 (1964), 580.

[3] Clark, *Farewell to an Idea*, 401.

tracked modern art's course in its equivocal relations with 'spectacle' defined as '*capital* accumulated until it becomes an image'.[4] Tom Raworth's recent poem 'Differences in Common' might be sardonically alluding to just such an idea: 'try | trading capital for an icon | effect'.[5]

Foster's remarks imply yet another familiar dilemma of avant-garde art: the more the world turns your work into taste and spectacle, the further you have to go with your scorched-earth policy to get any 'anti' effects worthy of the name. He is, however, inclined to be understanding of pop's anti-art antics—by underlining the likelihood that a category distinction was being preserved:

On the other hand, one might take the benign view that both fine art and commercial design benefited from this exchange of forms, and that the effect was to reinforce values that were, in fact, rather traditional—unity of image, immediacy of effect and so on.[6]

These observations on the classic pop artists—Foster lists alongside Lichtenstein (his article's subject), Warhol, Rosenquist, Hamilton, Richter, and Polke—form a starting point because their dilemmas were even more evident for the work of a slightly younger generation of artists, artists such as Jim Dine, with whom Raworth collaborated in the late 1960s. Both Dine and Raworth in their early work are redeploying and personalizing devices inherited from the 'historical' avant-garde. Though Dine referred to himself in 1966 as 'not a Pop artist',[7] his work is regularly discussed in books on the subject. Yet just as nothing is gained in insisting on the label, so I'm not implying that Raworth is, or was, or might have been a pop poet. Both artists did emerge, though, during that moment in the recent history of the contemporary arts[8]—and

---

[4] Guy Debord, cited in T. J. Clark, *The Painting of Modern Life: Paris in the Art of Manet and his Followers* (London: Thames & Hudson, 1990; rev. edn. 1999), 9. Lawrence Alloway, accredited with having coined the term 'pop art', was himself associated with the situationists. See also Thomas F. McDonough (ed.), *Guy Debord and the Situationist International: Texts and Documents* (Cambridge, Mass: MIT Press, 2002).

[5] Tom Raworth, *Meadow* (Sausalito, Calif.: Post-Apollo, 1999); *Collected Poems* (Manchester: Carcanet, 2003), 542.   [6] Hal Foster, 'Pop Eye', 7.

[7] Germano Celant and Clare Bell, *Jim Dine: Walking Memory 1959 to 1969* (New York: Guggenheim Museum, 1999), 196. Dine's work is discussed in (e.g.) Lucy R. Lippard, *Pop Art* (London: Thames & Hudson, 1970), Tilman Osterwold, *Pop Art* (Köln: Benedikt Taschen, 1991), and S. H. Madoff (ed.), *Pop Art: A Critical History* (Berkeley and Los Angeles, Calif.: University of California Press, 1997).

[8] The title to the Menil Collection exhibition catalogue—*Pop Art: U.S./U.K. Connections, 1956–1966* (Ostfildern-Ruit: Hatje Cantz, 2001)—offers a pair of bracketing dates for the pop era, though its beginnings were evident in work of the earlier fifties, and its aftermath may not yet have ended. All of the poems from *The Relation Ship* are from 1963–6. Some of those from *Nicht*

their oeuvres are in part inflected by a number of its characteristic strategies.

In a 1972 interview with Raworth, Barry Alpert asked the poet:

How appropriate do you think the artwork of Barry Hall, and Jim Dine, and Joe Brainard is for the books they worked on with you[?] What sort of sensibility do you think you share with them, or what qualities of a particular book were amplified or complemented by the artist involved?

In answering, Raworth went back to what now seems like a golden age of poetry book production, and to the first edition of *The Relation Ship*, published by Goliard Press in 1967 with art by Barry Hall:

I was more involved in those illustrations, we printed them together, and we were seeing one another nearly every day. They worked well, I thought. I liked seeing them in the book. I think the things Jim did in *The Big Green Day*, and the cover, were great. They're exactly like the sense of the book, abstract but precisely notated. Joe's drawings were his drawings. I mean he didn't have a text of the book. I trust those three people completely. Joe's worked because they're really still . . . nice in a book that's shifting sideways. The illustrations in *Lion Lion* were just things I had in my pockets—which fit into the shape of the book which is really notations on Spain and places and states of mind.[9]

The chronology to *Jim Dine: Walking Memory 1959 to 1969* notes that Dine and his wife Nancy moved to London in June 1967, and that the artist was at this time corresponding 'regularly with poets Ted Berrigan, Creeley, Kenneth Koch, and Ron Padgett'. Though the chronology fails to list Dine's contribution to *The Big Green Day*, published by Asa Benveniste in the following year, it does note that in 1969 'Dine's first book of poetry, *Welcome Home Lovebirds*, is published by Trigram Press', a book which was also 'illustrated with Dine's drawings'.[10]

Dine's interest in poetry can be detected from such witty works as 'The Sixteen Foot Line'—a panel painting of legs and shoes from 1965. He began writing poetry in 1966 when at Cornell. Poems like 'In a Green Suit', 'Portrait', 'Express', and 'Square', all from 1969, might almost have been written by Raworth himself—being composed with short punning phrases that are construed by means of a conceptual hopscotch:

War, Rosie?: Miscellaneous Poems 1964–69 also evidently fall within the bounds of that 1956–66 decade.

[9] 'Tom Raworth—An Interview Conducted by Barry Alpert', Spencer, Indiana, Feb. 11 1972, repr. in *Tom Raworth: An Exhibition* (Cambridge: Cambridge Conference of Contemporary Poetry 8, 1998), 8.

[10] Kara Vander Weg, 'Chronology' in Celant and Bell, *Jim Dine*, 236, 237.

working along   thinking things at a million second rate
talk makes me hoarse   so do cigarettes
black jet of fun   i cant stop seeing   it
red breaks out of the tape   touch my fingers   dont   yes[11]

This similarity could be attributed to a period or group style. Raworth's earlier poems, as Keith Tuma puts it, 'bear comparison with (and in my view surpass all but the very best) poetries associated with the so-called New York School' and 'with several Black Mountain poets'[12]—poets, that is, such as Dine's correspondents. Yet the shared manner may conceal a distinction in kind, for, despite the leaps and knight's moves, Dine's poems trace a broken line by means of what Mallarmé called 'la direction personelle enthousiaste de la phrase' (the enthusiastic personal direction of the phrase).[13] Despite the slightly stiff jumps, there's a continuity of assertive lyric presence across the parts, one which can also be heard in characteristic New York and Black Mountain work from the period.[14] Raworth's early poem dedicated to Jim and Nancy Dine, 'How Can You Throw it All Away on this Ragtime?', pays homage to a shared aesthetic freedom of association—but with a more fluidly rhythmic movement across the disjunctions, and a greater neutrality about who is talking and why:

he cannot move in clothes that are not his
trigger to many connections

of course the key slips through the grating
trust marginal thoughts[15]

---

[11] Dine, 'Square', in Celant and Bell, *Jim Dine*, 152.

[12] Keith Tuma, *Fishing by Obstinate Isles: Modern and Postmodern British Poetry and American Readers* (Evanston, Ill.: Northwestern University Press, 1998), 233. Raworth tends to underline his independence from such influences in the interview with Alpert (see e.g. 'Tom Raworth—An Interview', 9).

[13] Stéphane Mallarmé, 'Crise de vers', in *Mallarmé*, ed. A. Hartley (Harmondsworth: Penguin, 1965), 171.

[14] Consider e.g. the assertion of the first-person subject in Charles Olson's 'The Librarian' or 'The Twist' (*Selected Poems*, ed. R. Creeley (Berkeley and Los Angeles, Calif.: University of California Press, 1993), 86–8); in Frank O'Hara's 'In Memory of my Feelings', and any of his 'I do this, I do that' poems (*The Collected Poems*, ed. D. Allen (Berkeley and Los Angeles, Calif.: University of California Press, 1995), 252–7 ff.), or in much of Robert Creeley's *For Love* (*The Collected Poems 1945–1975* (Berkeley and Los Angeles, Calif.: University of California Press, 1982), 109–258), in Ed Dorn's 'On the Debt my Mother Owed to Sears Roebuck' or his 'Idaho Out' (*The Collected Poems, 1956–1974* enlarged edn. (San Francisco, Calif.: Four Seasons Foundation), 46–7, 107–22).

[15] Tom Raworth, *Nicht War, Rosie?: Miscellaneous Poems 1964–69* (Berkeley, Calif.: Poltroon, 1979), no. 23; *Collected Poems*, 51–2.

'I trust disparate elements going together',[16] Dine remarked in 1966, as if to underline a congruence of aesthetic outlook. Kit Robinson has drawn attention to the 'quick shifts of attention' in Raworth's earlier poems. Yet the degree of aesthetic yield in such work depends upon the distinctiveness of the elements and the nuances in the disjunctions between these 'specific, isolated points of view'[17] from and to which an engaged reader's attention shifts. Edward Lucie-Smith noted of the same work 'an elliptical quality reminiscent of Pierre Reverdy',[18] who wrote of the poetic image that 'Plus les rapports des deux réalités rapprochées seront lointains et juste, plus l'image sera forte' (The more the relations of the two realities brought together are distant and apt, the stronger will be the image).[19]

John Kerrigan is surely right to describe Raworth in the 1960s as 'a virtuoso of subversive paradoxes and quizzical epiphanies, playing revolutionary games with genre and form'. The critic, nevertheless, adopts a limiting term close to Hal Foster's: 'Though his early pieces sometimes lapse into verbal gadgetry, they are keen to push out the boundaries of how poetry should look and sound.'[20] This is one critical wisdom. However, it might be thought a little short on historical and geographical sweep. The typographical experiments of Pierre Albert-Birot, Guillaume Apollinaire's *Calligrammes*, Reverdy's and Vicente Huidobro's elaborately indented lines, and the experiments in sense derailment by Dadaists and Surrealists from Tristan Tzara to Benjamin Peret had already definitively pushed out the boundaries of how poetry should look and sound during the 'historical' avant-garde period. Those achievements were then reprised and consolidated in various personal-individualist directions in New York during the 1950s. Raworth's early work is inward with and well orientated in its allusion to such strategies, as at the end of 'November 1964':

> making jokes i secretly terrorized my children   i lay on the
> bed watching the sky change   peach to salmon   the clouds
> a dark blue   smoke blew across   a plane passed,
>   reflecting the sun

[16] Celant and Bell, *Jim Dine: Walking Memory 1959 to 1969*, 108.

[17] Kit Robinson, 'Tom Raworth', in Vincent B. Sherry (ed.), *Dictionary of Literary Biography*, xl, *Poets of Great Britain and Ireland since 1960*, 2 vols., pt. 2 (Detroit, Mich.: Gale Research, 1985), 467.

[18] Edward Lucie-Smith (ed.), *British Poetry since 1945* (Harmondsworth: Penguin, 1970), 366.

[19] Pierre Reverdy, 'L'Image', *Nord-Sud* (Mar. 1918), cited in M-L. Astre and F. Colmez (eds.), *Poésie Française* (Paris: Bordas, 1982), 379.

[20] John Kerrigan, 'Self-Reflections in the Poem's Pool', *Times Literary Supplement*, 19 Sept. 1997, 13.

> we land in the field   children
> run towards us as
> we remove our harnesses   they
> touch their fingers gently to the silk
> as it still moves[21]

The poem's solitary comma carefully nuances the syntactic relation across the line-ending and half a page width. Separated units often have syntactic continuity across their gaps, as in 'watching the sky change   peach to salmon'. The first person subject is not a guide marshalling the narrative elements, but one player among others: 'i secretly terrorized my children'. Raworth's art, at this stage, has continuities that are displayed as discontinuous, and discontinuities that may be presented continuously.

A quarter of a century later John Barrell speculated utopianistically that 'if continuous syntax is treated as if it were discontinuous, then the discontinuous can come to be heard, however uncertainly or provisionally, as continuous'. Taking mild issue with Colin MacCabe's review of *Writing* (1982), Barrell is contesting the politics of subjectivity embedded in its much more thoroughgoing disjunctivenesses: 'it is as impossible to imagine ourselves as emancipated from the coherence of self as it is to take seriously the notion that we are entirely constrained by it'.[22] Yet the ways of proceeding which prompted these reflections—Raworth's syntactic principle of no principles—can be sensed early. 'Continuation' from *The Big Green Day* has its share of disruptions and syntactic breaks ('corruption of instruction   don't want to hear it | shit even then he had misremembered it & | if he recalled the name i wouldn't know'), yet it comes to a close with a series of suddenly distended cadences and an unusually full rhyme:

> the only sound feet as the wind blows dust in the sunlight
> song of the regular bell and the still bodies burning under
>   the statue of verlaine
>
> but what i really care is that she came walking, walking
>   disguised as anyone
> a motorcycle passing early morning in the rain[23]

---

[21] Tom Raworth, *The Relation Ship* 2nd. edn. (London: Cape Goliard, 1969), unpaginated; *Collected Poems*, 16. I cite and discuss the Cape Goliard edition's lineation.

[22] John Barrell, 'Subject and Sentence: The Poetry of Tom Raworth', *Critical Inquiry*, 17 (winter 1991), 394, 392.

[23] Tom Raworth, *The Big Green Day* (London: Trigram, 1968), 36; *Collected Poems*, 36. I cite the Trigram edition's lineation.

This seems like a love poem that celebrates the recovery of a possibility for continuing ('now 14 years after . . . somehow expecting her to be there & recognizable'). The phrase 'disguised as anyone' is wonderfully thick with the sense that she can be seen in the two simultaneous aspects of otherness and recognition. The poem's shifts are themselves alive with a repertoire of possible moves; readers can't settle either into a centralized continuous subjectivity or, for that matter, a set-in-stone discontinuity. Among the qualities that keep the poem sounding so fresh is its being without formalistic orthodoxy of any evident colouring.

Raworth's observation that Dine's contributions to *The Big Green Day* are 'abstract but precisely notated' is perfectly to the point.[24] Aside from the collaged and screened buildings that appear on the cover and on the back page, there are four works. The first is printed in black on semi-transparent paper through which the title-page details can be read. It's a large ink blot with two smaller blots beside it like a minor archipelago. Around the back of the main island at irregular intervals Dine has hand-written the twenty-six letters of the alphabet in capitals followed by full stops. Facing the poem 'You've Ruined my Evening/You've Ruined my Life', the second shows a thumb- and four fingerprints which have been numbered, again with full stops: 1. 2. 3. 4. 5. The third—opposite 'The Lonely Life of the Lighthouse Keeper'—shows two casual and primitive line drawings annotated A. and B. The first of these, up at the top of the page, reads as a solid object on a ground, and looks vaguely phallic, while the second, down at the bottom, if read as hole, is a narrow vertical slot, and looks vaguely vaginal. Opposite the poem about a lonely lighthouse keeper, a man living in a phallic symbol, the Dine drawings may be illustrating the poem. Finally, opposite 'What is the Question', there are two drawings of what look like tufts of pubic hair, numbered 1. and 2. Dine's works in *The Big Green Day* (and the vaguely erotic prints used in the second edition of *The Relation Ship*) also exemplify a 1960s tendency to take sexual reference as liberationist—rather than, say, valorizing a niche for the adman to exploit. Though Dine's artworks are, more or less, abstract, they allude to the body, or to writing, or to both. In each case they are 'precisely notated' with the alphabet or with arabic numerals.

How are these works 'exactly like the sense of the book'? 'Here in Polynia' contains the lines 'hair, in a band, what became of her letters | inscribed in the cyrillic alphabet she had forgotten',[25] and four lines later:

---

[24] 'Tom Raworth—An Interview', 8.
[25] Raworth, *The Big Green Day*, 12; not in the *Collected Poems*.

'in the mementoes of my mind the decimal system has some uses'. 'Love Poem', similarly, makes play with the familiar form of a work in numbered parts—the play consisting in the fact that the first part has no number, the second is called 'section 2', and the next is numbered conventionally '3'. But then we get '4. continuing', 'on to 5', '6. (and approaching the bend)', then back to a conventional '7'. and finally '8. the end'.[26] The poem 'Collapsible' announces that there is 'nothing lonelier than hearing your own pop in another country',[27] while in 'These are not Catastrophes I Went Out of my Way to Look For' we encounter the poet studying one source for the iconography of pop art:

> no post today, newspapers and the childrens'
> comic, i sit
> in the lavatory reading heros the spartan
> and the iron man

While doing this he also smokes and examines 'new pencil marks on the wall, a figure four', then tells us that 'between my legs i read | levi stra | origina | quality clo'.[28] One of the poem titles, 'Wham!—The Race Begins', recalls the one-word exclamations of violent noise in comics, and the large Edwardian-advertising typeface used for the titles might be a part of the Lord Kitchener nostalgia in the British pop repertoire. These are no more than surface indications of ways in which the poems and the artworks are speaking similar languages of aleatory and creatively controlled gesture. Yet they do underline that the artfully judged Trigram Press edition of *The Big Green Day* constitutes a happy coincidence of compatible styles in different art forms within the same cultural moment.

II

Just as Dine's drawings of hair in *The Big Green Day* seem like an allusion to his own painting 'Hair' (1961), so too something like the fingerprints had appeared before. Öyvind Fahlström asked in 1963 if in Dine's 'Three Panel Study for Child's Room' the imprint of a child's hand on the canvas is 'a "fact" or an "object?" Is it an "event?" Is it a "popular" or "vulgar" way of painting?'[29] Fahlström had taken over Rauchenberg's studio at 128

---

[26] Ibid. 32–3; *Collected Poems*, 34–5.

[27] Ibid. 25; *Collected Poems*, 32.

[28] Ibid. 37; *Collected Poems*, 37.

[29] Öyvind Fahlström, cited in Brauer et al. (eds.), *Pop Art: U.S./U.K. Connections, 1956–1966*, 138.

Front Street in early 1961, so becoming a neighbour of Jasper Johns.[30] His questions are more a breathless way of covering the compatible options than an invitation to decide. The hand-print gesture too was by no means new when Dine deployed it. Johns's contemporaneous 'Study for Skin' pictures are from 1962, and the same artist's 'Skin with Frank O'Hara Poem' is from 1963–4. Yet there is a row of hand-prints clearly visible in Jackson Pollock's 'Number 1A' (1948) and Robert Storr has traced such kiddy-art gestures back to the Mexican muralist David Siquieros's experimental workshop in New York (1936), which Pollock attended.[31] The fingerprints in *The Big Green Day* take their place, then, like artful quotations, within a recognizable language that had been around for a number of decades.

'Three Panel Study for Child's Room' also adapts the collagist devices of Rauchenberg and Johns—themselves evolutions of cubist, Dadaist, and Surrealist methods—to an overtly personal allusiveness, in that it includes objects of childhood attached to the canvas: toy guns, a train, a car, and a Popeye statue. There is also an arrow and the words 'Chest of drawers goes here'. Jim Edwards, commenting on the picture, has suggested that 'The autobiographical sensibility of this work can also be seen as alluding to a personal iconography outside the usual sphere of Pop Art.'[32] Perhaps this is a polite nod in the direction of Dine's insistences that he is not a pop artist. It also seeks to distinguish between the anonymously public imagery of a Warhol Brillo Box, and the overtly personal and allusive approach to meaning in Dine's work of this period. Yet British pop artists, such as Sir Peter Blake, usually displayed private iconographic versions of public images—and this is also the case with a poem like Raworth's 'Claudette Colbert by Billy Wilder' where the references to 'flash gordon', for instance, crop up within what the poet himself called in the Alpert interview 'notations on . . . states of mind'.[33]

Equally, the minimal imagery in works by Johns of that time, as well as his painterly approach to texture and finish, point to refractedly personal

[30] See Kirk Varnedoe, *Jasper Johns: A Retrospective* (New York: Museum of Modern Art, 1996), 192.
[31] See Robert Storr, 'A Piece of the Action', in K. Varnedoe and P. Karmel (eds.), *Jackson Pollock: New Approaches* (New York: Museum of Modern Art, 1999), 45; and see T. J. Clark, *Farewell to an Idea*, 310–11 and fig. 184.
[32] Jim Edwards, catalogue commentary, in Brauer et al. (eds.), *Pop Art: U.S./U.K. Connections, 1956–1966*, 138.
[33] Tom Raworth, *Lion Lion* (London: Trigram, 1970); *Collected Poems*, 61. 'Tom Raworth—An Interview', 8.

themes.[34] It is, of course, one of the characteristic devices of pop to blur such distinctions between public and private. Popeye is a cartoon character for anyone, but the way particular children will appropriate that character for their life of play is both personal and autobiographical. Dine's and Raworth's approach can be read, though, with deep equivocation. T. J. Clark also recalled how in the 1960s and later 'The Situationists were primarily interested, in ways that have since become fashionable, in the possible or actual crisis of this attempt to regulate or supplant the sphere of the personal, private, and everyday.'[35] Do the artistic appropriations of popular objects and imagery resist the new consumer culture's attempts to 'regulate or supplant the sphere of the personal', or are they a cool capitulation to it? Raworth's early work allusively operates within this space of the public reference with personal reverberations, and all the indications are that it situates itself as 'subversive' and 'revolutionary' (to recall the terms of Kerrigan's review). But are the poems revolutionary in attempting to turn pop cultural products against themselves? Are they resisting the imagery that they appropriate? 'I Mean' from *The Relation Ship* doesn't unequivocally show any such tendency in its opening: 'all these americans here writing about america it's time to give | something back' or 'you gave me | the usual things, comics, | music, royal blue drape suits'. The next line appears to 'place' the straight world (as it used to be called) with the contrastive phrase 'what *they* ever give me but unreadable books?'. 'I Mean' ends with an imperative and a justification for it which may be drawn from Billy Wilder's *Love in the Afternoon*: 'follow me into the garden at night | i have my own orchestra'[36]—with a declaration of independence, that is, but from what exactly?

Interviewed by G. R. Swenson for *Art News* in 1963, Dine responded to a question about his attitude to pop: 'I don't deal exclusively with the popular image. I'm more concerned with it as a part of my landscape. I'm sure everyone has always been aware of that landscape, the artistic landscape, the artist's vocabulary, the artist's dictionary.'[37] The further Dine

---

[34] Johns's dark paintings from 1961–2 such as 'No', 'Good Time Charley', 'Painting Bitten by a Man', 'In Memory of My Feelings—Frank O'Hara', and 'Fool's House' may, for example, be interpreted as relating to the break-up of his relationship with Rauchenberg (see Varnedoe, *Jasper Johns*, 191, 388–9).

[35] T. J. Clark, *The Painting of Modern Life*, 9.

[36] Raworth, *The Relation Ship; Collected Poems*, 14–15. The italicized *they* is not in the later text. In his interview with Alpert, Raworth shows affection and respect for the Sam Fuller film *Pickup on South Street* alluded to in 'I Mean' ('Tom Raworth—An Interview', 13–14).

[37] Jim Dine, cited in 'From What is Pop Art? Part 1: Interviews by G. R. Swenson', in Madoff (ed.), *Pop Art*, 109.

goes along, the more he makes the visual artist sound like a writer. When it comes to 'my landscape ... vocabulary ... dictionary', isn't this as true of Raworth? His 1960s work is distinctly unlike contemporary pieces by, for example, Adrian Henri:

> And I saw DEATH in Upper Duke St
> Cloak flapping black tall Batman collar
> Striding tall shoulders down the hill past the Cathedral
> brown shoes slightly down at heel.[38]

Henri's use of pop images alongside public reference points like the cathedral reveals a sense of local community, a form of belonging, however improvised or attenuated. There is a consequent lack of inwardness that can be felt even here when the poet is striking what might have been a personal note by evoking this comic-book image of a capitalized 'DEATH'. Henri conjures the frisson of Americana in an ordinary Liverpool day. Raworth's work usually implies a more intimate sensibility at work—as again, for example, in 'Claudette Colbert by Billy Wilder': 'it's a chance i wouldn't miss for anything in the | wait in holland for | instance watching the windmills | that's more than flash gordon ever did'.[39]

There is a price to pay for this appropriation of the culturally invasive public icon as a personal or autobiographical symbol, as in Dine's use of the Popeye statue. The family feeling that might be alluded to in Dine's 'Three Panel Study for Child's Room' seems just that—an allusion. Raworth's early work is much possessed with children and childhood. 'Three' from *The Relation Ship* is a portrait of a parent and three kids, one of whom might be three years old:

> smell of shit when i lift him he knocks the book from my hand
> i hold him up she pulls at my leg the other comes in with a book
> he gives me his book picks up my book she pulls at his arm the other
> is pulling my hair i put him down he pulls at my leg she
> has taken my book from him and gives it to me i give him his book
> give her an apple touch the other's hair and open the door
>
> they go down the hall all carrying something[40]

Here the flat notation builds up a tension and then releases it, but without reference or even allusion to, never mind expression of, feeling that this

[38] Adrian Henri, 'Liverpool Poems', in *Collected Poems 1967 to 1985* (London: Allison & Busby, 1986), 31.
[39] Raworth, *Lion Lion; Collected Poems*, 61.
[40] Raworth, *The Relation Ship; Collected Poems*, 14.

occasion may or may not have generated. *The Relation Ship* in particular
(and *A Serial Biography* too) addresses matters of affect and affectlessness,
of vulnerability and invulnerability. Many of the poems, such as the
'*monday*' section of 'Six Days', worry about the speaker's lack of, or lack of
appropriate, feeling: 'i | was and still am addicted to self-pity'[41]. 'Anni-
versary' flatly states the alarmingly violent: 'i give you this bullet with
my name on it | how neatly it fits your mouth'; in the same poem, the
speaker idly commits a distinctly un-Buddhist act:

> just now not
> thinking, i touched the tip of my cigarette
> to the head of a moth walking by my paper knife
> & realised only when it spun and spun and fluttered
> what i had done.[42]

Then there's the line 'kitten i tried to drown holding it under the water—
it moved in the palm of my hand sound rising with the bubbles—a power
i didn't want' from the first part of 'Bitter Moon Dances';[43] or again in the
'*saturday*' of 'Six Days': 'there is nothing without touching',[44] which hangs
between a scepticism like that of doubting Thomas, a self-reference to the
poem's lineation, and a bit of raw sentimentality.

Lion Lion contains a drawing of a robot by Ben Raworth which appears
opposite the poem 'King of the Snow', a work shaped around a 'hunch-
back child' who 'gets finally to me'. In 'The Plaza and the Flaming Orange
Trees' the repeated exclamation 'daddy!'[45] is a quotation in which the
textual signs work to recess the exclamation within a frame where it can
signify without any clear lyrical ownership. Raworth's methods in these
early books increase the range and space of reference for the poem's field.
They do this with an egalitarian levelling of importance, so that the
reader is not guided to a prioritizing pattern; but this equalizing appears to
require for its working a flattening of affect within the lyric space. While
the title of Raworth's 1971 Cape Goliard Press publication, *Moving*, is
undoubtedly a pun—one that hinges together poetry in motion ('shifting
sideways') and poetry in emotion, it's by no means clear how unironically
relevant the second sense is to the book it names.

Here is Barrell, again, this time on Raworth's reading style: 'The equality of emphasis amounts to a refusal of all affect, a refusal which seems to

---

[41] Ibid. *Collected Poems*, 22.
[43] Ibid. *Collected Poems*, 3.
[45] Raworth, *Lion Lion*; *Collected Poems*, 54.

[42] Ibid. *Collected Poems*, 4.
[44] Ibid. *Collected Poems*, 26.

offer the words of the poem as an empty succession of empty signs.'[46]
Now it could be that—like a Mallarméan modernist who knows that
poems are made of words and not ideas or feelings—the affect is there,
but only *in* the words, not in their affectively loaded intonations. Keith
Tuma might be implying as much when he notes that Raworth's aesthetic is one in which 'tone, idiom, all allow us our temporary certainties'.[47]
However, T. J. Clark's sense of a crisis in attempts to 'regulate or supplant
the sphere of the personal, private, and everyday' might have a corollary
here too. Do Raworth's apparently affectless renditions of domestic
situations in *The Relation Ship*, for example, constitute responses to the felt
encroachment of a culture seeking to regulate and even supplant 'personal, private, and everyday' feeling? Did such a crisis in the languages of
personal affect move the poet away from dramatizing its expression into
a mode which allows only cool allusion to those very relationships which
most move, disturb, protect, and need protecting—relationships to family, friends, and colleagues which haunt the dedications, the epigraphs,
and frequently the texts of Raworth's writings?[48]

The aesthetic benefit of a cool approach, as Hal Foster's comments
suggest, is that it gives Raworth's early poems their equivalent of an
overall unity. The felt danger for his style is that it will lose a feel for the
necessary insouciance of this pop repertoire, precisely because of pop's
complicity with the 'spectacle industries', and will harden its discontinuous continuities into an in-your-face mode of keeping going. Suffering
something of a writing block at Yaddo in 1971, Raworth was reactively
dismissive of his work in poetry from the pop decade:

for ten years all I have done has been an adolescent's game, like the bright feathers
some male birds grow during the mating season. I look at the poems and they
make a museum of fragments of truth. And they smell of vanity, like the hunter's
trophies on the wall ('I shot that poem in '64, in Paris'). I have never reached the
true centre, where art is pure politics.[49]

Even if we were to take the poet at his word here, and describe the poems
as he does, there is no need to assume that this description entails its
implied evaluation. After all, there is something refreshingly honest about

---

[46] Barrell, 'Subject and Sentence', 393.

[47] Tuma, *Fishing by Obstinate Isles*, 238.

[48] Raworth's *Collected Poems* has as a dedication: 'This book is for my family and friends,
living and dead: small return for what they have put up with for forty years.'

[49] Tom Raworth, 'Letters from Yaddo', in *Visible Shivers* (Oakland and Novato, Calif.: O
Books with Trike, 1988), n.p.

the idea that a poet's early work contains showing off, or that individual poems which may have been hard to 'track down' stand out as memorable occasions for the young writer. What's more, 'a museum of fragments of truth' is rather a lot for a decade of poems to claim, and—as in Swinburne's rhyme about Collins's later work ('What brought good Wilkie's genius nigh perdition? | Some demon whispered—"Wilkie! have a mission."'[50])—it is possible to hope that artists will never make the mistake of trying to reach something as undesirable as the oxymoronic 'pure politics'.

J. H. Prynne's 'Foot and Mouth' addresses a sense in the mid-sixties of a commercial congruence in the pop idiom:

> Campbell's Cream of Tomato Soup, made I see at
> King's Lynn, Norfolk. Another fine local craft, you
> don't need to believe all you read about the New York
> art industry: 'the transfer of capitalistic production
> to the foreign market frees the latter completely from
> the limitations imposed by its own consumer capacity.'[51]

Prynne's allusion to Warhol and the cultural ambivalence of pop suggests why artists, particularly British ones, might well have wanted to take the aesthetics but leave the celebrations of shopping, fun, and the advertised way of life. It's worth noting that Ed Dorn, an important figure for both Prynne and Raworth, was also fiercely critical of Coca-Cola colonialism. Such a stance involved taking up positions on the mass of materials presented to the artist by contemporary consumer culture. In *Logbook* (1976), for instance, the text notes that 'The word I choose so precisely becomes next day the key word in an advertising campaign to sell a brand of stockings, because the word means *what comes to mind first*. And as a "writer" and an "artist" I should have sensed the direction of that word.'[52] This passage addresses the seemingly deluded desire of poets to escape the appropriative determinations of ideology by means of autonomous creative acts. They were expected to do this, according to at least one theory, by sticking to their intuition, an insight unique to each, which singles them out as having a vision worthy of expression.

[50] A. C. Swinburne, *Fortnightly Review*, 1 Nov. 1889, cited in the Introduction to Wilkie Collins, *Man and Wife* ed. N. Page (Oxford: Oxford University Press, 1995), p. vii.
[51] J. H. Prynne, *The White Stones* (Lincoln: Grosseteste, 1969), 77.
[52] Tom Raworth, 'Logbook page 399', in *Logbook* (Berkeley, Calif.: Poltroon, 1976); *Collected Poems*, 87.

Earlier in the previous decade, in 'Wedding Day', from *The Relation Ship*, Raworth had written:

> i made this pact, intelligence
> *shall* not replace intuition, sitting here
> my hand cold on the typewriter
> flicking the corner of the paper.[53]

A little later, in *A Serial Biography*, its narrator affirms, though in the simple-past tense: 'Intuition I still believed in above reason.'[54] The following decade, in the same section of *Logbook* referred to above, we read: 'Until the day I (   )ed that intelligence and intuition were the same, and passed through *that* fence.'[55] Dictionaries don't support the assertion that the two words are the same. They derive respectively from Latin verbs for looking at or perceiving, and for knowing as opposed to feeling or willing. Moreover, the distinction that Raworth deploys in 'Wedding Day' can be traced back at least to Kant's *Critique of Judgement*. Raworth might even be alluding to Benedetto Croce's answer to the question 'what art is', which he gives in the 'simplest manner':

art is vision or *intuition*. The artist produces an image or picture. The person who enjoys art turns his eye in the direction which the artist has pointed out to him, peers through the hole which he has opened for him, and reproduces in himself the artist's image.[56]

The immediate appeal of Croce's theory to a poet is well conveyed by Joseph Margolis's brief summary: 'the initial intuitive image (an emerging lyric awareness of what cannot be captured conceptually) argues for a distinctive cognitive identity between intuition and expression'.[57] Raworth may have been inclined to seek an aesthetic justification in lyric intuition, though he may not have always been able or even willing to keep his pact in these terms; and his poetic practice in any case indicates a disintegrating of any cognitive identity between intuition and overt expression.

[53] Raworth, *The Relation Ship*; *Collected Poems*, 6.
[54] Tom Raworth, *A Serial Biography* (London: Fulcrum, 1969), 16.
[55] Raworth, 'Logbook page 399', in *Logbook*; *Collected Poems*, 87.
[56] Benedetto Croce, *Guide to Aesthetics (Breviario di esthetica)* trans. P. Romanell (South Bend, Ind.: Notre Dame University Press, 1965), 8. At Yaddo in 1971 Raworth 'pulled down Maritain's *Creative Intuition in Art and Poetry* (and when else would I even look at a book like that?)'. That he pulled it down at all suggests an interest in the topic. What he will have found there suggests its limits (see 'Letters from Yaddo', in *Visible Shivers*, n.p.).
[57] Joseph Margolis, entry on Benedetto Croce in Ted Honderich (ed.), *The Oxford Companion to Philosophy* (Oxford: Oxford University Press, 1995), 11.

Raworth evidently likes to travel light, being inclined to call his poems 'notations', as he does in the interview with Barry Alpert, where he also explains that he prefers to write with his mind a blank: 'I really have no sense of questing for knowledge. At all. My idea is to go the other way, you know. And to be completely empty and then see what sounds.'[58] His definition of good work in this field would seem to be a poem that retains the freshness of its occasion in writing—in this case the 'Wedding Day' with its 'noise of a ring sliding onto a finger'. This freshness and intuitiveness is indicated stylistically by the relative lack of overt cohesion in the parts; yet it will also reveal an implicit coherence that can be sensed in the reading process:

> i wonder what's wrong with her
> face, she said, because
> there's nothing wrong with it really   i
> inhabit a place just to the left of that phrase.[59]

Raworth's youthful aesthetic looks like a working definition for poetry in which the imaginative action of the artist, the creative moment of bringing together disparate elements, delivers a uniquely poetic significance that could not be gained by any other means, and certainly not by the exercise of intelligence alone. Put another way, it's not a means for exercising intelligence, or deploying knowledge, but for recomposing the textures of experience—as in *Serial Biography* once more: 'Intuition I still believed in above reason. The *feel* of the thing. The oiled way it moved.'[60]

On 10 April 1968, in the course of a Norton lecture called 'A Poet's Creed', Jorge Luis Borges confesses to an early interest in Croce's aesthetic, but then declares that he withdrew from it to opt for allusion over expression:

Now I have come to the conclusion (and this conclusion may sound sad) that I no longer believe in expression: I believe only in allusion. After all, what are words? Words are symbols for shared memories. If I use a word, then you should have some experience of what that word stands for. If not, the word means nothing to you. I think we can only allude, we can only try to make the reader imagine.[61]

Although Borges claims that he came to this conclusion by abandoning a

---

[58] 'Tom Raworth—An Interview', 10.
[59] Raworth, *The Relation Ship; Collected Poems*, 6.
[60] Raworth, *A Serial Biography*, 16.
[61] Jorge Luis Borges, *This Craft of Verse* ed. C-A. Mihailescu (Cambridge, MA: Harvard University Press, 2000), 117.

mistaken belief in Croce's theory of expression, his picture of the writer inviting the reader to imagine with an allusion still has much in common with the account of art as intuition given by Croce. Borges's sense of an invitation to the reader equally brings back the consumerism problem. As Raworth puts it, 'The word I choose so precisely becomes next day the key word in an advertising campaign to sell a brand of stockings, because the word means *what comes to mind first*.'[62] Even if the artist's intuition has miraculously escaped ideological determination, there is no guarantee that the reader will be able to use it in an equally escaped fashion. Even unique expression has to be understood as available cultural allusion.

Turning for a moment to Raworth's 'Tracking (Notes)' of 1973, we may ask whether they aren't themselves in difficulties because they are instances of 'intelligence' in action, attempts to capture something conceptually: 'not rejecting *knowledge* but what (as in research) passes for knowledge and is but an illusion. The words (knowledge, intelligent etc.) must be redefined, or new words coined'. On the same page he asks: 'the connections (or connectives) no longer work—so how to build the long poem everyone is straining for?'[63] Here the poet seems to be uneasily adjusting himself to new conditions that will require a more sustained application of knowledge, intelligence, method, and purpose. Yet Raworth's ideas about how the connectives 'no longer work' or how words like 'knowledge' or 'intelligent' need redefining or scrapping are, precisely, counter-intuitive. They're so much more idea, and less experience.

The reader, as Croce's theory has it, then 'reproduces in himself the artist's image'.[64] No one is expecting Raworth to follow out Croce's prescription, and the fact that difficulties may be experienced in doing so equally reveals problems with the theory. Yet readers of his poetry do experience difficulties—and these can seem to derive from the relative lack of articulation, and the resultant equality of the parts that tacitly compose the aesthetically unified whole. Here a 'historical' avant-garde optimism about the creation of a new kind of reader, one formed through engagement with the jump-cut text, encounters the particular situations of actual, historically formed readers.

---

[62] Raworth, 'Logbook page 399', in *Logbook*; *Collected Poems*, 87.

[63] Tom Raworth, *Act* (London: Trigram, 1973), n.p. Raworth had noted that 'I can't write a long poem because I don't have any connections to make between whatever the bursts of energy are' ('Tom Raworth—An Interview', 4–5).

[64] Croce, *Guide to Aesthetics*, p. 8.

III

A connection between gaps in texts and various generation gaps is addressed in 'South America' from *Lion Lion*:

> as in the progress of art the aim is finally
> to make rules the next generation can break more cleverly   this morning
> he has a letter from his father saying "i have set my face
> as a flint against a washbasin in the lavatory. it seems to me
> almost too absurd and sybaritic" how they still don't know
> where power lies or how to effect change
> he clings to a child's book called 'all my things' which says:
> ball (a picture of a ball) drum (a picture of a drum) book (a picture of a book)[65]

This appears to sketch the Oedipal version of literary development, now a commonplace thanks to the ubiquity of Harold Bloom's theory of influence first published three years after *Lion Lion*. Perhaps these reflections on aesthetic conflict and change were prompted by Raworth's most sustained work of translation. He had translated poetry by Reverdy's contemporary and cubist-poet colleague Vicente Huidobro as part of his MA degree at the University of Essex, and later contributed prose renditions of his and many others' works to the *Penguin Book of Latin American Verse*.[66] Huidobro, like the muralist Diego Rivera, was in Paris (where 'South America' is set) during the cubist years. Paris is also where César Vallejo expects to die in 'Piedra negra sobra una piedra blanca' (Blackstone on a White Stone)—and where he did, in fact, die in 1938. 'South America' was 'written during the spring and summer of 1968', at about the time, that is, of the May Days in Paris. And it's in the poetry of South America by Vallejo and Neruda, for example, that 'historical' avant-garde styles and a commitment to revolutionary change most coincided.[67]

---

[65] Raworth, *Lion Lion; Collected Poems*, 59.

[66] Keith Tuma (ed.), *Anthology of Twentieth Century British and Irish Poetry* (New York: Oxford University Press, 2001), 613. Raworth's Huidobro translations are given as prose in Enrique Caracciolo-Trejo (ed.), *The Penguin Book of Latin American Verse* (Harmondsworth: Penguin, 1970), 101–9.

[67] T. J. Clark has given melancholy expression to what he sees as the fate of these coextensive efforts towards change: 'Some avant gardes believe they can forge a place for themselves in revolution, and have real truck with languages in the making; others believe that artists can be scientists, and new descriptions of the world be forged under laboratory conditions, putting aside the question of wider intelligibility for the time being. I do not see that either belief is necessarily (logically) misguided. It is just that in the actual circumstances of modernism—in modernity, that is—they have so far proved to be' (Clark, *Farewell to an Idea*, 10).

In Raworth's 'South America' it may be that 'they' are the older generation with their deference and trust for established power, qualities that seem then associated with a child's simplicity in taking a representation for the thing itself. The older generation is not only aesthetically to be outstripped, but this artistic revolution should include a cultural wise-up about representation that will produce an ideological shift as well. Yet, equally, 'they' could be the radical students of 1968—young people like the Dudley in 'Letters from Yaddo', who don't 'know the revolution's not coming by mail?' The penultimate poem in *Lion Lion* is 'Venceremos', one in which 'nothing changed' and, rather than a victorious coming together, we get a singular coming apart as the lion 'went five ways and left five different tracks'.[68] The reference to a child's book in 'South America' may also be a sardonic allusion to the politics of 'play power' (to borrow a phrase of 1970 from Richard Neville). The letter from 'his father', complete with allusion to Isaiah 5: 28, was actually received from Raworth senior, a devout Catholic convert. The poem can be read as equivocating between intergenerational stances. It ends in an oblique allusion to represented suffering:

> all one evening he draws on his left arm with felt-tipped pens
> an intricate pattern   feels how the pain does give protection
> and in the morning finds faint repetitions on the sheets, the inside
> of his thigh, his forehead   reaching this point
> he sees that he has written pain for paint   and it works better[69]

These lines have their own lightly concealed intricate pattern, moving from 'pain' to 'faint', then on to 'point' and to 'pain for paint'—which certainly works very well. In 'South America' is it possible, then, to detect through these hidden chimes an allusive sadness about the politics of generational difference and aesthetic change?

'Letters from Yaddo' also contains another piece of the poet's father's correspondence—correspondence that cuts in a number of pertinently conflictual ways. In his letter (transcribed by the poet into one to Dorn) Raworth senior confesses to a problem in appreciating his son's work:

There seems to have been a poetry explosion, and the resulting poeticised particles are too small for me to handle mentally with any satisfaction. Sometimes I seem to hover on the edge of a meaning to these minutiae of sensibility, but

---

[68] Raworth, 'Letters from Yaddo', in *Visible Shivers*, n.p; Raworth, *Lion Lion; Collected Poems*, 63.
[69] Raworth, *Lion Lion; Collected Poems*, 59.

finally it eludes me. Perhaps it is a private world that I am not supposed to enter. A pity, because beauty does not lose by being shared.[70]

Raworth's motives in transcribing the letter are not easy to judge. They display neither the desire to mock his father's reading abilities, nor to confess the failure of his art's capacity to communicate. Equally, the poet's father isn't seeking—like an outraged 'art lover' who doesn't know much about art but knows what he likes—to throw the pot of paint back in Whistler's face. Rather, he seems just saddened by the inability to make sense of these 'minutiae of sensibility'—a phrase which, by the way, acutely characterizes his son's work. What's more, that we have been here before is not lost on Raworth senior, for he adds apologetically: 'I hope you will not think of us as James Joyce thought of his aunt'. He then quotes Joyce's letter to the Aunt Josephine who had failed to acknowledge an inscribed copy of *Ulysses*. The parent who is having difficulty with his son's early books has evidently read either a selection of Joyce's letters or, perhaps more likely, Richard Ellmann's classic biography.[71]

As if to exemplify a couple of lines from 'Gaslight' in which 'someone else's song is always behind us | as we wake from a dream',[72] Raworth's father returns to his image later in the letter: 'I must have been thinking about your poems when I went to bed last night, because I dreamed that you had exploded Bridges' "London Snow" and I was trying to reconstruct it from the particles.'[73] Raworth's father may be attempting to piece together his son's poems with an aesthetics of reading that requires a poetry nearer to that which Croce would have assumed when he composed his aesthetic theory. Yet, equally, Raworth senior is admitting to doing what we all do when reading—working to compose meaning as we go along. This means, as Keith Tuma candidly puts it, that 'The pleasure one takes (or doesn't) in reading Raworth's texts . . . will be a matter of engaging the temporal processes of defamiliarization and destabilization and—equally—in our ability provisionally to configure the detail and nuance we pass in our motion through the text.'[74] Kerrigan saw reading Raworth in similar, but more emphatic, terms:

[70] Raworth, 'Letters from Yaddo', in *Visible Shivers*, n.p.

[71] James Joyce, *Selected Letters*, ed. R. Ellmann (London: Faber & Faber, 1975), 290–3; Richard Ellmann, *James Joyce* (1959), rev. edn. (Oxford: Oxford University Press, 1982), 538–9. Raworth's father is reported to have owned an early copy of the work that Joyce's Aunt Josephine didn't acknowledge in Tom Raworth, 'A Serial Biography: One', *The Wivenhoe Park Review*, 1 (winter 1965), 10–11).   [72] Raworth, *Act; Collected Poems*, 102.

[73] Raworth, 'Letters from Yaddo', in *Visible Shivers*, n.p.

[74] Tuma, *Fishing by Obstinate Isles*, 238.

Pursue his meanings too determinately, and you are frustrated by 'connectives' which don't work: even where syntax runs on, enjambing may not make sense. Approach the text too passively, and you are hypnotized by parataxis; the lines scroll by regardless, and nothing gets taken in. What seems needed is a style of attention which has got far enough beyond formalism to register the phrasal units as ventures and possibilities, tracks in 'an inexhaustibility of reference', rather than as the wreckage of something fragmented.[75]

Kerrigan's alternative to the wreckage nevertheless recognizes that to an ordinary reader 'fragmented' is likely to be the word that comes to mind, as it does in Raworth's own 'fragments of truth'—and as the poet's father implies with his 'poetry explosion'. Finding those 'minutiae of sensibility' too small to handle is then a recognizable description of such a reader's attempted attention to one of his son's poems. 'To practised avant-gardists', Kerrigan also notes, 'all this presents no problem.'[76] Readers used to such work position themselves confidently within the textual uncertainty, not anxiously reaching for fixities and definites. Yet Raworth's father's letter hardly illustrates the once supposed beneficial results of flabbergasting the bourgeoisie; rather, it makes a close relative feel somehow inadequate and raises a different, though equally familiar, question about the politics of difficulty. Raworth goes to look up the work he had exploded in his father's dream: 'So I went into the library to check on that "London Snow" poem. I found a collected Bridges on the shelf, and as I was reaching for it something distracted me.'[77] Here's the end of what he was distracted from:

> For now doors open, and war is waged with the snow;
> And trains of sombre men, past tale of number,
> Tread long brown paths, as towards their toil they go:
>   But even for them awhile no cares encumber
> Their minds diverted; the daily word is unspoken,
> The daily thoughts of labour and sorrow slumber
> At the sight of the beauty that greets them, for the charm they have broken.[78]

What's odd about the poem in the dream being this one is that it contains at its conclusion the notions both of 'beauty' and of something 'broken'—as it might be, exploded. This experience is being shared and dispelled by people walking to work, ordinary people by the sound of it

---

[75] Kerrigan, 'Self-Reflections in the Poem's Pool', 13.
[76] Ibid.
[77] Raworth, 'Letters from Yaddo', in *Visible Shivers*, n.p.
[78] Robert Bridges, *The Poetical Works*, 2nd. edn. (Oxford: Oxford University Press, 1953), 266.

too, with their 'cares', their 'thoughts of labour and sorrow'. Here Bridges might figure as a liberal straight man who provides Raworth's work with its perpetual foil. Yet, as the comparison with Joyce emphasized, we have been here before, and such contrasts themselves grow stale. As the poet himself writes in 'Gaslight', 'someone else's song is always behind us' and 'what we write is ever   the past'.[79] 'Wedding Day' and 'South America' have also become a part of literary history. The shrapnel from the explosion has fallen to earth, and the poems inhabit a place only a few decades to the left of 'London Snow'. All three poems are negotiating, in their different circumstances, with the personal, the private, and the everyday.

The quotation of his father's letter further underlines, if further under-lining were required, that Raworth's art is distinctively concerned with painful transits between public issues and the most minute and intimate notations of a life lived with others. Here is the opening to 'There are Lime-Trees in Leaf on the Promenade':

> we had come back from seeing one friend in the week
> they celebrated the twentieth anniversary of victory. fireworks
> parades.   and all across the town the signs the french
> people are not your allies mr. johnson   who were
> then, the old photographs.   garlanded the tanks with
> flowers now
> choke-cherry
>   a poison   we came
> separately home
>
> the children were there
> covered with pink blossoms like burned men[80]

Here 'the twentieth anniversary of victory' is VE Day. The American phase of the wars in Vietnam and the Liberation of Europe in 1944–5 are then rapidly located as a part of the poem's relevant context. Here the casual violence and difficulties with sentiment in *The Relation Ship* come fully into focus. The book, and with it much of Raworth's subsequent work, is an acknowledgement of complicity with, of probable helpless-ness in the face of, and a simultaneous resistance to violence and oppres-sion. These lines form an early and equilibrated example of a process which would be exacerbated with time—the infiltration of media culture

[79] Raworth, *Act, Collected Poems*, 102.
[80] Raworth, *The Relation Ship, Collected Poems*, 16–17.

into the personal, and, as a result, the personal suffered as public spectacle in lives which, nevertheless, struggle to sustain family members in a precarious affective environment.

Such a struggle is one sustained and sustaining theme in *The Relation Ship*, a theme culminating in the book's last poem, 'A Pressed Flower':

> evening
>> only the ground is dark, the sky still palest blue, and
> your grandfather whom i also love is perhaps dying
> these first weeks of the new year   because
> you are me i tear at you *how*
> can i channel it?   the children
> develop my faintly irritated voice[81]

The audible dotted lines of children and family in Raworth's earlier poetry, as well as the many dedications of work to relatives, friends, supporters, and fellow artists, produce a perhaps only apparent contradiction in the cultural significance of Raworth's oeuvre. While its procedures have embraced discontinuity for simultaneously cultural-critical and self-defensive ends, its framing devices (and, frequently, distinct elements in the texts too) have insistently alluded to the importance of human and emotional continuity. This is a further reason why MacCabe's sense of a 'joyful exploration of the release from the imaginary constraints of the coherent self' is an inaccurate account of even Raworth's most apparently disjunctive writing. Barrell saw with a lucid pessimism the predicament that his poetry may be obliged to inhabit:

We can perhaps see more clearly now than when MacCabe's review was written the impossibility—or so it seems at the moment—of choosing between the opposed accounts of the dispersed subjects of postmodernism, as emancipated from the tyranny of the requirement to produce and exhibit a perfect identity with themselves, or as the slaves and victims of a culture and economy which refuse to allow them even the illusion of selfhood.[82]

Perhaps a reason why there was and remains such an impossibility of choice here is because neither of these alternatives is either quite experientially real or at all culturally desirable. Asked to comment on the final pages of *The Relation Ship*, Raworth had this to say about 'A Pressed Flower': 'It was written a long time after the others, and it was there

---

[81] Raworth, *The Relation Ship*; *Collected Poems*, 27.
[82] Colin MacCabe, 'Dissolving the Voice', *Times Literary Supplement*, 1455, 30 Dec 1983, cited in Barrell, 'Subject and Sentence', 391; Barrell, ibid. 392.

because it was finally the end of that book . . . it was some sort of domestic end. And it still is.'[83] If Raworth has been able to stick with the commitments evident from his pact in 'Wedding Day', it will be because his work has not succumbed to an attitudinizing intelligence which would seek to valorize either the discontinuous or the continuous at the expense of the other. After all, meaningful growth and change at the personal and public levels will inevitably require, if they are to happen, the creative shaping of both. *Visible Shivers*, the book in which 'Letters from Yaddo' were finally to appear, is inscribed 'For | Mary Raworth, née Moore | (16th October 1902 to 3rd May 1983) | and | Thomas Alfred Raworth | (26th May 1904 to 30th October 1986)'.

[83] 'Tom Raworth—An Interview', 13.

CHAPTER 12

Roy Fisher's Last Things

I

Opening Roy Fisher's first hardback book of poetry, published in 1969, I found on the half-title page: '*the ghost of a paper bag*'. Leafing over a couple of pages, there it was again, this time looking like an epigraph to the collection, a volume called by its dust jacket *Collected Poems*, but by its title page and spine, give or take a pair of capitals: *collected poems 1968*. When I first stumbled upon this slim, eighty-page book I had never heard of Roy Fisher or read anything by him; but then, at nineteen, this was a common experience with volumes of collected poems. Yet his was so short, and since the dust jacket informed me that the author had been four in May 1935, I deduced that he had published his collected poems at the age of about thirty-eight. Nothing on the jacket blurbs suggested that he was dead, so what had happened? No sooner had Roy Fisher opened up shop, than he was pulling down the shutters. In fact, many one-book poets début with their last things, but the difference here was that this writer, who, I noted, had anyway published a prose book called *The Ship's Orchestra*, also appeared to know it at the time.

Reading on I came across that enigmatic phrase once more, this time as part of 'The Billiard Table'. The last poem in a section entitled 'Interiors with Various Figures', it describes a scene (partly prompted by a canvas of Braque's)[1] in which an 'I' and a 'you' confront an unnamed thing that seems to have slept the night on the billiard table. There is a 'mess of sheets on the green baize' which 'Suggests a surgery without blood', but, while the poem's 'you' keeps glancing at it, 'the tangle looks like abandoned grave-clothes'. Then comes the sentence including that half-title phrase:

---

[1] Roy Fisher, interview with Helen Dennis at University of Warwick Audio-Visual Centre, 9 May 1984, 130.

And watching it from where I sit
I see it's the actual corpse, the patient dead under the anaesthetic,
A third party playing gooseberry, a pure stooge, the ghost of a paper bag;
Something that stopped in the night.

(pp. 46–7)[2]

Placing first-person subject, verbs, and definite article ('I see it's the') in a commanding position at the beginning of the line starts an expectation that the correcting account will follow. Nevertheless, any security that 'I' knows better than 'you' what this mysterious thing might be is quickly dissipated in the sequence of predicates which grow more abstract and far-fetched as the list continues. The poem then changes both style and tack. The line shortens, the 'I' asks an unguarded question of the 'you' which hints that they may be married ('Have you ever felt | We've just been issued with each other | Like regulation lockers | And left to get on with it?'). The elusive object then becomes not the 'patient etherised upon a table' of T. S. Eliot's '. . . Prufrock', or a 'corpse', an empty tomb, or returning 'ghost' of literary and religious associations, but a newborn baby. The protagonists are described as 'Making unscheduled things like what's on the table'—not a planned pregnancy. The poem concludes with two lines like alternative endings. The former of these ('No longer part of us, it's still ours') catches the moment a couple find themselves with 'A third party playing gooseberry', their first child. The latter, with tacit reflexivity, unifies the over-identified target of the poem's imaginative trajectory with the implication that this is an as-yet-unnamed infant: 'Bring the milk jug, and let's christen it.'

Calling your first-born 'the ghost of a paper bag' would be cruel, but it's by no means a hopeless name for a book of verse, as Fisher explains:

I had first of all titled the collection 'The Ghost of a Paper Bag' as being the expressive title. Over the time it took to assemble and publish it, which was, I suppose, about three years, I wasn't writing at all and didn't imagine that I was going to write again. The exigencies of publishing brought up a possibility of calling it *Collected Poems*, and since I thought it probably was my total work, I let it be called *Collected Poems*. Typographically, I wanted the title 'The Ghost of a Paper Bag', which was still how I thought of the book, ghosted in in grey, but it got ghosted in in black on a page of its own, and it is still sort of drifting around there in the

---

[2] Parenthetical page numbers without other indication of source are to *Poems 1955–1987* (Oxford: Oxford University Press, 1988).

book. It looks like a motto but in actual fact it was the original title. It's always been reviewed as 'Collected Poems'.[3]

So this was 'the expressive title', but expressive of what? 'Something that stopped in the night', perhaps, or at any rate, something that stopped: 'I . . . didn't imagine I was going to write again.' The work gathered in this collection is the revenant of an everyday object, an object that has died in the unfamiliar way that paper bags do die and come back to haunt us. Though *Collected Poems 1968* is a largely paper container with a bundle of texts placed in it for safe keeping, the volume resembles more a carefully organized book than a round-up collection, an impression strengthened by comparing it with *Poems 1955–1980*—a publication which prints the texts in almost chronological order.

'Aside to a Children's Tale', a poem in rhyming quatrains about a funeral cortège passing through a city street, opens both volumes with an invocation of a last thing written when the poet was twenty-five. He had already composed floridly on this, my chapter's, theme in 'The Doctor Died', from the year before. Deaths had also touched other early pieces like 'The Military Graveyard in France' and 'The Lemon Bride', but with 'This dead march is thin | in our spacious street' the poet hits his stride, only to stop after four short verses:

> and four men like pigs
> bear high as they can
> the unguarded image
> of a private man;
>
> while broken music
> lamely goes by
> in the drummed earth,
> the brassy sky.   (p. 1)

Fisher's 'Aside to a Children's Tale' introduces a number of recurrent motifs and concerns, uppermost being the place of social and artistic formality in the cultural management of death. Though the final verse refers to a 'broken music', the two-stress metre and rhymes move to a mended theme. This not-so-broken music appears to be taken up and commented on by the next poem, 'Why They Stopped Singing'—a glance at the chronology of his writings indicating that during the fifteen months separating their compositions Fisher wrote only three uncollected pieces.

---

[3] 'Conversation with Roy Fisher: Eric Mottram', *Saturday Morning* (spring 1976), unpaginated, [1].

The title's seemingly programmatic resistance to musicality, a musicality that has been long associated with consolation and transcendence, may also acknowledge an involuntary stopping. In the book's second poem, lyric composition is detached from the rhythmic movement of music and, equally, the time-resisting stasis of visual art objects:

> They stopped singing because
> They remembered why they had started
>
> Stopped because
> They were singing too well   (p. 1)

The poem doesn't rhyme and is in no regular metre. The two-line stanza is little more than an ordering device for its spoken prose syntax. By stopping producing requiem-like lullabies, they, the poets, might have been learning to talk.

Turning to the close of *Collected Poems 1968*, a similarly careful ordering has been performed. The penultimate work, 'Three Ceremonial Poems', is a charm against entrapment. Fisher referred to the second of these as 'a sort of crummy classical art which then gradually breaks and flows',[4] but the 'crummy classical art' does appear to have been established by the end of the first. The evocation of 'Laurel bars, enamelled | with laurels, the bronze | on matted hair, blades | designed on guns' (p. 66) near its opening is capped with the closing image of a 'live mask plated over | Warrior, the stopped man' (p. 67). Fisher has commented on his attraction to images that are, or have, stopped:

> I'm fascinated by the element of arrest and the stopping of life in the picture, the photograph. Frozen movement interests me, partly because it seems to imply life. You look at something which is still, and you have to say: Alright, what is it still compared with?[5]

This comment was made after the publication of *Matrix* in 1971, when Fisher had come through his much-mentioned block of the later 1960s. Yet it would be more accurate to say that the poet has written at intervals from the edge of a permanent state of resistance. 'I tend to have a skeleton at the feast,' he has insisted, 'but to me it is a positive fact of writing, that one writes on the edge of a block, or under whatever the block is, the shadow of something.'[6] This shadow might be signalled by the poet's

[4] Jed Rasula and Mike Erwin, 'An Interview with Roy Fisher', in *Nineteen Poems and an Interview* (Pensnett: Grosseteste, 1975), 20.
[5] 'A Tuning Phenomenon: An Interview with Roy Fisher', *Sad Traffic*, 5 (1971), 33.
[6] *Saturday Morning*, [2].

attraction towards the static and choked off (like a skein that needs to be broken so that language can break and flow). In the second of 'Three Ceremonial Poems' a 'live mask plated over' is contrastively transformed to a 'Dark dust of shame | Raining down | Deep in the brickwork' which 'Changes its face' (p. 68). As if to keep commentators away from his ulterior motives, Fisher has tended to insist on the poem 'as art', a work which turns 'pity into an artistic composition'. This is merely true; yet, at a level which the poem doesn't articulate conceptually, 'Three Ceremonial Poems' shapes a transformative variation on satirical modernist militarism ('Stone, bronze, stone, steel, stone, oakleaves, horses' heels | Over the paving'[7]) with 'Absolute | Pity | Advancing' and 'shame | Raining down'. The 'stopped man' may well be dead, but pity and shame, with their present participles, have been set in motion. Thus, 'as art' the poem embeds an assumed ethics with political ramifications.

Collected Poems 1968 closes with 'After Working', making the poem figure as a postscript to the collection of work I had been reading. This point of organization is underlined by the poem's having figured as the opening piece in the Northern House pamphlet *The Memorial Fountain* (1966), whose contents are in this and other ways not replicated by the section of the book with that title.[8] 'After Working' is, unsurprisingly, a poem about being released from constraint. It describes how, looking up, 'The thoughts I'm used to meeting | at head-height when I walk or drive' (which being at 'head-height' have a social and communal familiarity) 'get lost here in the petrol haze | that calms the elm-tops'. Having managed a deflection away from what the poet is 'used to meeting', the poem then moves inward to the pictured 'half light of a night garage | without a floor'. Then onward it goes to conclude in darkness that is either the landscape of its starting point after sunset, or, freed from constraint, the territory of imagination. We follow it down past 'shores of what might be other | scummed waters | to oil-marked asphalt | and, in the darkness, to a sort of grass'. Once there, though, Fisher's poem and his *Collected Poems 1968* abruptly stop.

Nevertheless, finding a copy of *Matrix* made it evident that 'After Working' was not, in the chronologies of composition or publication, anything like Fisher's last thing. The not-absolutely-total writing block of the years in which he put together *Collected Poems 1968* proved to be one more of many stoppings to start again that have characterized the poet's

---

[7] T. S. Eliot, 'Coriolan', in *Collected Poems 1909–1962* (London: Faber & Faber, 1963),139.
[8] *The Memorial Fountain* (Newcastle upon Tyne: Northern House, 1966), 3–4.

creative life. Talking in 1977 Fisher admitted that 'I know my breath is short',[9] as if echoing the close of 'Seven Attempted Moves' with its 'Confinement, | shortness of breath. | Only a state of mind.' A person with short breath more frequently inspires and as frequently expires. These are also little deaths and reprieves experienced daily. This 'shortness of breath' is a 'state of mind' with 'Statues of it built everywhere', underlining the difficulty and necessity of the title's ' . . . Attempted Moves'. Escaping from tight corners into which it may have painted itself or scaling the walls of creative cul-de-sacs are situations that Fisher's sensibility characteristically finds itself needing to perform. The uncollected 'Kingsbury Mill' opens by wishfully thinking that 'If only, when I travelled, | I could always really move, | not take the apparatus'.[10] A comment on his style from some twelve years later implies that this wish has become the deed:

I'm not a spontaneous singer. I make sure when doing work of this kind that isn't discursive, by travelling light, that I have a medium which I have a feel for. *The Ship's Orchestra*, which is a bit dense for what I do now, was written in writing units—and you can see the length of them, two words, four or five lines of prose, occasionally a paragraph. It's quite simply beginning and then having the feel of the line, just as if you were drawing a line, until it ceased to be genuine, became fraudulent and just kept going by being inflated. I learnt to be honest with myself about the time I wrote *The Ship's Orchestra* and 'Interiors with Various Figures', and drop the line when it felt fraudulent.[11]

Even 'Continuity', written as Fisher was emerging from that block, figures images of stoppage: 'The fish-trap gives the waters form, | Minimal form, drawn on the current unattended, | The lure and the check.' The poet's forms, here, structure his lines upon those essential aspects of language use, the tiny stops and starts that give words significant shape, and the further poetic stops and starts of caesura, line-ending, enjambment, and stanza break. Yet no communication occurs if through these little deaths and resuscitations there is no flow, not of course for the trapped individual fish, but for the sustaining medium: 'So much free water.' The conundrums in this creative condition are contrastively related to the poet's recurrent material in the close of 'Continuity', where

[9] 'Roy Fisher Talks to Peter Robinson', *Granta*, 76 (June 1977), 17.
[10] 'Kingsbury Mill', in *The Memorial Fountain*, 13.
[11] 'Roy Fisher Talks to Peter Robinson', 17 (but citing the corrected text in Roy Fisher, *Interviews Through Time, and Selected Prose*, ed. T. Frazer (Kentisbeare: Shearsman, 2000), 74).

'The towns are endless as the waters are' (p. 71), and at the close of 'The Sky, the Sea':

> and beyond what has to be done
> there is nothing; the dusk
> free to come down,
> filled with cities of division.   (p. 96)

Fisher's longer works are all shaped by versions of his stop-start aesthetics. We find it in the collaged poems and prose fragments of *City* and the separately composed phrases, sentences, and paragraphs of *The Ship's Orchestra*; in those emblematically extreme fragmentary words, phrases, and passages of 'The Cut Pages' and the various sequences of lightly built lyrics. It is there in the thematically associated verse units of varying length that make up 'Wonders of Obligation' and the book-length *A Furnace*, which is composed by sequencing, with asterisk-marked pauses, passages of verse that vary in length from 3 to 101 lines. Thus, at the heart and lungs of his poetics is a cadence that might be called the temporary close. This is one that rounds off its passage, allowing breath to be drawn, preparatory, perhaps, to starting up again—as in 'Keats's death-mask | a face built out from a corner'. Yet then there's a stanza break, and these last words: 'If you're living | any decor | can make a wraith of you' (p. 110).

II

'Death is not an event of life':[12] these seven words begin by seeming to challenge a common assumption, but, once qualified ('Death is not lived through'), take on the air of a truism. So when Ludwig Wittgenstein was on active service with Austrian forces in the Great War what he came to understand by 'Der Tod' was: an individual's own death. There is no need to fear death: it cannot be experienced. Yet, equally truistic: dying is an event of life, as are other people's deaths. These, you *can* fear. And, while we're at it, you can fear the effect of your own death on others, such as those whom you love and who, you believe, love you: your death is an event of other people's lives. During the early 1960s Fisher 'decided that Wittgenstein's *Tractatus* was a very splendid sort of stylistic influence for one to adopt, and I paid far more attention to the *Tractatus* as a mode of

---

[12] Ludwig Wittgenstein, *Tractatus Logico-Philosophicus* (1922), trans. C. K. Ogden (London: Routledge, 1995), 185.

lineation, say, than to any poet'.[13] Robert Sheppard noticed this remark
and asked for clarification. His interviewee enthusiastically obliged:

You know how he writes it: the idea of a proposition which is about to hold firm
and then to be expanded on or qualified quite formally . . . That's what I'm talking about: lineation possibly in a conceptual, rather than a metrical, sense . . . It's
an utterly pragmatic, not theoretical, acknowledgment that I made to
Wittgenstein. I was just reading the English translation and just enjoying the
crack of it.[14]

This is no doubt true as far as it goes, which is to brush off any hint of a
claim to having developed a 'philosophy' or 'philosophy of composition'
from Wittgenstein's picture theory of elementary propositions.
However, numerous passages in Fisher's work indicate that he also paid
at least some attention to what the more aphoristic remarks in the latter
part of the *Tractatus* might mean, imply, or prompt—remarks such as
'Death is not an event of life. Death is not lived through.'

'As He Came near Death', the poem by Fisher that D. J. Enright picked
for *The Oxford Book of Death*, re-envisages spatial relations between a first
dying, then dead man and his relatives. 'As he came near death things
grew shallower for us', the poem begins, making dying an event of his life,
and his death an event of ours:

So he lay and was worked out on to the skin of his life and
        left there,
And we had to reach only a little way into the warm bed to scoop
        him up.   (p. 47)

Death is a creator of simultaneous intimacy and distance; Fisher conveys
this by at once drawing the participants close together ('things grew
shallower for us') and effecting a withdrawal into numbed isolation. The
intimate distance is further sharpened by details from the funeral:

Then the hole: this was a slot punched in a square of plastic grass
        rug, a slot lined with white polythene, floored with
        dyed green gravel.
The box lay in it; we rode in the black cars round a corner, got out
        into our coloured cars and dispersed in easy stages.

After a time the grave got up and went away.   (p. 47)

---

[13] *Saturday Morning*, [12].
[14] Robert Sheppard, *Turning the Prism: An Interview with Roy Fisher* (London: Damp Toads,
1986), 17–18.

If the last line parodies the Christian promise in the resurrection of the dead, it also figures a fading away of care in the dispersal of the living and the disappearance of the dead relative's grave. This final detachment is prepared for by a superficially uncomprehending distance in the narrating voice which recounts the events with a cultural inwardness that has, as it were, come out on the other side of the conventions—failing to take for granted the communal naturalization it nevertheless understands. Fisher's approach doesn't so much make routine and ritual strange, but draws out the strangeness in these cultural practices. One consequence is the poem's reducing to invisibility, at least partially or temporarily, the ties between people and things which make events of life conventionally intelligible: 'de-socializing art' (p. 186), as the poet himself puts it in his much later 'The Lesson in Composition'.

In an early, relatively socialized poem (incorporated into the collage of *City*) relative clauses shape the distances in a family disclosed through bereavement after a bombing raid. Fisher has disparaged this early work of 1957 for its unchallenging familiarity:

what happens to me is that I get people, more people as it were, reading me with more energy because I have written about an industrial city, because I have writ-ten at least one simple narrative poem about some of my relatives getting killed in an air raid. It's the thing most untypical of anything I believe about poetry that I ever wrote.[15]

This exaggeration was formulated to counter the version of his work being propagated at that time by Davie's pioneering critical study. 'The Entertainment of War'—whose memory-stimulating title was found in 'a newspaper editorial or a correspondent's report which I've lost'[16]—does, nevertheless, use a child's-eye view to turn away from any implied anger or bitterness at the wartime deaths it narrates. Unlike Dylan Thomas's poem of the Blitz, 'A Refusal to Mourn, the Death by Fire, of a Child in London', Fisher's stanzas needn't refuse to mourn: they barely register that cultural requirement and aren't tempted, directly at least, to fulfil it. The child's perspective sustained for the first nine of twelve verses is integral to the events described, the bombing and its aftermath, so that, despite the poem's conventional narrative mode, the family's existence is given perceptual density:

---

[15] *Nineteen Poems and an Interview*, 25.
[16] Interview with Helen Dennis, 129.

When I saw it, the house was blown clean by blast and care:
Relations had already torn out the new fireplaces;
My cousin's pencils lasted me several years.   (p. 18)

The corpse of the house is picked to the bone by relatives, and the poet as a boy is closely involved in the sharing out of the distant relations' property. Like so much of Fisher's work, 'The Entertainment of War' also intertwines mortality and style. The ambivalence caused by loss, grieved over or not, is formalized into patterns of proximity and distance, of being here, seeming to go away there, and of appearing then to come back, while having perhaps been here, or shifting back and forth between the terms, all the while.

The poem's observation that 'Never have people seemed so absent from their own deaths' (p. 19) touches Wittgenstein's remark—in this sudden death of an entire family where no experiences of dying or grieving involve their end with those who have survived. This, though, is how it felt to the poem's narrator remembering boyhood, not to an older relative:

But my grandfather went home from the mortuary
And for five years tried to share the noises in his skull,
Then he walked out and lay under a furze-bush to die.   (p. 19)

The circumstances of this grandfather's death are narrated with more detail in Fisher's autobiographical essay: 'there were perpetual ringing noises in his head. His trouble was probably tinnitus, but the general opinion—which he may have shared—was that he was losing his wits as he approached eighty.' The poet's relative either drifts off altogether or decides to make an end of it:

One January day, he disappeared, and the dog with him. Late the next day, and a dozen miles away in Sutton Park, the dog led a passerby to where he lay dying of exposure after a freezing night. I think everybody considered it a good death for him.[17]

There is no need to fear death: 'Death is not lived through'? But the threat or vicinity of death can be feared, as can its effects on others that survive. During the war Fisher's brother and brother-in-law 'spent years in danger' and the poet-to-be 'would engage in elaborate daily muttered rituals, which grew longer and longer, in order to ensure their safety,

[17] 'Roy Fisher 1930– ', in *Contemporary Authors (Autobiography Series)*, x (Detroit, Mich./New York/Fort Lauderdale, Fla./London: Gale Research, 1989), 81.

which I believed depended only on me'. Here the springs of art in childhood omnipotence fantasies, recognized as such, are succinctly outlined. Just as for so many who lived through those years, 'there was', Fisher adds, 'with the prolongation of stoicism, a deadening of areas of feeling'.[18] The boy narrator in 'The Entertainment of War' outlives the war death of his relations' family, then uses their total disappearance as a means for holding off fear:

> But had my belief in the fiction not been thus buoyed up
> I might, in the sigh and strike of the next night's bombs
> Have realized a little what they meant, and for the first time been afraid.

(p. 19)

Wittgenstein's remark in the *Tractatus* could be understood as a charm against the fear of extinction. Habitual accounts of Russian-formalist techniques in Fisher's oeuvre suppose that they are used to make experience more vitally perceived. Yet 'The Entertainment of War' and 'As He Came near Death' can be seen controlling, by giving an oblique perspective to, the emotions that are usually associated with the deaths of family members. In each case this is achieved by the adoption of a strategy that involves a calculated and partial non-understanding. 'As He Came near Death' fuses details from the poet's father's death in 1959 and his wife's grandmother's in 1964. It gives to them a paradoxical alien familiarity, as if being studied by an anthropologist not fully inside the forms of the culture being studied. Prompted by the *donnée* of its title, 'The Entertainment of War' exploits the *faux-naïf* potential in a boy's-eye view of sudden, violently public, yet also domestic and remotely familial death.

Two further sources of Fisher's sustained preoccupation with last things are suggested by the poet's autobiographical essay. The first of these is a bout of pneumonia survived at the age of twelve. 'That illness', which Fisher describes as 'a couple of months away from the world after passing through mortal danger' was 'a rite of passage':

it was as if I'd been somewhere unknown, and had come back altered. Wherever it was, it's the location of my imagination; it's still the place I have to find in order to write, and it's essential qualities never alter. It combines a sense of lyrical remoteness with an apprehension of something turbulent, bulky, and dark. There, I don't have to bother to grow older.[19]

[18] 'Roy Fisher 1930– ', 90.
[19] Ibid. 91.

There are many such objects or events and scenes in Fisher's work. One encounter predates by nine years the bout of pneumonia. In 'Rudiments' from 1979 the poet's father shows him first '*The Barge*', 'a dead black V in the murk, | gapped, with its bad face upturned'. The 'three- | year-old illiterate' and his dad are surrounded by 'turbulent, bulky, and dark' forms: 'Behind us, the biggest thing I'd ever seen, | the dark gas-holder | filled up the sky.' Finally, there is '*The Canal* itself':

> A black
> rippled solid, made of something
> unknown, and having the terrible property
> of seeming about to move,
> far under our feet. I'd never
> seen so much water before.   (p. 165)

This childhood thing which seems to be 'solid', but is also 'moving' and 'dark', provides an emblematic instance of shapes and forms, points of arrival and departure, in much of Fisher's work. We can find it in the night scenes of *City*, at the close of 'After Working', or in 'the sight of Brough | Keep, black as could be' that returns at the close of 'The Running Changes': 'there, once again, was Brough Castle | marking the turn south-ward, | and being dark' (p. 183).

The confinements of childhood illness and its requiring the sufferer to pass periods of time alone have helped prompt many a creative imagination, but a second source for Fisher's last things theme is distinctly more unusual. He describes how in early 1946 he decided that he was suffering from a form of undetectable tuberculosis and had no more than three years to live:

At all events, I now held the biggest of all my secrets. I was dead. No one must know. The shock would kill my parents, naturally; so delay their knowledge about it as long as possible. As the possessor of a deadly disease, I had the power of life and death over everybody I met.

The benefit of this 'hysteria', as Fisher calls it, was that it allowed him radically to 'revalue the currency of my dealings with my life: I renegotiated my contract'. In practical terms, this appears to have involved establishing a private self-importance ('the power of life and death over everybody') on the margins of his own existence: 'I'd had almost enough of life: I didn't want in, but I didn't want out strongly enough to commit suicide.' It is likely that many adolescents who are going to achieve things in the arts need to develop just such a secret self-importance that places them at a fluid distance from their surroundings. What is unusual about Fisher's way of achieving this is that he did it by imagining himself dead. This delusion lasted through the transition from grammar school to university:

When I left school my remote and disaffected manner earned me a beta-plus for Personality in place of the customary straight A awarded to Head Prefects. It was an unprecedented snub. I thought it no bad score, for a corpse.

At nineteen the university medical check and required visits to the local doctor made it quite plain that Fisher was, in fact, in reasonably good health: 'My game was up and I had to recognize it.' He describes how he then promptly forgot the delusion for two years: 'It was only then that I understood how mad I'd been, and it was the forgetting I found more frightening than the delusion itself.'[20]

'And there was another thing which was again merely personal', the poet observed in a discussion of inspiration for the composition of texts that went into *City*:

my father was dying, and he was very closely associated with the city, with these areas over a period of forty years. Seeing this life ending, and the inevitable process of turning up old photographs, old apprenticeship papers, extended time that made you realize more than usually how much the place was dependent upon very evanescent, temporal, subjective renderings of it, which might never BE rendered. And at that point my own lifetime was extended through his.[21]

Fisher's unpublished novel-fragment, *The Citizen*, contains an account of his father's last weeks, from which the 'Brick-dust in sunlight' (p. 20) passage of *City* was culled. At no point does the collage appear as an elegy for the poet's father, but there are moments when this 'merely personal' process of bereavement does touch the prose in that group of paragraphs: 'I look for things here that make old men and dead men seem young. Things which have escaped, the landscapes of many childhoods' (p. 20). Within the same sequence the work's 'Byronic'[22] narrating subject fends off a mock-gothic, or for that matter Hardyesque, sense that the dead can appear to us as revenants: 'I can see no ghosts of men and women, only the gigantic ghost of stone' (p. 21). Later in the collage Fisher's narrator-character attempts to distance himself from a further animating concern of nineteenth-century art; namely, the life and death cycle implied by organicist metaphors for cultures and societies:

---

[20] 'Roy Fisher 1930– ', 92–3 (three citations).
[21] *Nineteen Poems and an Interview*, 19.
[22] Ibid. 36.

Once I wanted to prove the world was sick. Now I want to prove it healthy. The detection of sickness means that death has established itself as an element of the timetable; it has come within the range of the measurable. Where there is no time there is no sickness. (p. 27)

As Wittgenstein puts it in that same proposition 6.4311: 'If by eternity is understood not endless temporal duration but timelessness, then he lives eternally who lives in the present.'[23] The teenage Roy Fisher had used the idea of his own death to keep the world at a distance by a fanciful management of time. The *City* passage hints at the need to rid itself of such temptations to a false omnipotence. Yet it contains a puzzling contradiction, for the detection of health—a concept which must lack meaning without the complementary concept of sickness—would also signify that 'death has established itself as an element of the timetable'. Just as the poet's imaginative hinterland, like the lyrical flights of poets who would 'so live ever',[24] is a place where he doesn't have to 'bother to grow old', this passage, conundrum and all, contains a desire to get beyond being in sickness and in health, 'out past' death, as a later poem puts it, revealing Fisher as by no means the first and surely not the last poet who has needed to announce that 'death shall be no more; Death thou shalt die'.[25]

III

J.-K. Huysmans's *À Rebours* contains a section in which the aesthete protagonist des Esseintes, as if attempting to outdo the pet lobster of Gérard de Nerval, has a tortoise studded with precious jewels; heavily underlining the narrative's message, the poor overwrought creature gives up the ghost. Discussing synaesthesia and the crudeness of olfactory imagery with Fisher in 1977 I was reminded of this same character's 'liqueur harmonica' and mentioned the book. 'I haven't read it,'[26] the poet replied. The son of a man who had been apprenticed to a paternalist jewellery firm in 1903, and who had been put to the craft as a boy because 'Jewellery of some sort had been the family trade for at least three generations',[27] Fisher will doubtless have noticed the interplay between luxurious artifice

---

[23] Wittgenstein, *Tractatus*, 185.

[24] John Keats, *The Complete Poems*, ed. J. Barnard, (Harmondsworth: Penguin, 1988), 452.

[25] John Donne, *The Complete English Poems*, ed. A. J. Smith (Harmondsworth: Penguin, 1971), 313.

[26] 'Roy Fisher Talks to Peter Robinson', 18.

[27] 'Roy Fisher 1930– ', 79.

and mortality in the aesthetics of symbolism. In his much-claimed fore-shadowing of 'The Death of the Author', Mallarmé described 'la dispari-tion élocutoire du poëte' as a ceding of the initiative to words, words which 's'allument de reflets réciproques comme une virtuelle traînée de feux sur des pierreries' (illuminate each other with reciprocal reflections like a virtual trail of fire on precious stones).[28] Fisher is, after all, a writer only a short distance from the 'two or three | generations of Symbolist poets' alluded to in *A Furnace* (*F* 24)[29] one of those 'Grotesquely called' and 'compelled | by parody to insist | that what image the unnatural | law had been stamping | was moving into Nature' (ibid.). Just as the 'Three Ceremonial Poems' evoked a 'live mask plated over', so *A Furnace* pic-tures an old couple close to death and their dog being 'beaten pewter'; it describes how the surviving husband's widowerhood 'was modern and quiet, his death | art'. What kind of art is it? That, for example, of the jewellery trade's electroplating: 'He was silvered. It was done' (*F* 26). 'Not that he actually enjoyed making jewellery', Fisher writes of his father, and his son's poetry too shows many signs of resistance to Western art's habitual buying of timelessness with precious obduracy.

There has been a slowly retrospective filling out to Fisher's 'death as art' studies: publication of *Matrix* collected the 'Five Morning Poems from a Picture by Manet', written twelve years earlier, while 'In Memory of Wyndham Lewis', also from August 1959, had to wait until *Poems 1955–1980*. Both sequences reveal that a thematic interest in the aesthetic rendering of mortal stoppage and how to sidestep it—though not the most congenial style for its articulation—were in place seven years before the 'Three Ceremonial Poems':

> Death music sounds for a boy by a stream,
> urgent as waves, as polished shoes,
> though amber screens of light shade him from time. (p. 10)

The last line sees in a visual image defence against dances to the music of time and inevitable death. Details in the previous two lines imply qualms about such a transformation. 'Death music' indicates a doubt about the reward of eternal art conferred on, for instance, Yeats's golden bird.

---

[28] Stéphane Mallarmé, 'Crise de vers', in *Mallarmé*, ed. A. Hartley (Harmondsworth: Penguin, 1965), 171. For an analysis of Roland Barthes's use of Mallarmé see Seán Burke, *The Death and Return of the Author: Criticism and Subjectivity in Barthes, Foucault and Derrida* (Edinburgh: Edinburgh University Press, 1992; 2nd edn., 1998), 8–10.

[29] Subsequent page references prefaced with an *F* are also to *A Furnace* (Oxford: Oxford University Press, 1986).

There is a dramatic act in the Irish poet's wish to be 'out of nature'; a death-defying posture. The 'boy by a stream' and the 'polished shoes' in Fisher's poem figure an interest in the specificity of lived circumstances, over which the music plays, giving an urgency to life in time, while threatening those circumstances with the death that will obliterate them: 'As in death, too, the world does not change, but ceases',[30] in the words of Wittgenstein's *Tractatus*.

'Once out of nature I shall never take | My bodily form from any natural thing,'[31] Yeats writes in 'Sailing to Byzantium'. The sea journey in progress is a one-way traffic: from life into art. The artifice, the golden bird, commands a music of unchanging forms. The emperor and attendants can make the bird sing, but can't themselves command the forms. 'Five Morning Poems from a Picture by Manet' examines the effect on life of such song. It feeds back on to the life that is supposed to enjoy such artifice the message of its unsensual music. These are also 'mourning poems'. Fisher has described his discomfort with the insistently heightened style of the sequence's fourth section:

for a long time I didn't publish that poem or think much about it. Because in terms of its style at that particular point it had a savage and black turn which didn't catch the tone of the way I usually think . . . in that poem, in fact, I talk about ordinary people who die and their death is given ceremony on an almost Yeatsian level. But they're certainly portrayed as dead who have been tricked and bamboozled by the world itself.[32]

Into the picture of an inhabited urban landscape comes the first person pronoun, deployed in this part as nowhere else in the 'Five Morning Poems . . .':

> Looking for life, I lost my mind:
> only the dead
> spoke through their yellow teeth
> into the marble tombs they lay beneath,
> splinters of fact stuck in the earth's fat rind. (p. 10)

The stanza begins by indicating that the mind is dispossessed by pressing home such understanding as only the dead may own. The gravestones are 'splinters of fact'—material objects which also serve to symbolize the

---

[30] Wittgenstein, *Tractatus*, 185.
[31] W. B. Yeats, 'Sailing to Byzantium', in *Collected Poems*, 2nd edn., ed. R. J. Finneran (Basingstoke: Macmillan, 1991), 194.
[32] *Nineteen Poems and an Interview*, 23.

only sure fact of life, its end. Living, according to the poem, seems closed to the understanding of the living. Similarly, as death completes a life, ending it, so it becomes a fact which, limited in time, can be understood. Because such understanding is useless to those still alive, 'I lost my mind' when 'looking for life'; the knowledge of the world that the dead have access to will not aid in living:

> Muttering, they told me how their lives
> from burial
> spiked back at the world like knives
> striking the past for legacies of wrong—
> the fiction of understanding worst of all.   (p. 10)

In 'Blood and the Moon' Yeats had asserted that 'wisdom is the property of the dead, | A something incompatible with life'.[33] In rewriting 'wisdom' as a more Stevens-like 'fiction of understanding' Fisher demurs at the 'Yeatsian level'. If his poem alludes to the lines by Yeats, it does so in order to contradict them. Not only does it say that the dead do communicate, but it states that they are not wise after the fact, and that if the dead do possess knowledge it may only be about how they have been 'bamboozled by the world itself'.

Fisher may slightly misremember his early poem here; the people who have died don't seem bamboozled by the world itself. Rather, according to the syntactically unstable final line of the third stanza, it seems to be the 'legacies of wrong' which do the bamboozling. Thus, it was the 'fiction of understanding' the world that misled them about the world. This fiction, identified with the dead, can also be associated with the aesthete's hope, that time can be transcended by means of an artwork's atemporal artifice. 'The fiction of understanding' may then be one of the knives that strike back at the world, at the reader of the poem and even its writer—via the stylistic and conceptual hand-me-down of an earlier period's poetry. Not only is Yeats echoed here, but Eliotic 'Thunder' too in 'Then I heard what the corpses said'. Almost three decades later, stripped of their rhythmic and lexical melodrama, these same figures 'come away | to the trench, | the dead in their surprise, | taking whatever form they can | to push across' and, as Fisher adds, unlike those earlier embittered and bamboozled ones, 'They've no news' (*F* 18).

Interviewers have turned more than once to the artistic sources for Fisher's mysterious 'Matrix' sequence of 1970. The poet had assumed

---

[33]   W. B. Yeats, 'Blood and the Moon', in *Collected Poems*, 239.

that everyone would know one such source. Elsewhere he was inclined to offer a lead: 'The cypresses, and the hooded figure, and the boat, and the place of the dead are out of a painting by a chap called Boechlin called *The Isle of the Dead* which is a popular late nineteenth-century piece of terrible painting.'[34] Fisher's adjectives 'popular' and 'terrible' roughly graph a mood in the third part of 'Matrix':

> This is where the dead
> are still supposed to make
> their disappearance:
>
> but always the same dead
> seem to be walking.
>
> Spectres of respect.   (p. 88)

Catching at the symbiotic relationship by which the dead thwart the living through the conventions of gothic art, that sardonic last phrase looks to have been found in the fact that 'spectre' and 'respect' are anagrams. As in the 'Five Morning Poems . . .', Fisher's work imaginatively inhabits Böcklin's painting, setting what had been the still paint of an evocative scene in motion:

> separate plots of twilight
> running the same destiny:
> the boat, with muffled oars,
> the hooded figure, B.D.,
> its hand upraised   (p. 89)

'B.D.' is not the initials of a name, but a qualification; the hooded figure is a priestly person who has received a Bachelor of Divinity, someone initiated in the theology that Fisher has elsewhere called a 'hoax area'.[35] The track of the poem takes in the architectural style of this hoax: 'a small classical temple | of the Lutheran cast', turning the teleology of absent last things into the aesthetic power of structures present in the world. The dark of the place where the dead are 'supposed to make | their disappearance', adding instant mystery with its twist on the expected words 'their appearance', is reorientated at the section's close:

[34] 'A Tuning Phenomenon', 32.
[35] *Nineteen Poems and an Interview*, 20; in his autobiographical essay Fisher describes 'an act which seems to me far more bizarre than my imaginary illness, but of which I'm more ashamed, since it was real, I joined a Christian church, on an intellectual whim' ('Roy Fisher 1930– ', 95).

> The mountains of the cypresses
> are the real dark of the path,
> humping their way higher;
>
> always a dark like that,
> set off by some artifice,
> growing.   (p. 89)

These closing lines redirect the reader towards a 'real dark': one produced by art's rendering of natural phenomena, as opposed, perhaps, to the unreal dark of an afterlife to which the dead go, or from which ghosts come. While Fisher's poem glancingly mocks a romantic cult of death by treating its conceptual markers as questions of style, it feeds on what it evokes. The quiet voicing of this passage does not overdramatize—as phrases like 'O sepia blooded-soldiers' (p. 12) or the 'ordure of decay' (p. 13) from 'In Memory of Wyndham Lewis' do—but its pared-back artifice is sustained by the spaciously gloomy mysteriousness of its source. If *A Furnace*, written over a decade after 'Matrix', 'will not give off much Gothic smoke' (*F* vii), it is because the long poem has found a strategy for the critical treatment of such material with far less of mockery's parasitic relationship to what it disparages.

A good deal of authority in human culture's history has rested, in the last resort, upon power over life and death. Earlier works of Fisher's had touched on complexes of assumption in our management of death. *A Furnace* confronts some of the cultural ideas that structure these powers—the ways, for example, that the clergy may have contributed to a willing, and seemingly needed, dispossession of the dead and of our own deaths:

>   Accept
> that the dead have gone away to God through
> portals sculpted in brass to deter,
> horrific. The signs of it, passably
> offensive in a cat or a herring,
> in a man are made out
> unthinkably appalling: *vide*
> M. Valdemar's selfless
> demonstration; drawn back and forth,
> triumphantly racked in a passage without
> extent, province of the agent,
> between antithesis and thesis.   (*F* 17)

M. Valdemar's demonstration is 'selfless' because 'It was his custom, indeed, to speak calmly of his approaching dissolution, as a matter neither to be avoided nor regretted.' The story's narrator, offering 'the *facts*' (as he tells us) of his experiment with mesmerism, puts his subject into a trance and has him speak from both sides of the edge of death: 'Yes;—no;—I *have been* sleeping—and now—now—I *am dead.*' His suspension somewhere, 'in a passage without | extent', between life and death is a literalized, pseudo-scientific enactment of the nineteenth-century's morbidified wish for immortality through art: 'It was evident that, so far, death (or what is usually termed death) had been arrested by the mesmeric process.' The story's ghastly allure, drawing the reader on towards a glimpse of the beyond which ends in Valdemar's horrific dissolution into 'detestable putridity'[36] is a version of Fisher's aversion to the placing of a fixed, dualistic barrier between life and death, turning a natural process between imprecisely delimited states into an iron curtain of separation and denial. *A Furnace* take the binary terms, subjects them to a sceptical blurring, and transforms them back into natural processes. His materials are, at times, gothic or, perhaps better, mock gothic, but his burner efficiently transforms them into a smokeless fuel.

Andrew Crozier has proposed that 'we should at least pause to ask if *A Furnace* does not arrive, finally, at a heterodox mysticism. Is its aim to annul the natural fact of death?' The critic would 'argue against such readings' because the poem contains no 'self-adequate symbolism'.[37] Perhaps so; but I would add that the 'aim to annul the natural fact of death' would qualify as another instance of infantile omnipotence in the absence of such symbols, and would be wishful even with them. After all, Donne's 'Death thou shalt die' evokes the Christian promise of eternal life, which can only be had, if at all, by first dying. John Matthias alluded to Crozier's pausing to ask, citing only as far as 'heterodox mysticism', so as to offer the counter-claim: 'It seems to me that it does.'[38] Are these views wholly incompatible? Fisher's later death studies need not aim to annul the natural fact of death, which might be just pie in the sky anyway, so as to qualify for the term 'heterodox mysticism'. The work that *A Furnace* does with the life–death binarism requires a basic, and 'by temper, realist'

---

[36] Edgar Allan Poe, 'The Facts in the Case of M. Valdemar', in *The Fall of the House of Usher and Other Writings*, ed. D. Galloway (Harmondsworth: Penguin, 1986), 351, 350, 357, 358, 359.

[37] Andrew Crozier, 'Signs of Identity: Roy Fisher's *A Furnace*', *PN Review*, 83, 18/3 (1992), 32.

[38] John Matthias, 'The Poetry of Roy Fisher', in J. Acheson and R. Huk (eds.), *Contemporary British Poetry: Essays in Theory and Criticism* (New York: SUNY, 1996), 56.

(p. 61), acceptance of death. Fisher's poem coolly acknowledges the necessary interrelation of the binary terms, their natural overlap, and the numerous ways (e.g. the 'involuntary memory' of genetics, dialect, environment, cultural and family traditions) that the dead of many centuries are actively present within and around us. It discovers mysticism in the patternings by which all our lives-and-deaths are part of the process. In this, too, his work extends a shadow cast by the early Wittgenstein: 'Not *how* the world is, is the mystical, but *that* it is.'[39]

Yet while the poet was working to identify cultural patterns in the various cults of death, others have played its literary junctures quite differently. His recent poem 'At the Grave of Asa Benveniste' begins by noting a 'Churchyard woman coming quickly from under the wall: | *You're looking for Plath*. No question-mark.'[40] Fisher had earlier lashed out at the exploitation of poets' suicides. On 22 January 1973, in conversation with Eric Mottram, he remarked that 'I think I've never written anything that I've kept, that was a straight reaction to an event, any thing in the world'.[41] However, on a prolific Friday just over a year before he seems to have composed 'Occasional Poem 7.1.72'. John Berryman threw himself off a bridge at about 9 a.m. in Minneapolis on that day. It is difficult not to think that Fisher's poem is a response to the news, as also to literary journalism about poetry and suicide: 'The poets are dying because they are told to die. | What kind of dirt is that?' Poets die just as everyone else, those pupils in 'One World', for example: 'By now, some are dead. I read of one | suicide and one broken skull.'[42] Fisher's angry occasional poem proposes that as a civilization which 'is filth' gets its hands on the controlling categories of 'taste', 'talent', and 'death', so the poets

> are going to be moving on out past talent,
> out past taste. If taste
> gets its gift wrappers on death—well—
> out past that, too. There are courts
> where nobody ought to testify.   (p. 99)

As when overtaking a parked car, 'to be moving on out past' something you must first acknowledge its presence there. Just how Fisher was to move 'out past' death in his poetry would take the composition of *A Furnace* to make clear.

---

[39] Wittgenstein, *Tractatus*, 187.
[40] *Poetry Review* 86/3 (autumn 1996), 28.
[41] *Saturday Morning*, [2–3].
[42] *Consolidated Comedies* (Durham: Pig Press, 1981), 8.

IV

'Inscriptions for Bluebeard's Castle', like its probable source in Béla Baláz's libretto for Bartók's opera, evokes, without ever directly stating, the central fact of Bluebeard and his murdered wives. In 'The Lake of Tears' we read that 'Day has turned to a silver mirror | whose dead extent the weeping | eyes could never see'. In 'The Treasure House', 'What | the sun touches | shines on forever dead | the dead images of the sun | wonderful'—an idea echoed in 'The Last Door' with its 'Moonlight the dead image of the day' (102–3). The word 'dead' in these brief passages, taken in the context of the poem's title, cannot help but evoke the dynamics of a moral tale about curiosity and fate which will be the death of Judith. Though human languages are indelibly suffused with the complexly conflictual ethics and morals of the cultures in which they are spoken, Fisher has seen a benefit in tactically 'de-moralizing' as well as 'de-socializing' literary art:

In this country people take a little bit of poetry, a little bit of literature, and if there's a moral in it, however crude, it will be taken, it will be coarsened still further... For my taste I moralize too much already.[43]

A good deal has been made of the poet's deploring this supposed simplifying tendency of readers and critics to take the moral, or equally of some poets to 'sloganize' their images. Crozier notes that 'his findings are kept provisional'.[44] Ian Gregson says his poems are 'indeterminate in their form and meaning' and present themselves as 'provisional statements leading to other provisional statements'.[45] Sean O'Brien cites Gregson and sums up the situation: 'Fisher is a markedly anti-foundationalist poet: we might say that his *modus operandi* depends on rejecting the idea of ends and purposes.' However, the critic, an admirer of Fisher's writings, if not some of the company they've tended to keep, adds that 'his work also reveals the mind's hankering after teleology'.[46]

Praise for the provisional, for the 'anti-foundationalist'—from these different critical perspectives—is bought at the cost of tacitly shoring up the very foundations which Fisher is said to be against, foundations represented by some demonized monger of definitive findings (often a

---

[43] *Nineteen Poems and an Interview*, 16.

[44] Crozier, 'Signs of Identity', 26.

[45] Ian Gregson, *Contemporary Poets and Post-Modernism: Dialogue and Estrangement* (Basingstoke: Macmillan, 1996), 172.

[46] Sean O'Brien, *The Deregulated Muse: Essays on Contemporary British and Irish Poetry* (Newcastle upon Tyne: Bloodaxe, 1998), 112.

travestied, ghostly Davie). As O'Brien's second thought demonstrates, the provisional is conveniently given its street value by being contrasted with systems of uttered verities about ends, purposes, and various last things. But what if, as so much of Fisher's poetry affirms, such systems are at best dubious illusions, nothing more than a 'hoax area'? Though the hankering that O'Brien detects may perhaps be construed out of *City* and other work from the 1960s, later writings, such as *A Furnace*, are less amenable to this view of Fisher as an experimentalist with recidivist backslidings towards 'ends and purposes'. There is, after all, Fisher's tendency, despite comments in interviews, to issue (however uncomfortably) definitive-sounding statements in poems: 'I want | to remark formally, indeed | stiffly, though not complaining, | that the place where I was raised | had no longer deference for water' (p. 161). In a world without foundations, such moments in Fisher's work constitute neither the uttering of gilt-edged securities nor the provisional 'takes' of an anti-foundationalist loosening a stiff world propped up on doubted—yet, by that token, needed—foundations. They are readings that neither ask for, nor require, future revision. Nor do they come offered as a tentative choice among Art's marvellous 'selection of skies' (p. 106).

Gregson concedes to Davie the assumption that Hardy, Larkin, and Fisher 'are all sceptics'.[47] Yet while Hardy and Larkin have poems such as 'The Oxen' or 'Church-Going' which insinuate the 'hankering' that O'Brien notes (suggesting that they are reluctant, nostalgic, or frightened poets wishing, but unable, to believe in such purposes and ends), Fisher seems a different brand of sceptic—more thorough, more like the 'honest doubt' of David Hume, with his arguments about causality, his distinction between fact and value, or his holding firm to atheism in the jaws of death and despite Boswell's obstinate questionings. Nor could it be said of Hume that his lack of belief in teleological foundations prevented him from making definitive statements. In the fully credited Heraclitean world of *A Furnace* all is flux and, as 'Handsworth Liberties' had earlier stated, 'in the crowd of exchanges' we not only 'can change' (p. 118) but can't avoid doing so. Definitive statements are, then, in any case, provisional (since everything is). So the provisional ones may as well be framed in as definitive a style as they need to be.

In his interview with John Tranter, Fisher notes of *A Furnace* that

There's an ongoing discussion of death, whether the reader likes it or not. I'm talking about death quite a lot, and I'm like this evangelist who's at your elbow,

---

[47] Gregson, *Contemporary Poets*, 171.

saying 'Talking about death . . . we just had this bit about sex and drink or whatever and birth, I was thinking about death while we were doing this, let's think
about death again a bit, and the burial of the dead.' I go back to it because that's
the thing I'm riding through the poem.[48]

Though Crozier rightly noted that the poem is not 'exclusively about last
things', he also observed that 'a main topic of *A Furnace*' is 'the connection
of the living to the dead, one's own life and death'.[49] Matthias remarked
that 'The Return', a section which 'no one to my knowledge, has traced
back to Ezra Pound's early poem of the same title or to Yeats's use of it in
A Vision, is uncanny in its dealings with the dead'.[50] Something of this
uncanniness can be evoked by noting that Fisher's poem is not so much,
and not only, concerned with 'the connection of the living to the dead',
but of the dead to the living. After all, the former can be subsumed under
the familiar sources and resources of poetic inspiration: active remembering. The latter takes seriously 'the life of the dead' (*F* 17) as not
merely a substitute vitality that the living attribute to them, but a range of
energies which impress them upon the living. The 'Who | shall own
death?' section of *A Furnace* explores some of the belief structures, or lack
of them, that had driven the poet's earlier stylistic approaches to the role
of death in culture:

> and Lazarus the test case. Only Almighty
> God could have worked that trick. Accept
> that the dead have gone away to God through
> portals sculpted in brass to deter,
> horrific.   (*F* 16–17)

Those 'portals sculpted in brass' are the shading in of his older theme, as,
later, are the descriptions of those local deaths: 'Had the three of them
been art, it would all have | been beaten pewter' (*F* 26). 'Death is not an
event of life', Wittgenstein asserted, but Fisher now contradicts that with
some of the knowledge familiar to poetry:

> that you are dead
> turns in the dark of your spiral,
> comes close in the first hours after birth,
> recedes and recurs often. Nobody
> need sell you a death.   (*F* 18)

---

[48] 'John Tranter Interviews Roy Fisher', *Jacket*, 1 (1997).
[49] Crozier, 'Signs of Identity', 26, 27.
[50] Matthias, 'Poetry of Roy Fisher', 56.

'Frozen movement', Fisher had said, 'interests me, partly because it seems to imply life.'[51] This passage works at loosening the hold of the life–death binarism by registering the interdependence of the concepts, the sense that through a human span they will recede and recur, that no one need sell you a death, because being alive your death is already implied and necessary. Even so, it may not be an event of your life, but it is the one event not of your life to which you are inescapably connected. It is also true that in the English language 'Nobody | need sell you a death', because the word 'death', if it is not to function abstractly, tends to takes an identifying genitive form: your death, the death of me. Shakespeare's Feeble encourages himself with the thought that 'we owe God a death', which is true enough if glossed as 'a man can die but once',[52] though (as *A Furnace* would prefer) not true if implying that death is on loan from some higher power. The supposed ownership of death by a transcendent force is described as a conceptual strategy by which civic authority can assert its cultural control over the citizenry, for: 'as if it were a military installation', they will 'specialize and classify and hide | the life of the dead' (*F* 17).

Fisher's remark in the Tranter interview that he's 'like this evangelist' offers a subject with more of a palpable design—'whether the reader likes it or not'[53]—than is usually supposed by criticism of his work devoted to the exposition of compositional strategies. Not that Fisher's writings had previously been devoid of such designs; there is, for example, the section in 'Wonders of Obligation' where 'I saw | the mass graves' prepared for those 'the air-raids were going to kill'. Having sidled into the passage with that vulnerable two-syllable line, 'I saw', Fisher gives it reiterative impetus in mid-flow:

> some will have looked down
> into their own graves on Sundays
>
> provided
> for the poor of Birmingham
> the people of Birmingham,
> the working people of Birmingham,
> the allotment holders and Mother, of Birmingham.
> The poor.   (p. 155)

---

[51] 'A Tuning Phenomenon', 33.
[52] *2 Hen. IV*, III. ii. 228–9.
[53] 'John Tranter Interviews Roy Fisher'.

If you take an adjective and put a definite article in front of it, you'll probably have a prejudice: 'The poor.' Fisher's sequence 'poor', 'people', 'working people', 'allotment holders and Mother' subjects the pigeonholing noun phrase to a mutedly angry scrutiny. Silkin could respond to this aspect of Fisher's work without difficulty, finding a 'sober dismay at the treatment individuals receive at the unkind hands of authority'.[54] There is a metaphor setting up the passage's main theme: 'mass graves dug | the size of workhouse wards'. The wartime surplus of death is found to be one of the routes by which a civic authority can impose itself on lives, using the methods of Poor Law social control:

> Once the bombs got you
> you were a pauper:
> clay, faeces, no teeth; on a level
> with gas mains,
> even more at a loss than before,
> down in the terraces between the targets,
> between the wagon works
> and the moonlight on the canal. (p. 156)

In the news documentary section of 'Stopped Frames and Set Pieces', the circumstantial detail of deaths appears to propel the composing attention into an aesthetic response: 'From the dead there were long runs of blood, right down into the gutters. Its brightness was astonishing, the gaiety of the colour' (p. 35). In the later poem 'the moonlight on the canal' has an initially similar brightness. Yet here the announced reluctance to 'sloganize ... an image'[55] homes in on a glanced at political-cultural point ('even more at a loss than before') through a change of perspective ('between the targets ... moonlight on the canal'). Fisher's turned colloquialism 'even more at a loss' finds a continuity between the puzzlement of the local people and their greater confusion when dead. His deft use of paired prepositions ('down in') puts the reader into the cockpit of a Dornier 217 or Heinkel 111 following the lit canal's map-reference point so as to hit the wagon works. They were as likely to be beginning the process of demolition and rehousing in this working-class district of Birmingham that had provided the source material for 'The Entertainment of War'.

If, in *A Furnace*, Fisher has been able to move 'out past' death, he has done so by getting beyond the debilitating reluctance of 'It is Writing', a

[54] Jon Silkin, *The Life of Metrical and Free Verse in Twentieth-Century Poetry* (Basingstoke: Macmillan, 1997), 305.
[55] *Nineteen Poems and an Interview*, 16.

poem which properly mistrusts the desire 'to glorify suffering' because 'it
could do it well'. Making definitive statements once more, the poet
mistrusts 'the poem in its hour of success, | a thing capable of being |
tempted by ethics into the wonderful' (p. 111). This counter-ethic has the
limitations of any negative injunction. Invoking what it rejects, its little
moral-aesthetic would commit the poet to avoidance tactics—tactics
such as those of the murderer in 'Barnardine's Reply':

> Barnardine, given his life back,
> is silent.
>
> With such conditions
> what can he say?
>
> The talk
> is all about mad arrangements, the owners
> counting on their fingers,
> calling it discourse, cheating   (p. 126)

This character, 'a dissolute condemned prisoner' in *Measure for Measure*,
makes an emblematic figure to take as the victim of experience sentenced
to him by higher suspect powers. Not inclined to 'Be absolute for
death',[56] as the Duke in a monk's disguise urges Claudio, but dissolute for
survival, Barnardine's 'sole insight into time | is that the right day for
being hanged on | doesn't exist' (p. 126). He may not influence his or
others' fates by talking, as variously the play's main characters can and
do. Rather, he defers the day of his execution by remaining drunk, in
which condition a priest cannot give him the last rites. Reprieved as part
of a puzzling plot wind-up in the final act, he exits without a line.
'Barnardine's Reply' represents this silence as the only suitable response
to the play's 'talk' called 'discourse' which is 'all about mad arrangements'.
The power of the authorities to arrange Barnardine's reprieve in *Measure
for Measure* appears so detached from the lives being arranged, that anyone
who experiences these is wholly unable to describe or comment on what
happens. As a phrase from 'In the Wall' has it, they are 'Seeing | what was
never to be said', and are 'lacking, in any case, | discourse' (p. 109).
Barnardine is a curious representative of those many urban figures in
Fisher's work who must try to avoid 'a bare-buttocked, incontinent, |
sunken-cheeked ending' (p. 98) within an environment and living conditions given as 'a free sample from the patentholders' (p. 126). But *A*

---

[56] *Measure for Measure*, dram. pers. and III. i. 5.

Furnace is by no means 'silent' on such issues of ownership and power; its achievement is to reinhabit the territory of the poet's earlier work, flushing into the open values and beliefs, implied or assumed, that had already inclined him to forms, methods, and subjects over many years. His long poem thus deploys, and frequently states, an evolved outlook, an ethics of attention to the world—one which is most tested, as an ethics tends to be, in its relations with death and the dead.

The later volume *Birmingham River* contains 'They Come Home', an episode originally part of the 'Core' section of *A Furnace*—which seems, naturally enough, to inhabit the spiritual climate of the long poem. Fisher has described this work as a 'straight autobiographical piece . . . about my wife Joyce's parents who had died within a fortnight of each other in 1980'.[57] Its relation to his 'engine devised, like a cauldron, or a still, or a blast-furnace, to invoke and assist natural processes of change' (*F* vii) appears in the double burning of the loved-ones' remains. First their ashes are brought home from the crematorium, releasing them from the grip of the civil authorities' version of how the dead are to be disposed of. The unflustered polemic of the poem evokes what may be done with the ashes as a project to keep our losses with us: 'by no means separate the dead | from anything'. This proposal takes on its own Heraclitean dimensions when—matter being neither created nor destroyed—some of the ashes are re-cremated with kitchen rubbish in a municipal-refuse disposal kiln:

> They're going again in a day or two:
>
> to be in part twice-burned
> in city flames; eight hundred
> degrees of the lance-burner
> under the oven's
> brick arch, and then whatever
> blast of the municipality
> lifts the remainder haze clear of Sheffield
> and over the North Sea.   (*B* 52)[58]

The dead parents, far from being 'out of nature' (as Yeats had hoped to be), come home to their daughter's domestic garden, where 'your | fingers and mine' are 'mixing your dead | in a layer across the topsoil'

[57] '"They are all gone into the world": Roy Fisher in Conversation with Peter Robinson', in *Roy Fisher, Interviews Through Time, and Selected Prose*, 111.
[58] This and subsequent page references prefaced with a *B* are to *Birmingham River* (Oxford: Oxford University Press, 1994).

(B 51)—via a thematically apt exhaust-pipe refit shop. Inside the car, they are jacked up with the vehicle. They come home not just into the ordinary life of their survivors, but home to nature, to the continuum of matter and energy of which we form a part, finally dispersed into the air we breath: 'by no means separate | from anything at all' (B 52).

A section from Fisher's recent 'The Dow Low Drop' puns on the drop of being hanged, by presenting in outline one of the poet's contemporaries at school who had perhaps miscalculated in an erotic game and died, self-hanged, wearing his mother's underwear. The poem imagines this person's future life:

> He's quieter. A good
> career in a science behind him
> following a narrow squeak in youth.
>
> I could greet him, dull idea,
> if I didn't believe my knowledge.[59]

This 'dull idea' evokes so as to fend off a dialogic encounter with the dead. Such poetic occasions have been revived with recourse to European epic traditions and in particular Dante's *Divine Comedy* on innumerable occasions over the past century, among the most recent being Seamus Heaney's 'Station Island' sequence. Fisher's lines eschew the tactical mock surprise in T. S. Eliot's adaptation of *Inferno* XV: 'What! are *you* here?'[60] The boy's death at fifteen is reported to his classmates:

> The censors of the day
> comforted the boys with *suicide*,
> *impatience, despair, tragedy.* Said
> nothing about the underwear.

The fear of this supposed perversion, implied in the censors' economy with the truth, is dispelled by the poem's even-pitched, unemphatic candour. Knowledge of a teleology which would have required those last things of judgement and punishment to structure its afterlife is implied, but fended off—not evoked for literary occasion furnishing. The poem is aware of this much-worked theme. However, it understands it as 'dull', perhaps from overuse. For this poem, the presence of the dead in the world of the living doesn't require an afterlife, merely a life, one in which such presences are felt without need of either doubt or surprise. The poet

---

[59] *The Dow Low Drop: New and Selected Poems* (Newcastle upon Tyne: Bloodaxe, 1996), 193.
[60] T. S. Eliot, 'Little Gidding', in *Collected Poems 1909–1962*, 217.

might have to greet 'My schoolmate, D., | forty-seven years hanged' only if 'I didn't believe my knowledge'.[61] This is a winning turn because knowledge—and that's what the line asserts it to be—doesn't usually require belief anyway.

In the work of *A Furnace* and after the poet has been quietly renegotiating for a secular culture what are nevertheless humanly necessary relations between the living and the dead. Yet while 'They Come Home' significantly revises the anthropology of 'As He Came near Death', the short poem 'Going', also from *Birmingham River*, was written from one of Fisher's more casually socialized perspectives:

> When the dead in your generation are still few,
> as they go, they reach back; for a while
> they fill the whole place with themselves,
> rummaging about, inquisitive,
> turning everybody on; bringing
> their eyes behind yours to make you see things for them.
>
> Now there are more, more every year,
> sometimes a month packed full with them
> passing through, first dulled, preoccupied, and then
> taken quickly to silence. And they're gone, that's all.   (*B* 10)

Not inclined to see this conclusion as contradicting the presentation of death and the returns of dead in *A Furnace* or 'They Come Home', Fisher has described this poem as one in which 'Death, the Sniper, was taking all the initiatives'.[62] Its composition and publication after the longer works nevertheless point to a poet not inclined to depend on the insights of his own previous work as the parameters of future perception. 'Going' remains alive to further ways in which death, for the living, is an event of life. Fisher's later poetry has not aimed to annul the natural fact of extinction, but by taking on 'Death, the Sniper' it has perhaps partially disarmed him.

Among Fisher's most recent writings are pieces that belong to the endgame of an oeuvre. In 'Item' the poet describes in passing the bodily effects of his stroke: 'One-handed | this year at least, and lame';[63] in the first of 'Four Songs from the Camel's Coffin' he states: 'I've come apart.'[64] Like 'The Collection of Things' with its 'cracked gold | high-

---

[61] *The Dow Low Drop*, 193.

[62] '"They are all gone into the world": Roy Fisher in Conversation with Peter Robinson', 112.

[63] 'Item', in *New Writing*, vi, ed. A. S. Byatt and P. Porter (London: Vintage, 1997), 302–5.

[64] *A Gallery for Gael Turnbull*, ed. Peter McCarey (Glasgow: Au Quai, 1998), 9.

heeled slipper' (*B* 1), 'At the Grave of Asa Benveniste' evokes the residual power of objects to carry meaning beyond the lives of their owners: 'Asa, | your hat's in the bathroom.'[65] What will survive of us is things, and these last things, like so much of his work, are things that will surely last. And, to end with, there is now a piece by Fisher called 'Last Poems':

> Thinning of the light
> and the language meagre;
> an impatient shift under the lines
>
> maybe to catch the way
> the lens, cold
> unstable tear, flattens and tilts
> to show codes of what may be flaring
> at the edge and beyond.
>
> Absence of self-pity suggests
> absorption in something or other
> new, never to be defined.
>
> But in all those years before
> what *was* his subject?[66]

While the opening lines sketch conditions of lack which might imply 'self-pity', its announced absence evokes the still vital possibility of 'absorption in something or other | new'. Fisher's way of approaching the new requires him to be wary of preventing its appearance by knowing what it might be. It is 'never to be defined' because to do so would prevent it from coming into literary being—as happens with the compositional demise outlined in the fifth of the 'Diversions': 'I saw what there was to write and I wrote it. | When it felt what I was doing, it lay down and died under me' (p. 133). So, then, 'what *was* his subject?' Nothing that you could know beforehand, but a thing at last made manifest by the works in which it is embedded.

Two of the great perennial subjects for poets have been love and death. In 'Of the Empirical Self and for Me', he writes that 'Even | love's not often a poem' (p. 125). From first to last, though, for Roy Fisher death often is.

[65] *Poetry Review*, 86/3 (autumn 1996), 29.
[66] *C.C.C.P.*8: Programme and Anthology of the Eighth Cambridge Conference of Contemporary Poetry, 24–6 Apr. 1998, 26.

Bibliography

Anderson, L., and Shapcott, J. (eds.), *Elizabeth Bishop: Poet of the Periphery* (Newcastle upon Tyne: Bloodaxe, 2002).

Alighieri, Dante, *The Divine Comedy*, trans. Charles Singleton (Princeton, NJ.: Princeton University Press, 1970).

Alley, Elizabeth and Williams, Mark (eds.), *In the Same Room: Conversations with New Zealand Writers* (Auckland: Auckland University Press, 1992).

Allott, Kenneth (ed.), *The Penguin Book of Contemporary Verse*, 2nd edn. (Harmondsworth: Penguin, 1962).

Auden, W. H., *The English Auden: Poems, Essays, and Dramatic Writings 1927–1939*, ed. E. Mendelson (London: Faber & Faber, 1977).

—— *Collected Poems*, ed. E. Mendelson (New York: Vintage, 1991).

—— *Prose and Travel Books in Prose and Verse, i. 1926–1938*, ed. E. Mendelson (Princeton, NJ: Princeton University Press, 1996).

Austin, J. L., *How To Do Things With Words*, 2nd edn., ed. J. O. Urmson and M. Sbisà (Oxford: Oxford University Press, 1975).

—— *Philosophical Papers*, 3rd edn., ed. J. O. Urmson and G. J. Warnock (Oxford: Oxford University Press, 1979).

Barrell, John, 'Subject and Sentence: The Poetry of Tom Raworth', *Critical Inquiry*, 17 (winter 1991).

Barzini, Luigi, *The Italians* (Harmondsworth: Penguin, 1968).

Baudelaire, Charles, *Le Spleen de Paris* (Paris: Éditions de Cluny, 1943).

—— *Intimate Journals*, trans. N. Cameron (Harmondsworth: Penguin, 1995).

Bedient, Calvin, *Eight Contemporary Poets* (Oxford: Oxford University Press, 1974).

Benjamin, Walter, *Illuminations* (New York: Schocken, 1969).

Bergson, Henri, *Oeuvres*, ed. A. Robinet (Paris: Presses Universitaires de France, 1970).

Bertolani, Paolo, *Incertezza dei bersagli* (Milan: Guanda, 1976).

Bertolucci, Attilio, *Viaggio d'inverno* (Milan: Garzanti, 1984).

Bishop, Elizabeth, *The Complete Poems 1927–1979* (New York: Farrar, Straus and Giroux, 1983).

—— *Collected Prose*, ed. R. Giroux (New York: Farrar, Straus and Giroux, 1984).

—— *One Art: Selected Letters*, ed. R. Giroux (New York: Farrar, Straus and Giroux, 1994).

Bishop, Elizabeth, *Conversations with Elizabeth Bishop*, ed. G. Monteiro (Jackson, Miss.: University of Mississippi Press, 1996).

Blake, William, *The Complete Poems*, ed. A. Ostriker (Harmondsworth: Penguin, 1977).

Bloom, Harold (ed.), *Elizabeth Bishop: Modern Critical Views* (New York: Chelsea House, 1985).

Borges, Jorge Luis, *This Craft of Verse*, ed. C-A. Mihailescu (Cambridge, Mass.: Harvard University Press, 2000).

Brauer, David E. et al. (eds.), *Pop Art: U.S./U.K. Connections, 1956–1966* (Ostfildern-Ruit: Hatje Cantz, 2001).

Breton, André, *Oeuvres Complètes*, i, ed. M. Bonnet et al. (Paris: Gallimard, 1988).

Bridges, Robert, *The Poetical Works*, 2nd. edn. (Oxford: Oxford University Press, 1953).

Brooker, Peter, *A Student's Guide to the Selected Poems of Ezra Pound* (London: Faber & Faber, 1979).

Browning, Robert, *The Poems*, ii, ed. J. Pettigrew and T. J. Collins (Harmondsworth: Penguin, 1981).

Buchan, James, 'The Great Letters of a Great Poet', *Spectator*, 7 May 1994.

Bullock, Alan, *Hitler: A Study in Tyranny* (1962) (Harmondsworth: Penguin, 1990).

Bunting, Basil, *Collected Poems*, 2nd edn. (London: Fulcrum, 1970).

—— *Uncollected Poems*, ed. R. Caddel (Oxford: Oxford University Press, 1991).

—— *Basil Bunting on Poetry*, ed. P. Makin (Baltimore, Md: Johns Hopkins University Press, 1999).

Burke, Seán, *The Death and Return of the Author: Criticism and Subjectivity in Barthes, Foucault and Derrida* (Edinburgh: Edinburgh University Press, 1992; 2nd edn. 1998).

Burman, Edward, 'The Culminating Sacrifice: An Interpretation of Allen Curnow's "Moro Assassinato"', *Landfall*, 153, 39/1 (Mar. 1985).

Burns, Robert, *The Poems and Songs of Robert Burns*, 3 vols., ed. J. Kinsley (Oxford: Oxford University Press, 1968).

Calder, Alex, 'Sacrifice and Signification in the Poetry of Allen Curnow', in M. Williams and M. Leggott (eds.), *Opening the Book: New Essays on New Zealand Writing* (Auckland: Auckland University Press, 1995).

Caracciolo-Trejo, Enrique (ed.), *The Penguin Book of Latin American Verse* (Harmondsworth: Penguin, 1970).

Carpenter, Humphrey, *A Serious Character: The Life of Ezra Pound* (London: Faber & Faber, 1988).

Cassam, Quassim, *Self and World* (Oxford: Oxford University Press, 1997).

Cavalcanti, Guido, *Rime*, ed. G. Cattaneo (Turin: Einaudi, 1967).

Celant, Germano, and Bell, Clare, *Jim Dine: Walking Memory 1959 to 1969* (New York: Guggenheim Museum, 1999).

Chaucer, Geoffrey, *The Works of Geoffrey Chaucer*, 2nd edn. ed. F. N. Robinson (London: Oxford University Press, 1966).

Churchill, Winston, *The Second World War*, 6 vols. (1948; rev. 1949) (Harmondsworth: Penguin, 1985).

Cioffi, Frank, *Wittgenstein on Freud and Frazer* (Cambridge: Cambridge University Press, 1998).

Clark, T. J., *The Painting of Modern Life: Paris in the Art of Manet and his Followers* (London: Thames & Hudson, 1990; rev. edn. 1999).

——*Farewell to an Idea: Episodes from a History of Modernism* (New Haven, Conn., and London: Yale University Press, 1999).

Coleridge, S. T., *Coleridge's Miscellaneous Criticism*, ed. T. M. Raysor (Cambridge, Mass.: Harvard University Press, 1936).

——*The Complete Poems*, ed. W. Keach (Harmondsworth: Penguin, 1997).

Collins, Wilkie, *Man and Wife*, ed. N. Page (Oxford: Oxford University Press, 1995).

Costello, Bonnie, *Elizabeth Bishop: Questions of Mastery* (Cambridge, Mass.: Harvard University Press, 1993).

Creeley, Robert, *The Collected Poems 1945–1975* (Berkeley and Los Angeles, Calif.: California University Press, 1982).

Crichton Smith, Iain, *The Notebooks of Robinson Crusoe* (London: Gollancz, 1975).

Croce, Benedetto, *Guide to Aesthetics (Breviario di estetica)*, trans. P. Romanell (South Bend, Ind.: Notre Dame University Press, 1965).

Crozier, Andrew, 'Signs of Identity: Roy Fisher's *A Furnace*', *PN Review* 83, 18/3 (1992).

Curnow, Allen (ed.), *The Penguin Book of New Zealand Verse* (Harmondsworth: Penguin, 1960).

——*An Incorrigible Music: A Sequence of Poems* (Auckland: Auckland University Press, 1979).

——*Selected Poems* (Auckland: Auckland University Press, 1982).

——*Look Back Harder: Critical Writings 1935–1984*, ed. P. Simpson (Auckland: Auckland University Press, 1987).

——*Selected Poems 1940–1989* (London: Viking, 1990).

——'Allen Curnow talks to Peter Simpson', *Landfall*, 175 (Sept. 1990).

——Unpublished letter to Peter Robinson, 28 May 1996.

——*Early Days Yet: New and Collected Poems 1941–1997* (Manchester: Carcanet, 1997).

Danto, Arthur C., 'The Art World', *Journal of Philosophy*, 61/19 (1964).

Davie, Donald, *Collected Poems 1950–1970* (London: Routledge & Kegan Paul, 1972).

——*Thomas Hardy and British Poetry* (London: Routledge & Kegan Paul, 1973).

——*The Poet in the Imaginary Museum*, ed. B. Alpert (Manchester: Carcanet, 1977).

——'Postmodernism and Allen Curnow', *PN Review*, 77, 17/3 (1991).

Davie, Donald, *Purity of Diction in English Verse* and *Articulate Energy* (Harmondsworth: Penguin, 1992).

—— *Collected Poems*, ed. N. Powell (Manchester: Carcanet, 2002).

Defoe, Daniel, *The Life and Strange Adventures of Robinson Crusoe*, part II (Boston, Mass.: David Nickerson, 1903).

—— *Robinson Crusoe*, ed. M. Shinagel (New York: Norton, 1994).

Desnos, Robert, *Destinée arbitraire*, ed. M-C. Dumas (Paris: Gallimard, 1975).

Dickey, James, *Poems 1957–1967* (New York: Collier, 1967).

—— *Babel To Byzantium: Poets and Poetry Now* (New York: Grosset and Dunlap, 1971).

Dijkstra, Bram, *Cubism, Stieglitz, and the Early Poetry of William Carlos Williams* (Princeton, NJ: Princeton University Press, 1969).

Donne, John, *The Complete English Poems*, ed. A. J. Smith, (Harmondsworth: Penguin, 1971).

Dorn, Edward, *The Collected Poems, 1956–1974*, enlarged edn. (San Francisco, Calif.: Four Seasons Foundation, 1983).

Eckermann, Johann Peter, *Gespräche mit Goethe in den Letzten Jahren seines Lebens*, Johann Wolfgang von Goethe, *Gedenkausgabe der Werke, Briefe und Gespräche*, xxiv, ed. E. Beutler (Zürich: Artemis, 1948).

Eliot, T. S., *The Sacred Wood: Essays on Poetry and Criticism* (London: Methuen, 1920).

—— 'Literature, Science and Dogma', *The Dial*, 82 (Mar. 1927).

—— *The Idea of a Christian Society* (London: Faber & Faber, 1939).

—— *Selected Essays* (London: Faber & Faber, 1951).

—— *On Poetry and Poets* (London: Faber & Faber, 1957).

—— *Collected Poems 1909–1962* (London: Faber & Faber, 1963).

—— *The Waste Land: A Facsimile and Transcript of the Original Drafts Including the Annotations of Ezra Pound*, ed. V. Eliot (London: Faber & Faber, 1971).

—— *The Letters of T. S. Eliot*, ed. V. Eliot (London: Faber & Faber, 1988).

Ellmann, Richard, *James Joyce* (1959), rev. edn. (Oxford: Oxford University Press, 1982).

Empson, William, *Argufying: Essays on Literature and Culture*, ed. J. Haffenden (London: Chatto & Windus, 1987).

—— *The Complete Poems* ed. J. Haffenden (London: Allen Lane, 2000).

Engelmann, Paul, *Letters from Ludwig Wittgenstein with a Memoir*, ed. B. F. McGuinness, trans. L. Furtmüller (Oxford: Blackwell, 1967).

Etter, Carrie, 'The Life of a Desk', *Times Literary Supplement*, 5235, 1 Aug. 2003.

Fallon, P., and Mahon, D. (eds.), *The Penguin Book of Contemporary Irish Poetry* (Harmondsworth: Penguin, 1990).

Feiling, Keith, *The Life of Neville Chamberlain* (London: Macmillan, 1946).

Feit Diehl, Joanne, *Elizabeth Bishop and Marianne Moore: The Psychodynamics of Creativity* (Princeton, NJ: Princeton University Press, 1993).

Fenton, James, *The Strength of Poetry* (Oxford: Oxford University Press, 2001).

Filreis, Alan, *Wallace Stevens and the Actual World* (Princeton, NJ: Princeton University Press, 1991).

Fisher, Roy, *The Memorial Fountain* (Newcastle upon Tyne: Northern House, 1966).

—— *Collected Poems 1968* (London: Fulcrum, 1969).

—— *Matrix* (London: Fulcrum, 1971).

—— 'A Tuning Phenomenon: An Interview with Roy Fisher', *Sad Traffic*, 5 (1971).

—— Jed Rasula and Mike Erwin, 'An Interview with Roy Fisher', in *Nineteen Poems and an Interview* (Pensnett: Grosseteste, 1975).

—— 'Conversation with Roy Fisher: Eric Mottram', *Saturday Morning*, 1 (spring 1976).

—— 'Roy Fisher Talks to Peter Robinson', *Granta*, 76 (June 1977).

—— *Consolidated Comedies* (Durham: Pig Press, 1981).

—— Interview with Helen Dennis at University of Warwick Audio-Visual Centre, 9 May 1984.

—— *A Furnace* (Oxford: Oxford University Press, 1986).

—— *Poems 1955–1987* (Oxford: Oxford University Press, 1988).

—— 'Roy Fisher 1930– ', *Contemporary Authors (Autobiography Series)*, x (Detroit, Mich./New York/Fort Lauderdale, Fla./London: Gale Research, 1989).

—— *Birmingham River* (Oxford: Oxford University Press, 1994).

—— *The Dow Low Drop: New and Selected Poems* (Newcastle upon Tyne: Bloodaxe Books, 1996).

—— 'At the Grave of Asa Benveniste', *Poetry Review*, 86/3 (autumn 1996).

—— 'Item', in *New Writing*, vi, ed. A. S. Byatt and P. Porter (London: Vintage, 1997), 302–5.

—— 'John Tranter Interviews Roy Fisher', *Jacket*, 1 (1997).

—— 'Three Songs from the Camel's Coffin', in Peter McCarey (ed.), *A Gallery for Gael Turnbull* (Glasgow: Au Quai, 1998).

—— 'Last Poems', *C.C.C.P.*8: Programme and Anthology of the Eighth Cambridge Conference of Contemporary Poetry, 24–26 April 1998.

—— *Interviews Through Time, and Selected Prose*, ed. T. Frazer (Kentisbeare: Shearsman, 2000).

Foden, Giles, 'Seriously Substantial', *Times Literary Supplement*, 14–20 Sept. 1990.

Forde, Victoria, *The Poetry of Basil Bunting* (Newcastle upon Tyne: Bloodaxe, 1991).

Fortini, Franco, *Insistenze: Cinquanta scritti 1976–1984* (Milan: Garzanti, 1985).

Foster, Hal, 'Pop Eye', *London Review of Books*, 24/16, 22 Aug. 2002.

Fountain, Gary, and Brazeau, Peter, *Remembering Elizabeth Bishop: An Oral Biography* (Amherst, Mass.: University of Massachusetts Press, 1994).

Gannon, Franklin R., *The British Press and Germany, 1936–1939* (Oxford: Oxford University Press, 1971).

Gardner, Philip and Averil, *The God Approached: A Commentary on the Poems of William Empson* (London: Chatto & Windus, 1978).

Gasset, José Ortega Y, *The Dehumanization of Art* (New York: Doubleday, 1956).

Ginsborg, Paul, *A History of Contemporary Italy: Politics and Society 1943–1988* (Harmondsworth: Penguin, 1990).

Glover, Jonathan, *I: The Philosophy and Psychology of Personal Identity* (Harmondsworth: Penguin, 1988).

Goldensohn, Lorrie, *Elizabeth Bishop: The Biography of a Poetry* (New York: Columbia University Press, 1992).

Graham, W. S., 'Notes on a Poetry of Release', *Poetry Scotland*, 3, July 1946.

—— *Collected Poems 1942–1977* (London: Faber & Faber, 1979).

—— 'From a 1949 Notebook . . .', *Edinburgh Review*, 75 (1987).

—— ' "Dear Pen Pal in the distance": A Selection of W. S. Graham's Letters', ed. R. Grogan, *PN Review*, 73, 16/5 (1990).

—— *Uncollected Poems* (Warwick: Greville, 1990).

—— *Aimed at Nobody: Poems from Notebooks*, ed. M. Blackwood and R. Skelton (London: Faber & Faber, 1993).

—— *The Nightfisherman: Selected Letters*, ed. M. and M. Snow (Manchester: Carcanet, 1999).

—— *New Collected Poems*, ed. M. Francis (London: Faber & Faber, 2004).

Gregson, Ian, *Contemporary Poets and Post-Modernism: Dialogue and Estrangement* (Basingstoke: Macmillan, 1996).

Griffiths, Richard, *Fellow Travellers of the Right, British Enthusiasts for Nazi Germany 1933–1939* (Oxford: Oxford University Press, 1983).

Habib, M. A. R., *The Early T. S. Eliot and Western Philosophy* (Cambridge: Cambridge University Press, 1999).

Hacker, P. M. S., *Insight and Illusion: Themes in the Philosophy of Wittgenstein*, rev. edn. (Oxford: Oxford University Press, 1989).

—— *Wittgenstein: Connections and Controversies* (Oxford: Oxford University Press, 2001).

Haffenden, John (ed.), *Viewpoints: Poets in Conversation with John Haffenden* (London: Faber & Faber, 1981).

—— 'Sexual Types of Ambiguity: William Empson in Japan', *Areté: The Arts Tri-Quarterly*, 6 (autumn 2001).

Hamilton, Ian (ed.), *The Oxford Companion to Twentieth-Century Poetry in English* (Oxford: Oxford University Press, 1994).

Harmon, William, *Time in Ezra Pound's Work* (Chapel Hill, NC: University of North Carolina Press, 1977).

Harrison, Victoria, *Elizabeth Bishop's Poetics of Intimacy* (Cambridge: Cambridge University Press, 1993).

Heaney, Seamus, *Preoccupations: Selected Prose 1968–1978* (London: Faber & Faber, 1980).

—— *The Government of the Tongue: The 1986 T. S. Eliot Memorial Lectures and Other Critical Writings* (London: Faber & Faber, 1988).

—— *The Redress of Poetry: Oxford Lectures* (London: Faber & Faber, 1995).

Henri, Adrian, *Collected Poems 1967 to 1985* (London: Allison & Busby, 1986).

Herbert, George, *The Complete English Poems*, ed. J. Tobin (Harmondsworth: Penguin, 1991).

Herrnstein Smith, Barbara, *Contingencies of Value: Alternative Perspectives for Critical Theory* (Cambridge, Mass.: Harvard University Press, 1988).

Hill, Geoffrey, *The Lords of Limit: Essays on Literature and Ideas* (London: André Deutsch, 1984).

—— *The Enemy's Country: Words, Contexture, and other Circumstances of Language* (Oxford: Oxford University Press, 1991).

—— *New and Collected Poems* (Boston, Mass.: Houghton Mifflin, 1994).

Hogg, James, *Songs by the Ettrick Shepherd 1831*, in J. Wordsworth (ed.), *Revolution and Romanticism, 1789–1834* (Oxford: Woodstock, 1989).

Honderich, Ted (ed.), *The Oxford Companion to Philosophy* (Oxford: Oxford University Press, 1995).

Hynes, Samuel, *The Auden Generation: Literature and Politics in England in the 1930s* (London: Faber & Faber, 1976).

Inness, Julie C., *Privacy, Intimacy, and Isolation* (New York: Oxford University Press, 1992).

Isherwood, Christopher, *Christopher and His Kind 1929–1939* (London: Eyre Methuen, 1977).

James, Henry, *Maud-Evelyn, The Special Type, The Papers, and Other Stories* (London: Macmillan, 1923).

Johnson, Lionel, *Poetical Works of Lionel Johnson* (London: Elkin Matthews, 1915).

Johnson, Samuel, *The Complete English Poems*, ed. J. D. Fleeman (Harmondsworth: Penguin, 1971).

—— *Lives of the English Poets: A Selection*, ed. J. P. Hardy (Oxford: Oxford University Press, 1971).

—— *The History of Rasselas, Prince of Abissinia* ed. D. J. Enright (Harmondsworth: Penguin, 1976).

Jonson, Ben, *The Poems*, ed. G. B. Johnston (London: Muses Library, 1954).

Joyce, James, *Dubliners* (Harmondsworth: Penguin, 1956).

—— *A Portrait of the Artist as a Young Man* (Harmondsworth: Penguin, 1960).

—— *Selected Letters*, ed. R. Ellmann (London: Faber & Faber, 1975).

—— *Poems and Shorter Writings*, ed. R. Ellmann, A. Walton Litz, and J. Whittier-Ferguson (London: Faber & Faber, 1991).

Kalstone, David, *Five Temperaments: Elizabeth Bishop, Robert Lowell, James Merrill, Adrienne Rich, John Ashbery* (New York: Oxford University Press, 1977).

—— *Becoming a Poet: Elizabeth Bishop with Marianne Moore and Robert Lowell*, ed. R. Hemenway (London: Chatto & Windus, 1989).

Kavanagh, Patrick, *Selected Poems*, ed. A. Quinn (Harmondsworth: Penguin, 1996).

Keats, John, *Letters of John Keats to his Family and Friends*, ed. S. Colvin (London: Macmillan, 1935).

—— *The Complete Poems*, ed. J. Barnard (Harmondsworth: Penguin, 1988).

Kelly, L. (ed.), *Poetry and the Sense of Panic: Critical Essays on Elizabeth Bishop and John Ashbery* (Amsterdam and Atlanta, Ga.: Rodopi, 2000).

Kerrigan, John, 'Self-Reflections in the Poem's Pool', *Times Literary Supplement*, 19 Sept. 1997.

—— and Robinson, P. (eds.), *The Thing about Roy Fisher* (Liverpool: Liverpool University Press, 2000).

Koch, Philip, *Solitude: A Philosophical Encounter* (Chicago and La Salle, Ill.: Open Court, 1994).

Larkin, Philip, *Required Writing: Miscellaneous Pieces 1955–1982* (London: Faber & Faber, 1983).

—— *Collected Poems*, ed. A. Thwaite (London/Hessle: Faber & Faber/Marvell, 1988).

Lawrence, D. H., *The Complete Poems*, ed. V. de Sola Pinto and F. W. Roberts (Harmondsworth: Penguin, 1977).

Leader, Zachary, 'Raising Ron Cain: How Amis and Larkin mocked their own Movement', *Times Literary Supplement*, 5066, 5 May 2000.

Lippard, Lucy R., *Pop Art* (London: Thames & Hudson, 1970).

Lisboa, E., and Taylor, L. C. (eds.), *A Centenary Pessoa* (Manchester: Carcanet, 1995).

Lloyd, T. O., *Empire to Welfare State: English History 1906–1985*, 3rd edn. (Oxford: Oxford University Press, 1986).

Lombardi, Marilyn May, *The Body and the Song: Elizabeth Bishop's Poetics* (Carbondale and Edwardsville, Ill.: Southern Illinois University Press, 1995).

Longenbach, James, *Stone Cottage: Pound, Yeats, and Modernism* (New York: Oxford University Press, 1988).

Longley, Edna, *Louis MacNeice: A Study* (London: Faber & Faber, 1988).

Lopez, Tony, 'On "Malcolm Mooney's Land" by W. S. Graham', *Ideas and Production*, 4 (Dec. 1985).

—— 'Reading W. S. Graham's "Implements"', *Swansea Review*, 1 (Apr. 1986).

—— 'W. S. Graham: an Introduction', in *Edinburgh Review*, 75 (1985).

—— *The Poetry of W. S. Graham* (Edinburgh: Edinburgh University Press, 1989).

Lowell, Robert, *Selected Poems*, rev. edn. (New York: Farrar, Straus and Giroux, 1977).

—— *Collected Prose*, ed. R. Giroux (New York: Farrar, Straus and Giroux, 1987).

Lowry, Elizabeth, 'Belonging Down There', *Times Literary Supplement*, 4929, 19 Sept. 1997.

Lucie-Smith, Edward, *British Poetry since 1945* (Harmondsworth: Penguin, 1970).

MacCabe, Colin, 'Dissolving the Voice', *Times Literary Supplement*, 1455, 30 Dec. 1983.

McDonald, Peter, *Louis McNeice: The Poet in his Contexts* (Oxford: Oxford University Press, 1991).

McDonough, Thomas F. (ed.), *Guy Debord and the Situationist International: Texts and Documents* (Cambridge, Mass: MIT Press, 2002).

Machado, Antonio, *Selected Poems*, trans. Alan S. Trueblood (Cambridge, Mass.: Harvard University Press, 1982).

—— *Poesías completas*, 10th edn. (Madrid: Espasa-Calpe, 1984).

MacInnes, Mairi, *Splinters* (Reading: University of Reading Printing School, 1953).

—— *Admit One* (London: Putnam, 1956).

—— [as Mairi McCormick], 'First Representations of the Gamma Alcoholic in the English Novel', *Quarterly Journal of Studies on Alcohol*, 30/4 (Dec. 1969).

—— *Herring, Oatmeal, Milk & Salt* in *Quarterly Review of Literature*, poetry series, iii, T. and R. Weiss (eds.) (Princeton, NJ: 1981).

—— *The House on the Ridge Road* (Boston, Mass.: Rowan Tree, 1988).

—— *Elsewhere & Back: New & Selected Poems* (Newcastle upon Tyne: Bloodaxe,1993).

—— *The Quondam Wives* (London and Baton Rouge, La.: Louisiana State University Press, 1993).

—— *The Ghostwriter* (Newcastle upon Tyne: Bloodaxe, 1999).

—— *The Pebble: Old and New Poems* (Urbana and Chicago, Ill.: University of Illinois Press, 2000).

—— *Clearances: A Memoir* (New York: Pantheon, 2002).

MacNeice, Louis, *Modern Poetry: A Personal Essay* (Oxford: Oxford University Press, 1938).

—— *The Poetry of W. B. Yeats* (Oxford: Oxford University Press, 1941).

—— *The Strings are False: An Unfinished Autobiography* (London: Faber & Faber, 1965).

—— *Varieties of Parable* (Cambridge: Cambridge University Press, 1965).

—— *Collected Poems*, ed. E. R. Dodds (London: Faber & Faber, 1979).

—— *Selected Literary Criticism*, ed. A. Heuser (Oxford: Oxford University Press, 1987).

—— *Selected Prose of Louis MacNeice*, ed. A. Heuser (Oxford: Oxford University Press, 1990).

Madoff, Steven Henry (ed.), *Pop Art: A Critical History* (Berkeley and Los Angeles, Calif.: University of California Press, 1997).

Makin, Peter, *Bunting: The Shaping of his Verse* (Oxford: Oxford University Press, 1992).

Mallarmé, Stéphane, *Oeuvres complètes*, ed. H. Mondor and G. Jean-Aubry (Paris: Gallimard, 1945).

—— *Mallarmé*, ed. A. Hartley (Harmondsworth: Penguin, 1965).

Mandelstam, Osip, *Selected Essays*, trans. S. Monas (Austin, Tex.: University of Texas Press, 1977).

Manhire, Bill, 'Blood in the Blood', *NZ Listener*, 29 Sept. 1979.

——*Zoetropes: Poems 1972–82* (North Sydney: Allen & Unwin, 1984).

Marsack, Robyn, *The Cave of Making: The Poetry of Louis MacNeice* (Oxford: Oxford University Press, 1982).

——'A Home in Thought: Three New Zealand Poets', *PN Review*, 46, Cambridge Poetry Festival special issue, 12/2 (1985).

Marvell, Andrew, *The Poems*, ed. H. MacDonald (London: Routledge & Kegan Paul, 1952).

Matthias, John, 'The Poetry of Roy Fisher', in J. Acheson and R. Huk (eds.), *Contemporary British Poetry: Essays in Theory and Criticism* (New York: SUNY, 1996).

Mendelson, Edward, *Early Auden* (London: Faber & Faber, 1981).

Miller, Chris, 'Allen Curnow as Post-Modern Metaphysical', *PN Review*, 105, 21/7 (1995).

Millier, Brett C., *Elizabeth Bishop: Life and the Memory of It* (Berkeley and Los Angeles, Calif.: University of California Press, 1993).

Milton, John, *Paradise Lost*, ed. A. Fowler (London: Longmans, 1971).

Monk, Ray, *Ludwig Wittgenstein: The Duty of Genius* (London: Jonathan Cape, 1990).

Montale, Eugenio, *L'opera in versi*, ed. R. Bettarini and G. Contini (Turin: Einaudi, 1980).

——*Le occasioni*, ed. D. Isella (Turin: Einaudi, 1996).

Moore, A. W., *Points of View* (Oxford: Oxford University Press, 1997).

Moore, Marianne, *The Complete Poems*, ed. C. Driver (Harmondsworth: Penguin, 1982).

——*The Selected Letters*, ed. B. Costello et al. (New York: Knopf, 1997).

Morrison, Blake, *The Movement: English Poetry and Fiction of the 1950s* (Oxford: Oxford University Press, 1980).

Nabokov, Vladimir, *Strong Opinions* (New York: Vintage, 1990).

Nagel, Thomas, *Mortal Questions* (Cambridge: Cambridge University Press, 1979).

——*The View from Nowhere* (Oxford: Oxford University Press, 1986).

——*Equality and Partiality* (Oxford: Oxford University Press, 1991).

Nashe, Thomas, *The Unfortunate Traveller and Other Works*, ed. J. B. Steane (Harmondsworth: Penguin, 1972).

Nietzsche, Friedrich, *The Gay Science*, ed. B. Williams (Cambridge: Cambridge University Press, 2001).

Norman, Charles, *Ezra Pound* (London: MacDonald, 1969).

O'Brien, Sean, *The Deregulated Muse: Essays on Contemporary British and Irish Poetry* (Newcastle upon Tyne: Bloodaxe, 1998).

O'Hara, Frank, *The Collected Poems*, ed. D. Allen (Berkeley and Los Angeles, Calif.: University of California Press, 1995).

Olson, Charles, *Selected Poems*, ed. R. Creeley (Berkeley and Los Angeles, Calif.: University of California Press, 1993).

O'Neill, Michael, and Reeves, Gareth, *Auden, MacNeice, Spender: The Thirties Poetry* (Basingstoke: Macmillan, 1992).

Oppen, George, *The Selected Letters*, ed. R. Blau DuPlessis (Durham, NC: Duke University Press, 1990).

Orr, Peter (ed.), *The Poet Speak: Interviews with Contemporary Poets* (London: Routledge & Kegan Paul, 1966).

Osterwold, Tilman, *Pop Art* (Köln: Benedikt Taschen, 1991).

Palattella, John, 'Heavy Lifting', *London Review of Books*, 23/11, 7 June 2001.

Paulin, Tom, *Thomas Hardy: The Poetry of Perception* (Oxford: Oxford University Press, 1975).

Perloff, Marjorie, *Wittgenstein's Ladder: Poetic Language and the Strangeness of the Ordinary* (Chicago, Ill.: University of Chicago Press, 1996).

Perse, Saint-John, *Oeuvres complètes* (Paris: Gallimard, 1972).

Phillips, Adam, *On Flirtation* (London: Faber & Faber, 1994).

Pocock, J. G. A., 'Removal from the Wings', *London Review of Books*, 19/6, 20 Mar. 1997.

Poe, Edgar Allan, *The Fall of the House of Usher and Other Writings*, ed. D. Galloway (Harmondsworth: Penguin, 1986).

Pound, Ezra (ed.), *Active Anthology* (London: Faber & Faber, 1933).

—— *Guide to Kulchur* (1938) (New York: New Directions, 1970).

—— *Selected Poems*, ed. T. S. Eliot (London: Faber & Faber, 1948).

—— *The Selected Letters of Ezra Pound 1907–1941*, ed. D. D. Paige (New York: New Directions, 1950).

—— *The Literary Essays of Ezra Pound*, ed. T. S. Eliot (London: Faber & Faber, 1954).

—— and Spann, Marcella (eds.), *Confucius to Cummings: An Anthology of Poetry* (New York: New Directions, 1964).

—— *Pound/Joyce: The Letters of Ezra Pound to James Joyce*, ed. F. Read (New York: New Directions, 1970).

—— *Gaudier-Brzeska: A Memoir* (1916) (New York: New Directions, 1970).

—— *Selected Prose 1909–1965*, ed. W. Cookson (London: Faber & Faber, 1978).

—— *Ezra Pound and Dorothy Shakespear: Their Letters*, ed. O. Pound and A. Walton Litz (London: Faber & Faber, 1984).

—— *The Cantos of Ezra Pound*, 4th coll. edn. (London: Faber & Faber, 1987).

—— *Ezra Pound and Japan: Letters and Essays*, ed. S. Kodama (Redding Ridge, CN: Black Swan, 1987).

—— *Ezra Pound and Margaret Cravens: A Tragic Friendship 1910–1912*, ed. O. Pound and R. Spoo (Durham, NC: Duke University Press, 1988).

—— *Personae: The Shorter Poems*, rev. edn., ed. L. Baechler and A. Walton Litz (New York: New Directions, 1990).

Prynne, J. H., *The White Stones* (Lincoln: Grosseteste, 1969).

Quartermain, Peter, *Basil Bunting: Poet of the North* (Durham: Basil Bunting Poetry Archive, 1990).

Rachewiltz, Mary de, *Discretions* (London: Faber & Faber, 1971).

Raffel, Burton, *Ezra Pound: Prime Minister of Poetry* (Hampden, Conn.: Archon, 1984).

Rathmell, John, 'Charles Tomlinson', *Prospect* (winter 1960).

Raworth, Tom, 'A Serial Biography: One', *The Wivenhoe Park Review*, 1 (winter 1965).

—— *The Relation Ship* (1968), 2nd. edn. (London: Cape Goliard, 1969).

—— *The Big Green Day* (London: Trigram, 1968).

—— *A Serial Biography* (London: Fulcrum, 1969).

—— *Lion Lion* (London: Trigram, 1970).

—— *Moving* (London: Cape Goliard, 1971).

—— *Act* (London: Trigram, 1973).

—— *Logbook* (Berkeley, Calif.: Poltroon, 1976).

—— *Nicht War, Rosie?: Miscellaneous Poems 1964–69* (Berkeley, Calif.: Poltroon, 1979).

—— *Visible Shivers* (Oakland and Novato, Calif.: O Books with Trike, 1988).

—— *Tom Raworth: An Exhibition* (Cambridge: Cambridge Conference of Contemporary Poetry, 8, 1998).

—— *Meadow* (Sausalito, Calif.: Post-Apollo, 1999).

—— *Collected Poems* (Manchester: Carcanet, 2003).

Reverdy, Pierre, 'L'Image', *Nord-Sud* (Mar. 1918), cited in M-L. Astre and F. Colmez (eds.), *Poésie Française* (Paris: Bordas, 1982).

Rhees, Rush (ed.), *Recollections of Wittgenstein* (Oxford: Oxford University Press, 1984).

Rich, Adrienne, *On Lies, Secrets, and Silence: Selected Prose 1966–1978* (New York: Norton, 1979).

Ricks, Christopher, *The Force of Poetry* (Oxford: Oxford University Press, 1984).

—— *Essays in Appreciation* (Oxford: Oxford University Press, 1996).

—— *Allusion to the Poets* (Oxford: Oxford University Press, 2002).

Riley, Bridget, *Dialogues on Art* (London: Zwemmer, 1995).

Rimbaud, Arthur, *Oeuvres Complètes*, ed. A. Adam (Paris: Gallimard, 1972).

Robinson, Peter, 'Ezra Pound and Italian Art', in D. Humphries (ed.), *Pound's Artists: Ezra Pound and the Visual Arts in London, Paris and Italy* (London: Tate Gallery, 1985).

—— *In the Circumstances: About Poems and Poets* (Oxford: Oxford University Press, 1992).

—— *Poetry, Poets, Readers: Making Things Happen* (Oxford: Oxford University Press, 2002).

—— 'Very Shrinking Behaviour: The Poetic Collaboration of William Empson and Chiyoko Hatakeyama', *Times Literary Supplement*, 5233, 18 July 2003.

Rosenthal, M. L., *Sailing into the Unknown: Yeats, Pound, and Eliot* (New York: Oxford University Press, 1978).

Ruskin, John, *Works* ed. E. T. Cook and A. Wedderburn, Library Edition, 39 vols. (London: George Allen et al., 1903–12).

Ruthven, K.K., *A Guide to Ezra Pound's Personae* (1926), (Berkeley and Los Angeles, Calif.: University of California Press, 1969).

Schmidt, Michael, *An Introduction to Fifty British Poets* (London: Pan, 1979).

—— 'Charles Tomlinson', *PN Review*, 52, 13/2 (1986).

—— (ed.), *A Calendar of Modern Poetry*, PN Review, 100, 21/2 (1994).

—— and Jones, Peter (eds.), *British Poetry since 1970* (Manchester: Carcanet, 1980).

Sciascia, Leonardo, *L'affaire Moro* (Palermo: Sellerio, 1978).

Searle, John R., *Speech Acts: An Essay on the Philosophy of Language* (Cambridge: Cambridge University Press, 1969).

—— *Expression and Meaning: Studies in the Theory of Speech Acts* (Cambridge: Cambridge University Press, 1979).

—— *The Construction of Social Reality* (New York: Free Press, 1995).

Sereni, Vittorio, 'A Letter from Vittorio Sereni', *PN Review*, 5, 5/1, 1977.

—— *Selected Poems of Vittorio Sereni*, trans. M. Perryman and P. Robinson (London: Anvil, 1990).

—— *Poesie*, ed. D. Isella (Milan: Mondadori, 1995).

Shakespeare, William, *The Complete Works*, ed. S. Wells and G. Taylor (Oxford: Oxford University Press, 1988).

—— *Shakespeare's Sonnets*, ed. K. Duncan-Jones (London: Nelson, 1997).

Sheppard, Robert, *Turning the Prism: An Interview with Roy Fisher* (London: Damp Toads, 1986).

Sherry, Vincent B. (ed.), *Dictionary of Literary Biography*, xl, *Poets of Great Britain and Ireland since 1960*, 2 vols. (Detroit, Mich.: Gale Research, 1985).

Silkin, John, *The Life of Metrical and Free Verse in Twentieth-Century Poetry* (Basingstoke: Macmillan, 1997).

Sinfield, Alan (ed.), *Society and Literature 1945–1970* (New York: Holmes and Meier, 1984).

Smither, Elizabeth, 'New Zealand: Pocket of Poetry', *PN Review*, 41, 11/3 (1984).

Stallworthy, Jon, *Louis MacNeice* (Oxford: Oxford University Press, 1995).

Stevens, Wallace, *The Collected Poems* (London: Faber & Faber, 1955).

—— *Opus Posthumous*, rev. edn. ed. M. J. Bates (London: Faber & Faber, 1990).

Stevenson, Anne, *Elizabeth Bishop* (New York: Twayne, 1966).

Stock, Noel, *The Life of Ezra Pound* (Harmondsworth: Penguin, 1974).

Stokes, Adrian, *The Critical Writings*, 3 vols., ed. L. Gowing (London: Thames & Hudson, 1978).

Swigg, Richard, *Charles Tomlinson and the Objectivist Tradition* (Lewisberg, Pa.: Bucknell University Press, 1994).

Symons, Julian, *The Thirties and the Nineties* (Manchester: Carcanet, 1990).

Taylor, Charles, *Sources of the Self: The Making of the Modern Identity* (Cambridge: Cambridge University Press, 1989).

Tennyson, Alfred, *The Poems of Tennyson*, 3 vols., ed. C. Ricks (London: Longmans, 1987).

Terrell, Carroll F., *A Companion to the Cantos of Ezra Pound*, 2 vols. (Berkeley and Los Angeles, Calif.: University of California Press, 1980/1984).

Terry, Arthur, *Antonio Machado: Campos de Castilla* (London: Grant and Cutler, 1973).

Thomas, Dylan, *Collected Poems 1934–1952* (London: J. M. Dent, 1952).

Tóibín, Colm, 'The South', *London Review of Books*, 16/15, 4 Aug. 1994.

Tomlinson, Charles, *Castilian Ilexes: Versions from Antonio Machado*, Introd. by Henry Gifford (Oxford: Oxford University Press, 1963).

—— *Renga: A Chain of Poems by Octavio Paz, Jacques Roubaud, Edoardo Sanguinetti, and Charles Tomlinson* (Harmondsworth: Penguin, 1979).

—— *Some Americans: A Personal Record* (Berkeley and Los Angeles, Calif.: University of California Press, 1981).

—— *Poetry and Metamorphosis* (Cambridge: Cambridge University Press, 1983).

—— *Translations* (Oxford: Oxford University Press, 1983).

—— *Collected Poems* (Oxford: Oxford University Press, 1985).

—— *The Return* (Oxford: Oxford University Press, 1987).

—— 'Charles Tomlinson at Sixty: In Conversation with Richard Swigg' in *PN Review* 59, 14/3 (1987).

—— *American Essays: Making It New* (Manchester: Carcanet, 2001).

Travisano, Thomas J., *Elizabeth Bishop: Her Artistic Development* (Charlottesville, Va: University of Virginia Press, 1988).

Tuma, Keith, *Fishing by Obstinate Isles: Modern and Postmodern British Poetry and American Readers* (Evanston, Ill.: Northwestern University Press, 1998).

—— (ed.), *Anthology of Twentieth Century British and Irish Poetry* (New York: Oxford University Press, 2001).

Unamuno, Miguel de, *The Tragic Sense of Life*, trans. J. E. Crawford- Flitch (New York: Dover, 1954).

Valéry, Paul, *Degas Danse Dessin* (Paris: Gallimard, 1938).

—— *Oeuvres*, ii, ed. J. Hytier (Paris: Gallimard, 1960).

—— *The Art of Poetry*, trans. D. Folliot, *The Collected Works*, ed. J. Matthews, vii (Princeton, NJ: Princeton University Press, 1985).

Vallejo, César, *Selected Poems*, ed. S. Hart (London: Duckworth, 2000).

Varnedoe, Kirk, *Jasper Johns: A Retrospective* (New York: Museum of Modern Art, 1996).

—— and Karmel, Pepe (eds.), *Jackson Pollock: New Approaches* (New York: Museum of Modern Art, 1999).

Vinson, J., and Kirkpatrick, D. L. (eds.), *Contemporary Poets* (London and New

York: St Martin's, 1975).

Weaver, Harriet Shaw (ed.), *The Egoist, An Individualist Review*, 2–3 (New York; Kraus, 1967).

Wedde, Ian, and McQueen, Harvey (eds.), *The Penguin Book of New Zealand Verse* (Auckland: Penguin, 1985).

Welch, John, 'The Life of It', *PN Review*, 138, 27/4 (Mar.–Apr. 2001).

Wheeler-Bennett, John W., *The Nemesis of Power: The German Army in Politics 1918–1945* (London: Macmillan, 1954).

——*Munich, Prologue to Tragedy* (London: Macmillan, 1966).

Whitman, Walt, *The Complete Poems*, ed. F. Murphy (Harmondsworth: Penguin, 1986).

Williams, Bernard, *Problems of the Self: Philosophical Papers 1956–72* (Cambridge: Cambridge University Press, 1973).

——*Moral Luck: Philosophical Papers 1973–1980* (Cambridge: Cambridge University Press, 1981).

Williams, William Carlos, *The Collected Poems*, i, ed. A. Walton Litz and C. MacGowan (New York: New Directions, 1986).

Winters, Yvor, *In Defence of Reason* (Athens, Ohio: Ohio University Press, 1947).

Wittgenstein, Ludwig, *Tractatus Logico-Philosophicus* (1922), trans. C. K. Ogden (London: Routledge & Kegan Paul, 1995).

——*Lectures and Conversations on Aesthetics, Psychology and Religious Belief*, ed. C. Barrett (Oxford: Blackwell, 1966).

——*Zettel*, trans. G. E. M. Anscombe, ed. G. E. M. Anscombe and G. H. Von Wright (Oxford: Blackwell, 1981).

——*Culture and Value*, rev. 2nd edn., trans. P. Winch, ed. G. H. von Wright et al. (Oxford: Blackwell, 1998).

——*Philosophical Investigations*, 3nd edn., trans. G. E. M. Anscombe (Oxford: Blackwell, 2001).

Wollheim, Richard, *Art and its Objects*, 2nd edn. (Cambridge: Cambridge University Press, 1980).

——*The Thread of Life* (Cambridge: Cambridge University Press, 1984).

Wordsworth, William, *The Prose Works of William Wordsworth*, 3 vols., ed. A. B. Grosart (London: Moxon, 1876).

——*The Poetical Works of William Wordsworth*, 5 vols., ed. E. de Selincourt and H. Darbishire (Oxford: Oxford University Press, 1940–49).

——*The Poems*, 2 vols., ed. J. O. Hayden (Harmondsworth: Penguin, 1977).

Yeats, W. B., *The Variorum Edition of the Poems of W. B. Yeats*, ed. P. Allt and R. K. Alspach (New York: Macmillan, 1971).

——*The Collected Poems*, 2nd edn., ed. R. J. Finneran (Basingstoke: Macmillan, 1991).

Index

Lightning Source UK Ltd.
Milton Keynes UK
08 September 2010

159587UK00006B/7/P